THE GURU GRANTH SAHIB

THE GURU GRANTH SAHIB

CANON, MEANING AND AUTHORITY

Pashaura Singh

OXFORD
UNIVERSITY PRESS

OXFORD
UNIVERSITY PRESS

Oxford University Press is a department of the University of Oxford.
It furthers the University's objective of excellence in research, scholarship,
and education by publishing worldwide. Oxford is a registered trademark of
Oxford University Press in the UK and in certain other countries.

Published in India by
Oxford University Press
22 Workspace, 2nd Floor, 1/22 Asaf Ali Road, New Delhi 110002, India

First Edition published in 2000
Oxford India Paperbacks 2003
13th impression 2023
Digitally Printed in 2024

ISBN-13 (print edition): 978-0-19-566334-1
ISBN-10 (print edition): 0-19-566334-9

ISBN-13 (eBook): 978-0-19-908773-0
ISBN-10 (eBook): 0-19-908773-3

Typeset in Giovanni
by Eleven Arts, Keshavpuram, New Delhi 110 035 Printed in India by
Manipal Technologies Limited, Manipal

To
the Loving Memory
of my parents

Sardar Ishar Singh
Sardarni Dalip Kaur

CONTENTS

List of Figures   x

List of Tables   xi

Preface and Acknowledgements   xii

Note on Orthography   xv

Glossary   xvii

SECTION ONE
CANON

1. INTRODUCTION   3
   Revelation of the Bani and its Verbal Expression   7
   Transmission of the Bani and Compilation of   15
      the Adi Granth
   Canon Formation in the Sikh Tradition   23
   Sikh Studies   26

2. A SURVEY OF EARLY MANUSCRIPTS   28
   Pre-Canonical Stage   32
   First Canonical Text   53
   Post-Canonical Traditions   61
   Final Canonical Text   81
   Conclusion   81

3. TEXTUAL ANALYSIS   83
   Mul Mantar   84
   Liturgical Texts   90
   Guru Nanak's *Suhi* Hymn   102
   Guru Arjan's *Tilang* Hymns   106

Guru Arjan's *Ramakali* Hymn   114
Conclusion   122

4. RAGA ORGANIZATION OF THE ADI GRANTH   125
   Devotional Music in the Sikh Tradition   128
   Final Sequence of the Ragas in the Adi Granth   136
   Selection of Ragas and the *Raga-Mala*   145
   Conclusion   149

5. GURU ARJAN'S EDITORIAL PERSPECTIVE   151
   Doctrinal Consistency   152
   The Ideal of the Balanced Life   161
   Optimistic Sikh View   165
   The Inclusive Ideal   167
   The Concern for Independent Identity   174
   Conclusion   175

6. SCRIPTURAL ADAPTATION IN THE ADI GRANTH: 177
   ISSUES OF THE BHAGAT BANI
   Collection of the Bhagat Bani   179
   Selection of the Bhagat Bani   188
   Conclusion   201

7. THE ADI GRANTH TRADITIONS AND   203
   CANON FORMATION
   Lahore Recension   206
   Banno Recension   212
   Damdama Recension   222
   The Standard Version of the Adi Granth   224
   Printed Version of the Adi Granth   230
   Conclusion   234

SECTION TWO
MEANING

8. THE MEANING OF GURBANI: 239
   A FOCUS ON HERMENEUTIC TECHNIQUES

Major Schools of Scriptural Interpretation   242
Recent Trends in Scriptural Interpretation   257
Conclusion   261

SECTION THREE
AUTHORITY

9. THE GURU GRANTH SAHIB: 265
THE PLACE OF SCRIPTURE IN THE SIKH TRADITION
Oral Experience of the Sikh Scripture   267
The Word as Guru   271
The Role of the Scripture in Sikh Ceremonies   275
The Ultimate Authority   278
Conclusion   280

10. CONCLUSION   282

Bibliography   289

Index   303

FIGURES

Figure 2.1   Genealogy of the Adi Granth   30

Figure 8.1   Theoretical Schema for Various
              Hermeneutic Techniques   259

Figure 9.1   Movement of the Bridegroom and the Bride
              Around the Guru Granth Sahib   276

TABLES

Table 3.1	Evolution of the *Anand* from Early Manuscripts	100
Table 4.1	'Index of Indices' in the Kartarpur Manuscript	141
Table 7.1	Manuscripts of the Banno Recension	220

PREFACE AND ACKNOWLEDGEMENTS

This study seeks to answer three closely related questions in the process of canon-formation in the Sikh tradition: How did the text of the Adi Granth come into being? What is the meaning of *gurbani*? How did the Adi Granth come to be the Guru Granth Sahib?

I began to grapple with the first two questions in the course of my doctoral research thesis 'The Text and Meaning of the Adi Granth' at the University of Toronto in 1991. As soon as I received my first appointment at the University of Michigan in 1992, I found that my doctoral thesis had already become the focus of a worldwide debate within the Sikh community and scholarly circles. Although the nature of the debate was mostly polemic, it raised further questions about the concept of revelation, the method of textual analysis and the academic study of sacred scriptures. In fact, the censure of scholarly research on the Adi Granth was intimately linked with the complex political situation of Punjab, and it brought the whole issue of academic freedom into sharper focus. In this study, I try to respond to some of these issues from an academic perspective. Although I do not claim to have discovered satisfactory answers to all the questions raised in the debate, I have tried to stick to the three questions of my inquiry.

The most rewarding experience in this study has been the opportunity to work with Professor W.H. McLeod, an eminent historian of the Sikh tradition. Arguably the foremost academic in the field of Sikh studies, Professor McLeod taught me skills that have added expertise to scientific inquiry. He guided me through every phase of this study with great sensitivity. He patiently read my early drafts, provided extensive comments and saved me from many errors. To him, I owe a particular debt of gratitude and I acknowledge it with warmest thanks. I am profoundly grateful to Professor N. Gerald Barrier for his comments on an earlier draft of this study. Special thanks are due to Professor Joseph T. O'Connell, who has always provided me with stimulating feedback and watched my progress very carefully. I am thankful to my son, Maninder Pal Singh, for drawing the figures of this study and helping me with problems related to my computer.

During the difficult period of the controversy over my doctoral thesis, a number of academic institutions and colleagues supported me wholeheartedly. I am particularly thankful to the Canadian Society for the Study of Religion, the American Academy of Religion and the South Asia Council of the Association for Asian Studies for upholding my right to free inquiry. Professors Harjot Oberoi, N. Gerald Barrier, Arthur W. Helweg, Paul Wallace, John W. Spellman, Verne A. Dusenbery, Harold G. Coward, Ronald W. Neufeldt, Milton Israel, Karen Leonard, Bruce LaBrack, Louis E. Fenech, Vishva B.L. Sharma, Thomas R. Trautmann, Victor Lieberman, Nicholas B. Dirks, Donald J. Munro, Donald S. Lopez Jr., Peter E. Hook, Madhav Deshpande, Pradeep Chhiber, Tahsin Siddiqi, Gurudharam Singh Khalsa, Harbans Singh, Attar Singh, J.S. Grewal, Mohinder Singh, Piar Singh, Madanjit Kaur, Amritjeet Singh and Sulakhan Singh Dhillon provided me with unflinching support at a time when my academic freedom was at stake. I am grateful to all of them.

I thank the Social Sciences and Humanities Research Council of Canada, Ottawa, for providing me with doctoral and post-doctoral fellowships during the course of my research and writing. Appreciation is also extended to the Department of Asian Languages and Cultures and the Center for South and Southeast Asian Studies, University of Michigan, for the summer research grants that made my visits to India and England possible. I am greatly indebted to the family of Sardar Bhajan Singh Sandhu for their hospitality during my stay with them in England. I also acknowledge with thanks the moral support received from Mrs Gurdev K. Attariwala, Dr G.S. Attariwala, Dr Mann Singh Nirankari, Principal Bhagwant Singh, Manjit Singh Pannu, Ajeet Nahal, Gurmale Singh Grewal, Lushman Singh Grewal, Dr Jaswant Singh, Dr Trilochan Singh, Baldev Singh Dhaliwal, Raman Kaur, Dr Virinder Singh Grewal, Dr Sukhbir Singh, Dr Shivdev Singh, Dr Rishpal Singh Aujla, Dr Amrik Singh Chattha, Dr Jaswinder Kaur Chattha and Professor Satnam Singh Bhugra.

An earlier short version of chapter 6 was published as 'Scriptural Adaptation of the Adi Granth' in the *Journal of the American Academy of*

Religion, LXIV/2 (1996). One section of chapter 3 was published as 'Guru Arjan's Ramakali Hymn' in the *Journal of the American Oriental Society*, 16.4 (1996), while another section from chapter 2 was published in an earlier form as 'An Early Sikh Scriptural Tradition: The Guru Nanak Dev University Manuscript 1245' in the *International Journal of Punjab Studies*, Vol. 2, No. 1 (1994).

My special thanks go to my publishers, the Oxford University Press, New Delhi. In particular, I am extremely grateful to Rasna Dhillon and Kaushik Das Gupta, both of whom are responsible for overseeing the project with extraordinary care.

My wife, Baljeet Kaur, deserves special gratitude for her unfailing love, support and sympathetic endurance throughout my studies. I also acknowledge warmly the patience of my children, Manpreet Kaur, Maninder Pal Singh and Kiratpreet Kaur. They have sustained me through this whole period of research and writing. Finally, I owe the greatest debt to my parents, particularly my mother, who sowed the seed of gurbani within me in my childhood. I dedicate this study to their loving memory.

Pashaura Singh
University of Michigan, Ann Arbor

NOTE ON ORTHOGRAPHY

I n this study, many terms and words from the Arabic, Persian, Sanskrit, Hindi and Punjabi languages have been used. Terms common to Punjabi and other north Indian languages have been transliterated in their Punjabi forms, that is, *shabad* instead of *sabda* (divine word), *bani* instead of *vani* (divine utterance), *bhagat* instead of *bhakta* (devotee), *shalok* instead of *sloka* (couplet or stanza). The exceptions are a few instances in which a Sanskrit or Hindi form has secured an established place in English usage, for example, *bhakti* (loving devotion), *karma* (action), and *raga* (melodic organization). These terms have been used in their anglicized forms. All other terms are italicized, although they do not have appropriate diacritical marks in the text.

Except where otherwise indicated, the translations of scriptural quotations are my own, with editorial assistance received from Professor W.H. McLeod. In these translations I have also relied on three translated versions of the Adi Granth: Gopal Singh, *Sri Guru Granth Sahib*, 4 vols. (Delhi: Gur Das Kapoor, 1962); Manmohan Singh, *Sri Guru Granth Sahib*, 8 vols. (Amritsar: Shiromani Gurdwara Prabandhak Committee, 1962–9); and Gurbachan Singh Talib, *Sri Guru Granth Sahib*, 4 vols. (Patiala: Punjabi University, 1984–90). The most commonly used abbreviation in this study is AG, which refers to the Adi Granth. For all quotations from the Adi Granth, I have used the text printed in *Shabadarath Sri Guru Granth Sahib Ji*, which follows the standard Adi Granth pagination of the 1430-page text. The reference M1, *Tilang* 5, AG, p. 722, for instance, means that the passage is from the hymn numbering 5, in measure *Tilang*, by Guru Nanak, on page 722 of the Adi Granth. The code-word mahala (or simply M) with an appropriate number identifies the composition of each Guru. The works by Guru Nanak, Guru Angad, Guru Amar Das, Guru Ram Das, Guru Arjan and Guru Tegh Bahadur are indicated by M 1, 2, 3, 4, 5, and 9 respectively. All the Gurus sign their compositions 'Nanak' in the Adi Granth. Again, the reference *Var Sarang* 1 (16) defines the position of the *shalok* in the *var*, that is, the first shalok of the sixteenth stanza of *Var Sarang*. The var of the Adi Granth is a distinctive genre, which is constituted by a series of stanzas (*pauris*). Each pauri is preceded by a number of subsidiary stanzas called shalok. Another abbreviation used in this study is CE, which stands for common era. Except where otherwise mentioned all dates are CE.

Most of the time only English translations of scriptural passages are given. In certain instances, however, the transliterated versions of the original are also given side by side where it is absolutely necessary for the sake of the argument.

GLOSSARY

Adi Granth	The Guru Granth Sahib, the sacred scripture of the Sikhs compiled by Guru Arjan in 1603–4.
Akal Purakh	The one beyond time; Sikh concept of the divine being analogous to God.
Akal Takhat	Timeless throne; seat of temporal authority of the Guru (especially Guru-Panth) located on the premises of the Harimandir Sahib or Golden Temple at Amritsar.
akhand path	Unbroken reading; an uninterrupted recitation of the entire Guru Granth Sahib by a relay of readers.
amrit	Nectar of immortality; the sanctified water used in the initiation ceremony of the Khalsa.
amrit-dhari	A Sikh who has taken amrit; an initiated member of the Khalsa.
amrit sanskar	The initiation ceremony of the Khalsa.
Anand Karaj	The Sikh marriage ceremony.
Anand Sahib	A forty-verse liturgical composition of Guru Amar Das in *Ramakali* mode. Its short version, first five verses and the last one, is usually recited at the completion of every Sikh service or ceremony.
Ardas	Petition; the daily Sikh prayer recited at the conclusion of every Sikh ceremony.
arti	Adoration; Guru Nanak's hymn in *Dhanasari* mode which is part of the late evening prayer, *Kirtan Sohila*.
Asa	A raga; one of the sections of the Adi Granth.
astapadi	An Adi Granth shabad of eight verses with a refrain.
avatar	A descent; incarnation of a deity, usually Vishnu.
baba	Father or grandfather; a term of affection and respect, often used for religious figures (including the Adi Granth) as well as within the family.
Bala janam-sakhis	One of the extant collections of *janam-sakhi* anecdotes.
bani	Utterance; works of the Gurus and the bhagats recorded in the Adi Granth.

benati chaupai	A liturgical composition which forms part of the evening prayer, *Rahiras Sahib*, is actually from the *Pakhayan Chritar* ('Tales of the Wiles of Women') of the Dasam Granth.
Bhagat	Devotee, one who practises bhakti.
bhagat bani	The utterances of the poet-saints of bhakti, sant and sufi origins, which (along with the compositions of the Sikh Gurus) are recorded in the Adi Granth.
bhai	Brother, title of respect given for piety and/or learning.
Bhairau	A raga; one of the sections of the Adi Granth.
bhakti	Belief in, adoration of a personal god.
bhog	The ceremony which concludes a complete reading of the Guru Granth Sahib. In early manuscripts bhog marks (usually the symbol of *IK Oankar* or other saffron marks) are found at the end of the volume.
chaunki	A division of each day in the larger gurdwaras in which a particular selection of bani is sung. There are five chaunkis each day.
chaupad	An Adi Granth shabad consisting of four verses with a refrain.
chauri	A fan made from yak hair or peacock feathers which is waved over an open Guru Granth Sahib, designating the royal authority of the scripture.
chhant	A lengthy Adi Granth shabad, commonly of four or six lyrical verses.
darshan	Audience; appearance before eminent person, sacred object, etc.
Dasam Granth	Book of the tenth Guru, the scripture whose authorship is attributed to Guru Gobind Singh or his time.
dhadhi	Village bard or minstrel.
dharam (dharma)	Religious and panthic duty.
dharamsala	Place of worship for early Sikh panth (later gurdwara).
dhrupad	Fixed word; a musical style which became popular in north India during the fifteenth and sixteenth centuries.
gaddi	Cushion; seat of authority.
Gauri	A raga; one of the sections of the Adi Granth.
giani	A learned person, especially well versed in Sikh scriptures.
granth	Book or religious scripture, especially the Guru Granth Sahib.
granthi	A reader of the Guru Granth Sahib; the functionary in charge of a gurdwara.

gurbani	Compositions of the Gurus.
gurbani kirtan	Devotional singing of the Gurus' compositions.
Gurbilas	Praise of the Guru; hagiographic narratives of the lives of the sixth and tenth Gurus, stressing their role as warriors.
gurdwara	The Guru's door, the Sikh place of worship; the temple or house in which the Guru Granth Sahib is kept.
gurmat	The view of the Guru, the sum total of the Gurus' teachings; the doctrines referred to as Sikhism.
gurumata	The Guru's intention, a resolution passed by the Sarbat Khalsa (q.v.) in the presence of the Guru Granth Sahib.
gurmukh	One who faces towards the Guru; a follower of the divine, of the Guru.
Gurmukhi	From the Guru's mouth; the script in which the compositions of the Gurus were first written. It has become the script in which Punjabi is written by most Sikhs, and by some others.
gurpurb	Celebration of the birth or death anniversary of one of the ten Sikh Gurus.
Guru	A spiritual 'preceptor', either a person or the divine inner voice. The divine Guru became manifest in the form of ten human Gurus (from Guru Nanak to Guru Gobind Singh) and now persists in the form of the twin doctrine of Guru-Granth and Guru-Panth.
Guru Granth Sahib	The Adi Granth, specifically in its role as Guru.
Guru Khalsa	The Khalsa in its role as Guru.
Guru-Panth	The Panth in the role of Guru.
Hari	Name of God.
Harimandir Sahib	The Golden Temple at Amritsar.
hartal	Deletion; a yellow-greenish paste used for deletion in the manuscripts of the Adi Granth.
hatha-yoga	Yoga of force; the yogic discipline practised by the adherents of the nath tradition.
haumai	I-ness, my-ness, self-centred pride.
hukam	Divine order; a passage from the Guru Granth Sahib chosen at random; cf. *vak*.
IK-Oankar	The one being; benedictory formula from the Adi Granth.
Jaijavanti	A raga; a section of the Adi Granth. This is the last raga of the standard version of the Sikh scripture.
Jat	Punjabi rural caste, numerically dominant in the Sikh Panth.

jathedar	Commander of a Sikh takhat; or the leader of a military band or a group of Sikh protesters.
kabitt	A poetic metre.
kanphat yogi	Split-ear yogi; follower of Gorakhnath and adherent of the nath tradition.
karah prasad	Sacramental food made of flour, sugar and clarified butter, prepared in a large iron dish (*karahi*). It is distributed after each gurdwara service.
karam (karma)	The destiny or fate of an individual, generated in accordance with deeds performed in his/her present and past existences.
katha	Homily.
Kaur	Princess, a name used by female members of the Khalsa, as a parallel to Singh (lion) for men.
Khalsa	The religious order established by Guru Gobind Singh in 1699.
khande di pahul	Baptism of double-edged sword as initiation to the Khalsa.
Khatri	A mercantile caste of the Punjab.
kirtan	Singing of hymns.
lakh	One hundred thousand.
langar	The community kitchen attached to every gurdwara from which food is served to all, regardless of caste or creed; the meal served from such a kitchen.
lav (pl. lavan)	Circumambulating the Guru Granth Sahib as part of a marriage ceremony.
mahala	Code word used to distinguish works by different Gurus in the Adi Granth. For instance, Guru Nanak, as first Guru, is designated 'Mahala 1' or simply 'M1'; the second Guru, Angad, is designated as 'M2' and so on.
mahant	The head of a religious establishment in the Udasi sect; the proprietor of a historical gurdwara until disestablishment in 1925.
Majh	A raga associated with the Majha region of the Punjab; one of the sections of the Adi Granth.
Majha	Middle; the area of central Punjab lying between the Beas and Ravi rivers.
Malwa	The plains tract extending south and southeast of the Satluj river, particularly the area occupied by Ferozepur, Ludhiana and Patiala districts.
man	The complex of heart, mind and spirit; common Indian word.

manji	Preaching office of the early panth.
man-mukh	One who faces towards the uncleaned *man*, that is, a degenerate person.
mantra	A scriptural verse in praise of the divine. It is normally used as a sacred formula to invoke divine grace.
masand	Administrative deputy acting for the Guru. The post was introduced by Guru Ram Das and the incumbents served faithfully for some time, but later became corrupt and were disestablished by Guru Gobind Singh.
Mina	Rascal; a follower of Prithi Chand, eldest son of Guru Ram Das, and a pretender to the office of Guru.
miri-piri	Temporal-spiritual, the Sikh doctrine that maintains that the Guru possesses temporal as well as spiritual authority. It goes back to the sixth Guru, Hargobind, who symbolically donned two swords, one for each type of authority.
nam	The divine name, a summary term expressing the total being of Akal Purakh.
nam japan	Devoutly repeating the divine name.
nam simaran	The devotional practice of meditating on the divine name or nam.
namaz	Muslim prayer, especially prescribed daily prayers.
Nanak-panth	The community of Guru Nanak's followers; the early Sikh community; (later) members of the Sikh community who do not observe the discipline of the Khalsa.
Naqshbandi movement	Muslim revivalist movement introduced into India during the late sixteenth century, vigorously promulgated by Shaikh Ahmad of Sirhind (1564–1624).
nath tradition	Yogic sect of considerable influence in the Punjab prior to and during the time of the Sikh Gurus; practitioners of hatha-yoga.
nawab (navab)	Governor; lord; prince.
nirankar	Without form, a name of Akal Purakh used by Guru Nanak.
nirguna	Without qualities, formless, non-incarnated; cf. saguna.
nirmala	A sect of celibate Sikhs which commanded particular strength in the nineteenth century.
nit-nem	The Sikh daily liturgy.
Panth	The key word refers to the Sikh community; path, way or system of religious belief.
paramarath	Sublime meaning; the technique of scriptural inter-

	pretation which provides the spiritual meaning of a particular hymn.
paratal	Changing of drum-rhythms; hymns of the Adi Granth which must be sung in paratal style based on the changing of drum-rhythms.
pauri	Stanza of a var.
pothi	Tome, volume.
prabandha	An ancient musical style which was characterized by the rigour of its rules leaving no place for improvisation.
Prabhati	A raga; one of the sections of the Adi Granth.
prasad	Sacramentally offered food; cf. karah prasad.
puranamashi	The night of the full moon.
Puratan	One of the extant collections of janam-sakhi anecdotes.
purvang	First portion; the musical scale in which the vadi is in the lower tetrachord.
raga	Musical mode or melodic organization, a series of five or more notes on which a melody is based.
raga-mala	The garland of musical modes, a controversial text containing the list of eighty-four ragas of north India noted at the end of the Guru Granth Sahib.
ragi	Sikh hymn singer.
rahau	Refrain; the rahau-verse is repeated during the musical performance. It represents the central theme of the whole hymn.
Rahiras	The supplication, the evening prayer.
rahit	The code of conduct of the Khalsa.
rahit-nama	Recorded version of the rahit.
Ramakali	A raga; a section of the Adi Granth.
rumala (romila)	A cloth for covering the Guru Granth Sahib (q.v.).
sabha	Society, association.
sach khand	The realm of truth.
saguna	With qualities, possessing form; cf. nirguna.
sahaj	The condition of ultimate bliss resulting from the practice of nam simaran.
samvadi	Co-sonant; usually fourth or fifth pitch above vadi.
sampraday	Doctrine, system of belief; group holding particular beliefs; sect.
sangat	Congregation, group of devotees.
sansar	Transmigration.
Sant	One who knows the truth; a pious person; an adherent of the sant tradition.
	One renowned as a teacher of gurmat.

sant tradition	A devotional school of north India which stressed the need for inner religion as opposed to external observance.
Sarbat Khalsa	The entire Khalsa, representative assembly of the Khalsa.
sat	Truth; true; common Indian word.
satinam	The name is truth.
sat-nam	[Your] name is truth.
satsang	An assembly of true believers; congregation.
seva	Service offered in a gurdwara.
seva-panthi	Fellowship of service; member of the Sikh sect founded by Bhai Ghahnayya, a disciple of Guru Gobind Singh. During the siege of Anandpur, Bhai Ghahnayya toured the battlefield, carrying water to wounded friend and foe alike.
shabad	Word; a hymn of the Adi Granth.
shabadarath	Meanings of words; synonyms of difficult words.
shabad kirtan	Hymn singing in Sikh tradition.
shabad vichar	Reflection on the word; the mode of interpretation of the hymns of the Adi Granth.
shalok	A short composition (normally a couplet) from the Adi Granth (q.v.).
Shiromani Gurdwara Prabandhak Committee	The Sikh organization which controls the main gurdwaras in Punjab and Haryana (commonly referred to as the SGPC).
Shiv, Shiva	The god, who in western usage is usually spelt Siva.
Siddh, Siddha	Eighty-four men believed to have attained immortality through the practice of yoga and to be dwelling deep in the Himalayas. They figure in the janam-sakhis, where they are confused with naths.
Singh Sabha	Reform movement initiated in 1873. The Singh Sabha became an arena for a struggle between the conservative Sanatan Sikhs and the radical Tat Khalsa.
Siri raga	A raga; one of the sections of the Adi Granth. This is the first raga of the standard version of the Sikh scripture.
So Dar	A selection of five hymns from the Adi Granth sung during the early evening. It is part of the evening prayer, Rahiras.
So Purakh	A selection of four hymns from the Adi Granth recited as part of the evening prayer, Rahiras.
Sorathi	A raga; a section of the Adi Granth.
sufi	A Muslim mystic order.

takhat	Throne; one of the five centres of temporal authority within the panth. The five takhats are located at Amritsar, Anandpur Sahib, Damdama Sahib (Bhatinda district), Patna Sahib (Bihar) and Hazur Sahib, Nander (Maharashtra).
tika	Commentary.
tirath	A place of pilgrimage with water.
Udasi	Adherent of the Udasi panth, an order of ascetics (normally celibate) who claim Siri Chand as their founder (Guru Nanak's eldest son).
uttrang	The musical scale in which vadi is in the upper tetrachord.
Vadahans	A raga; a section of the Adi Granth.
vadi	Sonant; the most important pitch in a raga.
Vahiguru	Praise to the Guru, the modern Sikh name for God (wonderful lord).
Vaishnava	Believer in, practitioner of bhakti, directed to the god Vishnu in one of his incarnations (either Ram or Krishan).
vak	Saying; a passage from the Guru Granth Sahib chosen at random; cf. hukam.
var	Ode, a poetic form. An Adi Granth arrangement consisting of stanzas (pauris) with preceding shaloks.
viakhia	Exegesis; extended commentary on a particular hymn from a particular angle.
zat	Caste, an endogamous group.

SECTION ONE

CANON

INTRODUCTION

A book is only 'scripture' insofar as a group of persons perceive it to be sacred or holy, powerful and portentous, possessed of an exalted authority, and in some fashion transcendent of, and hence distinct from, all other speech and writing.[1]

What is scripture? How does it come into being? How does it acquire its canonical status? What is its relationship with the community of believers? How does the community appropriate, interpret and keep the canon alive? These are some fundamental questions that have fascinated the human imagination for centuries. Each religious tradition has addressed these questions in its own way. While reading the literature of the major religious traditions of the world, I was struck by the paucity of any systematic literature produced in response to these questions in my own tradition. It was this quest for satisfactory answers to these questions that inspired me to look at the Sikh tradition more closely. The purpose of the present study is, therefore, to understand various issues related to the concept of scripture from the Sikh perspective.

The Adi Granth is the sacred scripture of the Sikh community. Literally the word *granth* means a religious book. The adjective *adi*, or first has been appended to distinguish this Granth from the second sacred scripture of the Sikhs, the Dasam Granth, which contains the works attributed to the tenth (*dasam*) Guru, Gobind Singh. In Sikh usage, however, the Adi Granth is normally referred to as the Guru Granth Sahib, which implies a confession of faith in the scripture as Guru. As the manifest body of the Guru it carries the same status

---

[1]William A. Graham, *Beyond the Written Word: Oral Aspects of Scripture in the History of Religion* (New York: Cambridge University Press, 1987), p. 5.

and authority as did the ten Gurus from Guru Nanak (1469–1539) to Guru Gobind Singh (1666–1708). It has become the symbol of ultimate sanctity for the Sikh community, and is treated with the most profound respect when it is installed ceremonially in a gurdwara (Guru's door), the Sikh place of worship, or in private Sikh homes. It should, however, be emphasized that the reverence of the Adi Granth as Guru lies not in the text, but in the minds and hearts of the Sikhs.[2] This theme will be elaborated in the final section of this study which discusses the role of the Adi Granth in the corporate and personal lives of the Sikhs.

Let us now examine the theoretical framework related to the general notion of scripture in academic discussion. Literally, the word scripture (from the Latin *scriptura*, a writing) means holy writ, holy writing, or sacred book. In scholarly discourse, however, the concept of scripture is usually used to refer to a canonical text, whose boundaries were fixed long ago, and whose authority within the community of believers is unquestioned. In this context, William Graham makes the point that scripture is a relational concept. He argues that a text becomes scripture only in an active and subjective relationship to persons, and as part of a cumulative communal tradition. From a historian's point of view, the sacredness of a book is not an *a priori* attribute of a text but one that is realized historically in the life of communities who respond to it as something sacred or holy. We cannot conceive of any text as being sacred or authoritative in isolation from a community.[3] Indeed, to describe a text as canonical is to acknowledge its authority for the adherents of that particular religion. It is quite possible that members of one religion may read or admire the sacred scripture of another religion, and feel that they have gained valuable insights from it, but it is only those who belong to that community of faith who regard that scripture as having authority over the way they live or the beliefs they hold.[4]

The main focus in the study of scripture until recently has been on the methods of critical analysis which determine the cultural, historical, and literary influences that gave rise to individual texts. In recent years, however, scholars have shifted their focus from the *content* of religious texts to the *forms* of scriptural traditions. They

[2]cf. Wilfred Cantwell Smith, *What Is Scripture?: A Comparative Approach* (Minneapolis: Fortress Press, 1993), pp. 89–91.

[3]Graham, *Beyond the Written Word*, p. 5.

[4]Jean Holm, 'Introduction: Raising the Issues', in Jean Holm with John Bowker, eds, *Sacred Writings* (London: Pinter Publishers, 1994), p. 2.

are now moving 'beyond the tendency to delimit scripture to the black and white text of "holy writ" and to embrace a broader conception that can also account for such representations of scripture as a supratextual cosmological principle.'[5] Therefore, the study of a text as scripture is not only concerned with its textual problems, the reconstruction of its history, and its contextual meaning, but also with its ongoing role in the cumulative tradition of a religious community, both as a normative source of authority and as a prodigious living force.

The distinction between scripture and text becomes clear in Wilfred Cantwell Smith's recent work, *What Is Scripture?*, in which he emphatically states that scriptures are not merely texts. He argues that scripture is a human activity in which people make a text into scripture by treating it in a certain way.[6] In his analysis, Smith defines scripture as a trilateral term referring to 'a relation—an engagement—among humans, the transcendent, and a text,' thereby stressing the human dimension along with the traditional emphasis on the divine origin of any sacred text. He then affirms that

Scripture has functioned symbolically. It has served as a channel for something beyond itself. One cannot understand any symbol simply by studying that symbol. Nothing is "objectively" a symbol, and its meaning does not lie in itself. It lies in the hearts, minds, lives of those persons and groups for whom it is symbolic (and not in those persons and groups, their neighbors—or perhaps their children—for whom it is not symbolic. This double fact keeps history from being dull!).[7]

In analysing the place of scripture in human life, Smith goes beyond the tendency to define scripture solely in terms of textual categories, and looks at the concept from a broader comparative perspective by taking into consideration various examples from the history of different religious traditions. He maintains that scripture functions not simply as a text but as a symbol of the transcendent, that is, as a supratextual source of authority for a religious community. However, his treatment of Sikh scripture is limited to only two brief paragraphs[8] which (although quite significant in an erudite work like his) reflects the general tendency on the part of scholars to either treat the Sikh tradition briefly or ignore it completely.

[5]Barbara A. Holdrege, *Veda and Torah: Transcending the Textuality of Scripture* (Albany: SUNY Press, 1996), p. 5.

[6]Smith, *What Is Scripture?*, p. 18.

[7]ibid., p. 239.

[8]ibid., pp. 196–7.

Here, our main focus is on the text of the Adi Granth. In particular, we shall try to understand the process of canon-formation in the Sikh tradition. Before we venture to address this issue, however, we need to define the key terms and basic concepts related to this study. The contents of the Adi Granth are normally referred to as *bani* (utterance), or as *gurbani* (the utterance of the Guru). The most frequently employed phrase *dhur ki bani* (utterance from the beginning) refers to the transcendental origin (or ontological status) of the hymns of the Adi Granth. This particular understanding of revelation is based upon the doctrine of the *sabad*, or divine word, enunciated by Guru Nanak and the succeeding Gurus. According to this doctrine, sabad is the vehicle of communication between Akal Purakh (the timeless being, God) and an awakened individual. The inspired utterance of the Guru (gurbani) or bhagat (*bhagat bani*) embodies this divine word. The term used for the divine word itself thus came to be applied to the composition that gave it expression.[9] Thus any individual hymn from the Adi Granth is invariably called a sabad which may be defined as an expression of the experience of the divine truth in verbal form. The word sabad is used in an anglicized form shabad in this study. Similarly, *salok* has been rendered as shalok.

Recently, it has been argued that the Punjabi word bani is a feminine noun and hence it refers to the feminine principle in the Sikh vision of revelation. For instance, Nikky-Guninder Kaur Singh's findings lay emphasis on the feminine dimension of the Sikh scripture:

Bani, feminine in its imagery, feminine in its tone, set in musical patterns that remain in harmony with the rhythm of nature in its daily and seasonal motions, permeates through the senses into the very depths of a person and leads to ecstatic disclosures.[10]

In her analysis, however, Nikky Singh does not mention that the Punjabi word sabad is a masculine noun. Does it (like other key terms of masculine gender such as *nam* or divine name, *hukam* or divine order, *raga* or musical measure, Guru or divine preceptor and so on) highlight the masculine dimension of revelation? It is indeed difficult to offer an argument about the nature of divine revelation on the basis of the gender of a community's terminology. Nevertheless, Nikky Singh's work provides us with a much needed

---

[9]W.H. McLeod, *Early Sikh Tradition* (Oxford: Clarendon Press, 1980), p. 288.

[10]Nikky-Guninder Kaur Singh, *The Feminine Principle in the Sikh Vision of the Transcendent* (Cambridge: Cambridge University Press, 1993), p. 248.

feminist perspective on Sikh tradition. She has employed gender-free language for the first time in her analysis of the scriptural passages and their translations.

REVELATION OF THE BANI AND ITS VERBAL EXPRESSION

The concept of revelation is an important factor in the ascription of authority to sacred texts. It is based on the assumption that the texts possess absolute authority if they have a very special origin, that is, if they have originated from a divine source. In its basic sense, revelation may be defined as 'a divine communication shaped to the interests and values of a particular society at a particular time,' and the proper content of revelation may be understood as the 'nature of an object of supreme value, of a final goal for human life, and of the way to achieve this goal'.[11] As textual critics or historians, however, we have no independent method to determine the nature of revelation. The only way we can understand the truth-claims of revelation in different religious traditions is to allow the scriptural texts to speak for themselves. Although these conflicting truth-claims are beyond the province of the history of religions, we can try to understand their impact on the historical development of a particular religious community. In this section, therefore, our primary concern is to understand the concept of revelation from the Sikh perspective. In particular, we shall try to address the following questions: What is the relationship between the revealed message and its verbal expression? Can human language describe adequately the divine message?

In order to fully comprehend the idea of how Akal Purakh reveals the divine word to the Guru or bhagat through direct communication and how that word becomes the primary focus in the evolution of the Sikh community, we need to examine the actual works of the Gurus from the Adi Granth. Let us consider, for instance, the first two lines from Guru Nanak's *Tilang* hymn:

> As the bani of the Lord comes to me so do I proclaim its knowledge (*gian*), O Lalo! From Kabul he (Babur) has descended with sin as his marriage-party and forcibly demanded a dowry, O Lalo!
>
> (M1, *Tilang* 5, AG, p. 722)

The actual context of this utterance is said to be a battlefield on which Babur's invading army defeated Indian forces. Here, Guru

---

[11] Keith Ward, *Religion and Revelation* (Oxford: Clarendon Press, 1994), pp. 24, 30.

Nanak is responding to an actual life-situation with his profound inner experience. In tune with Akal Purakh, he reflects on the situation at hand, and communicates his deep knowledge (gian) to the people through the medium of the spoken language. The divine message is thus conveyed in common parlance reflecting the cultural code of that time. Indeed, the typical use of the word gian indicates how the bani inspired Guru Nanak's own thought processes as he pondered the situation in a particular historical context.

In the celebrated *Japji* Guru Nanak maintains that the glory of Akal Purakh is sung under such aspects as are relative to the endowments of the seeker.[12] In other words, Akal Purakh reveals himself to the devotee in terms of the constitution and faculties of the human mind, and in accordance with the needs of the age. Indeed, no mode of cognition is capable of understanding reality-in-itself; what is apprehended is relative to the mode of apprehension, which determines the form in which reality is known.[13] These points are made explicit in the clear distinction which Guru Nanak makes throughout his works between the divine message (bani) and its expression in actual words (*akhar*). In his *Patti Likhi* (thus was the slate written), for instance, Guru Nanak proclaims that 'those who through the grace of the Guru understand the divine mystery behind these letters (*akhar*) erase the debt [of karma] from their heads.'[14] Thus it is the meaning behind the words (*akhar*) and not the words themselves that constitute the locus of revelation in Sikhism. Similarly, in his *Bavan Akhari* (the fifty-two letters) Kabir maintains that 'these letters (*akhar*) will vanish whereas those [mystic] syllables are beyond these letters.'[15] These scriptural passages clearly indicate a differentiation between the medium of expression (akhar) and the divine message, a message which is by its very nature inexpressible. More precisely, language is primarily an instrument for articulating an approximation to the divine message.

The second Guru, Angad (1504–52), composed only sixty-two shaloks of bani during the thirteen years of his guruship. These shaloks throw considerable light on the historical situation of the Sikh Panth (community). He employed the word bani for the 'nectar-like utterances' (*amrit bani*) of Guru Nanak and marked the doctrinal

[12]M1, *Japu* 3, AG, pp. 1–2.

[13]Jasbir Singh Ahluwalia, *The Sovereignty of Sikh Doctrine* (New Delhi: Bahri Publications, 1983), p. 46.

[14]M1, *Ragu Asa Patti Likhi*, AG, p. 432. Also see Guru Nanak's *Japji* 19, AG, p. 4.

[15]Kabir, *Gauri Purabi Bavan Akhari*, AG, p. 340.

boundaries of the Sikh faith in strict conformity with the message of his predecessor. In a particularly striking instance, he describes the nature of divine revelation and makes a clear distinction between the Vedas and the compositions of the Guru:

Shalok M 2
Discourses on the stories from the Vedas discuss sins and merits. People are recompensed according to their deeds and thereby they descend into hell or ascend into heaven. Caught up in notions of high and low castes, the world strays in delusion. The nectar-like *bani* which expounds the nature of ultimate reality (*tatu*) has come (*ai*) through enlightenment and deep meditation. The one who is Guru-oriented (*gurmukh*) has uttered it and has known it, and [only those] blessed with divine grace praise it and meditate on it. According to the divine order all is created; according to the divine order all is preserved; and according to the divine order its innermost parts are perceived. Only when one's self-centredness (*haumai*) is shattered, O Nanak, is one recorded in divine reckoning. (1)
(M2, *Var Sarang* 1 (16), AG, p. 1243)

Here the term 'Vedas' is probably used as a general term for Hindu religious texts, which stress the inexorable nature of the law of karma, the consequences of good and bad karma as heaven and hell, and institutional discrimination on the basis of caste and gender. Guru Angad may be alluding here to the Vedic injunction that Shudras and women are prohibited from even hearing the Vedas.[16] In contrast to the worldview of many Hindu texts, Guru Angad claims the exclusive status of bani which delivers all people from the shackles of karma and from the discriminatory aspects of the caste system through divine grace. He stresses the functioning of the divine order (hukam) in human affairs, which overrides the law of karma. Indeed, for the Sikh Gurus, the law of karma is not inexorable. It is subject to the higher principle of hukam (divine order) which is defined as 'an all-embracing principle, the sum total of all divinely instituted laws; and it is a revelation of the nature of God.'[17] Further, Guru Angad maintains that the bani came (ai) to those awakened individuals who had achieved the perfect state of enlightenment through the grace of the Guru. Thus by stressing the inspired nature of bani Guru Angad laid down doctrinally, the requirement for the compilation of the Sikh scripture parallel to the

[16]Thomas B. Coburn, '"Scripture" in India', in Miriam Levering, ed., *Rethinking Scripture: Essays from a Comparative Perspective* (Albany: SUNY Press, 1989), p. 107.
[17]See W.H. McLeod, *Guru Nanak and Sikh Religion* (Oxford: Clarendon Press, 1968), p. 203.

Vedas.[18] Furthermore, by his time the bani had already acquired an exclusive status within the Sikh Panth, and it had become the focus of congregational worship.

The next substantial contribution to the bani, however, came from the third Guru, Amar Das (1479–1574), who composed 907 hymns, drawing his inspiration from the 974 hymns of Guru Nanak.[19] He enveloped the bani of the first Guru in his own, and thereby laid the foundation for its long survival.[20] He employed the word bani far more frequently than Guru Nanak did, and in many more crucial contexts. To be precise, Guru Amar Das used the word 170 times, as against 62 in Guru Nanak's larger number of hymns.[21] In the first place, he used it in its conventional sense of a composition by one of the Gurus: 'Come, dear Sikhs of the true Guru, sing the true bani of the Guru, the best bani of all banis!'[22] Secondly, Guru Amar Das identified it with the formless lord (*nirankar*) himself: 'Hail, hail the bani, which itself is the formless lord. There is nothing else its equal.'[23] Here, the bani is represented not as gross speech but as subtle impulses of sound reverberating forth from the formless one (nirankar). In other words, the bani functions as the living voice of Akal Purakh which resounds throughout creation.

Finally, Guru Amar Das used the term bani more frequently for the universal bani which perpetually exists through all ages and in all places. It is itself held as an object of devotion: 'Love the bani of the Guru. It is our support in all places and it is bestowed by the creator himself.'[24] For Guru Amar Das, Guru Nanak's bani was the pre-eminent example of the universal bani, which exists eternally through all ages. He explicitly states:

> True is the bani of that servant [of the lord], which has pervaded the world through the word of the Guru. Its true report has resounded throughout the four ages. Imbued in the divine name, his servant stands revealed.

(M3, Basant 7, AG, p. 1174)

[18]Surjit Hans, *A Reconstruction of Sikh History from Sikh Literature* (Jalandhar: ABS Publication, 1988), p. 48.

[19]Taran Singh, ed., *Guru Granth Ratnavali* (Patiala: Punjabi University, 1975), p. 14.

[20]Christopher Shackle, 'The First Restatement of the Bani', *The Sikh Courier* (London, Autumn–Winter 1985), p. 72.

[21]ibid., p. 73.

[22]M3, *Ramakali Anandu* 23, AG, p. 920.

[23]M3, *Var Gujari*, 1 (18), AG, p. 515.

[24]M3, *Prabhati* 7, AG, p. 1335.

The divine word (sabad) is thus the underlying inspiration of the universal bani, which together with the Guru is the instrument of liberation throughout the ages. In this context, Christopher Shackle aptly maintains that it is Guru Amar Das's formulation of the doctrine of the bani to which one should look for the first overt expression of reverence for the bani's physical form. This tendency was ultimately to lead to the fusion of bani and Guru in the traditional proclamation of Guru Gobind Singh that both were to be exclusively embodied in the Guru Granth Sahib.[25]

During his brief ministry of seven years, the fourth Guru, Ram Das (1534–81), contributed a total of 679 hymns and expanded the range of available musical modes or *ragas* by adding eleven new ones, which were not used by the earlier Gurus. He used the key word gurbani (Guru's utterance) in its modern sense for the first time. In his compositions the identification of the bani with the Guru becomes quite explicit:

> The bani is the Guru and the Guru the bani, and the nectar (amrit) permeates all the bani. When the Guru utters the bani and the believer responds with faith, then shall it be seen that the Guru bears him to freedom.[26]

(M4, *Nat Astapadian 4*, AG, p. 982)

This verse of Guru Ram Das clearly foreshadowed the doctrine of Guru-Granth which came to be fully developed when, according to well-founded tradition, Guru Gobind Singh installed the Adi Granth as Guru before he passed away in 1708. This acknowledgement of the scripture as Guru made *de jure* what was in a sense already *de facto*.

The fifth Guru, Arjan (1563–1606), covered a large span of human experience during his twenty-five years of guruship and composed 2218 hymns, which makes him by far the largest contributor to the scripture.[27] In fact, the popular expression *dhur ki bani* (utterance from the Beginning) comes from his *Sorathi* hymn:

> This utterance (bani) has come from the beginning. It has effaced all anxiety from my heart. The supreme being is kind and compassionate. Says Nanak: the lord has revealed the truth.

(M5, *Sorathi 13*, AG, p. 628)

[25]Shackle, 'The First Restatement of the Bani', p. 73.
[26]Cited in W.H. McLeod, ed. and trans., *The Chaupa Singh Rahit-nama* (Dunedin: University of Otago Press, 1987), p. 204.
[27]Taran Singh, *Guru Granth Ratnavali*, p. 14.

Here, the bani is portrayed as existing prior to the revelation, since the beginning of creation, as the instrument of creative power through which Akal Purakh brought forth the universe. Thus the expression dhur ki bani refers to the primordial wisdom as a living force and the immediate source of creation. Indeed, this statement of Guru Arjan has become the standard view of the divine origin of the Sikh scripture. That is why he did not regard the Adi Granth as an ordinary compilation: 'The book is the abode of the Supreme Lord.'[28] In fact, the Adi Granth was granted an especially sacrosanct and authoritative status when Guru Arjan installed it in the newly built Harimandir, now known as the Golden Temple of Amritsar.

Let us now briefly put this inquiry into a comparative perspective. Providing a global perspective on the understanding of the revealed nature of scripture, Wilfred Cantwell Smith maintains that

Scripture begins on high, and has found its way down to us, or such. The Qur'an that Muslims revere is originally on a heavenly tablet, from before the beginning of time. In fact, the standard way of referring to it is that it "came down"— or rather, was sent down. The Zohar speaks of the Torah as primordially without division into words, and only later unfolding into its verbal form. Veda, as we have seen, has been sounding from all eternity; the *rsis* captured some part of it. And so on.[29]

Clearly, the various religious communities across the globe maintain the divine status of their respective scriptures in one way or another. Each scripture is, however, a partial manifestation of the divine intention in a specific cultural context. The echoes of the Sikh idea of the universal bani may be heard in Smith's description. Further, the revelation in the Adi Granth has its heritage in the rich concept of sabad (sacred sound) in Indian thought.[30] It may be noted that Smith places too much emphasis on similarities, and does not pay much attention to the differences that give each tradition its unique character and identity.

In order to fully understand the current debate over the issues of divine revelation versus textual analysis, we need to examine different approaches towards the inspired nature of scriptural texts. For instance, the entry on divine revelation in *The Encyclopaedia of Sikhism* reads:

[28]M5, *Sarang* 90, AG, p. 1226.
[29]Smith, *What Is Scripture?*, p. 234.
[30]W. Owen Cole and Piara Singh Sambhi, *The Sikhs: Their Beliefs and Practices* (London: Routledge & Kegan Paul, 1978), p. 52.

Revelation is defined as the way God discloses and communicates Himself to humanity. There are different views on how he does this. The Hindu belief is that God occasionally becomes incarnate as an *avatar* and thus communicates Himself through his word and action while living on this earth. For the Muslims the revelation consists in actual words in the form of direct messages conveyed from God through the angel Gabriel, to the Prophet. Another belief is that God communicates not the form but the contents of the words, i.e., knowledge, to man. A related view is that, as a result of the mystic unity they achieve with Universal Self, certain individuals under Divine inspiration arrive at truths which they impart to the world. The Gurus did not subscribe to the incarnation theory ... nor did they acknowledge the existence of angels or intermediaries between God and man. They were nevertheless conscious of their divine mission and described the knowledge and wisdom contained in their hymns as God-given ... It is in this sense that Bani is revelation for the Sikhs. It is for them God's Word mediated through the Gurus or Word on which the Gurus had put their seal. The Bani echoes the Divine Truth; it is the voice of God ... [31]

This is a general statement on the issue of divine revelation with explicit reference to Hindu and Muslim traditions, but with implicit reference to the Sikh concept of revelation that 'God communicates not the form but the contents of the words, i.e., knowledge, to man.' Accordingly, the Sikh Gurus were conscious of their divine mission, and they described the 'knowledge and wisdom' contained in their hymns as divinely inspired. Although the above statement fails to take into account the rich tradition of Vedic revelation (*sruti*, what is heard), it certainly lays emphasis on the role of an avatar as the medium of divine revelation in the Hindu tradition. In the Muslim case, it makes the point that revelation takes place in the form of actual words being conveyed to the Prophet through an angel, Gabriel. In this context, Harold Coward aptly maintains that in Islam 'there is no notion of an inspiration from God that is then clothed and uttered in the best words a human mind can create.'[32] In the Qur'an, he argues, Muhammad receives a direct, fully composed revelation from God, which he then recites to others.[33] Evidently there are different notions of revelation in different religious contexts.

Certain participants in the current scholarly debate on the Adi Granth text have a different notion of revelation, a notion which

[31]Harbans Singh, ed., *The Encyclopaedia of Sikhism*, Vol. 1 (Patiala: Punjabi University, 1992), p. 276.

[32]Harold Coward, *Sacred Word and Sacred Text: Scripture in World Religions* (Maryknoll, New York: Orbis Books, 1988), p. 82.

[33]ibid.

they may have picked up from the Islamic tradition (or from the Christian literalist interpretation of the Bible). In their discourse, they seem to superimpose Islamic concepts on Sikh tradition and maintain that actual words were revealed to the Gurus rather than the content of the words (that is, knowledge). They further maintain that 'a change in revealed bani is a theological contradiction.'[34] This shift in understanding is a move to a much narrower interpretation of the kind of revelation entailed in the Adi Granth text. The new model is less Indian and less Sikh than Qur'anic. According to this interpretation the text itself is revealed, given to the Gurus directly by Akal Purakh. That is, perfect words had been delivered in an unchangeable form and consecrated in a perfect scripture. Such an approach removes all space for viewing the creation of the text as a historical process. In fact, this particular notion of revelation cannot be sustained in the light of variant readings that we encounter in the Adi Granth and also in the collation of certain pre-canonical texts. The most illuminating instance is the appearance of Guru Nanak's *So Dar* (that door) hymn in three different versions in the standard version of the Adi Granth, one in the morning prayer (*Japji*), the other in the evening prayer (*So Dar Rahiras*) and the third in the Asa Raga.[35] The count of variants in this text alone goes up to thirty-one. It would seem arbitrary and naive to claim that the *So Dar* hymn was revealed to Guru Nanak on three different occasions in three different versions. There are other such instances in the Adi Granth where certain hymns appear at two different places with remarkable text variants.

In this context, Piar Singh aptly argues that the 'Sikh revelation cannot claim to have come in those very linguistic units in which it is found recorded in the Holy Scripture.'[36] In order to address the issue of 'variant readings', therefore, he offers the following definition of revelation: 'when in tune with the Universal Consciousness, revelations came to the Gurus in ideas, concepts or truths, which the Gurus put in common parlance and broadcast them for the benefit of the people at large.'[37] This definition is in line with the

---

[34]Kharak Singh, ed., *Abstracts of Sikh Studies* (Chandigarh: Institute of Sikh Studies, January 1993), p. 17.

[35]M1, *Japu* 27, AG, p. 6; *So Daru Ragu Asa* 1, AG, pp. 8–9; *Ragu Asa Gharu 1 So Daru* 1, AG, pp. 47–8.

[36]Piar Singh, *Gatha Sri Adi Granth and the Controversy* (Grandledge, Michigan: Anant Education and Rural Development Foundation, Inc., 1996), p. 149. (Hereafter refered to as *Gatha*)

[37]ibid., pp. 149–50.

self-understanding of the Gurus themselves, and makes perfect sense in the light of several examples of differing versions of the text where the same meanings have been expressed in different words. This will be discussed later in the third chapter of this study.

In sum, there has historically been a differentiation between the divine message—that is to say, the full intent or meaning of the scripture revealed to the Gurus—and the actual language of the Adi Granth. This understanding is based on the assumption that the process of recording or striving to articulate divine inspiration will inevitably entail some process of reduction. This position is historically in accordance with Indian thought about sacred texts; the Veda, for example, is believed to have been given at the moment of creation, but the Veda that we now have in hand is less than the fullness of that Veda.[38] Such an approach would assume that humans have had some hand in shaping the Vedic or Sikh hymns now on record. It should, however, be emphasized that the Gurus' personal beliefs about the inspired nature of their utterances have always promoted the self-understanding of the evolving Sikh Panth during the last five centuries with respect to the revealed character of Sikh scripture.

TRANSMISSION OF THE BANI AND COMPILATION OF THE ADI GRANTH

The compilation of the Adi Granth was the culmination of a process that had already begun in Guru Nanak's lifetime during the period when he resided at Kartarpur, a religious commune that he founded on the right bank of the River Ravi in the Punjab. The community of disciples (Sikhs) that first grew around him at Kartarpur during the early decades of the sixteenth century received the message of liberation through religious hymns of unique genius and notable beauty. Stressing the originality of Guru Nanak's hymns, W.H. McLeod perceptively remarks:

Plainly there is much that is profoundly original in the hymns which we find recorded under his [Guru Nanak's] distinctive symbol in the Adi Granth. There is in them an integrated and coherent system which no other Sant has equalled; and there is a beauty which no other Sant has matched.[39]

[38]See Holdrege, *Veda and Torah*, pp. 29–32.
[39]W.H. McLeod, *The Sikhs: History, Religion, and Society* (New York: Columbia University Press, 1989), p. 31.

The earliest Sikh community began to use these hymns in devotional singing (*kirtan*) as a part of congregational worship. In this context, J.S. Grewal has aptly pointed out that the use of Guru Nanak's compositions in Sikh liturgy developed logically and historically into the compilation of the Adi Granth by Guru Arjan in 1604.[40]

Guru Nanak frequently regarded himself as the herald of Akal Purakh, proclaiming the glory of the divine word: 'The *dhadi* (minstrel) openly proclaims the glory of the divine word (sabad).'[41] He repeatedly asserted that his sayings were the result of direct communication from Akal Purakh,[42] and thus instructed his disciples to have faith in the bani of the true Guru as the truth and the path to self-realization.[43] Such a deep consciousness of divine inspiration must have created an urgency to preserve the bani through oral as well as written media. It was quite natural for the first Sikhs to memorize the Guru's hymns and to express their faith by showing their allegiance to the revealed message of their Guru. So there came into being an oral tradition of transmitting the poetic compositions of Guru Nanak, which is prevalent among Sikhs even today. Moreover, the contribution of modern research to the area of oral tradition has now firmly established that scripture can be transmitted orally with relatively little change, provided certain conventions are observed. These include specific memory training, mnemonic devices, control over the recital by certain members of the audience, and a preference for poetry rather than prose.[44]

There are certain references in the hymns of Guru Nanak that point towards the existence of a written tradition during his lifetime. He maintained that one might lose the divine word through oral recitation alone if one has not written it down to preserve it.[45] It is, however, important to note that the Gurmukhi script in its present form was almost non-existent before Guru Nanak. Indeed, his composition *Patti Likhi* in the *Asa* mode formed the basis of the Gurmukhi characters, which were used in recording his works.[46]

[40]J.S. Grewal, 'A Perspective on Early Sikh History', in Mark Juergensmeyer and N. Gerald Barrier, eds, *Sikh Studies: Comparative Perspectives on a Changing Tradition* (Berkeley: Berkeley Religious Studies Series and Graduate Theological Union, 1979), p. 36.

[41]M1, *Var Majjh* 27, AG, p. 150.

[42]M1, *Vadahansu Chhant* 1, AG, p. 566: 'I speak only when you inspire me to speak, O Lord.'

[43]M1, *Maru Solahe* 8, AG, p. 1028.

[44]McLeod, *Early Sikh Tradition*, p. 106.

[45]M1, *Vadahansu Chhant* 1, AG, p. 566.

[46]M1, *Ragu Asa Patti Likhi*, AG, pp. 432–4.

This composition is a kind of acrostic which Guru Nanak composed to match the letters of the alphabet. In fact, the original Gurmukhi script is a systematization of *lande/mahajani* business shorthands, of the kind Guru Nanak must have used professionally as a young man.[47] It was also known as *takari*. According to a note on the opening folio of *Sarang* mode in the second volume of the Goindval pothis, Guru Angad formulated the Gurmukhi script under the supervision of Guru Nanak to record the compilation of the Guru's hymns (bani).[48] This was an emphatic rejection of the superiority of Devnagari and Persian scripts (along with Sanskrit and Persian languages), and the hegemonic authority they represented in the scholarly and religious circles of that time. The use of the Gurmukhi script certainly added an element of demarcation and self-identity to the early Sikh tradition.

In Guru Nanak's compositions the inscription of the divine name is an important theme in itself.[49] In one of his shaloks, for instance, he praises those scribes who devoted themselves to writing the divine name:

> Blessed is the paper, blessed the pen. Blessed is the pot which contains the blessed ink. The scribe is blessed, O Nanak, who writes the true divine name.
>
> (M1, *Var Malhar* 1 (28), AG, p. 1291)

This verse clearly suggests that the written tradition of the transmission of bani must have begun during Guru Nanak's lifetime. Elsewhere, he even chastises those scribes who made a living by copying the bani and selling it as incantation: 'A curse on those who write the divine name and sell it [for profit].'[50] These scribes had misunderstood the essential purpose of bani which was meant to be distributed freely.

It is possible that Guru Nanak himself wrote down his compositions. Unlike many religious figures of his day he was not illiterate,[51] and no one can deny the organizational skills which he developed in his professional training as a Khatri businessman. Bhai Gurdas has recorded that Guru Nanak used to carry a book (*kitab*) of his own compositions on his missionary tours, although the manuscript of this collection is no longer extant.[52] The Sodhi family

---

[47]For more details, see G.B. Singh, *Gurmukhi Lipi da Janam te Vikas* (Chandigarh: Panjab University, 1972).

[48]Pinjore Pothi, f. 216.

[49]M1, *Siri Ragu* 6, AG, p. 16.

[50]M1, *Var Sarang* 1 (20), AG, p. 1246.

[51]McLeod, *Guru Nanak and the Sikh Religion*, p. 227.

[52]*Varan Bhai Gurdas*, 1: 32.

of the village Guru Har Sahai, in Ferozepur district, who are the direct descendants of Prithi Chand (Guru Arjan's elder brother), claimed to have in their possession this first written pothi, which unfortunately was reported to have been lost in a train theft in 1970.[53] However, nothing much can be stated with certainty without sufficient information concerning the contents of this volume. There exists no known manuscript of Guru Nanak's compositions written in his own hand or in his lifetime.

The consolidating process within the Panth had, however, gone so far that the idea of a religious community having sacred writings was in due course appropriated and absorbed from the parallel examples of the Hindu and Muslim communities of the Punjab. In this context, the first definite attempt by the Sikh tradition to record a single collection of approved works was evidently made during Guru Amar Das's period. The reason for this was that there were growing problems of access to and authenticity of the bani in the rapidly expanding Sikh community throughout India. Secondly, there was a demand for copies of the bani in various Sikh *sangats* (congregations). Bhai Gurdas gives the names of Pandha and Bula as the singer and scribe of the third Guru who made copies of the hymns of the Gurus for distribution among Sikhs.[54]

Thirdly, there are indications that some schismatic groups circulated hymns under the name of Nanak with the intention of winning a following of loyal Sikhs. There exist some specimens of such hymns in an early manuscript. For instance, a fifteen-verse composition *Sri Ragu Mahal 3 Chhant* is attributed to Guru Amar Das, but is not included in the standard version of the Adi Granth. This may have originated from the circles of schismatic groups.[55] Guru Amar Das thus voiced a general warning against the circulation of 'unripe utterances' (*kachi bani*): 'Apart from the [compositions of the] true Guru all bani is spurious. Those who recite it are spurious; likewise those who hear it and those who propagate it.'[56] Therefore, to counter the threat of spurious hymns becoming popular among the Sikhs and to provide authentic versions of the bani for the community, Guru Amar Das undertook the task of collecting the sacred works of his own composition and of the previous Gurus,

---

[53]Giani Gurdit Singh, *Itihas Sri Guru Granth Sahib: Bhagat Bani Bhag* (Chandigarh: Sikh Sahit Sansthan, 1990), pp. 559–61.

[54]*Varan Bhai Gurdas*, 11: 16.

[55]See Bhai Gurdas Library, Rare Books Section, GNDU, MS # 1245, ff. 101b–103b.

[56]M3, *Ramakali Anandu* 24, AG, p. 920.

together with selections from compositions of some bhagats. He prepared the so-called Goindval pothis, at least two copies of which are still extant with the descendants of the third Guru.

Although the Goindval volumes provided a substantial nucleus for formulating the scripture, there were other collections of the Gurus' hymns that were preserved by devout Sikhs and must have been available to Guru Arjan for inclusion in the Adi Granth. The index of the Kartarpur manuscript of the Adi Granth clearly states that the text of the introductory *Japu* (of Guru Nanak) was copied from a manuscript written by Guru Ram Das.[57] It seems that Guru Ram Das also made copies of collections of bani. Moreover, among the Sikhs there was a professional class of scribes who copied the works of the Gurus: 'Those hands are pure and holy, my soul, which are used in writing the praises of the lord.'[58] Thus, by stressing the devotional and religious significance of writing bani, Guru Ram Das raised the status of the scribes, who were otherwise held in low esteem in India. Furthermore, like his predecessor, Guru Ram Das also warned against the circulation of 'unripe utterances' among the Sikhs: 'Those who in imitation of the true Guru make false utterances are fools, and they are destroyed by their lies.'[59] This continuing threat of spurious hymns must have hastened the process of the compilation of the Adi Granth under his successor.

Guru Arjan inherited a large body of sacred verse when he assumed the office of guruship in 1581. He was filled with admiration when he found priceless gems and inexhaustible treasure in what had been preserved by his predecessors: 'After opening the treasure of my spiritual father and grandfather, I looked at it, and then I realized the divine treasure in my own heart, mind and soul (*man*).'[60] Here the reference to the ancestral treasure (*piu dade ka khajana*) may suggest that Guru Arjan received at least two sets of manuscripts of bani, one belonging to his father, Guru Ram Das, and the other to his maternal-grandfather, Guru Amar Das. The works of the first three Gurus, together with the bhagats, were grouped together in the Goindval pothis. Since Guru Ram Das was not represented in these volumes, Guru Arjan may have had access to at least a second manuscript, containing the works of his father. All such documents

[57]Bhai Jodh Singh, *Sri Kartarpuri Bir de Darshan* (Patiala: Punjabi University, 1968), p. 4.

[58]M4, *Bihagara Chhant* 4, AG, p. 540.

[59]M4, *Var Gauri* 9 AG, p. 304.

[60]M5, *Gauri* 31, AG, pp. 185–6.

containing the works of his predecessors would have been an important source of inspiration for Guru Arjan right from the beginning of his ministry. Acquaintance with this earlier corpus of hymns would have facilitated his own composition of a large number of short lyrical pieces (sabads) which could be easily memorized.

The process of the creation of a scripture is, of course, linked with the question of why Guru Arjan made the decision to prepare an authorized volume. The traditional answer to this question is that he did so in response to the threat of the Minas—the descendants of his elder brother Prithi Chand, and their followers—who were circulating spurious hymns under the name of Nanak.[61] However, this answer appears for the first time in several eighteenth-century sources, namely the *Bansavali-nama* (1769), written by Kesar Singh Chhibbar, and the *Chaupa Singh Rahit-nama* (1765), coming from the same Chhibbar tradition.[62] This tradition reflects an eighteenth-century Sikh understanding of the compilation of the Adi Granth, which was carried into nineteenth-century Sikh sources. There is, however, no contemporary evidence to support the contention that the Minas were involved in the propagation of spurious hymns. The Miharvan *janam-sakhi* and other literature from their circle appeared long after the compilation of the Adi Granth in 1604.[63] Even the threat of circulation of apocryphal writings, which had been coming from certain groups within the Panth since the days of Guru Amar Das, does not appear to have been the major factor in the compilation of the Adi Granth, though it may have prompted the process of compilation to a certain extent.

The compilation of the Adi Granth and its acceptance as scripture is better understood, not as the response to a threat, but as part of a more complex process of consolidation and crystallization[64] which the Sikh tradition had been undergoing from the Kartarpur period of Guru Nanak's life. This process reached another milestone in the

---

[61]For details on the Mina sect, see McLeod, *Guru Nanak and the Sikh Religion*, pp. 18–19, n. 4.

[62]Rattan Singh Jaggi, ed., 'Bansavali Nama Dasan Patshahian Ka', *Parakh: Research Bulletin of Punjabi Language and Literature*, Vol. II (Chandigarh: Panjab University, 1972), p. 51 and McLeod, trans., *The Chaupa Singh Rahit-nama*, pp. 92 and 173, nos 248–9.

[63]For more details, see McLeod, *Guru Nanak and the Sikh Religion*, pp. 18–21.

[64]I had earlier used the word crystallization to describe an emerging religious community from Wilfred Cantwell Smith's article, 'The Crystallization of Religious Communities in Mughal India,' *On Understanding Islam: Selected Studies* (The Hague: Mouton Publishers, 1981), pp. 177–96. The change to the word consolidation comes from Smith's latest work, *What Is Scripture?*, p. 47.

history of the Panth during the period of the fifth Guru. As J.C. Archer puts it: 'the bare fact of canon-making has significance in itself. The Sikhs were intent upon a book.'[65] The primary intention of Guru Arjan was to create an authoritative text for the Sikh community through which it could understand and assert its unique identity. By doing so he could affix a seal on the sacred word to preserve it for posterity and also frustrate any attempts by schismatic groups to circulate spurious hymns for sectarian ends.

In his article 'Scripture as Form and Concept,' Wilfred Cantwell Smith refers to the general idea of a set of divinely inspired utterances cast in a fixed written form, but suitable for oral presentation. He argues that scripture as a religious phenomenon gradually emerged and developed in the Near East in a process of consolidation, the virtually complete stage of which comes with the Qur'an. He then suggests that the creation of Sikh scripture was manifestly influenced by the Qur'an:

When we say that in the Qur'an this process culminates, we do not mean to suggest that it altogether stops at that point. Almost a thousand years later the Granth Sahib, the scripture of the then emergent Sikh community in India, the form of it and the concept of it and its place in the personal piety and corporate polity of the Sikh community over the next three or so centuries, until today, were manifestly influenced in turn by the Qur'an: the scripture as a form and a concept in the religious life of the Muslims with which the Sikh movement emerged as continuous. That movement was continuous also, in another way and perhaps less closely, with the Hindu.[66]

Smith's view may be acceptable if we limit ourselves to the general category of scripture as a form and a concept. The creation of a unified scripture for the Sikh community was certainly suggested by the surrounding Islamic tradition. This compositional influence may be seen among early Sikh scribes who followed the Qur'anic tradition of illuminating the margins and the opening folios of the manuscripts of the Adi Granth. It may also be seen in the place that Adi Granth occupies in the personal piety and corporate polity of the Sikhs. But apart from this peripheral influence, there is no evidence of any direct influence of the Qur'an on the structure or content of the Sikh scripture. For instance, the raga organization of the Adi Granth can be understood only in the context of Indian religious

---

[65]John Clark Archer, *The Sikhs in Relation to Hindus, Moslems, Christians, and Ahmadiyyas: A Study in Comparative Religion* (Princeton: Princeton University Press, 1946), p. 146.

[66]Smith, *What Is Scripture?*, p. 48.

literary traditions. The Qur'an does not provide the model for the organization and content of the Adi Granth. Smith seems to put too much emphasis on the Muslim influence in the formation of the Adi Granth, both absolutely and relatively to the Indian scriptural precedent. He argues that Sikh scripture's 'form, status, role in practice, and metaphysical interpretation in theory, have approximated more closely to Western counterparts, including especially the Qur'an, than have any other within India.'[67] Elsewhere, he provides a somewhat balanced perspective: 'The scripture's close-to-supreme place in Sikh life is reminiscent of the Near Eastern scriptural tradition, even though of course analogies also with Hindu patterns are discernible—aside from the basic uniqueness of the Sikh orientation, which can be quite special.'[68] Indeed, it is evident from the works of the Gurus that they were self-consciously involved in the creation of a new scripture parallel to both the Vedas and the Qur'an.

In this context, Frits Staal argues that the Sikh scripture has a janus head—with one face looking in the Indian direction with respect to the sacredness of sound and the other face looking in the direction of western monotheistic religions, particularly Islam, with respect to the emphasis on written texts. Thus it implicitly challenges analytic dichotomies that rigidly oppose oral and written texts, or sound and meaning, or that which foresees an inevitable evolutionary movement between them.[69] Moreover, the historical context of the compilation of the Adi Granth was the cultural environment of Mughal India, which stressed the presence of a revealed scripture as part of the definition of a religious community. In this context, Smith aptly points out that 'the Islamic movement had settled down, following a period of violent aggression in India, to some centuries of a pervasive and collaborative cultural presence—culminating in the brilliance of Mughal empire.'[70] In fact, Emperor Akbar's peaceful reign provided the historical context in which the Sikh scripture came into being.

In order to understand the textual process that went into the creation of a new scripture for the newly developing Sikh community

[67]ibid., p. 201.

[68]ibid., p. 197.

[69]Frits Staal, 'Comments: The Concept of Scripture in the Indian Tradition', in Juergensmeyer and N.G. Barrier, eds, *Sikh Studies*, pp. 123–4. Also see Verne A. Dusenbery, 'The Word As Guru: Sikh Scripture and the Translation Controversy', *History of Religions*, 31(4)(May 1992): 387.

[70]Smith, *What Is Scripture?*, p. 201.

at the beginning of the seventeenth century, we shall return to the actual examination of the old manuscripts in the following chapters. Evidently, Guru Arjan produced the first canonical text (*Adi bir*) of the Adi Granth in 1604. The manuscript bearing this date is still in existence at Kartarpur,[71] in Jalandhar district of Punjab, in the possession of the Sodhi descendants of Dhir Mal. That is why it is commonly known as the Kartarpur bir (recension) of the Adi Granth. The earliest reference to Guru Arjan's compilation is in a manuscript, Baba Ram Rai's bir (written in 1659 and now preserved at Dehradun), where it is mentioned as the granth of the fifth Guru (*panjaven mahale ka granth*). The second important reference can be found in the following note from a manuscript, written by a Sikh named Ram Rai (different from Baba Ram Rai) in 1692 during the period of Guru Gobind Singh and now preserved at Patna Sahib: 'The "Great Granth" (*vada granth*), which was written by Gurdas Bhalla at the dictation of Guru Arjan, was evidently known to scribes as the benchmark for authenticating their own copies of the Adi Granth.'[72] This note specifically mentions for the first time, the name of Bhai Gurdas as being the amanuensis of the fifth Guru. In addition, Guru Arjan had the help of Bhai Buddha, a surviving member of the original Kartarpur community and therefore, a valuable link with the living voice of Guru Nanak.[73] Bhai Buddha's personal witness to the authenticity of the bani must have played an important role in discriminating between genuine and apocryphal writings.

CANON FORMATION IN THE SIKH TRADITION

The purpose of the present study is threefold. The first section seeks to reconstruct the history of the text of the Adi Granth, and specifies the various factors that may have prompted the fifth Guru to collate an anthology of devotional literature. It begins with the examination of early manuscripts and applies the profile method to classify them into their appropriate family-groups.[74] It analyses sections of the Adi Granth and seeks to deduce some of Guru Arjan's editing

---

[71]This is not the Kartarpur in which Guru Nanak spent his later years (which is now in Pakistan), but a town in Jalandhar district founded by Guru Arjan.

[72]For details, see next chapter.

[73]Bhai Buddha's involvement in the project of preparing the scripture seems to be established by his handwriting on the decorated folio of GNDU MS # 1245. See Chapter 2 for details.

[74]For details, see Chapter 2.

principles, particularly his approach to the inclusion of the bhagat bani (utterances of the bhagats, such as Kabir, Namdev, Ravidas, Shaikh Farid and various other medieval Indian poets of sant, sufi and bhakti origin) in the Sikh scripture. More specifically, this study addresses the issues surrounding certain problematic texts that have been the main focus of scholarly debate till now. It also examines various factors that led to the emergence of three different traditions of the Adi Granth after its original compilation in 1604, and then to its eventual standardization. This study, therefore, addresses basic issues of assimilation, redaction, and canonization in the Sikh scriptural tradition. Understanding how the Sikh scripture emerged tells us about the process of canonization in general, as well as about the particular dynamics of the Sikh tradition.

In any academic discussion of scriptural traditions, the term canon has two meanings—norm and list, both of which connote definitive and authoritative writings. A canon not only distinguishes between what is to be accepted and what is to be rejected but also differentiates between two kinds of scriptural authority in a religious tradition. We can characterize this difference in terms of absolute and relative authority: the absolute authority of the canonical scriptures over and against the relative authority of other works from the same tradition. Thus the concept of canon may be defined as follows: a collection of texts, the authority of which is related to the authority of other texts from the same religion as absolute to relative.[75] It should, however, be emphasized that a text becomes canonical precisely by virtue of its application in the present context. In other words, the whole canonical process by which the various scriptures reach their final form is governed by what Brevard Childs has called the principle of actualization, that is, the 'process by which an ancient historical text ... derives chiefly from a need to "update" an original tradition.'[76] Thus we shall try to understand the process of updating the text of the Adi Granth during the different stages of its canonization. Indeed, the major part of this study focuses on the issue of canon-formation in Sikh tradition.

The second section of this study seeks to examine different interpretations of the Adi Granth that may be discerned in various

[75]Rein Fernhout, *Canonical Texts: Bearers of Absolute Authority: Bible, Koran, Veda, Tipitaka,* trans. by Henry Jansen and Lucy Janson-Hofland (Amsterdam and Atlanta, GA: Editions Rodopi B.V., 1994), pp. 2–7.

[76]Brevard S. Childs, *Introduction to the Old Testament as Scripture* (Philadelphia: Westminster Press, 1979), p. 79.

works from the seventeenth century to the present day. It addresses the question of how historical meanings relate to the true meaning of the Adi Granth. However stable the text of the Sikh scripture might be, its interpretation has varied at different times and places. This is true not of the Sikh tradition alone, but of any religious tradition one might name. In this context, Gerald Bruns remarks that scriptures are structurally oriented away from an original intention toward the manifold possibilities of future understanding. They possess an openness to future interpretation that is characteristic, for example, of a good law.[77] This study argues that the text of the Adi Granth has an enduring potential for further interpretation. Each generation of interpreters has drawn out its meaning from a particular angle. Thus, plurality of interpretations of the Adi Granth has always been a part and parcel of the Sikh tradition.

The third section of this study deals with the issue of authority of the Adi Granth. It has been discussed earlier that a text is canonical not by virtue of being the final, correct and official version, but because it becomes binding on a religious community. The whole point of canonization of a text is to underwrite its authority with respect to the present and future in which it will reign supreme as a binding text. In this context, Gerald Bruns argues that the distinction between canonical and non-canonical is not just a distinction between authentic and unauthentic texts—that is, it is not reducible to the usual opposition between the inspired and the mundane, the true and the apocryphal, the sacred and the profane. On the contrary, it is a distinction between texts that are forceful in a given situation and those that are not. Therefore, from a hermeneutical standpoint, in which the relation of a text to a historical situation is always of primary interest, the theme of canonization is power.[78] Indeed, to inquire into the canonization of the Adi Granth is to ask how it came to possess its power over the Sikh Panth. This study, therefore, examines the role of the Adi Granth as Guru in the personal piety, liturgy and corporate life of the Sikhs. It addresses the basic issue of how scripture functions as a supratextual source of authority. The Adi Granth has given the Sikhs a sacred focus upon which to reflect and in the process discover the meaning of life as Sikhs. Hence it has always been a decisive factor in the search for a distinctive Sikh identity.

[77]Bruns, *Hermeneutics*, p. 76.
[78]ibid., pp. 65–6.

SIKH STUDIES

The present study is a continuation of the academic debate on certain issues of scriptural analysis in the field of Sikh studies. It must be seen in the historical context of research done in the last hundred years or so as a result of the impact of the scientific and rationalist influence of western education.[79] In fact, the Singh Sabha movement was primarily a Sikh response to western cultural impact, and it made a major contribution to identity consciousness in the colonial period. Charan Singh's *Bani Biora* (1908) was the first major study on the text of the Adi Granth. It presents statistical data under seventy-four sub-headings. For instance, his findings on the various ragas of the Adi Granth may be understood in the context of the *Raga-mala* debate that had already become the focus of scholarly attention at that time. G.B. Singh wrote his pioneer work on the manuscripts of the Adi Granth in 1944, and Jodh Singh responded to the issues raised in that work in 1947.[80]

Further, Teja Singh and Sahib Singh addressed the issue of the compilation of the Adi Granth and based their arguments primarily on internal evidence. They were influenced by the west and applied the method of form criticism to the text of the Adi Granth.[81] Surinder Singh Kohli's *A Critical Study of the Adi Granth* (1961), Taran Singh's *Sri Guru Granth Sahib da Sahitak Itihas* (Literary History of Sri Guru Granth Sahib, 1968), Mohinder Kaur Gill's *Guru Granth Sahib di Sampadan Kala* (The Art of the Compilation of the Guru Granth Sahib, 1975) and Piara Singh Padam's *Sri Guru Granth Prakash* (Splendour of Sri Guru Granth, 1977) focus on different aspects of the Adi Granth from various research perspectives. Basically these works are descriptive rather than analytical in nature.

Furthermore, the issue of variant readings of the Adi Granth has always attracted great scholarly attention. The Shiromani Gurdwara Prabandhak Committee (SGPC) itself sponsored a research work *Sri Guru Granth Sahib Ji dian Santha-sanchian ate Puratan Hath-likhat Pavan Biran de Paraspar Path-bhedan di Suchi* (List of the variant

---

[79]For a useful survey of works on the text of the Adi Granth, see Piar Singh, *Gatha Sri Adi Granth* (Amritsar: Guru Nanak Dev University, 1992), pp. 33–68.

[80]See G.B. Singh, *Sri Guru Granth Sahib dian Prachin Biran* (Lahore: Modern Publications, 1944) and Bhai Jodh Singh, *Prachin Biran Bare: Bhullan di Sodhan* (Lahore: Lahore Book Shop, 1947).

[81]See Teja Singh, 'Sri Guru Granth Sahib di Rachna,' *Gian Amrit* (Amritsar, June 1956) and Sahib Singh, *Adi Bir Bare* (Amritsar: Singh Brothers, 1970).

readings of the text of Sri Guru Granth Sahib on the basis of old manuscripts) in 1977. Similarly, the editor of the *Singh Sabha Patrika*, Giani Gurdit Singh published three special issues of *Path-Bodh Ank* (August, September and October, 1979) and three facsimiles of the Guru Har Sahai pothi for the first time. He then published some more facsimiles of this earlier pothi and the two extant Goindval pothis in his *Itihas Sri Guru Granth Sahib: Bhagat Bani Bhag* (1990), thereby bringing the issue of variant readings of certain pre-canonical texts into sharper focus.

More recently, Piar Singh and Gurinder Singh Mann have employed analytical approaches to understand the making of Sikh scripture. The former follows a sceptical approach in his analysis while the latter veers towards a traditional approach, although both of them make extensive use of manuscript evidence. Piar Singh bases his enquiry exclusively on the evidence of 'earlier compilations and old codices' and stresses that 'the tradition may be kept in sight but it alone need not be the decisive factor.'[82] This approach, he argues, would 'provide a real insight into the stages through which the revealed word had to pass to acquire its present form, at the hands of its earlier compilers and adorers.'[83] Gurinder Singh Mann, on the other hand, establishes traditions in his analysis and makes profuse use of traditional sources and oral family histories. He skirts the issue of variant readings and instead focuses on the 'three phases of the evolution of the Sikh sacred text,' represented by the Guru Har Sahai pothi, the Goindval pothis and the Kartarpur pothi.[84] Throughout his arguments, Mann plays down the role of Guru Arjan in the creation of the first canonical text. The present study takes issue with these two scholars on a number of points. It tries to strike a balance between the two approaches offered by the sceptical left-wing and the traditional right-wing scholarship. It is hoped that it will fill a significant gap in our understanding of the process of canon-formation in Sikh tradition.

[82]Piar Singh, *Gatha*, p. 2.

[83]ibid.

[84]Gurinder Singh Mann, *The Goindval Pothis: The Earliest Extant Source of the Sikh Canon* (Cambridge, MA: Harvard Oriental Series, 1996), p. 43.

2

A SURVEY OF EARLY MANUSCRIPTS

Bani, as we find it compiled and codexed in earlier birs, does not show any one to one correspondence in their texts, nor in their format. Text-variants abound, and recensions differ materially ... Not much is known about the earlier pothis and compilations that were available to Guru Arjan and Bhai Gurdas. The tradition mentions Baba Mohan Pothis only. Yet, it cannot be denied that there definitely were many more collections and *sporadic compilations*, vestigial footprints of which may be, more or less, discerned in all earlier birs. Their presence throws a flood of light on the proclivities—preferences, insights, and modalities of the earlier compilers.[1]

Academic discussion on the text of the Adi Granth has so far been focused on the so-called Kartarpur–Banno debate. It started in 1944 when G.B. Singh, an official in the postal service with an avowed interest in the Punjabi language and old manuscripts, set about marshalling evidence to challenge the authenticity of the Kartarpur manuscript as being the original text of the Adi Granth prepared under Guru Arjan's supervision and recorded by Bhai Gurdas. He suggested that the Banno bir or recension, which is believed to have been prepared by a Sikh named Banno (hence its name Banno bir), represents the original text.[2] He made this claim without examining the Kartarpur manuscript, and this fact alone provided sufficient reason for Sikh scholars to disregard his pioneer work. It is, however, important to note that the Kartarpur–Banno debate originated in a polemical context (*khandan–mandan*), which was the characteristic feature of those days, when the Arya

[1]Piar Singh, *Gatha*, pp. 32–3, 34–5.

[2]G.B. Singh, *Sri Guru Granth Sahib dian Prachin Biran*. For details on the debate see Nripinder Singh, *The Sikh Moral Tradition* (Delhi: Manohar Publishers, 1990), pp. 225–36.

Samajis and Sikhs frequently attacked each other's faith. G.B. Singh seemed to be serving the Arya Samaj interests as evidenced by his defence of Dayanand's arguments in his book.[3] Since then much of the energy of Sikh scholars has been devoted to proving the authenticity of the Kartarpur bir.[4]

The Kartarpur–Banno debate is, however, misdirected, for the following reasons. First, the most significant point which is generally missed in this debate is the fact that there were three, not just two, major recensions of the written text of the Adi Granth. This becomes clear after a preliminary survey of seventeenth-century manuscripts. Secondly, the debate largely relies upon tradition and random speculation rather than careful research. Finally, the major weakness of this debate is that the textual problems are dealt with in isolation, without any reference to Guru Arjan's editorial policy, by means of which he produced the first canonical text of the Adi Granth. In other words, it does not take into account the textual process through which the Adi Granth came into being.

Here, it is my intention to discuss another issue which goes beyond the Kartarpur–Banno debate. I propose that it is more fruitful to focus on the history of the text of the Adi Granth than to decide prematurely what the original reading was. In this context, Edwards Hobbs makes an observation on the goal of textual criticism: 'One is interested in the history of the text not just to decide what the original reading was but to see how the tradition dealt with the same concerns that people have today.'[5] Therefore, the reconstruction of the textual history of the Adi Granth will help us to understand the *rédaction* process that was at work behind the whole operation of formulating an authoritative text. It is also interesting to observe from the examination of old manuscripts, that the later scribes, who failed to understand that process, struggled with problematic texts and responded by tampering with the text of the Adi Granth. These scribes (and their groups within the Panth) were primarily responsible for the different recensions of the Adi Granth.

---

[3]ibid., p. 68.

[4]Bhai Jodh Singh, *Prachin Biran Bare* and *Kartarpuri Bir*; Sahib Singh, *Adi Bir Bare* (Amritsar: Singh Brothers, 1970) and Daljeet Singh, *Essays on the Authenticity of Kartarpuri Bir and the Integrated Logic and Unity of Sikhism* (Patiala: Punjabi University, 1987).

[5]Edwards Hobbs, 'An Introduction to Methods of Textual Criticism', in Wendy Doniger O'Flaherty, ed., *The Critical Study of the Sacred Texts* (Berkeley: Berkeley Religious Studies Series and Graduate Theological Union, 1979), p. 23.

It should also be emphasized at the outset that the process of compilation of the Adi Granth seems to have started much earlier than tradition would have us believe, and it must have continued throughout Guru Arjan's period of guruship. This is the conclusion one draws from a comparative analysis of old manuscripts of the Adi Granth. Guru Arjan evidently worked over certain pre-canonical traditions before he produced the first authoritative text in 1604. In the last two years of his life, he added to the scripture a number of self-composed hymns (which are not mentioned in the index of the

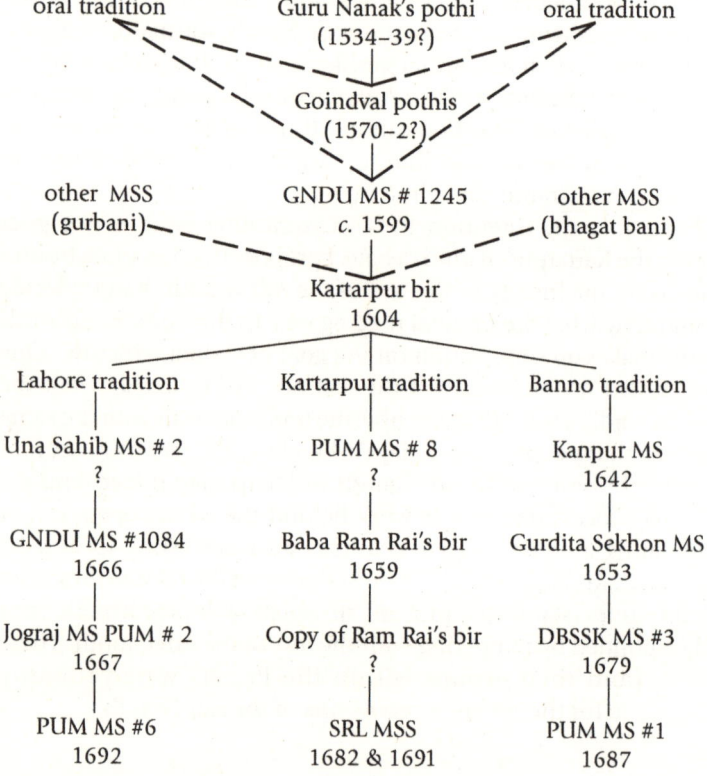

Figure 2.1 Genealogy of the Adi Granth

PUM = Punjabi University Museum, Patiala. GNDU = Guru Nanak Dev University, Amritsar. DBSSK = Dr Balbir Singh Sahitya Kendra, Dehra Dun. The 'Gurdita Sekhon MS' is in the possession of Mahant Gopal Singh of Tikana Sri Bhai Ramkishan, a Seva-panthi sect, Patiala. 'Una Sahib MS' is in the possession of Baba Sarabjot Singh Bedi, Una Sahib, Himachal Pradesh. SRL MSS = Manuscripts at the Sikh Reference Library, Amritsar.

Kartarpur MS) and some hymns by the bhagats before he died in 1606.[6] In order to understand this process more thoroughly, we may begin with the genealogical tree of the text of the Adi Granth.

At the top of the diagram (Figure 2.1) stands Guru Nanak's original pothi which was most probably written during the Kartarpur period. It is followed by the Goindval pothis, which provided a principal source for the compilation of the scripture. Then comes a rare manuscript in draft form, preserved at Guru Nanak Dev University in Amritsar, on which Guru Arjan seems to have worked to finally produce the text of the Adi Granth. It is highly likely that there were other such manuscripts of gurbani as well as of bhagat bani which have not survived. A detailed description of the location and the brief history of various manuscripts is given under the following four sections: (a) pre-canonical stage; (b) first canonical text; (c) post-canonical traditions; (d) final canonical text.

Before we begin the study of ancient documents, however, it will be useful to enumerate certain basic assumptions of manuscriptology. First, to determine the age of the manuscript from external features only is no merit in itself; it is merely a promise of merit. At times external features could be misleading. The real merit of the manuscript, therefore, lies in its contents, and this is what the textual critic must judge the manuscript by. In other words, the age of the text of a manuscript is more significant than the age of the manuscript itself. Second, the standard rule of 'short reading' may be helpful to place manuscripts that are not dated in their proper chronological order. Third, the rule of difficult reading may be equally applied to determine the age of the manuscript. Fourth, geographical origin of the manuscript and the subsequent history of its movement must always be kept in mind while estimating the value of the document. Finally, the argument of orthography must take precedence over other traditional explanations in placing the documents in their proper historical context.[7]

Further, in order to classify various manuscripts into their textual families, we shall employ the celebrated 'profile method.' This method is accepted as a superior enterprise in textual criticism for three reasons. First, this method takes into consideration all units of variations, and the profiles that are formed include both the shared and the unique readings. Second, it is also a valid means of grouping

[6]For details, see Bhai Jodh Singh, *Kartarpuri Bir*, pp. 5–6.

[7]The first three points have been taken from Hobbs, 'An Introduction to Methods of Textual Criticism,' pp. 1–27.

manuscripts in all text types. Third, it can be employed successfully in the formation of tentative groups and their profiles through quantitative analysis of internal evidence of readings rather than the external evidence of manuscripts.[8] It is in the light of this theoretical background that the examination of various manuscripts of early Sikh scriptural tradition will be undertaken.

PRE-CANONICAL STAGE

1. Guru Nanak's Pothi

According to tradition, Guru Nanak prepared a pothi of his own compositions during the Kartarpur period. In particular, the janam-sakhi traditions report that he passed on this volume to Guru Angad at the time of his succession.[9] The Sodhi family of Guru Har Sahai village in the district of Ferozepur claimed to have in its possession this original pothi until 1970 when it was reported to have been stolen in a train-theft. Giani Gurdit Singh has four photocopies of certain folios of the Guru Har Sahai pothi in his book *Itihas Sri Guru Granth Sahib*. He further claims to have examined the volume on different occasions before its loss.[10] Our primary concern is with the contents of this volume which might help us to determine whether or not it can be definitively identified with Guru Nanak's pothi.

The most significant point relates to the inscription on the opening folio of the Guru Har Sahai pothi which describes the earliest form of the *Mul Mantar*.[11] It reads:

The One Supreme Being (*IK Oankar*)
True Name, the Creator (*sach nam kartar*)
Baba Nanak (*Baba Nanak*)

Indeed, this short form of the *Mul Mantar* may have originated in the liturgical context. The early Sikhs must have recited it rhythmically (*ikk o-a-n-k-a-r// sach nam kartar//*) while meditating upon the divine name in the congregation (sangat). In the *Prabhati* hymn, for instance, Guru Nanak explicitly urges his followers to 'recite the true name of

---

[8]Paul R. McReynolds, 'Establishing Text Families', in *The Critical Study*, pp. 111–12.

[9]Kirpal Singh, ed., *Janam-sakhi Parampara* (Patiala: Punjabi University, 1969), pp. 57, 184–5.

[10]See Giani Gurdit Singh, *Itihas Sri Guru Granth Sahib: Bhagat Bani Bhag* (Chandigarh: Sikh Sahit Sansthan, 1990), pp. preface (facing p. xi), 3, 10, 14, and 559–60.

[11]For a photocopy of its facsimile, see ibid. (facing p. xi). Giani Gurdit Singh provides a different reading of this inscription (*IK Oankar satinam–Baba Nanak*).

the creator' (*bolahu sachu namu kartar*).[12] Although this unique and short form of the Mul Mantar places the Guru Har Sahai pothi before the writing of the Goindval volumes, the use of the signature Baba Nanak indicates that it was written by a Sikh scribe rather than by the Guru himself.

Secondly, in his inaugural address at the function to understand the correct readings of gurbani (Path-bodh Samagam) at Amritsar in 1979, Giani Gurdit Singh presented a photocopy of a facsimile of Guru Har Sahai pothi containing a shalok from *Var Asa*. The shalok reads as follows:

> There is one supreme being (*IK Oankar*)
> known by grace through the true Guru (*satgur parsadi*).

What kind of service is this in which the fear of the Master does not depart? One is called a servant (*chakaru*), Nanak, [if] one is absorbed in the love of one's Master.[13](1)

This shalok with slight linguistic variation appears under the distinctive symbol of Guru Angad in *Var Asa*.[14] It is instructive to note that this shalok is recorded independently in the Guru Har Sahai pothi. It points to an early stage when the distinctive code-word *mahalu* or *mahala* had not yet been introduced into the writing system. Incidentally, the early reading of this shalok appears in the Guru Nanak Dev University manuscript (1245) in *Var Asa*.[15]

Thirdly, regarding the contents of the Guru Har Sahai pothi, Giani Gurdit Singh reports that the volume comprises two sections. The opening section, which is of particular interest to our study, includes only the writings of Guru Nanak, beginning with the *Japji* and ending with a hymn in the *Tukhari* mode. There is no raga organization in this section. The second section of the Guru Har Sahai pothi includes the works of Guru Amar Das, Guru Ram Das and a large number of hymns of the bhagats. Giani Gurdit Singh further assures us that this section was later appended to the original text of the manuscript and is written in a different hand.[16] On the basis of this information,

---

[12]M1, *Prabhati* 9, AG, p. 1329.

[13]For a photocopy of this fascimile, see Giani Gurdit Singh, ed., *Singh Sabha Patrika* (October 1979), facing p. 24

[14]M2, *Var Asa* 2 (23), AG, p. 475. The word *sevak* (servant) is used for *chakar* (servant) in the standard version and there is additional word *ji* (if) in the second line.

[15]GNDU MS 1245, f. 452a.

[16]Cited in Gurinder Singh Mann, 'The Making of Sikh Scripture' (Ph.D. thesis, Columbia University, 1993), p. 47.

Gurinder Singh Mann has argued that 'if the Harsahai pothi was not the original manuscript that the early seventeenth-century sources attribute to Guru Nanak, it may have been a copy of the manuscript that represented the core of the Sikh scriptural corpus.'[17] Throughout his arguments Mann has freely taken recourse to traditions in making the claim that the Guru Har Sahai pothi was by Guru Nanak. It must be stated here that traditions are notoriously unreliable sources for historical data. One should, therefore, be cautious in relying upon a work that exhibits a general lack of historical awareness and an inability to see the all-important difference between statements based on evidence and tradition.

Finally, the issue of orthography is crucial to determine the authenticity of the Guru Har Sahai pothi. Giani Gurdit Singh does not provide any facsimiles from the first section of the volume other than the short version of the Mul Mantar, although he took these photographs in 1960. It is quite natural for any traditional scholar to be extremely cautious in revealing the information which might prove detrimental to his/her standing in orthodox circles. The other three facsimiles—containing Kabir's hymn in the *Sri* mode (*pada gusain kabir ka*), Madan Mohan Sur Das's *pada* and the death-dates of the first three Gurus—belong to the second section of the pothi. Piar Singh suggests that the writing style of these three facsimiles is closer to that of Baba Mohan's pothis.[18] For the purpose of intensive palaeographic arguments, however, we need more evidence about the script of the first section. It will then be possible to offer a final assessment about the Guru Har Sahai pothi. For the time being we must suspend our judgement on the issue of its identity with Guru Nanak's pothi.

2. The Goindval Pothis

The author of *Mahima Prakash* (1776), Sarup Das Bhalla, writes for the first time about Guru Arjan's retrieval of the Goindval pothis from the custody of Baba Mohan (hence they are also called as Mohan pothis) for the purpose of preparing the first canonical text of the Adi Granth.[19] This tradition is then repeated in all later nineteenth-century Sikh sources. Two volumes of the Goindval pothis are still extant and in the possession of the descendants of Guru

---

[17]ibid., pp. 50–1.

[18]Piar Singh, *Gatha* (*Sri Adi Granth*), p. 117.

[19]Sarup Das Bhalla, *Mahima Prakash: Bhag Duja*, eds Gobind Singh Lamba and Khazan Singh (Patiala: Punjab Language Department, 1971), pp. 358–61.

Amar Das—one volume is preserved with the Bhalla family of Jalandhar and the second is in the possession of a collateral family living in Pinjore. A photocopy of the Jalandhar volume is kept at the Punjabi University Library, Patiala. This is normally referred to as Volume I. It begins with the *Suhi* raga followed by *Prabhati, Dhanasari, Basant, Bhairo, Maru,* and *Tilang.* The Pinjore pothi, known as Volume II, has four ragas, namely *Ramakali, Sorathi, Malar* and *Sarang.* These two volumes consist of 300 and 224 folios respectively, some of which are totally blank.[20]

Traditionally, the Goindval pothis were written during the period 1570-2 by Baba Sahansram, son of Baba Mohan and grandson of Guru Amar Das. However, the actual date given on Volume I, which is kept at Jalandhar, is *sambat* 1652 *magh vadi* 1, corresponding to January 1595, the period of Guru Arjan. Thus, there is the question of the authenticity of the two available pothis as to whether or not these are the original volumes prepared under the supervision of the third Guru or just copies of the original. Giani Gurdit Singh, who has examined the two volumes very closely, has suggested that the date given on Volume I was inserted later when they were procured by Guru Arjan for use in the compilation of the Adi Granth.[21] The actual writing of the Goindval pothis, he argues, took place prior to Guru Ram Das's assumption of guruship, which is indicated by his handwriting and the marginal note on folio 94 of Volume II: 'Jeth Chand, your enraptured slave' (*gulam mast tainda Jeth Chand*).[22] Although Jeth Chand was the original name of the fourth Guru, it is not certain whether he actually wrote this note in his own hand on a blank folio or whether it was a later insertion by the Bhalla family to lend credibility to the pothis in order to extract donations.

On the authority of Baba Prem Singh of Hoti, Gursharan Kaur Jaggi argues that although the writing of these volumes started in sambat 1629 (1572) at the instance of Guru Amar Das, it continued till sambat 1652 (1595) when four hymns were added by Baba

---

[20]For more details, see Gursharan Kaur Jaggi, ed., *Babe Mohan valian pothian* (Delhi: Arsi Publishers, 1987); Piar Singh, *Gatha Sri Adi Granth*, pp. 71–112; and Gurinder Singh Mann, *The Goindval Pothis: The Earliest Extant Source of the Sikh Canon* (Cambridge, MA: Department of the Sanskrit and Indian Studies, Harvard University, 1996).

[21]Giani Gurdit Singh, *Itihas Sri Guru Granth Sahib*, p. 563.

[22]For a facsimile of this autograph, see Piar Singh, *Gatha Sri Adi Granth*, p. xxiii, Plate IX. The autograph is in takri/lande script without any vowel-signs. The writing does not seem to be old.

Sahansram.[23] Piar Singh, on the other hand, argues that the presence of two hymns attributed to Guru Ram Das and one to Guru Arjan date these pothis to Guru Arjan's time.[24] The use of different pens at a number of places suggests that the hymns were written at different times, and that this process continued for a long time. Gurinder Singh Mann has discussed the issue of dating at length and concludes that 'the task of compiling these pothis was accomplished during the final years of Guru Amar Das's life and that Bawa Prem Singh's view as to their 1570–2 dating appears to be correct.'[25]

A careful examination of the opening folio of Volume I reveals that the date was inserted later in the text in a different hand. It stands out from the rest of the text, which was written by the scribe who recorded the Guru's blessing (*bar*) on the decorated folio of Volume I:

There is one supreme being, known by grace through the true Guru (IK *Oankar satgur prasadi*). Sambat 1652 magh vadi 1. The pothi was written for Guru Ambir (Amar) Baba. The [true] name, the creator, the fearless one and the formless one! Beyond birth and death, self-existent. (1)

This blessing was given by Guru Baba [Nanak] to Guru Angad, who gave it [to the third Guru], three generations have given it. Whosoever contemplates the bani with his inner being will be liberated in life (*jivan-mukat*). Both of his ambitions [in this world and the next] will be achieved [and] he will find comfort [in this life]. He will not be wanting in anything. He will be liberated [and] will go to the presence of the Guru. The supreme Lord is the one [who gives] this sound counsel. There is absolutely no doubt about it. Know this thing to be true. If any one deserts our rightful succession to [the office of] the Guru and adheres to someone else he will certainly go to hell.[26]

In the first place, this text explicitly states that the pothi was written at the instance of Guru Ambir (Amar) Baba.[27] In Punjabi culture the word Baba is used for grandfather in family relationships and its present context suggests that the scribe was the grandson of the third Guru. In its religious sense it refers to a revered figure. Guru Nanak was generally known as Baba Nanak to his followers. Thus the phrase

[23]See Gursharan Kaur Jaggi, *Babe Mohan valian Pothian*, p. 51.

[24]Piar Singh, *Gatha Sri Adi Granth*, p. 112.

[25]For an extended discussion on the dating-issue, see Mann, *The Goindval Pothis*, pp. 18–25.

[26]The word *hundi* literally means cheque or bill of exchange. It is a legal document. Here it refers to the hereditary succession.

[27]Like the Punjabi word ambrit for amrit, here Ambir stands for Amar in the village community.

Guru Baba in the text specifically refers to Guru Nanak. More generally the word Baba is used as a term of address, meaning sir, father, master. In the Adi Granth, the word Baba is mostly used for Akal Purakh.[28] In each usage, the context is crucial to its meaning.

Secondly, the mention of the blessing (bar) by three generations (*tiha pirian*) of Gurus in the past tense indicates that the text of the blessing was written after the death of Guru Amar Das to make the claim to the office of guruship. The use of the word hundi is quite revealing because it suggests that the descendants of the third Guru were making a hereditary claim as they challenged Guru Ram Das. In designating his son-in-law as Guru, Guru Amar Das had bypassed his own sons, Baba Mohan and Baba Mohri. Whereas Mohri accepted his father's decision and fell at the feet of Guru Ram Das, Baba Mohan established his own guruship at Goindval.[29] It should be noted that the line of guruship established by Guru Nanak was not hereditary in the first three successions. The hereditary pattern was asserted after Guru Ram Das. Nevertheless, the succession in each case went to the most suitable candidate, not automatically from father to eldest son. Moreover, it was always the decision of the reigning Guru to nominate his successor. The text of the above blessing clearly indicates that Baba Mohan did not accept the guruship of Guru Ram Das and that he was challenging him by invoking the customary law of primogeniture.

We are primarily concerned in this study with the contents of the two available volumes of the Goindval pothis, which are very important for any understanding of the process of compilation of the Adi Granth. These two volumes are still the oldest manuscripts at our disposal. The style of the Gurmukhi script would place these documents in the second half of the sixteenth century, as is demonstrated by the fact that the vowel-signs were not fully developed when these volumes were written. The letters of the Gurmukhi script are still in their early lande or takari forms. However, these two volumes do not contain all the compositions of the first three Gurus. Presumably, Guru Arjan had access to more than two volumes. Giani Gian Singh reported in the *Tavarikh Guru Khalsa* about the Goindval pothis that he had seen in Patiala in sambat 1952 (1895). The raga sequence of one volume beginning with the *Ramakali* raga does

---

[28]M1, *Asa Astapadian* 11, AG, p. 417: 'O Lord, to Thee we offer salutation!' (*ades baba ades*).
[29]Sundar, *Ramakali Saddu*, AG, p. 924.

match one of the available pothis, but the second volume of Gian Singh's description, which begins with the *Siri* raga, is certainly different from the present volumes. It is believed to be no longer extant.[30] There is, however, the possibility that private collectors still hold manuscripts that may yet produce additional volumes of the Goindval pothis (perhaps the remaining two).

Gurinder Singh Mann's work provides a generally accurate description of the contents of the two available volumes, although one may not agree with him on every point. For instance, his acceptance of Giani Gurdit Singh's assertions about the identification of the writings of Gulam Sadasevak with those of Guru Ram Das (before he actually became the Guru) is questionable. First, if Baba Mohan himself crossed out the writings of Jeth Chand/Gulam Sadasevak from the pothis in his possession (as is evidenced from the actual crossings in the volumes), then why did he not cross out Guru Ram Das's alleged autograph on folio 94 of the second volume? How could he tolerate the autograph of his rival in his own pothis? In fact, these deleted compositions were written in competition with the fourth Guru, and the author Gulam Sadasevak may well be Baba Mohan himself.[31] These writings were crossed out much later (perhaps in the eighteenth century) when the Bhalla family wanted to establish the sacred status of their ancestors in the eyes of the Sikh rulers.[32] It was at that time that the alleged autograph of Guru Ram Das was written on the blank folio to extract donations from Sikhs.[33] It is no wonder that the tradition of opening the volume at the same folio is still current in the Bhalla family of Pinjore when they show it on the full-moon day (*puranmashi*) every month. Second, the poetic style of these compositions is flattering and plodding, unlike the authentic bani of Guru Ram Das. Finally, Guru Ram Das's warning against the circulation of 'unripe utterances' (kachi bani) among the Sikhs must be understood in the context of the struggle for legitimacy.[34] Piar Singh

[30] Giani Gian Singh, *Tavarikh Guru Khalsa* (Patiala: Bhasha Vibhag, 2nd edn, 1970), p. 394.

[31] For the full text of these fourteen hymns attributed to Gulam/Sadasevak, see Mann, *The Goindval Pothis*, pp. 102–16. For Mann's arguments on this issue, see pp. 24 and 152, n. 65.

[32] Also see Surjit Hans, *A Reconstruction of Sikh History from Sikh Literature* (Jalandhar: ABS Publications, 1988), p. 286.

[33] Piar Singh questions the genuineness of this autograph. See his *Gatha*, p. 20.

[34] M4, *Var Gauri* (9), AG, p. 304.

also maintains that although the hymns in the name of Gulam and Sadasevak bear Nanak as their pen name, 'their authorship is, however, enigmatic.'[35]

Most importantly, in the section of *Maru* raga there are only ten hymns of Guru Nanak and Guru Amar Das to be found in the Jalandhar pothi, but in the corresponding raga section in the Kartarpur volume there are seventy-six hymns. Thus there is a difference of sixty-six hymns that must be explained. Why did the compiler of the Jalandhar pothi not include all the hymns of the Gurus in the *Maru* raga? Were those hymns not available to him at the time of the compilation of his volume? In the case of other ragas, however, Gurinder Mann provides us with a comparative chart (Table 7) of the number of hymns of the Gurus in the extant Goindval pothis and the Kartarpur manuscript. On the basis of this chart, he makes the following assertion:

[T]here is only a minimal difference between the number of hymns of the Gurus included in the extant Goindval pothis and those that appear in the Kartarpur pothi.... The actual difference thus is limited to three hymns that appear in the Goindval pothis but not in the Kartarpur pothi, and five hymns that are present in the Kartarpur pothi but are not available in the extant Goindval pothis.[36]

Here, we must be cautious in accepting Mann's arguments as he seems to be overstating the case. The difference of sixty-six missing *Maru* hymns is so large that it makes his assertions questionable. Mann is fully aware of this problem and that is why he excludes *Maru* raga from his discussion since it 'presents special complications.'[37] His selective use of data does not offer any solution to certain unresolved textual issues.

In the light of the above discussion, the two available volumes must be regarded as copies rather than as the original Goindval *pothis*. Mann's assertion that these volumes were written *ad seriatim* is another significant factor which clearly indicates that they were copied from the original manuscript or some other source much later.[38] W.H. McLeod aptly points out that a scribe copying from an

---

[35]Piar Singh, *Gatha*, p. 20.
[36]Mann, *The Goindval Pothis*, pp. 36–7.
[37]ibid., p. 36.
[38]See ibid., p. 33. The original compilation must have been done in a discontinuous manner due to the complexity of the selection process.

existing manuscript will naturally follow the procedure of continuous writing and in doing so he is unlikely to leave gaps.[39] Indeed, there did exist other copies of the original volumes in the late sixteenth century, since Guru Amar Das encouraged the distribution of the copies of gurbani freely, and Pandha and Bula were well known as the scribe and singer among the audience.[40] The original Goindval pothis went to Guru Ram Das at the time of succession, which is clearly indicated in the testimony of Sundar's *Saddu* in the *Ramakali* mode: '[The true Guru] gave Ram Das Sodhi the apostolic mark and the "token" of Guru's true word.'[41] The token of Guru's true word (*gur sabadu sachu nisanu*) in the text refers to the written collection of gurbani in the form of the Goindval pothis. These pothis went to Guru Arjan, along with Guru Ram Das's own collection at the time of his succession. Guru Ram Das's manuscript has not survived; neither have the original Goindval pothis. The two available volumes survived because they became the sacred relics of the Bhalla family. In this context, W.H. McLeod's cautious assessment of these volumes is quite significant: 'Although the two extant volumes are certainly old, the question of their being original copies remains to be definitively proven.'[42] More recently, Pritam Singh has compellingly argued that Guru Arjan did not use the two available pothis in the compilation of the Adi Granth.[43]

Let it not be supposed that I am trying to diminish the value of the two available volumes by raising the question of their authenticity. This is certainly not my intention. I am fully convinced that these volumes contain the earliest writings of the first three Gurus and the bhagats. These manuscripts are of fundamental importance in any attempt to understand the history of the textual evolution of the Adi Granth. Moreover, they contain all the compositions of the first three Gurus in the available ragas that are found in the standard version of the Adi Granth. Furthermore, there is a clear textual relationship between these volumes and the text of the Kartarpur version of the Adi Granth through the Guru Nanak Dev University manuscript,

---

[39]W.H. McLeod, 'The Sikh Scriptures: Some Issues', in Mark Juergensmeyer and N.G. Barrier, eds, *Sikh Studies: Comparative Perspectives on a Changing Tradition*, p. 102. This is in contrast to the Kartarpur manuscript where writing was done in a discontinuous manner, moving between sections rather than strictly *seriatim*.

[40]*Varan Bhai Gurdas*, 11: 16.

[41]Sundar, *Ramakali Saddu* 5, AG, p. 923.

[42]W.H. McLeod, *Historical Dictionary of Sikhism* (Lanham, MD and London: Scarecrow Press, Inc., 1995), pp. 88–9.

[43]Pritam Singh, ed., *Ahiyapur Vali Pothi*, Vol. I (Amritsar: Guru Nanak Dev University, 1998), pp. 234–9, 299.

MS 1245. For our purposes, the text of these volumes, particularly the writings of the first three Gurus and the bhagats, belong, to the original Goindval pothis.

3. The Guru Nanak Dev University (GNDU) MS 1245

This manuscript was purchased in 1987 by Guru Nanak Dev University from Harbhajan Singh and Harcharan Singh Chavla, antique and manuscript dealers in Bazar Mai Sevan (now Jallianwala Bagh), Amritsar, at a cost of Rs 7500 at the recommendation of Piar Singh. It was entered in the catalogue of rare collections of Bhai Gurdas Library on 30 March 1987, with accession No. MS 1245. In his two-page recommendation Piar Singh stated on 21 March 198 7: 'This bir (recension) is very unique (*vilakhan*) and deserves to be secured for the library.' MS 1245 bears neither the signature symbol of its writer nor the year of its writing. Not much information about the history of its circulation is available. Generally speaking, people in India do not have a genuine concern for locating and preserving old manuscripts, except for a few private owners. Thus there is nothing unusual about the lack of information regarding the actual history of the manuscript. During my doctoral research, I examined the manuscript for two days on 30 and 31 May 1990, at the rare books section of the Guru Nanak Dev University Library. Although the manuscript was still intact in its original (re)binding, it had become so brittle that it required the immediate attention of experts for its proper care and preservation. I have in my possession a number of photographs of this manuscript which were taken with the permission of the University authorities at Amritsar.

3.1. External Features of the Manuscript

In order to place the document in its proper historical perspective, let us begin with the study of its external features. The opening four folios of the manuscript are profusely decorated with artwork. Particularly, the finely illuminated octagonal circle (*astakari chakkar*) on the second folio reflects the geometric art motifs, which are normally seen in the manuscripts of the late sixteenth and early seventeenth centuries. In the medieval art motifs, for instance, the astakari chakkar is a symbolic representation of the entire universe, ordered into eight cardinal points, with a divine guardian at each of them.[44] One can see such art motifs reflected in the opening

---

[44]See David Gordon White, 'Predicting the Future with Dogs', in Donald S. Lopez Jr, ed., *Religions of India in Practice* (Princeton, NJ: Princeton University Press, 1995), pp. 291–2.

folios of the Goindval volumes and the Kartarpur manuscript. In decorating the opening folios of the written collections of gurbani the Sikh scribes were, in fact, following the contemporary example of the magnificently calligraphed and illuminated copies of the Qur'an.

Secondly, the introductory note written at the beginning of the manuscript claims that 'there is a benedictory autograph written in Guru Hargobind's blessed hand on the fourth leaf.'[45] However, an examination of the manuscript reveals that a different piece of paper, containing the Mul Mantar written in Guru Tegh Bahadur's hand, was pasted much later on the fourth decorated page.[46] The owner of the manuscript must have received the autograph from the ninth Guru and pasted it in the blank folio of his scriptural relic to preserve it for posterity. The presence of this autograph, however, cannot be used to make the claim that the document was written during Guru Tegh Bahadur's period.[47] Rather, it proves another significant point— that the owner of the manuscript belonged to the mainline Sikh tradition.[48]

Third, the dealer's note claims that the manuscript contains a hymn written in Bhai Buddha's hand on the third decorated page. The insertion was perhaps to follow a contemporary Muslim tradition in which the Qur'anic *fatiha* was written by a revered figure at the time of writing a new copy of the Qur'an. In this case the following hymn of Guru Amar Das, which appears in a slightly different form in *Var Vihagara*, is written on the third page of the manuscript in a different hand:[49]

The devotees of the Guru eternally serve the true one by remaining absorbed in spontaneous love day and night. Always in joy, they sing the praises of the true lord from the innermost core of their hearts. The divine Beloved

---

[45]GNDU MS 1245. See the manuscript note by Harbhajan Singh and Harcharan Singh Chavla.

[46]The handwriting of the Mul Mantar tallies exactly with the writing style of Guru Tegh Bahadur, given in Ganda Singh (samp.), *Hukam-name* (Patiala, 1967), p. 75.

[47]See Kharak Singh, ed., 'Blasphemous Attacks', *Abstracts of Sikh Studies* (January 1993), p. 22.

[48]Piar Singh, for instance, maintains that the compiler had no connection with any dissident group of Miharban or Ram Rai. See his *Gatha Sri Adi Granth*, p. 170.

[49]The manuscript note by Harbhajan Singh and Harcharan Singh Chavla claims that Bhai Buddha wrote this hymn in his own hand. However, no evidence is cited in support of this claim.

abides within them as it is written in their destiny by the creator from the very beginning. In his grace, Nanak, the Lord himself has granted union to them.

(M3, Var Vihagara 1(8), AG, p. 551)

If the dealer's claim that Bhai Buddha wrote this hymn in his own hand is based on sound family tradition, then we may assume his involvement in the creation of the scripture. It is quite possible that the manuscript was placed in the custody of Bhai Buddha and his descendants may have preserved it as a scriptural relic. However, Sant Baba Darshan Singh, the present incumbent at the seat of Bhai Buddha, has no knowledge of this manuscript.[50] It means that the family had long forgotten the tradition, perhaps when they disposed of the manuscript to some dealer due to its incomplete nature.

Fourth, folio 1255a of the manuscript contains the dates of the demise of the first five Gurus. The long eulogistic description of Guru Amar Das's death is particularly noteworthy. This may indicate that the scribe was a close associate of the third Guru, possibly a member of the Bhalla family or a descendant of a *Manji-bardar*, a Sikh missionary appointed by the third Guru.[51] Balwant Singh Dhillon associates this manuscript with the Mina tradition but there is no evidence to support this contention.[52] If this were the case, there should have been some reference to Prithi Chand or Miharban in the list of the dates of demise of the Gurus. Moreover, an extra-canonical hymn in the *Asa* mode refers to the Minas as instigating Sulhi Khan to attack the Guru's establishment: 'They [Minas] approached the [Mughal] ruler to attack us. They created a false propaganda with the show of worldly wealth'.[53] How can such a hymn be included in the manuscript if it is a Mina collection? Furthermore, the similarity of the *Japji* text to Harji's *Japu Parmarath* points towards the possibility that both were perhaps copied from a common earlier source. It does not prove the Mina origins of the GNDU text at all.

Finally, a careful examination of the manuscript reveals that the entire writing work has been done by one hand only. The handwriting

---

[50]See Kharak Singh, 'Blasphemous Attacks', p. 16.

[51]Piar Singh, *Gatha Sri Adi Granth*, p. 169.

[52]Balwant Singh Dhillon, 'Myth of an Early Draft of the Adi Granth (MS 1245)', *Abstracts of Sikh Studies* (July 1993), pp. 84–5.

[53]GNDU MS 1245, f. 398. This hymn specifically refers to the incident when Sulhi Khan's horse bolted and fell into the brick-kiln. Also see M5, *Bilaval* 104, AG, p. 825.

of the scribe is exceptionally neat and legible. The Gurmukhi orthography is still in the process of development. To a large extent, its style is very similar to the Gurmukhi script of the Kartarpur manuscript. The most distinctive difference, however, is in the formation of certain letters and the vowel-signs. For instance, a dot is used for the vowel-sign *kanna* (a) instead of a half vertical stroke, whereas the vowel-sign *hora* (o) is still written in its archaic form. The vowel *ura* (u) is written with an open end like the symbol of *oankar*, whereas the vowels *aira* (a) and *iri* (i) are written in their early takari forms. Similarly, the consonant *chhachchha* (chh) is still written in its earlier sharda form, while the other consonants such as *haha* (h), *ghaggha* (gh), *chacha* (ch), *nana* (n) and *lala* (l) are written in their early takari forms.[54] Thus on the basis of archaic orthography, the GNDU manuscript can be placed between the Goindval pothis and the Kartarpur bir.

3.2. *Dating of the Manuscript*

For the purpose of the dating of MS 1245 we need to examine actual contents along with its external features. Piar Singh has rightly dated this document as prior to the writing of the Kartarpur bir in his examination of the manuscripts of the Adi Granth. However, his dating of the Kartarpur bir to the period of the sixth Guru is wrong.[55] That manuscript was certainly completed in 1604 and this date is recorded in the handwriting of the primary scribe who prepared the table of contents. We shall further discuss the contents of the Kartarpur bir in the next section.

On the basis of the table on folio 1255a of MS 1245 containing the dates of demise of the first five Gurus, Piar Singh argues that this manuscript was written immediately after Guru Arjan's death. This assertion may be questioned on the following grounds. First, the table is written on the blank folio before the end of the manuscript. This is not conventional. In most of the early manuscripts the table of dates pertaining to deaths is either found at the very beginning (immediately after the contents page) or at the very end of the volume. In the present case, it was most probably written on the blank folio after Guru Arjan's death, which provided the historical context to record these dates for posterity. Even in the Kartarpur bir the table of dates recording the death of the first five Gurus was entered much later, and its entry in the table of contents was recorded

---

[54]For details, see Piar Singh, *Gatha Sri Adi Granth*, p. 173.
[55]ibid., p. 204.

with a different pen. From the photograph of this folio (which is in my possession) of the Kartarpur bir, it is quite evident that the words *joti joti samavane ka chalitar* (death dates of the Gurus on folio 41) were certainly inserted later in the table of contents. Bhai Jodh Singh confirms this fact.[56]

Second, the actual contents of the GNDU volume clearly suggest its compilation before 1604, the year of the completion of the Kartarpur bir. Although the bulk of Guru Arjan's hymns are available in the GNDU volume, there are instances of recording of only the opening lines of his hymns, followed by blank spaces. Clearly, these hymns were not available to the scribe in their final form. Moreover, four hymns of Guru Arjan in *Devgandhari* raga (*Thakur hoi ap dayal; Apune satgur pahi binau kahia; Anath nath prabh hamare;* and *Prabh ihai manorath mera*) and three other hymns—one each in *Gujari* (*Tun samarath saran ko data*), *Suhi* (*Darasan ko lochai sabh koi*) and *Bilaval* (*Mu lalan siu prit bani*) ragas respectively—are not to be found in the GNDU volume. These hymns were added in the later Kartarpur manuscript. Similarly, the absence of several other shaloks and hymns in the GNDU volume clearly places the document historically before the Kartarpur bir.[57] More evidence of this nature will be provided in the next section.

Finally, let us try to date the GNDU manuscript. There are certain hymns by Guru Arjan which refer to events in the life of Guru Hargobind.[58] Their presence in the GNDU volume clearly indicates that it was compiled after 1595, the year of Guru Hargobind's birth. Thus, we may historically place the document somewhere between 1595 and 1604. In his doctoral thesis, Gurinder Singh Mann has suggested that the GNDU manuscript was prepared in or around the year 1600.[59] There is a popular story in the Sikh tradition that some people told Emperor Akbar that Guru Arjan was compiling a book in which Muslim and Hindu prophets were reviled. When the emperor met the Guru towards the end of 1598, he had seen some collection of Sikh writings and found nothing objectionable in it.[60]

---

[56]Bhai Jodh Singh, *Kartarpuri Bir*, p. 4.

[57]For a complete detail of missing hymns, see Balwant Singh Dhillon, 'Myth of an Early Draft', pp. 89–91.

[58]For details, see Hans, *A Reconstruction of Sikh History*, pp. 140, 148, 158 and 170.

[59]Mann, 'The Making of Sikh Scripture', p. 87.

[60]Teja Singh and Ganda Singh, *A Short History of the Sikhs* (Patiala: Punjabi University 1989), pp. 31–2. According to Badauni and Sujan Rai, the meeting took place at Goindval (see *Khulasatut Twarikh*, p. 425 and *Akbarnama*, p. 514).

Perhaps it was the GNDU manuscript under preparation at that time. We may thus safely suggest 1599 as the date of its compilation.

3.3. *Internal Features of the Manuscript*

The manuscript has a total of 1267 folios. It is in the form of an incomplete draft on which the compiler seemed to be working. At a number of places the plan of the layout may be seen from the recording of only the first lines of certain hymns, followed by blank spaces. Such instances can be seen in folios 207a–b, 769b–770a, 1066b, 1236a–1242a, 1245b–1246a, 1247a–1248a, 1254a–b and 1262b. This manuscript is known for its variant readings. There are a number of texts in this volume that were revised in the final version of the Adi Granth. It also contains certain extra-canonical hymns which were edited out in the final version.[61] The issue of extra-canonical hymns requires detailed analysis in itself, and will be discussed in a separate study. Some of the major characteristic features of MS 1245 are given under the following sub-headings.

3.3.1. Introductory Section

This section opens with liturgical prayers. The morning prayer contains Guru Nanak's *Japji* and the evening prayer consists of '*So Dar* and four hymns' (*sodaru tatha chare sabad*). Like the Kartarpur bir, MS 1245 does not contain the *So Purakh* text (a collection of four hymns, the first two of them by Guru Ram Das and one each by Guru Nanak and Guru Arjan respectively). This clearly indicates that it became part of the evening prayer after the compilation of the Adi Granth in 1604. Again, the late evening prayer (*Sohila*) is not to be found in the introductory section of MS 1245. Thus the liturgical section of this volume clearly points towards an earlier stage of its evolution.

3.3.2. The Main Section

The main section has a different raga sequence, and the index of hymns of each raga-section is written separately at the beginning of that section. Obviously the convention of writing the index had begun by this time, since there is no index of hymns to be found in the Goindval volumes. For instance, on the basis of a discrepancy between the sequence of certain hymns composed in *Siri* raga in the index and their actual position in the main text, Piar Singh argues that the compiler of this manuscript was certainly copying its index from some other source.[62] This supports the general assumption of

---

[61]For details, see Piar Singh, *Gatha Sri Adi Granth*, p. 144–72 and Balwant Singh Dhillon, 'Myth of an Early Draft', pp. 1–92.

[62]Piar Singh, *Gatha Sri Adi Granth*, p. 143.

manuscriptology that scribes usually copied from more than one manuscript. It may also reflect the pre-canonical stage of a particular document. Moreover, the discrepancy between the index and the text is frequently encountered in the early manuscripts of the *Sur Sagar*.[63] Even Bhai Jodh Singh records a number of such instances from the Kartarpur manuscript.[64]

MS 1245 begins with the *Siri* raga followed by the usual *Majh, Gauri, Asa, Gujari, Devgandhari, Bihagara* and *Vadahans* ragas. Thereafter, it diverges from the standard pattern and follows its own sequence of *Dhanasari, Jaitasari, Sorathi, Kalayan, Nat-narain, Todi, Bairari, Tilang, Gond-bilaval, Suhi, Bilaval, Ramakali, Mali-gaura, Maru, Kedara, Tukhari, Bhairau, Basant, Sarang, Malar, Kanara* and *Prabhati* ragas. Particularly, the position of *Sorathi, Kalayan* and *Nat-narain* (placed here as 11th, 12th and 13th in the raga sequence) changes in the standard version, where they are placed as 9th, 29th and 19th respectively. It is, however, important to note that this manuscript does contain all the major thirty ragas of the Adi Granth. Once the sequence of these ragas was fixed in the Kartarpur volume in 1604, it was faithfully followed in all later manuscripts.

In the GNDU volume each raga has subdivisions based on the length of the compositions, beginning with the short pada genre, followed by other poetic forms (*astapadi, chhant* and other longer works), and ending with the longer *var* or ballad. Evidently the present sequence of subdivisions had already developed when this manuscript was written. It is, however, important to note that Guru Amar Das's *Anandu* (Bliss) is located on folio 881a after Guru Nanak's *Siddh Gost* and before *Var Ramakali* of the third Guru. In this respect the GNDU volume follows the sequence of the second volume of the Goindval pothis.[65] This close correspondence clearly shows a textual relationship between the two documents. In the final text of the Adi Granth, however, Guru Arjan juxtaposed the *Anandu*, Guru Amar Das's hymn of joy, and the *Saddu* (Call), Sundar's dirge on the Guru's death, to stress the theme of a balanced life.

Status of the Vars (Ballads)
The GNDU manuscript contains a total number of twenty-one vars (including the mention of the ballad by Satta and Balvand), which is one less than the twenty-two of the standard version of the Adi

---

[63]Professor Kenneth E. Bryant of the University of British Columbia shared this information with me.

[64]Bhai Jodh Singh, *Kartarpuri Bir*, pp. 5–6.

[65]Piar Singh, *Gatha Sri Adi Granth*, p. 94.

Granth. It does not contain Guru Arjan's *Var Basant,* which unlike other vars, has only three stanzas. It is important to note that this var was recorded in a blank folio in the Kartarpur manuscript much later, and there is no mention of this var in the index.[66] Let us examine certain distinctive features of the vars in the GNDU volume.

In the first place, the vars of this manuscript are still in their pre-canonical stage. For instance, the shaloks in the vars are not assigned their proper authorship such as M1, M2, M3, M4, and M5. It is quite noteworthy that this convention was later introduced with a different pen in the text of the vars in the Kartarpur bir.[67] In certain cases in the GNDU text, the shaloks have yet to be selected for the *pauris* (stanzas). For instance, in folios 482b, 483a and 483b, there are blank spaces to be filled in with the shaloks for the pauris numbering 18, 20 and 21 respectively in the var of Guru Amar Das in the *Gujari* mode. These blank spaces clearly illuminate the textual process of the vars being fixed for the first time in the GNDU volume. This process acquires an added significance from the fact that vars are not to be found in the two available Goindval pothis.

Secondly, there is an interesting instance in this volume where the compiler had written an editorial note after the twenty-seventh stanza of Guru Nanak's *Var Malhar.* The note on folio 1182a reads: 'This stanza is [actually] number twenty-eight' (*eh pauri athaihavi aisai*). This note clearly indicates that the last stanza numbering 28 (*sabho varatai chalati chalatu vakhania*), which was added by Guru Arjan himself to the *Var Malhar,* should change places with Guru Nanak's stanza numbering 27 (*tun ape api varatada api banat banai*) in the final text. In the standard version of the Adi Granth, the title of the stanza numbering 27 reads: 'The new stanza by the fifth Guru' (*pauri navin mahala 5*). The position of this stanza of Guru Nanak is fixed at the end.[68] This editorial process also proves another significant point that there is a close correspondence between the GNDU volume and the Kartarpur bir. Thus it establishes a clear textual relationship between these two manuscripts.

Thirdly, seven vars of the GNDU volume are assigned specific heroic tunes (*dhunis*) to which they are supposed to be sung. In most cases, these tunes are not written at the beginning of their text

[66]Bhai Jodh Singh, *Kartarpuri Bir,* pp. 37 and 110.

[67]ibid., pp. 52, 54, 61, 72, 75, 76, 78, 80, 82 and 90. Bhai Jodh Singh rightly points out that the authorship of the shaloks was not recorded in the original inscribing of the vars, but was inserted later with a thin pen.

[68]M1, *Var Malhar* (27/28), AG, p. 1291.

in different raga sections, rather they are mentioned in the index only.[69] In the two cases of Guru Nanak's *Var Malhar* and Guru Ram Das's *Var Vadahans*, however, the tunes are specifically stated at the beginning of their texts in addition to the index entries. It should be emphasized here that the two additional heroic tunes were assigned to Guru Nanak's *Var Majh* and Guru Arjan's *Var Ramakali* in the later Kartarpur volume.

Finally, there is no recording of such words as *sudh* (pure or correct) or *sudh kichai* (make corrections) at the end of the vars in the GNDU text, thus reflecting the pre-canonical nature of this document. This convention was used for the first time in the Kartarpur manuscript by Guru Arjan to mark his personal approval of the content, form and organization of the vars in particular raga sections. This is quite evident from the inscription of sudh in the margins at the end of sixteen vars in the Kartarpur bir.[70] It also highlights the editorial process through which the blank spaces in the vars of the GNDU text were duly filled in the Kartarpur volume.

Status of the Bhagat Bani

The most distinctive feature of the GNDU volume is that it contains the writings of the Gurus and those bards closely associated with the Sikh court. Apart from the panegyrics (*savayye*) of the bards in praise of the Gurus, it contains Mardana's shalok as well as Sundar's *Saddu* (Call). The var by Satta and Balvand in the *Ramakali* mode is not to be found in the main text, although its mention has been made at the end of the index. This was definitely incorporated in the later Kartarpur manuscript. Piar Singh maintains that the compiler of the GNDU manuscript acknowledged only the bani of the Sikh Gurus and the Sikh bards.[71] Similarly, Gurinder Singh Mann argues that the 'GNDU pothi may have been the result of a decision to drop the writings of non-Sikh saints from the Sikh canon.'[72] This suggestion raises important questions: does this mean that the compiler was drawing a line between Sikh and non-Sikh writings of the bhagats? Was there any tension between the followers of the

[69]GNDU MS 1245, ff. 160 (M5, *Var Gauri*), 343 (M1, *Var Asa*), 457 (M3, *Var Gujari*), 524 (M4, *Var Vadahans*), 1098 (M4, *Var Sarang*), 1151 (M1, *Var Malhar*) and 1185 (M4, *Var Kanara*).

[70]Bhai Jodh Singh, *Kartarpuri Bir*, pp. 55, 62, 73, 76, 78, 80, 83, 93, 99, 105, 113, 115 and 116. The only exception is the recording of sudh at the end of Guru Arjan's hymns in the *Todi* raga (f. 532).

[71]Piar Singh, *Gatha Sri Adi Granth*, p. 171.

[72]Mann, 'The Making of Sikh Scripture', p. 91.

bhagats and the Sikhs that led to the exclusion of the bhagat bani from the Sikh scriptural tradition at that particular moment? Was the Sikh community's self-consciousness heightened at that time to such an extent that it revised its earlier inclusive ideal provided by the Goindval pothis? In raising these questions, however, one must be cautious against reading too much into that particular situation.

It is true that the GNDU volume does not contain bhagat bani as such. We may suggest that Guru Arjan's primary concern was to fix the hymns of the Gurus first, and then to deal with the issue of the hymns of the bhagats. However, the presence of Kabir's shaloks in *Var Gujari*, *Var Bihagra* and *Var Ramakali*, followed by Guru Amar Das's responses to the issues raised by the bhagats, provides clear evidence that the compiler of this volume had every intention of including bhagat bani in the Sikh scriptural tradition. Six shaloks of Kabir are included in Guru Arjan's *Var Ramakali*. Further, Guru Arjan's *Basant* hymn (*sun sakhi mani japi piar*), praising the devotion of non-Sikh saints as an inspiration to meditate upon the divine name, appears in the GNDU volume. Furthermore, in one of his hymns in the *Bhairau* mode, Guru Arjan uses the signatures of Kabir, since he adapts certain verses of the bhagat and addresses the issue of independent Sikh identity. Thus the bhagat bani was certainly not anathema to the compiler of the GNDU volume. Presumably, he was collecting the hymns of the bhagats separately in another volume to include them later in the final recension. This is perhaps the reason why the Kartarpur manuscript does not contain the index of the individual hymns of bhagat bani, which was included *en bloc* after the Gurus' works at the end of each raga section.

3.3.3. The Epilogue

The arrangement of the concluding section of this volume is not yet fixed, nor is its content determined. In the first place, the titles of the epilogue of the volume appear in their earlier forms, which were standardized in the Kartarpur volume. For instance, the title of the Gurus' shaloks in excess of the vars is written as *Salok Varan Te Bahari* in folio 1232a. In a similar manner, the title of the panegyrics by a bard named Kali in praise of Guru Angad appears as *Savayye Guru Angad Ke Kalai Bhatti Kite*.[73]

Secondly, in the text *Salok Varan Te Bahari*, there are thirty-five shaloks of Guru Nanak, the opening lines of sixty-two shaloks of Guru Amar Das, twenty-eight shaloks of Guru Ram Das and

---

[73]GNDU MS 1245, f. 1263b. For other titles see ff. 1263a, 1264b, 1265b and 1266b.

twenty-two shaloks of Guru Arjan, followed by the opening line of the *Mundavani*. Apart from certain variant readings, some shaloks are missing in this section. There are also certain extra-canonical shaloks in this volume. All these points clearly refer to its pre-canonical stage.

Thirdly, the text *Salok Sahanskriti Ke* has sixty-two stanzas of Guru Arjan, some of which are written with opening verses (numbering 13, 14, and 43–62) only, leaving blank spaces to be filled later. Guru Nanak's shaloks are not to be found in this text. It is followed by twenty-four stanzas of Guru Arjan's *Gatha* (verses 6–22 are written with opening lines only). Then comes the table of dates of the demise of the first five Gurus in folio 1255a, which was written unconventionally before the end of the manuscript. This was perhaps inserted later in the blank folio.

Fourthly, an extra-canonical text *Ratan-Mala* attributed to Guru Nanak is found in folio 1257a, but it was edited out in the final version of the Adi Granth due to its emphasis upon *hatha-yoga* ideals. This is followed by eleven panegyrics composed by Guru Arjan. Then come twenty-two stanzas of Guru Arjan's *Phunahe* and the opening lines of nine stanzas of his *Chaubole*.

Fifthly, there are twenty panegyrics by Guru Arjan in praise of Guru Nanak (*Mahale Pahile Ke Guru Arjan Ke Mukhavak*), which are found at two different places in this volume in folios 1259a–1260b and 1263a–1263b. The panegyrics by the bards (*Bhattan De Savayye*) in praise of the Gurus are still in their earlier short form. The manuscript contains only thirty-two panegyrics as compared with 123 savayyas found in the standard version of the Adi Granth. By the time this manuscript was written, some of the bards had not yet appeared in the court of the Guru.

Finally, Guru Arjan's concluding shalok (*tera kita jato nahin*) is not to be found in this volume. Obviously this shalok was composed in gratitude at a time when the final text of the Adi Granth was prepared in 1604. It comes after the *Mundavani* in the Kartarpur manuscript.

All these internal features of MS 1245 place the document well before the writing of the Kartarpur bir. However, Balwant Singh Dhillon refers to certain features such as repetitions, omissions, apocrypha, and the discrepancy between the index and text to discredit MS 1245 as a legitimate source in the compilation of Sikh scripture. His arguments are based on the premise that in order to maintain the traditional view it would be best for the faithful to deny the very existence of early manuscripts. For instance, he completely fails to understand the issue of variant readings of certain hymns in the following observation:

Similarly in raga *Bhairo* the lines of hymn No. 51 (*hari ke log sada gun gavahi*) have been inverted, and at the end [an] abortive attempt has been made to record another hymn which begins with the original first line (*bhai kau bhau paria*) of this hymn. Evidently, the scribe, in his attempt to confuse the hymns of Guru Arjan, had split the text of some hymns into two to compose a new hymn.[74]

Here the author attributes the motive of forgery to the scribe of the GNDU manuscript. This is simply not the case. One can see the same *Bhairo* hymn (*Bhairo Mahala 5: hari ke log sada gun gai tini kau milia puran dham*) repeated in the Kartarpur bir in folio 836/1 with the marginal note: 'This hymn is repeated here, its actual place is at [number] fifty-two' (*ehu sabad duharagati charia hai bavanjah hai*).[75] The hymn that appears at number 52 in folio 834/1 (*Bhairo Mahala 5: bhai kau bhau paria simarat hari namu*) differs slightly from the above hymn in terms of wording and sequence of lines. The following three conclusions can be drawn from this interesting instance. First, Guru Arjan himself fixed the final reading of his *Bhairo* hymn in the Kartarpur bir and crossed out the second reading in folio 836/1. His editorial note further highlights the extraordinary care with which the scripture was prepared. Second, the commonality of the variant readings of certain hymns in the GNDU volume and the Kartarpur bir establishes a clear textual relationship between the two documents. The issue of variant readings of certain hymns will be discussed at length in the next chapters. It will be shown that this variation was the result of the liberty taken by Sikh musicians in devotional singing.

In sum, the GNDU manuscript represents the pre-canonical stage of Sikh scriptural tradition. It is still in its incomplete form, and illuminates the textual process through which the evolution of the Sikh scripture took place. Its textual relationship with the Goindval pothis and the Kartarpur bir is quite obvious. It is of rare value to the textual critic. Although the manuscript soon became irrelevant to mainstream Sikhs because of its incomplete nature, it survived as a scriptural relic. The history of its movement still needs to be

---

[74]Balwant Singh Dhillon, 'Myth of an Early Draft', pp. 79–80.

[75]See Bhai Jodh Singh, *Kartarpuri Bir*, 108. For other such instances, see Kartarpur MS, ff. 96/2, 415/1, 483/1, 511/1 and 550/2.

explored. There were other such manuscripts, 'vestigial footprints of which may be discerned,' as Piar Singh argues, in all earlier compilations such as the Bahoval pothi and Pahinda Sahib's bir.[76] All these documents reflect the fluid state from which the various structures of organization and the final form of various hymns emerged in the first canonical text of the Adi Granth.

FIRST CANONICAL TEXT

The Kartarpur Manuscript

The Kartarpur manuscript is generally held to be the document actually inscribed by Bhai Gurdas at the dictation of Guru Arjan and that is why it has attracted so much scholarly attention for the last fifty years.[77] The editorial comments in this manuscript, which are unique and revealing, are not to be found in any other manuscript. We shall now discuss some of its characteristic features. First, the date of completion of the volume is recorded at the head of the table of contents as follows: 'Having completed the pothi, [the scribe] has reached [to the indexing of it] on sambat 1661 *miti bhadau vadi ekam 1*'. On the basis of my personal examination of the Kartarpur bir on 14 May 1990, I can confirm that there was no tinkering with the original recording of this entry. I have in my possession the photograph of this folio of the table of contents of the Kartarpur manuscript. This date corresponds to 1 August 1604. It is worth noting here that the word used for the volume is pothi, which was the generic term employed for Sikh scripture at that time.

Second, the manuscript has a total of 974 folios. The system of folio numbering is unique. One should always keep in mind that on opening the volume the two pages—one on the left and the other on the right, constitute one leaf. The number of the leaf is given on the left page following the Sanskritic tradition, which constitutes folio 1a or 1/1 (Jodh Singh's method) of the first folio and the right page becomes folio 1b or 1/2. Jodh Singh suggests that folios were numbered before the actual writing began, and that groups or clusters

---

[76]For more details on these two manuscripts, see Piar Singh, *Gatha*, pp. 120–34.

[77]John Clark Archer, 'The Bible of the Sikhs', *The Review of Religion* (London, January 1949), pp. 115–25; C.H. Loehlin, 'A Westerner looks at the Kartarpur Granth', *Proceedings of the Punjab History Conference*, First Session (Patiala: Punjabi University, 1966), pp. 93–6 and his paper entitled 'Textual Criticism of the Kartarpur Granth' in Juergensmeyer and Barrier, eds, *Sikh Studies*, pp. 113–18.

of folios (approximately 123 clusters, each cluster consisting of eight folios) were allocated in advance to particular raga sections and sub-divisions within each section.[78] This is evident from the recurrence of blank spaces (of which 226 folios are entirely blank and some others partly blank) in the manuscript, particularly those found at the conclusion of distinct sections of the volume.

Third, there are explicit references to the autographs of Guru Arjan and Guru Hargobind in the index as follows: (a) 'The autograph of the fifth Guru is on folio 45'; (b) 'The autograph of the sixth Guru is on folio 540.' The actual recording of the Mul Mantar in Guru Arjan's hand is to be found on the decorated folio 29/1 which, according to Bhai Jodh Singh, was the result of new numbering done at the time of fixing the borders and binding the volume again. Similarly, the autograph of Guru Hargobind in the form of the Mul Mantar is to be found on another decorated folio 541/1 in the middle of the volume. The reason for the discrepancy seems to be the fact that this leaf was fixed on the reverse side at the time of re-binding. Guru Hargobind's autograph in the Kartarpur volume clearly indicates, first, his involvement in the creation of the scripture, and secondly, his designation as the sixth Guru of the Sikhs. Guru Arjan may have taken this step to ensure succession in the wake of the rivalry with his elder brother, Prithi Chand. His intention to designate his only son as his successor may be seen in the hymn which he composed to celebrate the latter's birth.[79] Piar Singh has, however, insistently argued that the presence of the autograph of the sixth Guru takes the manuscript to a later period rather than the period of Guru Arjan.[80] If that was the case, how can we explain the mention of the autograph of the fifth Guru in the index? It is quite possible that a new index was prepared on a new leaf after the death of Guru Arjan when the autograph of the sixth Guru was also included in the volume. The primary scribe of the manuscript, Bhai Gurdas, was alive during the period of the sixth Guru.

Fourth, a careful examination of the manuscript suggests that

[78]See Bhai Jodh Singh, *Kartarpuri Bir*, Introduction, p. h (Punjabi letter *haha*). Jodh Singh's method of numbering has been questioned by Piar Singh, Gurinder Mann and Randhir Singh in their works. However, one should keep in mind that the scribes of the Sanskrit manuscripts usually put the leaf number on the left-hand side rather than on the conventional right-hand side. I have seen a number of manuscripts of the Adi Granth where leaf numbers are given on the left-hand side. Obviously their scribes followed the Sanskritic tradition.

[79]See M5, *Asa* 7, AG, p. 396.

[80]Piar Singh, *Gatha*, p. 95.

the whole operation of recording was conducted in a discontinuous manner, moving between sections, each of which was carefully read by Guru Arjan before he was able to pronounce it sudh (pure, correct). The actual recording of sudh in the margins in a different hand can be seen in folios 161/1, 256/1, 259/1, 365/1, 402/2, 406/1, 434/2, 460/2, 496/1, 532/2, 648/2, 723/1, 728/2, 804/2, 884/1, 901/2, and 916/1 at the end of the var which usually concludes the works of the Gurus in each section, that is, before the works by the bhagats begin. It is worth noting that in later manuscripts the recording of sudh became part of the actual text instead of the margins. This is also the case in the modern printed editions of the Adi Granth.

Fifth, in the *Dhanasari* mode there is one hymn by Guru Amar Das (*nadari kare tan simaria jai*) which is composed in response to Guru Nanak's hymn (*kiun simari sivaria nahin jai*) in folio 499/2. It is clearly indicated in the index in folio 10/2 that the fourth hymn in the section of Guru Nanak's hymns is that of the third Guru (*chautha sabad mahale 3 ka*). To reinforce this authorship there is another editorial comment in folio 10/2 in the margin, facing the section of the hymns of the third Guru, saying that 'this number 1 hymn [of the third Guru] is written among the hymns of the first Guru at the fourth place' (*eh number 1 sabad mahale 1 vich likhia chauthe than*). Similarly, there is a marginal note on folio 778/2, indicating that 'the right place of the twenty-second *Solaha* belongs to Guru Nanak's hymn which is currently located on folio 799/2' (*22 baihavan solaha pati 799/2 sahi hai/ mahale 1/ pahile ka*). The editorial comment in the index in folio 16/1 further clarifies that the 'hymn (*kudarati karnaihar apara*) of folio 799 should come at number 22.' Other such comments explaining the position of certain hymns can be seen in folios 694/1, 788/1, 804/2 and 805/1.

Sixth, at a number of places Guru Arjan discards a version of one or the other of his own hymns and points out that the final version of the same is to be found somewhere else. For instance, there is a marginal note in folio 836/1 referring to one of Guru Arjan's hymns: 'This hymn is repeated here; its actual place is at [number] fifty-two' (*ehu sabadu duharagat charia hai bavanja hai*). The actual hymn in folio 836/1 reads:

Bhairo Mahal 5
People of God always sing the divine praises, and they have found the perfect dwelling-place. Every one desires to see the servant [of God] day

and night, even Dharamraj, the god of death, becomes sanctified. (1) Even fear [within oneself] gets scared through meditation on the divine Name. All diseases of three qualities [of Maya] have disappeared, and the tasks of the servant have been accomplished. (1). Refrain. Lust, anger, greed, attachment, slander and pride—all go away in the company of true devotees. One meets such saintly people through great fortune, I am sacrificed to them, O Nanak, all the time. (2.58.1)

The final version that appears at number 52 in folio 834/1 differs slightly from the above hymn in terms of wording and sequence of lines, and it is found in the standard version of the Adi Granth.[81] Other such notes can be seen in folios 96/2, 415/1, 483/1, 511/1, and 550/2. In this context, Piar Singh has raised the issue of the deletion of Guru Arjan's *Asa* hymn (*har jan line prabhu chhadae*) in folio 306/2 of the Kartarpur manuscript. He argues that the inclusion of this hymn and its later deletion are still very enigmatic: 'A question arises whether the fifth Guru himself did not know that this particular hymn was not by him.'[82] If Piar Singh had examined the Kartarpur bir himself he would have known that the same hymn appears at number 31 in the index (f. 7/1) and the text (ff. 296/2–297/1, AG, p. 378). It was only its second occurrence (f. 306/2) that was deleted with the use of *hartal* (a yellow-greenish paste used for deletion), and its mention in the index at number 94 (f. 7/1) was crossed out with a pen.

Seventh, there are four instances where Kabir's verses are either crossed out with a pen or erased with the use of hartal. A shalok (*dhari ambar vich belari*) was incorporated in a different hand on the right hand corner just below the Mul Mantar in Kabir's *Var Satt* (Seven Days) in *Gauri* raga in folio 275/1, but later it was deleted with the use of hartal. This shalok can still be read under the deletion paste. Second, Kabir's hymn in folio 374/2 in *Asa* mode (*dekhahu loga hari ki sagai*) is crossed out with a pen. Third, only two lines of Kabir's hymn appear in folio 497/2 in *Sorathi* raga (*audhu so jogi gur mera*) which are deleted with a pen. Fourth, a shalok (*kabir ram nam ke patantarai*) was incorporated in folio 943/2 at the end of Kabir's shaloks with a different hand, but it was crossed out with a pen. An editorial comment explains that 'this is

---

[81]M5, *Bhairau* 52, AG, p. 1151.

[82]Piar Singh, *Gatha*, p. 101. Similarly, Gurinder Mann, who has examined the Kartarpur bir, argues that 'Guru Arjan did not like the text of the hymn and decided to obliterate it' (see 'The Making of Sikh Scripture', p. 208). He also failed to notice that only the second occurrence of this hymn was deleted.

just an ordinary shalok' (*eh salok aime hai*), which may indicate that it was not approved by the Guru.[83] In a similar manner, the Mira Bai hymn (*man hamaro badhio kaval nainu*), which was written in a different hand in folio 810/2 at the end of *Maru* raga, was deleted with a pen. The issues behind these deletions will be discussed in detail in the sixth chapter.

Eighth, there are only two lines of Guru Arjan's *Ramakali* hymn (*ran junjjhanara gau sakhi hari ek dhiavahu// satguri tum sevi sakhi mani chindiara phalu pavahu//*) in folio 703/1. Although the scribe has used a different pen, this couplet is in the same hand as the text which precedes it. It is followed by a blank space which extends to more than two folios and there is no deletion of any sort. The use of a different pen and the absence of its mention in the index clearly indicate that this couplet was added after the compilation of the scripture in 1604 and before Guru Arjan's death in 1606. Another such example is the recording of a single line of Surdas's hymn (*chhadi man hari bimukhan ko sangu*) in the *Sarang* mode in folio 885/2. Here too the scribe has used a different pen. The opening line of Surdas's hymn is followed by four blank lines in the manuscript, which could accommodate the remainder of the hymn. Again, there has been no deletion at this point. The single line is followed by Guru Arjan's comment on Surdas (*hari ke sang basse hari lok*) which is in response to the issue raised by the bhagat in his hymn.

Finally, the letters and the vowel-signs of the Gurmukhi script appear to have greatly developed by the time the Kartarpur volume was written in 1603–4. A comparative analysis of the earlier manuscripts (Goindval pothis and the GNDU MS 1245) and the Kartarpur manuscript has revealed that Guru Arjan standardized the Gurmukhi script when he prepared the final text of the Adi Granth. For instance, a half-vertical stroke is used for the vowel-sign *kanna* instead of a dot. The use of *kanaura* (au) was also introduced. Certain Sanskrit conventions such as the omission of *aunkar* (u) with *ura* is encountered at some places. The vowel *aira* (a) and the consonant *chhachhha* (chh) are, however, still written in forms which resemble the corresponding takari letters.

Bhai Jodh Singh's work, *Sri Kartarpuri Bir de Darasan*, gives a scrupulously accurate description of the manuscript and provides

[83]Giani Gurdit Singh, *Itihas Sri Guru Granth Sahib*, p. 502. Bhai Jodh Singh has given a slightly different reading of the comment in his *Kartarpuri Bir* on page 119 (*eh salok agge hai*, this shalok lies ahead). This does not seem to make sense in the present context.

comprehensive and meticulous notes on the text. At one crucial point, however, he adds his own interpretation to his description to solve a textual problem.[84] It is important to note that this manuscript is variously known as the Kartarpur version, the Bhai Gurdas version, or the Adi bir (first or original version). Before falling into the hands of Dhir Mal, who brought it to Kartarpur for the purpose of establishing his own guruship after the death of Guru Harkrishan, it was known as the granth of the fifth Guru (*panjaven mahale ka granth*), and it was kept at Kiratpur by the seventh and the eighth Gurus.[85] Its presence in Kiratpur is evident from certain notes in Baba Ram Rai's bir which was written in 1659 during Guru Har Rai's period. Under the circumstances, it is misleading for Gurinder Mann to argue that the Adi bir remained in the custody of Dhir Mal at Kartarpur from the 1630s.[86] In this context, Piar Singh rightly argues that it is unlikely that Guru Hargobind 'should have readily parted with the acknowledged insignia of guruship for all the ten long years he passed at Kiratpur.'[87] If he carried the original bir with him when he left Amritsar after his skirmishes with the Mughal army, how could he leave it at Kartarpur when he moved his centre to Kiratpur? Dhirmal was hardly sixteen years old, in 1643 when he received a revenue-free grant from the Mughal emperor Shah Jahan 'who was evidently seeking to sow discord in the Panth.'[88] It was then that he became suspect in the eyes of Guru Hargobind who appointed his younger brother Har Rai as the seventh Guru in 1644. After this event, Dhir Mal's activities became a menace to the mainline Sikh community. It is more likely that he captured the original volume and brought it to Kartarpur as part of his strategy to lay claim to the office of guruship after Guru Harkrishan's death in Delhi.

Much ink has been spilt on the question of the authenticity of the Kartarpur bir. Due to its association with Dhir Mal it has suffered at the hands of both categories of scholars, that is, those who had the opportunity to examine it personally and those who failed to have access to the manuscript. On the one hand, we have the traditional historian Rattan Singh Bhangu, who wrote in the middle of the nineteenth century that both the original Amritsari granth and the Damadami granth had been carried off by Afghans in 1762

[84]For details, see Chapter 3, p. 118.
[85]G.B. Singh, *Prachin Biran*, pp. 169–70.
[86]Mann, 'The Making of Sikh Scripture', pp. 94–6.
[87]Piar Singh, *Gatha*, p. 79.
[88]McLeod, *Dictionary*, p. 72.

during the battle of the Great Holocaust (*vadda ghalughara*).[89] He did not acknowledge anything associated with the Dhirmalias as genuine and was simply reflecting the bias of the Khalsa against the reprobate groups. On the other hand, his two contemporaries, the authors of *Suraj Prakash* (1843) and *Gurbilas Chhevin Patashahi* (1840), had certainly seen the Kartarpuri bir at the Moti palace of Maharaja Ranjit Singh in Lahore and duly acknowledged its genuineness.[90]

In the present century, Bhai Kahn Singh Nabha, the celebrated Singh Sabha scholar, raised the question of the authenticity of the Kartarpur bir, and he was followed by a long line of other scholars who expressed their doubts even without examining the manuscript.[91] It was Bhai Jodh Singh who came to its defence with his thorough examination of the manuscript. He was followed by Daljeet Singh who became too dogmatic in his attitude towards a particular view of the creation of Sikh scripture. He maintained that the Kartarpur bir consisted of the actual words uttered by the Gurus and was recorded under the direct supervision of Guru Arjan. Indeed, his approach represents the fundamentalist variety in the strict sense of the word. More recently, Piar Singh has provided a strong rebuttal to Daljeet Singh's arguments and set aside the authenticity of the Kartarpur bir with his scholarly approach. Although Piar Singh could not have access to the Kartarpur bir—a single weakness in his analysis—he drew his conclusions from an examination of a large number of early manuscripts of the Adi Granth and other secondary sources. No textual critic can afford to ignore his arguments, even though one might not agree with him on every point. For instance, he argues that the autograph of the fifth Guru and the index leaf are lifted documents. His arguments are based on some original photographs of these folios that I supplied him upon his request. He interpreted them in his own way in order to buttress his claims. The main problem with the present state of the Kartarpur bir is that it was laminated in 1956–7 through a 'preservation operation.'[92] All

[89]Rattan Singh Bhangu, *Sri Guru Panth Prakash*, ed. Jeet Singh Sital (Amritsar: Sikh Itihas Research Board, SGPC, 1984), p. 459. Also see Piar Singh, *Gatha*, p. 78.

[90]For details, see Chapter 7, p. 229.

[91]For details, see Mann, *The Goindval Pothis*, pp. 137–8, n. 1.

[92]The preservation was done by Basant Singh Rekhi at the instance of Sodhi Amarjit Singh who had approached Vidya Sagar Suri, the records-keeper of the Punjab. The note reads: 'This respected Bir of Siri Guru Granth Sahib is preserved by Shri Basant Singh Rekhi, [through the] period from 18.5.1956 to 31.10.1956 and from 21.4.1957 to 16.5.1957.' The note was written and signed on 16 May 1957. The

its folios were framed and pasted on different papers before lamination. Thus it is difficult to agree with Piar Singh's arguments based on the external features of the manuscript. His arguments about the text of the Kartarpur bir, however, require a detailed response, and we shall return to them at different points in our analysis.

There are some rare manuscripts preserved at Patna Sahib, the birthplace of Guru Gobind Singh, the text of which was claimed to have been corrected by comparing it with the text of the original volume. For instance, the following note from a manuscript written by a Sikh named Ram Rai, son of a goldsmith named Uttam Chand, in sambat 1749 (1692) illuminates the process of textual transmission.

This granth is the copy of the granth of Fateh Chand, Fateh Chand's granth is the copy of the Puhkar [or Pushkar] granth. The Puhkar granth is corrected by comparing it with the great granth, which was inscribed by Gurdas Bhalla at the dictation of the fifth Guru. If someone corrects his granth with the help of the [great] granth, his granth will be correct. Even then if someone wants to correct his granth, he should do so by comparing it with the granth of Jagana Brahman. As compared with other granths, the granth of Jagana Brahman has been corrected [with the great granth]. The Puhkar granth is [also] corrected by comparing it with the granth of Jagana Brahman.[93]

The following points emerge from this text. First, the concern for the correctness of the copy of the Adi Granth seems to have been widespread in the Sikh community in the late seventeenth century. Second, the great granth (*vadda granth*), which was written by Gurdas Bhalla at the dictation of Guru Arjan, was evidently known to the scribes as the benchmark for authenticating their own copies of the Adi Granth.[94] Third, the note specifically mentions, for the first time, the name of Bhai Gurdas as being the amanuensis of the fifth Guru. Fourth, the copies of the Adi Granth were popularly known by the names of the scribes (like Fateh Chand and Jagana Brahman) as

---

manuscript can now last for the next four to five hundred years without any further process of preservation. However, there is an urgent need for making a microfilm of it, copies of which could be made available in different libraries for scholarly use.

[93]Piara Singh Padam, *Sri Guru Granth Prakash* (Patiala: Kalam Mandir, 2nd edn, 1990; 1st edn, 1977), p. 105. For further details on this manuscript, see Piar Singh, *Gatha*, pp. 339–42.

[94]Giani Gurdit Singh claims to have in his possession an old manuscript which carries a similar note: 'This granth has been corrected by comparing it with the Adi Granth, so keep the spellings and the vowel-signs intact'. The Adi Granth here refers to the Adi bir. See *Itihas Sri Guru Granth Sahib*, p. 412.

well as places (like Puhkar or Pushkar). In particular, Jagana Brahman seems to have enjoyed a great reputation for writing the correct (sudh) copies of the Adi Granth in the seventeenth century. Incidentally, Bhai Gurdas has mentioned the name of Jagana Brahman in the list of Guru Arjan's devout Sikhs.[95] He originally belonged to Agra where he must have received his education in Sanskritic learning. He is reputed to have fought bravely in the battle of Amritsar at the bidding of Guru Hargobind.[96]

In sum, it may be stated that the concern for the authentic copy of the Adi Granth reflects a situation in which other versions of the text of the Adi Granth were widely in use by different groups within the Sikh community. The Lahore recension differs from the Kartarpur version only in its concluding section. It has a different order, sometimes ending with the shaloks of Kabir and Farid, and sometimes with the panegyrics in praise of the Gurus. The Banno recension, however, contains extra material which is not to be found in the other two versions.

POST-CANONICAL TRADITIONS

1. Kartarpur Tradition

1.1. *The Punjabi University Museum (PUM) Manuscript # 8*

This manuscript is the earliest extant copy of the Kartarpur tradition. Although there is no colophon which can be used to date it, certain indications suggest that the volume was written after the compilation of the Kartarpur manuscript, possibly during Guru Arjan's lifetime. For instance, it does not contain Guru Tegh Bahadur's hymns. Further, it has a conventional entry in the index as follows: 'The *Japu* was copied directly from the manuscript written in Guru Ram Das's hands' (*japu sri Guru ramdas ji ke dasakhatan ka nakal*). This entry seems to be the characteristic feature of all manuscripts of the Kartarpur tradition, which challenges the bold claim made by Daljeet Singh that 'no other bir [apart from the Kartarpur bir] records these words.'[97] There are other points which emerge from an actual examination of the volume.

The main characteristics of this volume may be described as follows. First, the manuscript has a total of 564 folios. Its recording

---

[95]*Varan Bhai Gurdas*, 11: 27.
[96]Piar Singh, *Gatha Sri Adi Granth*, pp. 341–2.
[97]See *Essays*, p. 13.

was carried out strictly *seriatim* by copying from the Kartarpur manuscript. Like its predecessor, it contains the actual noting *sudh* (pure, correct) in a different hand in the margins. The most important instance is the recording of *sudh kita* (corrections made) in the margin of folio 130a at the end of Guru Arjan's *Var Gauri* in contrast with the noting of *sudh kichai* (make corrections) in the Kartarpur text in the margin of folio 259a, which shows that it was a further revision of the Kartarpur manuscript. It also records the formula 'by the grace of the true Guru' (*satgur prasadi*) at the conclusion of the liturgical text *So Dar* in folio 5a. The same formula can be found in the Kartarpur MS in folios 51/2 and 52/2. It clearly indicates that the copying of the bani was regarded by the early Sikh community as a devotional activity, and its completion was normally marked by the scribal formula 'by the grace of the true Guru' (satgur prasadi) at the end of the section.[98]

Second, it contains the liturgical text *So Purakh*, which is not to be found in the Kartarpur text, signifying that it was written at a time when the evening prayer, Rahiras, was further extended with the inclusion of *So Purakh* in Sikh worship. Third, only two lines of Guru Arjan's *Ramakali* hymn are to be found in folios 373b–374a. There is no blank space or deletion at this point. Fourth, Mira Bai's hymn in the *Maru* raga is not to be found in this volume. Fifth, a single line of the Surdas hymn is to be found in folio 509b, and it is followed by Guru Arjan's commentary hymn on Surdas.

Sixth, the final shalok (*tera kita jato nahin*) forms part of a group of extra shaloks by Guru Arjan in the epilogue (*Salok Varan Te Vadhik*) instead of coming after the *Mundavani*. This clearly indicates that this shalok gradually became a part of Sikh liturgy in the evening prayer, and then acquired its usual place after the *Mundavani*. In this case, either the scribe has followed an earlier convention or has consciously diverged from the Kartarpur text by keeping the *Mundavani* as the seal at the end. There is yet another possibility, that a new leaf containing these liturgical texts was added in the Kartarpur manuscript at a time when their sequence was fixed by Guru Arjan. This is indicated by the fact that a new pen was used while writing the *Mundavani* and the concluding shalok in folio 973/1 of the Kartarpur volume. Further, the following leaf (ff. 973/2–974/1) does not have the usual lines indicating margins on both sides.[99]

[98]Also see British Library (BL), MSS Or. 2748. In this volume the scribal formulae (*sri satguru gribnivaz* or *vahiguru gribnivaz* or simply *vahiguru*) can be seen on folios 39b, 104a and 161a.

[99]See Bhai Jodh Singh, *Kartarpuri Bir*, p. 122.

Seventh, it does not contain the controversial *Raga-mala*, which throws new light on its inclusion in the Kartarpur manuscript. The *Raga-mala* text may have been included much later, at the very end by the same scribe at the instance of Guru Arjan. This is evident from the way its entry has been made in the index. Some words of this entry have been written vertically in the margin, which is a clear case of later insertion.[100]

Eighth, the manuscript contains an apocryphal text (*Para Ras Rakhsu*), describing the indigenous process of preparing mercury oxide, a medicinal preparation, at the end of the volume on an extra blank folio after the folio numbered 574b. It is in the same hand, though written in slightly bolder letters. This single fact evidently links this manuscript with the Kartarpur bir, since this medicinal prescription (*Para Ras Rakhsu*) is also to be found in the original volume in folios 21b–22a. It is a recipe for converting mercury into medicinal ash (*kushta* or *bhasam*), which is considered a panacea for several diseases. Perhaps the scribe followed a contemporary Muslim tradition of writing such medicinal formulae in the blank folios, which were then inserted in the binding to preserve the manuscripts of the Qur'an.[101]

Finally, the Gurmukhi script goes back to the early seventeenth century as is evident by the use of the dot (or small circle 'o') for the vowel-sign *kanna* most of the time. The writing is the same throughout the text except at the end, when a different hand has inserted the apocryphal text (*Hakikati Rah Mukam Raje Sivanabh Ki*) on the extra blank page. There is, however, no mention of it in the index, and it was definitely incorporated in the volume much later. In the Kartarpur volume the last entry in the index on folio 2/2 reads: 'The *Raga-mala* and [an account of the way to the abode of] Raja Sivanabh in Sin(g)hla-dip in folio 974.' Some of the words of this entry (*Sivanabh Raje Ki vidhi*) are written vertically in the margin as there is no space for them in the next line, where a new heading of the index of indices (*tatakara tatakare*) of the ragas begins. There is, however, no such text *as Sin(g)hla-dip Sivanabh Raje Ki Vidhi* to be found after the *Raga-mala* in the Kartarpur manuscript. Two explanations may be offered here. First, the last words in the entry (*Tatha Sin(g)hla-dip Sivanabh Raje Ki Vidhi*) were added much later

---

[100]Piar Singh, *Bhai Jodh Singh: Jivan ate Rachana* (Patiala: Punjabi University, 1983), p. 84.

[101]Bhai Jodh Singh, 'A Note on Kartarpur Granth', *Proceedings of Punjab History Conference*, First Session (Patiala: Punjabi University, 1966), p. 97.

to make an attempt to include this apocryphal text in the scripture, but it was somehow turned down. Second, the inclusion of this text was not approved by Guru Arjan himself, although its mention had already been made in the index entry.[102] Whatever the case may be, it is certain that the last words in the index entry were written in an unconventional way. The entry for the text *Sin(g)hla-dip Sivanabh Raje Ki Vidhi* should have been distinguished from the *Raga-mala* entry, if it was to be included in the scripture.

The Punjabi University acquired this manuscript from Bhai Durga Singh of Patiala. The following words are inscribed in gold letters on the binding: 'Presented with loving affection to [his] grandson Avtar Singh by Ghannaya Singh, the servant of servants [of the Guru].' Evidently the manuscript remained in the family as a precious possession and was handed down to successive generations. Bhai Durga Singh's ancestry may be traced back to Bhai Dharam Singh Daddhiala, a devout Sikh follower of Guru Gobind Singh, who was a scribe as well as a singer.[103]

1.2. Baba Ram Rai's Bir

G.B. Singh examined Baba Ram Rai's bir, completed on 29 March 1659 (sambat 1716 varkhai mah vaisakh vadi 1), and recorded his findings in his book in 1944. He cites three very important marginal notes from this manuscript to show that it was corrected by comparing it with the text of the granth of the fifth Guru (*Panjaven Mahale Ka Granth*).[104] One of these notes is quite useful in understanding the textual problem of Mira Bai's hymn in the Adi Granth. The scribe has inserted the hymn in a small hand at the end of *Maru* raga, but upon comparison with Guru Arjan's volume, he makes the following comment: 'Mira Bai's hymn is not to be found in the granth of the fifth Guru' (*mira bai ka sabad panjavain mahalai ke granth nahin*). This note clearly indicates that the scribe of Baba Ram Rai's bir found Mira Bai's hymn crossed out in the original volume. It is quite understandable that the scribes would take note of specific corrections done in the original volume so that they might not repeat them in their own copies. However, Piar Singh interprets this note in his own way to argue that Mira Bai's hymn did not figure in

---

[102]There is another such instance in the Kartarpur manuscript in folio 963/1 where a new heading *paran-sangali mahala* 1 is written in Persian script, but there is no such text to be found there. The folio is totally blank. Presumably the text was not approved by Guru Arjan due to questions concerning its authorship.

[103]Piara Singh Padam, *Sri Guru Granth Prakash*, p. 106.

[104]G.B. Singh, *Prachin Biran*, pp. 169–70.

the original manuscript, and hence he questions the authenticity of the Kartarpur bir.[105]

The second note appears at the end of Ravidas's hymn (*sukh sagar suritar chintamani*) in *Maru* raga, which was missed in the first recording. After its inscription in the margin, the following note is written: 'This hymn has been copied from the granth of the fifth Guru' (*ih sabad panjaven mahale ke giranth uparahu likhia*). Evidently, the original volume was consulted in making certain corrections in Baba Ram Rai's bir.

The third note raises the interesting issue of the authorship of four shaloks of Guru Nanak which now appear under the symbol of the third Guru in the standard version of the Adi Granth. In Baba Ram Rai's bir all the shaloks, that were in excess of the vars (*Salok Varan Te Vadhik*), were copied from the original volume. At the end of the shaloks of Guru Ram Das, the following colophon appears: 'All these shaloks have been copied from the granth of the fifth Guru' (*itane salok panjaven mahale ke giranth uparahu likhe*). The authorwise count of the shaloks runs as follows: M1 = 37, M3 = 63, and M4 = 30. In the standard version of the Adi Granth, however, this counting is given as follows: M1 = 33, M3 = 67, and M4 = 30. This discrepancy clearly indicates that the last four shaloks of Guru Nanak were added to the list of Guru Amar Das's shaloks (*abhiagat eh na akhiai., abhai niranjan param padu, hovan pandit jotaki,* and *brahaman kaili ghatu*). It is important to note the use of hartal even in the Kartarpur bir at the end of Guru Nanak's shaloks (f. 967/1). This was certainly done after the period of Guru Har Rai, perhaps when the original volume fell into the hands of Dhir Mal. There must have been questions concerning the authorship of those four shaloks within different groups of the Panth. For devout Sikhs, however, it hardly matters if those shaloks are by Guru Nanak or by Guru Amar Das.

Some of the important features of Baba Ram Rai's bir are as follows: First, there is an autograph of Guru Har Rai before the index. Second, it has the conventional entry of the Kartarpur tradition regarding the 'copying of the *Japu* directly from the manuscript written in Sat Guru Ram Das Ji's hands' (*japu sri satiguru ramdas ji ke dasakhatan ka nakal*). Third, it contains the liturgical text *So Purakh*, indicating that it had already become part of the introductory section of the Adi Granth. Fourth, it follows the standard order of thirty ragas and concludes with the normal sequence of *Salok Sahaskriti*

---

[105]See Piar Singh, *Gatha*, p. 50.

(shaloks in sahaskriti idiom), *Gatha* (story), *Phunahe* (hymns with special repetition), *Chaubole* (discourse with four listeners), Kabir's shaloks (243), Farid's shaloks (130), Guru Arjan's savayyae (9+11= 20), panegyrics by Bhatts (9, 10, 22, 60 and 21 = 122), *Salok Varan Te Vadhik*, *Mundavani*, *Raga-mala* and *Var Basant* (*mahala 1*). The scribe has wrongly attributed *Var Basant* to Guru Nanak. In fact, it is the composition of Guru Arjan. There is no apocryphal text in this volume.[106] Evidently, *Var Basant* of Guru Arjan was originally included at the end of the Sikh scripture. It was included later in the Kartarpur bir in the *Basant* mode (f. 854/2) in the middle of a blank folio before the compositions of the bhagats.

1.3. Manuscript Copy of Baba Ram Rai's Bir

The followers of Baba Ram Rai made copies from his bir, one of which is preserved at Gurdwara Dasmesh Bhavan, Sri Guru Singh Sabha, Dehradun. This manuscript was hidden in a forest near Dehradun at the time of the episode of Nanakana Sahib in 1921 by the followers of Baba Ram Rai who feared that the Akalis might take over their establishment. In the meanwhile it came into the hands of Bhai Wazir Singh, who donated it to the management of Gurdwara Dasmesh Bhavan.

Some of the characteristic features of the copy of Baba Ram Rai's bir are as follows. First, there is no colophon by which the manuscript can be dated. It is undoubtedly a copy of the Kartarpur version, and does not contain the compositions of Guru Tegh Bahadur. The first entry in the index reads: 'The Japu is copied from the manuscript written in Sri Guru [Ram]Das's hand.'[107] This entry seems to have become a convention in the Kartarpur tradition. Second, the list of the dates of the demise of Gurus includes Ram Rai as the eighth Guru, not Guru Harkrishan.[108] This reflects the situation of a parallel line of guruship based on the possession of a copy of the Adi Granth.

Third, only two lines of Guru Arjan's *Ramakali* hymn (*hari ek*

---

[106]For details, see G.B. Singh, *Prachin Biran*, pp. 167–77. Also see, Piar Singh, *Gatha*, pp. 258–61. The manuscript is in the possession of Mahant Inderesh Charan Das of Baba Ram Rai's *dera* at Dehradun. Gurinder Mann's information that it is at Singh Sabha Gurdwara in Dehradun is incorrect. *The Goindval Pothis*, p. 160, n. 99.

[107]The copyist failed to understand this convention and deleted the word Ram with hartal to make it look like Gurdas.

[108]Gurdwara Sri Guru Singh Sabha, Dehradun, MS copy of Baba Ram Rai's bir, f. 657b. The death date of Guru Har Rai is followed by the entry: 'Sri Guru Ram Rai Ji, the creator lord, died on the eighth light day of the month of *bhadon* in sambat 1744 [1687]'.

dhiavahu run junjjhanara gau sakhi// satguri tum sevi sakhi mani chindiara phalu pavahu//) in a slightly different order are to be found in the margin of folio 452a, written in a different hand. Presumably these were omitted consciously by the scribe in the first instance, appreciating the textual problem they presented because of their incomplete nature.

Fourth, the Mira Bai hymn in *Maru* raga is deleted by the use of hartal on folio 530a. Fifth, even the single line of Surdas's hymn in the *Sarang* mode is omitted. Here, the scribe seems to have decided to leave out the incomplete hymn. Only the commentary hymn of Guru Arjan on Surdas is to be found in folio 589b.

Finally, a single couplet of Kabir (*dhari ambari vich belari*) at the beginning of his *Var Satt* in *Gauri* mode in folio 185a and Trilochan's hymn in *Gujari* raga (*naunidhi parasi*) have been deleted by the use of hartal. These were deleted presumably because they are not to be found in the Kartarpur manuscript (the couplet of Kabir is deleted there, and the hymn of Trilochan, which may have been copied from some other volume of the Lahore recension, does not appear in the Kartarpur manuscript at all).

An examination of this copy of the Adi Granth clearly indicates that its predecessor, Baba Ram Rai's bir, was certainly corrected by comparison with the granth of the fifth Guru. It seems to point to another fact, that the Adi bir was at Kiratpur with Guru Har Rai when Baba Ram Rai's bir was prepared.[109] Piar Singh has given the details of another copy of the Adi Granth which was corrected by comparison with the Adi bir.[110]

2. Lahore Tradition

The earliest textual example of this tradition was the manuscript written in sambat 1667 (1610) during Guru Hargobind's period. It was popularly known as Lahori bir because it was prepared in Lahore.[111] W.H. McLeod refers to this copy of the Adi Granth as Adi bir (Kartarpur version), which was not the case.[112] It was preserved at the Sikh Reference Library in Amritsar, which was destroyed in

[109]For another copy of Ram Rai's bir written in sambat 1742 (1695), see G.B. Singh, *Prachin Biran*, pp. 177–8.

[110]See Piar Singh, *Gatha Sri Adi Granth*, pp. 210–18.

[111]Piar Singh (*samp.*), *Adi Sakhian* (Ludhiana: Lahore Book Shop, 3rd edn, 1983; 1st edn, 1969), p. 78.

[112]W.H. McLeod, 'Hakikat Rah Mukam Raje Sivanabh Ki', *Proceedings of Punjab History Conference*, Fourth Session (Patiala: Punjabi University, 1970), p. 102.

1984 during Operation Bluestar. Fortunately, a detailed report concerning this manuscript had already been prepared in 1969.[113] This report describes the sequence of the concluding section of the manuscript after the text of *Chaubole* as follows: (1) *Salok Varan Te Vadhik*, (2) Guru Arjan's *Mundavani*, (3) Guru Arjan's concluding shalok, (4) panegyrics by the fifth Guru, (5) panegyrics by the bards in praise of the Gurus; (6) Kabir's shaloks; and (7) Farid's shaloks. Another distinguishing feature of this manuscript was that it contained an extra-canonical hymn of Trilochan in *Gujari* mode (*naunidhi parasi*).

G.B. Singh examined another manuscript of this tradition, popularly known as Bura Sandhu's recension. Although his findings are very useful in understanding this recension, his dating of the manuscript to 1605, based on a misleading colophon, is mistaken. The colophon reads as follows.

The Granth Sahib was completed in the presence of Sri Guru Ji. It was written by Bhai Bura Sandhu in the presence of the fifth king. Bhai Milkhi, a resident of Peshawar, got this volume written [for himself]. Whosoever gets the opportunity to see (*darsan*) this Granth Sahib, will be blessed with a unique vision (*darsan*) of Guru Nanak Sahib Ji's body. Please forgive me for any mistakes. Sri Vahiguru Ji is the Eternal Truth. [The Granth Sahib] was completed in sambat 1662 (1605).[114]

This colophon is definitely a forgery for the following reasons. First, it gives only the year of writing of the volume, not the more precise dating that was customary in manuscripts of the period. Secondly, instead of writing the date at the beginning of the index it is written unconventionally at the end of the volume on a new leaf, which is a clear case of later interpolation. Thirdly, the word Granth Sahib came to be used for the Sikh scripture much later. Originally it was known as the pothi, which is quite evident from the index of the Kartarpur manuscript.[115] The colophon, we may surmise, was intended to make a claim to an earlier period for the sake of collecting the offerings of the Sikhs. Piara Singh Padam, who examined the same manuscript in the possession of Bawa Arjan Singh at Sharifpura in 1948, concluded that it was in fact written in sambat 1711 (1654).[116]

[113]Swami Harnam Das, *Adi Sri Guru Granth Sahib Ji dian Puratan Biran te Vichar* (Kapurthala: Ramesh Chander Suri, 1969), pp. 106–8.

[114]G.B. Singh, *Prachin Biran*, pp. 110–11.

[115]Kartarpur MS, f. 2/2. Also see, Bhai Jodh Singh, *Prachin Biran Bare*, pp. 97–8.

[116]Piara Singh Padam, *Sri Guru Granth Prakash*, p. 101. Also see Piar Singh, *Adi Sakhian*, p. 79.

The concluding section of Bura Sandhu's bir runs as follows. After the text of *Chaubole*, the sequence diverges from the standard pattern: *Salok Varan Te Vadhik*, Kabir's shaloko, Farid's shaloks, and panegyrics in praise of the Gurus. Most importantly, Guru Arjan's var in *Basant* mode is recorded at the end of the volume, rather than at its appropriate place in the section on raga *Basant*. It should be emphasized that the Lahore tradition is also popularly known as the Bura Sandhu tradition of the Adi Granth. Let us now return to the actual examination of some of the manuscripts of this tradition.

2.1. *Una Sahib Manuscript # 2*

This manuscript is preserved by Baba Sarabjot Singh Bedi at Una Sahib, Himachal Pradesh. There is no colophon which can be used to date it. Some of the important features of this manuscript are as follows. First, in folio 15a, two entries are made concerning the autographs of Guru Hargobind (*nisanu mahala* 6) and Guru Gobind Singh (*nisanu mahala* 10), both of which, being on different pieces of paper, are pasted in folio 16a. The writing of the manuscript seems to have begun during the period of the sixth Guru (1606–44), and it was certainly completed before the death in 1675 of Guru Tegh Bahadur, whose complete works were added later at the end of the volume in folios 562b–565a.

Second, only two lines of Guru Arjan's hymn in *Ramakali* mode are to be found in folio 359a. Third, the Mira Bai hymn in *Maru* raga is not to be found in this volume. Fourth, the single line of Surdas's hymn which seems to have been consciously omitted in the first instance, was written in a different hand after Guru Arjan's commentary hymn on Surdas in folio 493b. Fifth, there are no specified tunes (dhunis) at the beginning of different ballads (vars) except the var in *Ramakali* mode in folio 367a. Sixth, the concluding shalok forms a part of Guru Arjan's group of extra shaloks, which is followed by the *Mundavani* in folio 543a. The concluding section ends with panegyrics by the bards in praise of the Gurus.

Finally, the entry of the dates of demise of the ten Gurus on folio 567b also contains two conspicuous names which throw some light on the origin of the tradition. They are as follows: (a) 'Sri Satguru Sach Ji died on Friday, the ninth light day of the month of *magh* in sambat 1732 [1675]', (b) 'Sri Satguru Sajada Mal Ji died on Sunday, the second light day of the month of *manghar* in sambat 1777 [1720].' Evidently these two persons, Sach Ji and Sajada Mal Ji, were revered as Gurus by their followers, who constituted a sect within the Panth.

Who were they? Were they Udasis or masands? The answers to these questions may provide a clue to an understanding of the origin of this tradition. In fact, the possession of this copy of the Adi Granth by the Bedi family may suggest that it was used by the Udasis themselves or a sect associated with them, who seem to have come closer to the Panth as a result of Guru Hargobind's efforts at reconciliation. It is quite possible that the Udasis were responsible for this version of the Adi Granth.

2.2. *Guru Nanak Dev University (GNDU) Manuscript # 1084*

The manuscript was written in sambat 1723 (1666), and at least two different sets of handwriting can be discerned in this volume. The Gurmukhi script can probably be ascribed to the seventeenth century because a dot is used in place of the vowel-sign *kanna*. The following features are worth noting. First, the text of *So Purakh* is missing in this volume. Second, the two lines of Guru Arjan's *Ramakali* hymn which are written in the margin in folio 293b, are consciously omitted in the first instance. There is a marginal note above these lines which states that 'this hymn has been written here by mistake' (*ehu sabadu pasi likhia bhulli*), which clearly suggests that the scribe was puzzled by seeing just two lines of an incomplete hymn in the volume that he was using to make his own copy. Presumably he wrote the two lines in the margin, along with his comment, much later.

Third, although Mira Bai's hymn is to be found in this volume in folio 351b, the single line of Surdas's hymn has been omitted. Again, the scribe seems to have been puzzled by the incomplete hymn, which he decided to leave out. Here the scribe fails to acknowledge the authorship of Guru Arjan in his commentary hymn on Surdas in folio 398b. Rather, he attributes that hymn to Surdas (*Bani Bhagat Surdas Jiu Ki: hari ke sang basse hari lok*). This also shows that he was puzzled to find Guru Arjan in the midst of the bhagat bani. Fourth, there is an extra-canonical hymn of Namdev in the *Dhanasari* mode (*sat samund ja ki hai kirani*) in folio 222b.

Fifth, the sequence of the concluding section changes after the text of *Chaubole*. It runs as follows: (a) *Salok Varan Te Vadhik*, (b) panegyrics by the fifth Guru, (c) panegyrics by the bards in praise of the Gurus, (d) Kabir's shaloks, (e) Farid's shaloks, and (f) *Raga-mala*. The complete works of Guru Tegh Bahadur were incorporated much later between the panegyrics of the bards and the shaloks of Kabir by adding new folios. It should be emphasized that there is no mention of *Raga-mala* in the index of the volume. It seems to have been added later, probably at the time of the addition of the works of Guru Tegh Bahadur.

Finally, the concluding shalok of Guru Arjan is written after the *Mundavani*. There is a very significant marginal note here which states: 'This shalok must be written after the *Mundavani*, it is the final one' (*ehu saloku mundavani dai picchai likhana orak da*). The note clearly indicates that the earlier convention of including this shalok in Guru Arjan's group of extra shaloks must be replaced with this new convention, which may have its origin in the Sikh liturgy of evening prayer.

2.3. Jograj Manuscript, Punjabi University Museum # 2

The manuscript was completed in 1667 (sambat 1724 magh vadi ekam 1) by Jograj, who died in 1671 (sambat 1728 magh vadi chauth 4) on a Sunday. The scribe seems to have enjoyed a high reputation in the community because his death is mentioned along with the deaths of eight Gurus (f. 2b). In folio 2a, a different piece of paper, containing the Mul Mantar written by Guru Tegh Bahadur, is pasted.

There is another piece of information given in folio 3b, said to be a copy of Guru Har Rai's writing:

Copy of the words written by the seventh Guru (*sataven mahale kian akharan ki nakal*):
Shalok: Keep your hope of succour focused only on the one lord, my *man*, and discard all other hope. Meditate, Nanak, on the divine name and all your tasks will be accomplished.
These words were proclaimed in writing by the Guru at the time of succession to the throne [of Guru Nanak] in the morning hours of Tuesday, in the month of the last days of *poh* [December/January], at Thapal Dera in Sirmor. He who reflects upon these words will be blessed. His cycle of birth and death will be broken. This is the Guru's *vak* [commandment].

This note refers to an important moment in Sikh history when Guru Har Rai went to Thapal in Sirmor (Nahan) soon after his succession to the throne [of Guru Nanak] and proclaimed his first teaching in the form of a vak or commandment. It also throws considerable light on the tradition of receiving a vak from the Guru. Jograj seems to have felt the need to record this for posterity in his volume of the Adi Granth. Moreover, this note corroborates the testimony of the contemporary Persian chronicle *Dabistan-i-Mazahib*: 'In the year one thousand and fifty five (Hijri), when Najabat Khan, son of Shah Rukh Mirza, having mobilized an army, under the orders of Shah

Jahan, invaded the territories of Tara Chand and made the Raja a prisoner, Guru Har Rai went to Thapul in the territories of Raja Karam Prakash near Sirhind.'[117] Evidently, the Guru did not want to 'embroil himself in an armed conflict between the chief of Hindur (Nalagarh) and the Mughal commandants who invaded his territories.'[118]

The following important features concerning this manuscript may be noted. First, the index of the manuscript on folio 4b shows that it concludes with Shaikh Farid's shaloks, and does not contain the *Raga-mala*. But this volume was later converted into the Banno version by adding the apocryphal texts as well as the *Raga-mala* at the end. Second, the works of Guru Tegh Bahadur were incorporated in different raga sections, sometimes by adding new folios and sometimes by writing in the margins. In particular, raga *Jaijavanti* was inserted after the *Jaitsari* mode in the margin in folio 315a.

Third, the two lines of Guru Arjan's *Ramakali* hymn are not to be found in folio 423b in this volume. Jograj seems to have consciously omitted them because of their incomplete nature. Fourth, the extra-canonical hymn of Trilochan in *Gujari* mode (*naunidhi parasi*) was interpolated in the margin of folio 234b much later, in a different hand. Fifth, no hymn of Mira Bai is to be found in the *Maru* raga in folios 525a–525b. Sixth, the scribe has consciously omitted the single line of Surdas's hymn in *Sarang* mode. Only the commentary hymn of Guru Arjan on Surdas is to be found in folio 583a.

Finally, the manuscript was written in the Kiratpur area by a devout Sikh, Jograj, who was quite popular in the Sikh community. Evidently, he deliberately omitted the problematic texts from the volume. The later addition of apocryphal texts at the end indicates that the Lahore recension was declining and the Banno tradition was coming to the fore within the Panth.

2.4. The Punjabi University Museum Manuscript # 6

The manuscript was completed in 1692 (sambat 1749 savan sudi ekam 1) on a Tuesday during the days of Guru Gobind Singh. It is very neatly written, has few corrections, and appears to be in a single hand throughout. All the texts in the volume are to be found on exactly the same folios as are given in the index. The dates of the demise of the Gurus contain the following important note in folio 27a after the entry of Guru Arjan's death: 'This is a copy of the writing of the eighth

[117]Ganda Singh, trans., 'Nanak Panthis', *The Punjab: Past and Present*, Vol. 1, part 1 (April 1967), pp. 67–8.

[118]J.S. Grewal, *The New Cambridge History of India II.3: The Sikhs of the Punjab* (Cambridge: Cambridge University Press, 1990), p. 67.

Guru, the creator lord, who wrote with his own special hand' (*mahale atthaven* (8) *ji ka nakalu hai khas kalam apani hathin likhia kartai purakhi*). The note refers to the first recording of the entries of the dates of the deaths of Baba Gurdita and Guru Hargobind, which was done by the eighth Guru himself in the original copy of the Adi Granth.[119]

The manuscript is also remarkable because there is very little use of hartal to be found in it, the one instance being the deletion of the Mul Mantar in folio 7b. Other characteristic features of the text of this volume are as follows. First, the most significant point concerning this volume is that the bani of Guru Tegh Bahadur is to be found at the appropriate places in different raga sections, the only exception being the place of *Jaijavanti* raga which comes after *Jaitsiri* mode in folio 322a.

Second, only two lines of Guru Arjan's *Ramakali* hymn are to be found in folio 405a. Third, Mira Bai's hymn in *Maru* raga is not to be found in folio 472a, where it should be, had it been included. Fourth, Guru Arjan's commentary hymn on Surdas is written first in folio 525b, and is then followed by a single line of Surdas with a special new heading (*Sarang// Ik Oankar satigur prasadi// chhadi man hari bimukhan ko sangu//*) at the end of the raga. It clearly indicates that the scribe was fully aware of the incomplete nature of Surdas's hymn, but faithfully copied the single line in his volume.

Fifth, there are no specified tunes (dhunis) at the beginning of different ballads (vars) except the var in *Malar* mode in folio 535a. Sixth, the concluding shalok forms a part of Guru Arjan's group of extra shaloks in folio 575b. It is then followed by the shaloks of the ninth Guru, including one couplet attributed to Guru Gobind Singh (*Mahala Dasavan* (10)// *balu huo bandhan chhutai sabhu kachhu hot upai//sabh kachhu tumare hath mai tum hi hoi sahai//54//*) in folio 576b. Thereafter comes the *Mundavani* in folio 576b, which is followed by Kabir's shaloks, Farid's shaloks, Guru Arjan's savayyae and the panegyrics by the bards in praise of the Gurus. There is no *Raga-mala* at the end of this manuscript.

Finally, it appears that this volume was copied from the Kangarh manuscript, which was written in sambat 1718 (1661) at Kiratpur.[120]

---

[119]This entry in the Kartarpur manuscript is in a child-like hand, particularly the eulogistic description of Guru Hargobind's death which must have been written at the instance of Guru Har Rai. See Kartarpur MS, f. 25/2. A photograph of this folio is in my possession.

[120]For a detailed analysis of the Kangarh manuscript, see G.B. Singh, *Prachin Biran*, pp. 178–95.

That is why this tradition is sometimes referred to as the Kiratpur recension of the Adi Granth.

3. Banno Tradition

3.1. *Kanpur Manuscript*

The manuscript held at Gurdwara Bhai Banno Sahib, Jawahar Nagar, Kanpur, is believed by its custodians to be the first copy of the Adi bir, prepared by Bhai Banno. Pritam Singh examined this manuscript for a period of five days on three different occasions in 1981–2, and recorded his findings in his article 'Bhai Banno's Copy of the Sikh Scripture'.[121] The description of the contents of the manuscript in the second column of the table he devised for his analysis, is very useful for our purpose. But his use of traditions as identifiers of the Banno version in the first column is questionable. It is, therefore, not possible to agree with him on all the conclusions he draws from his examination.

Pritam Singh points out that the date of writing of the manuscript was tampered with in such a way that the original year sambat 1699 (1642) was made to look like sambat 1659 (1602). The purpose of this tampering was to show that it was written in an earlier period.[122] A team of scholars from Guru Nanak Dev University, Amritsar, who examined the Kanpur manuscript, concluded that the original date of its writing was sambat 1699 (1642).[123] The majority opinion, which is based on the examination of the Kanpur manuscript, accepts that date as the time of the preparation of the Banno bir.[124]

Some of the characteristic features of the Kanpur manuscript are as follows. First, it does not contain the liturgical text *So Purakh*, which may indicate that it might have been copied from the Adi bir prepared by Bhai Gurdas, now kept at Kartarpur. Second, a close look at Guru Arjan's hymn in the *Ramakali* raga in folio 319a reveals that it originally contained only the first two lines, but later the hymn

---

[121]Pritam Singh, 'Bhai Banno's Copy of the Sikh Scripture', *Journal of Sikh Studies*, Vol. xi, no. ii (Amritsar: Guru Nanak Dev University, August, 1984), pp. 98–15.

[122]ibid., p. 104. Also see Piar Singh, *Adi Sakhian*, pp. 78–9. The author argues that the tampering with the date sambat 1699 can be easily seen with the help of a magnifying glass. For an actual photograph of the index folio of the Banno volume, see Piar Singh, *Gatha Sri Adi Granth*, Plate XXIV. The facsimile was provided by Dr Winand M. Callewaert, who has a microfilm of the complete Banno text.

[123]See Appendix B, in Daljeet Singh, *Essays*, pp. 83–7.

[124]ibid., pp. 46–9. G.B. Singh claims that the original date that was tampered with was sambat 1648 (1591). See *Prachin Biran*, p. 147. However, this early date of the compilation of the Banno text cannot be accepted.

was completed by adding twenty-two more lines in a smaller hand. Third, Mira Bai's hymn in *Maru* raga is to be found in folio 369a. Fourth, originally there was only the single line of Surdas's hymn in folio 414a, but some other hand completed the hymn much later. Fifth, all of the works of Guru Tegh Bahadur were added at the end in a different hand and on a different type of paper. Some of these hymns, however, were incorporated in the appropriate raga sections wherever possible. Sixth, the *Mundavani* and the final shalok are in folio 464b in their proper sequence. After them come the following apocryphal texts: (a) three shaloks attributed to Guru Nanak (*jit dar lakh muhammada*), (b) twenty-two extra-canonical shaloks of Guru Nanak (*bai atash ab khak*), (c) *Ratanmala* (*asan sadh niralam rahai*), and (d) *Hakikat Rah Mukam Raje Siva Nabh Ki*. Seventh, the *Raga-mala* is to be found after the apocryphal texts and before the traditional recipe for the preparation of the ink (*Siahi Ki Bidhi*) at the end of the volume. This is a normal feature of all Banno texts.

Finally, the most significant instance of deletion in this volume is Guru Amar Das's *Solaha* (*agam agochar beparavahe*) in folios 351b–352a, which is assigned a new position numbering 23 in serial order. In the Kartarpur volume the reallocation of the same *Solaha* is indicated by marginal notes in the index in folio 16/1 and in the text in folio 778/1. This fact alone makes the Kanpur volume a direct copy of the Adi bir.[125]

The Kanpur manuscript was copied from the Adi bir during the period of Guru Hargobind. This is indicated by the index entry referring to his autograph as follows: 'the benedictory autograph of the sixth Guru is in folio 34' (*nisanu Guru ji ke dasakhat mahala 6*). The actual autograph in the form of the Mul Mantar, written on a different piece of paper, is pasted in the decorated folio 33b.[126] The extra material found in this copy of the Adi Granth was clearly a later interpolation, which was done at a time when it was converted into the Banno text. This is an example of what Northrop Frye calls devout faking.[127] G.B. Singh also makes the point that in the old volumes of the Banno version, which had already been written prior

---

[125]A detailed description of the Kanpur MS is given in Rajinder Singh Bal, *Bhai Banno Darpan ate Khare vali Bir* (Jalandhar: 82/3-d Central Town, 1989), pp. 95–110.

[126]There is another decorated folio 369a with the mul mantar in the centre. The custodians of the manuscript claim that this second autograph belongs to Guru Arjan, but there is no mention of it in the index or anywhere else in the text. See ibid., pp. 102–3.

[127]Northrop Frye, *The Great Code: The Bible and Literature* (San Diego: A Harvest/ HBJ Book, 1983; 1st edn, 1981), p. 163.

to sambat 1732 (1675), the apocryphal texts are to be found in the concluding folios in the handwriting of some other writer.[128]

There is yet another convention which is to be found in the index of the Banno texts showing the position of the copy numbered in order from the Adi bir, written by Bhai Gurdas at the dictation of Guru Arjan. For instance, the entry in the Kanpur manuscript reads: 'The *Japu* is copied from the copy of the manuscript written in Guru Ram Das's hand' (*japu Guru ramdas jiu ke nakal ka nakal*).[129] It clearly indicates that this volume is a direct copy of the Adi bir. Perhaps this convention was created for the first time by a group within the Panth, which tried to promote the Banno version. In the same manner, the dates were also changed or rewritten to make the claim that this particular copy of the Adi Granth was written much earlier.

3.2. Gurdita Sekhon Manuscript, Tikana Bhai Ramkishan, Patiala

The manuscript is preserved by Mahant Gopal Singh of Tikana Sri Bhai Ramkishan, a seva-panthi sect of Patiala. It was written in 1653 (sambat 1710 miti harh sudi 14) by Gurdita Sekhon of Udhovala for the sangat of Guru Har Rai. This is evident from the following note that appears in folio 760a:

Gurdita, the slave, falls at the feet of the whole sangat of the Guru. Accept my humble submissions. I have written only those words that I know. Forgive me [for any mistakes] for the sake of the Guru and the sangat. May I always remember the Guru. Gurdita the Jat, a resident of Udhovala, Sekhon by caste, seeks your benevolence. May the Guru dwell in our remembrance through every breath. I have written the granth with the blessings of the sangat of Guru Har Rai.[130]

The custodians of the manuscript trace their origin to Bhai Ghanahyya (a devout Sikh follower of the ninth and the tenth Gurus and the originator of the sect of seva-panthis), who devoted his entire life to the mission of serving his fellow-beings in the name of the Guru. There was indeed a tradition among the seva-panthis of writing copies of the Adi Granth. Bhai Addhan Sahib (*addhan-shahi* ink is named after him), the second successor of Bhai Ghanahyya after

---

[128]G.B. Singh, *Prachin Biran*, p. 350.

[129]Giani Rajinder Singh Bal, *Khare vali Bir*, p. 119.

[130]The phrase *Guru Har Rai ji ki sangat ka sadaka* may also mean 'with the blessed company of Guru Har Rai.' If this was the case, Guru Har Rai must have given his autograph to the scribe. This did not happen for the reason that the copy was not written in the company of the Guru.

Bhai Seva Ram, and Bhai Lorinda Sahib, were two seva-panthi scribes who devoted their lives to making copies of the Adi Granth.

Some of the characteristic features of this recension of the Adi Granth are as follows. First, the conventional entry in the index states that the present copy is fourth in order from the original (*siri Guru ji ramdas ke dasakhatan ka nakalu tha tis ka nakalu tis ke nakalu ka nakalu*). There is also a reference in the index to the autograph of the Guru without specifying it (*nisanu Guru ji ke dasakhat mahala*), which shows that Gurdita was not able to receive the autograph of Guru Har Rai as he claims in the above note. However, a piece of paper containing the Mul Mantar written by Guru Tegh Bahadur is pasted with decorated borders in folio 19a.[131] The list of the dates of demise of the first six Gurus is given in folio 14b, which clearly indicates that the manuscript was definitely written during the period of the seventh Guru.

Second, neither the text of *So Purakh* nor the works of the ninth Guru are to be found in this volume. Third, the complete hymn of Guru Arjan in *Ramakali* raga is to be found in folio 478a. Fourth, Mira Bai's hymn in *Maru* raga is to be found in folio 581a. Fifth, there is only one line of Surdas's hymn in this volume in folio 665b. It is followed by Guru Arjan's comment on Surdas.

Sixth, the *Mundavani* and the final shalok are in folio 756b, which are followed by the apocryphal texts in folios 756a–758a in a different sequence: (a) three shaloks attributed to Guru Nanak, (b) twenty-two extra-canonical shaloks, (c) *Hakikat Rah Mukam*, and (d) *Ratanmala*. The title of (b) is given as 'Discourse with Malar' (*gosati malar nali hoi*) in the index entry, whereas the mention of *Hakikat Rah Mukam* is totally omitted, which may indicate that it was added much later in the text.[132] Seventh, the *Raga-mala* is to be found in folio 759b, followed by the traditional recipe for the preparation of the ink at the end of the volume in folio 760a.

Finally, this volume of the Adi Granth has remained in the custody of the seva-panthis, who brought it from Shahpur in the Sargoda district of Pakistan at the time of partition. Bhai Ramkishan, who died in 1945, was highly reputed among the Sikh community of

---

[131]Mahant Gopal Singh insists that the Mul Mantar was written by Guru Har Rai, which is not correct. It tallies exactly with the style of Guru Tegh Bahadur as given in the *Hukam-name*. Also see the report on this volume in Giani Maha Singh, ed., *Khalsa Samachar*, Vol. 60, no. 45 (Amritsar, October 8, 1959), pp. 1–2 and 7.

[132]For a detailed analysis of the text, see McLeod, 'Hakikat Rah Mukam Raje Sivanabh Ki', pp. 96–105.

that area, and his establishment was named after him as 'Tikana Bhai Ramkishan, Shahpur'. It clearly points towards an area closer to Gujrat district, where the Banno version was quite popular.

3.3. Dr Balbir Singh Sahitya Kendra Manuscript # 3

The manuscript was written in 1679 (*sambat 1736 varkhai mahi assu sudi 3*), only four years after Guru Tegh Bahadur's death in 1675. Some of its characteristic features are as follows. First, the conventional entry in the index clearly states that its position is third in order from the original volume of the Adi Granth (*japu Guru ramdas jiu ke nakalu ka nakalu tha tis ka nakalu*). Although there is a mention of the autograph of the Guru in the index (*nisan Guru ji ke dasakhat*), the decorated folio at the beginning of the manuscript remains blank since the scribe was not able to get the autograph of Guru Gobind Singh.

Second, the liturgical text *So Purakh* is to be found in folio 28b. This volume contains the works of Guru Tegh Bahadur at their appropriate places in different raga sections, which indicates that the decision to include them had already been taken by Guru Tegh Bahadur before he left for Delhi in 1675, and that it was implemented by Guru Gobind Singh immediately after his death. G.B. Singh describes another volume that was written in 1675 (*sambat 1732 miti agahan vadi 7*), and completed about seventeen days after Guru Tegh Bahadur's death. It contains his works at appropriate places in various ragas. G.B. Singh suggests that the ninth Guru himself gave instructions before he left for Delhi that his bani should be included in the Adi Granth.[133] In the light of this fact, the Damdama tradition that Guru Gobind Singh did so in 1705 becomes questionable.

Third, there are two extra hymns of Trilochan and Namdev, which are to be found in folios 242b and 312a. The Namdev hymn is written in the margin in a different hand, and is a clear case of later interpolation. Fourth, at the conclusion of the *Jaitsiri* raga the scribe had started writing the title of Guru Tegh Bahadur's *Jaijavanti* raga in folio 319b, but he stopped there and wrote a note that it could be found in folio 589. This raga was then written before the *Prabhati* mode in folio 589b. The shift clearly indicates that the place of *Jaijavanti* raga was not fixed by that time.

Fifth, the complete hymn of Guru Arjan in the *Ramakali* raga is to be found in folio 412a. Sixth, Mira Bai's hymn in *Maru* raga is to be found in folio 492a. Seventh, there is only one line of Surdas's

---

[133]See G.B. Singh, *Prachin Biran*, pp. 215–34.

hymn in this volume in folio 556a. It is followed by Guru Arjan's comment on Surdas. Eighth, there are some extra-canonical shaloks of Guru Tegh Bahadur in this volume in folios 633a–634a, which are deleted with hartal but which can still be read under the deletion paste.[134]

Finally, the *Mundavani* and the final shalok are in folio 634b, which are followed by the apocryphal texts in folios 634b–637a. The *Raga-mala* is to be found in folio 637b, followed by the traditional recipe for the preparation of the ink at the end of the volume in folio 638a.

This volume is another variation of the Banno recension, which includes extra-canonical hymns of Trilochan and Namdev. These hymns are generally found in the Lahore tradition. Some shaloks were also floating around in the oral tradition in the name of Guru Tegh Bahadur. This reflects a situation of some confusion in the Sikh community with respect to the status of certain hymns of the bhagats and those of Guru Tegh Bahadur.

3.4. Punjabi University Museum Manuscript # 1

This manuscript was written in 1687 (*sambat 1744 magh vadi 1*), during the period of Guru Gobind Singh. The colophon points to the autograph of the tenth Guru, which is to be found on a piece of paper pasted in folio 26b. It reads:

The supreme being is one. The Guru is true (*IK Oankar Guru Sati*).

G (*gagga*) signifies Gobind and conveys the message that one should contemplate the divine qualities and remember Him with each breath. Friend! do not delay. Who knows how long this body may last?

Here Guru Gobind Singh employed the shalok of Guru Arjan as his autograph. Evidently, there was a tradition of getting the inaugural benedictory autograph from the Guru at the time of initiating the project of making a copy of the Adi Granth. Sometimes the scribes succeeded in getting the autograph, and sometimes they did not. The Guru's autograph cannot be regarded as his approval of the volume, however, because he would not have read the whole volume before giving his autograph.

An examination of this volume reveals the following important features. First, the colophon clearly indicates that this volume is third

---

[134]For details, see my 'The Text and Meaning of the Adi Granth' (Ph.D. thesis, University of Toronto, 1991), pp. 56–7. For other examples of apocryphal shaloks attributed to Guru Tegh Bahadur, see IOL, MSS Panj. D2, ff. 698a, 699a and 699b.

in order from the original volume of the Adi Granth (*japu Guru ramdas jiu ke nakalu ka nakalu nakalu*). Second, the liturgical text *So Purakh* is to be found in folio 33a. Third, the extra hymn of Trilochan was entered in the volume in folios 269b–270a, but later deleted with hartal. However, it can still be read. The deletion clearly indicates that there was a controversy in the Sikh community over the status of this hymn.

Fourth, the works of Guru Tegh Bahadur are to be found at their proper places in the ragas. Some of these are incorporated in between the lines of the text. The *Jaijavanti* raga comes after the *Jaitsiri* mode in folio 350a. Fifth, the complete hymn of Guru Arjan in the *Ramakali* raga, written in a small hand on a different piece of paper, was pasted in the text much later in folio 459a. Originally there were only the first two lines in bold letters. A photograph of the page clearly indicates how the later addition stands out from the rest of the text in folios 459a–459b.[135] This process of conversion points to the fact that the Banno version was coming into prominence within a section of the Panth during the time of Guru Gobind Singh.

Sixth, Mira Bai's hymn in *Maru* raga is to be found in folio 545b. Seventh, at first this volume had just a single line of Surdas's hymn, but later some other scribe completed it in a small hand. Still later it was deleted with hartal leaving only the first line in folio 615b. It is followed by Guru Arjan's comment on Surdas and reinforces our assumption that the scribes, who failed to understand Guru Arjan's editorial insights, struggled with the problematic texts.

Eighth, there is one shalok attributed to Guru Gobind Singh among the couplets of Guru Tegh Bahadur in folio 700b. Ninth, the *Mundavani* and the final shalok are in folio 700b. These are followed by the apocryphal texts in folios 700b–704a. Tenth, the *Raga-mala* is to be found in folios 704a–704b, followed by two blank pages. Then, at the end of the volume in folio 706a, comes the traditional recipe for the preparation of the ink.

In sum, this copy of the Adi Granth is yet another variation of the Banno text. It should be noted that once the reputation of the Banno version became widespread within some sections of the Panth, copies of other versions were changed to bring them in line with it. This seems to have been the situation during the last quarter of the seventeenth century.

---

[135]There are in my possession a number of photographs of this manuscript which were taken with the permission of the University authorities at Patiala.

FINAL CANONICAL TEXT

There is clear manuscript evidence that Guru Gobind Singh made an attempt to standardize the text of the Adi Granth and thus prevent the circulation of three different versions of it during his period. Although the decision to include the compositions of his father was taken by Guru Tegh Bahadur himself, it was the tenth Guru who closed the canon during the last decades of the seventeenth century at a place called Damdama in Anandpur. In the recent past, there have been manuscripts of this version, written in 1682 and 1691 respectively, and preserved at the Sikh Reference Library, Amritsar. Unfortunately, these rare manuscripts were destroyed during Operation Bluestar in 1984. We shall return to the reports concerning the contents of these manuscripts in Chapter 7. Moreover, there still exist a number of manuscripts of the eighteenth century around Anandpur and Damadama (Bhatinda) areas, the main centres of Sikh activities in the late seventeenth and early eighteenth centuries, which belong to this final version of the Adi Granth.[136] It should be emphasized, however, that the closing of canon did not mean that other versions of the Adi Granth went out of circulation in the eighteenth and nineteenth centuries.

CONCLUSION

The foregoing examination of the early manuscripts reveals the evolution of the text of the Adi Granth through different historical phases. The written tradition of the bani seems to have begun during Guru Nanak's lifetime. It is not yet certain whether the first section of the Guru Har Sahai pothi was identical to Guru Nanak's pothi or whether it was simply a later copy of the early corpus of Sikh scriptural tradition. By the time of Guru Amar Das, however, we are on certain ground, and the Goindval pothis provided a principal source for the compilation of the Sikh scripture. The two extant copies of the Goindval pothis contain the earliest form of the writings of the first three Gurus and the bhagats. The GNDU MS 1245 is another important document which reflects the pre-canonical stage of Sikh scriptural tradition. It illuminates the textual process through which the evolution of Sikh scripture took place. There were other such

---

[136]See Gurinder Singh Mann, 'The Making of Sikh Scripture', pp. 18, 40, 125–6. Also see, Piar Singh, *Gatha Sri Adi Granth*, pp. 324–32, 343–7.

documents (which have not survived), and there are certain extant manuscripts (such as the Bahoval pothi), which reflect the fluid state from which the various structures of organization and the final form of various hymns emerged in the first canonical text of the Adi Granth.

Guru Arjan seems to have worked on several pre-canonical traditions to produce the first canonical text of the Adi Granth in 1604. This great granth (*vadda granth*) of the fifth Guru was used by various scribes as a touchstone to authenticate their own copies of the Adi Granth in the seventeenth century. An examination of the Kartarpur manuscript indicates that its contents were frequently revised through the use of hartal and other methods such as crossing the lines out with a pen. Certain compositions were added later which were composed by Guru Arjan after 1604. On the whole, the raga organization and the final form of various hymns were fixed in the Kartarpur bir. I still stand by the claims of the originality of this document, although there are certain textual problems that need to be addressed. We shall return to them in the later chapters.

This analysis also shows that there was no unity of the Adi Granth text to be found among its different versions during the last quarter of the seventeenth century. Each group within the Panth tried to legitimize its version of the Adi Granth by pasting an autograph of the Guru at the beginning of each copy. In many instances, the scribes (and their groups within the Panth) failed to understand the editorial insights of Guru Arjan and struggled with the problematic texts. They were primarily responsible for the different versions of the text of the Adi Granth. Of all the three competing versions of the text that were being used by different groups within the Panth, it appears that the Banno version was gaining importance at the end of the seventeenth century and the beginning of the eighteenth. There are, however, some basic questions that still need to be addressed: how do we explain the origins of the Adi Granth traditions? What were the reasons for the predominance of the Banno version of the Adi Granth in the late-seventeenth-century or eighteenth-century Sikh community? Answers to these will be proposed in the seventh chapter. In the next chapter, however, we shall provide a textual analysis of certain portions of the Adi Granth.

3

TEXTUAL ANALYSIS

From a strictly orthodox point of view the Adi Granth is the manifest body of the Guru and many who accept it as such will be strongly inclined to regard its text as inviolate. For the scholar, regardless of his personal beliefs, a text recorded or transcribed by human hands must always be open to textual analysis in the expectation that original meanings may have been obscured or errors committed in the process of writing.[1]

Textual analysis is an acknowledged discipline in academic study of sacred texts of world religions. The text of the Adi Granth is thus an important focus for scholarly inquiry. By employing this method one can reconstruct its history by addressing the fundamental question of how the text came into being. It is also possible to understand the *rédaction* process that was at work behind the whole operation of formulating an authoritative text. One can also determine the errors committed by the scribe in the process of copying, as well as the intentional tampering with the text by some later scribes. However, one should always keep in mind that textual analysis is not a branch of mathematics, nor indeed an exact science at all. It deals with matters that are neither rigid nor constant but rather fluid and variable. It is certainly not susceptible to hard and fast rules.[2] It is, therefore, not surprising that at times different scholars may provide different perspectives while using the same data.

The recently published *Encyclopaedia of Sikhism* describes the role of Guru Arjan in the creation of a new scripture as follows.

[1]W.H. McLeod, 'The Sikh Scriptures: Some Issues', in *Sikh Studies: Comparative Perspectives on a Changing Tradition*, pp. 99–100.

[2]Christopher Key Chapple, 'Reading Patanjali Without Vyasa: A Critique of Four Yoga Sutra Passages,' *Journal of the American Academy of Religion*, 62(1) (Spring 1994): 85–105. The author cites A.E. Housman in the beginning to make the point.

The making of the Granth involved sustained labour and rigorous intellectual discipline. Selections had to be made from a vast mass of material. What was genuine had to be sifted from what was counterfeit. Then the selected material had to be assigned to appropriate musical measures, edited and recast where necessary, and transcribed in a minutely laid-out order. Guru Arjan accomplished the task with extraordinary exactness.[3]

Although this citation describes the creation of the Sikh scripture in a more or less traditional way, it does explicitly state that the process involved editing and recasting of certain hymns. We shall discuss this process in detail in this section. The textual variations in some of the hymns as they appear in the Goindval pothis and in the early manuscripts of the Adi Granth are quite illuminating. We shall examine them by comparing the relevant texts and manuscripts in order to understand the process of the making of the Sikh canon.

MUL MANTAR

The Mul Mantar, or root formula with which the Adi Granth opens, is the basic theological statement of the Sikh faith. It consists of different epithets, all of which are traditionally understood as characterizations of the ultimate reality, or Akal Purakh. According to the orthodox view, the Mul Mantar was created in its present form by Guru Nanak himself. For instance, Pritam Singh writes: 'In the Sacred Book of the Sikhs also, one may come across any number of divine attributes, but those which must have struck the founder, Guru Nanak, as the most prominent and essential, were woven by him in a short rhythmic composition, called the Mul Mantra, the seminal formula, consisting of 14 basic structural units.'[4] The number fourteen here may refer to the sacred number of fourteen jewels (*chaudan ratan*) of Indian thought.

The examination of early manuscripts has revealed, however, that the text of the Mul Mantar has evolved through different phases. For instance, the earlier form that appears in the two available copies of the Goindval pothis reads as follows.

IK Oankar satguru parsadu
sachu namu kartaru nirbhau nirikaru akal murati ajuni sambhau.[5] (1)

---

[3]Harbans Singh, ed., *The Encyclopaedia of Sikhism*, Vol. I (Patiala: Punjabi University, 1992), p. 190.

[4]Pritam Singh, ed., *Sikh Concept of the Divine* (Amritsar: Guru Nanak Dev University Press, 1985), p. vii.

[5]See Gurinder Singh Mann, *The Goindval Pothis: The Earliest Extant Source of the*

There is one supreme being, known by grace through the true Guru.

The true name, the creator, the fearless one and the formless one! The timelss one, never incarnated, and self-existent. (1)

Sometimes there is an additional phrase 'by the grace of the perfect Guru' (*Guru pure ke parsadu*) at the end of this text,[6] but nowhere does this form of the Mul Mantar correspond to the standard version given in the Adi Granth. Evidently this was the form that was current during the period of Guru Amar Das.

The origin of the major components of the earlier form of the Mul Mantar as given in the Goindval pothis, however, can be traced directly from the works of Guru Nanak. First, the numeral ('IK') at the beginning of the Mul Mantar represents the unity of the ultimate reality, a concept which Guru Nanak interprets in monotheistic terms. It affirms that the supreme being is one without a second. This is quite evident from the following statement: 'My Master is the one. He is the one, brother, and he alone exists.'[7] Similarly, the symbol Oankar has its origin in Guru Nanak's lengthy work Oankar in the measure *Ramakali Dakkhani*, which gives particular meaning to it.[8] Accordingly, Oankar is the foundational word (sabad), which is the basis of the whole creation and represents in seed form all scriptural revelation.

Second, the most important word used by Guru Nanak to express the nature of divine revelation in its totality is nam (the name), frequently linked with sachu (truth) to give the compound form sachu-namu.[9] It is understandable that the compound sachu-namu (the true name), which indicates the eternal reality, should have become part of the basic theological statement of the Sikh faith. Guru Nanak himself identifies the Mul Mantar with the divine name.[10] The word sachu was very much in vogue during his times, and is thus frequently used in his works.

Third, Guru Nanak frequently employs such terms as kartar (creator), *akal* (timeless) and nirankar (formless) for the supreme

---

Sikh Canon (Cambridge, MA: Department of Sanskrit and Indian Studies, Harvard University, 1996), pp. 194 and 205.

[6]ibid., p. 204.

[7]M1, *Asa 5*, AG, p. 350.

[8]M1, *Rag Ramakali Dakhani Oankaru*, AG, pp. 929–38.

[9]W.H. McLeod, *The Sikhs: History, Religion, and Society* (New York: Columbia University Press, 1989), p. 50.

[10]M1, *Maru Solihe 20*, AG, p. 1040.

being in his works. The following statements may provide the basic units in the earlier form of the Mul Mantar:

The fearless one, the formless one, the true name—who has created the entire world! (*nirbhau nirankaru sachu namu// ja ka kia sagal jahanu//*).[11]

There is one supreme being, the true name—with whom is determined true justice!' (*eka murati sacha nau//tithai nibarai sachu niau//*).[12]

The detached one, never incarnated, and self-existent! He is attained only through the Guru's teachings, O Nanak! (*api atiti ajoni sambhau nanak gurmati so paia//*).[13]

Fourth, in Guru Nanak's usage the Guru is the voice of Akal Purakh, mystically uttered within the human heart, mind and soul (*man*).[14] The phrase satguru parsadu, therefore, conveys the meaning that the true Guru reveals himself through grace. By the time of Guru Nanak's successors, however, the range covered by the term Guru extended from the personal Guru to the concept of an eternal Guru and on to identification with the supreme being himself. Thus the additional phrase *Guru pure ke parasadu* (by the grace of the perfect Guru) may refer more specifically to the personal Guru than to the divine Guru. Its use may reflect a situation in which competing claims to the office of guruship were being made. This was certainly done by Baba Mohan who challenged the authority of Guru Ram Das. It is no wonder that he added the additional phrase in his pothis. This single fact dates the writing of the two available volumes to a later period and makes them out to be copies of original Goindval pothis.

On the whole, the basic elements of the earlier form of the Mul Mantar come from the works of Guru Nanak. Presumably he himself formulated it during the Kartarpur period, when the first Sikh community started using it in prayers. The most significant point is that it lays emphasis on the formless (nirankar) aspect of ultimate reality. For Guru Nanak the word nirankar is of utmost importance, which is quite evident from its occurrence in his description of the 'realm of truth' (sach khand), the fifth and the final stage in the soul's spiritual ascent.[15] Further, Guru Nanak's frequent use of the word kartar (creator) for the supreme being is quite evident from

[11] M1, *Var Asa* 2 (5), AG, p. 465.

[12] M1, *Basant Ast.* 3, AG, p. 1188.

[13] M1, *Maru Solahe* 21, AG, p. 1042.

[14] W.H. McLeod, *Guru Nanak and the Sikh Religion* (Delhi: Oxford University Press, reprint, 1976; 1st edn, Clarendon, 1968), p. 199.

[15] M1, *Japu*, AG, p. 8. Also see ibid., pp. 172, 223–4.

his works. Towards the end of his life he founded a village on the right bank of the Ravi river, and named it Kartarpur, the dwelling-place of the creator. According to the janam-sakhi traditions, early Sikhs who visited the Guru at Kartarpur would greet each other by saying 'Kartar! Kartar!'[16] In fact, Guru Nanak himself used to greet his followers in the same way and inspire them to recite the divine name to achieve liberation in life: 'Recite the true name of the creator. Then you will not have to come [into this world] again and again' (*bolahu sach nam kartar//phir bahur na avan var//*).[17] Furthermore, the expression *sachu namu kartar* echoes the earliest form of the Mul Mantar, available in the beginning of the Guru Har Sahai pothi.[18]

Guru Ram Das invoked the divine attributes of the Mul Mantar in one of his compositions. The original verse resembles the text of the Mul Mantar and, similarly, it is free of any metrical or rhyme scheme. It reads as follows:

japi man nirbhau// sati sati sada sati// nirvairu akal murati// ajuni sambhau// mere man anadini dhiai nirankar nirahari//

Contemplate the fearless one, my *man*, who is true, true and always true. Devoid of enmity, the timeless one, never incarnated and self-existent! Meditate day and night on the formless one, my *man*, who is above any need of sustenance.

(M4, Sarang 11, AG, p. 1201)

The comparison of this text with the earlier form of the Mul Mantar given above clearly indicates the addition of the word *nirvair* (without enmity), which Guru Ram Das employs to put emphasis on the divine attribute of benevolence. Although Guru Nanak also employs the word nirvair for the supreme being in his *Ramakali Dakkhani Oankaru*,[19] it is used more frequently in the compositions of Guru Ram Das.[20] This may reflect his firm resolve to counter the hostility of his rivals with the spirit of love and friendliness.[21] Thus a new emphasis is placed upon the benevolent nature of ultimate reality.

[16]See Piar Singh, *Gatha*, p. 134.

[17]M1, *Prabhati* 9, AG, p. 1329.

[18]See the photocopy in Giani Gurdit Singh, *Itihas Sri Guru Granth Sahib: Bhagat Bani Bhag* (Chandigarh: Sikh Sahit Sansthan, 1990), preface.

[19]M1, *Ramakali Dakkhani Oankaru*, AG, p. 931.

[20]See Gurcharan Singh, *Adi Granth Shabad-anukramanika*, Vol. 2 (Patiala: Punjabi University, 1971), pp. 1526–7.

[21]Surjit Hans, *A Reconstruction of Sikh History from Sikh Literature* (Jalandhar: ABS Publication, 1988), pp. 106–10.

In this context, Piar Singh argues that the use of the word nirvair was 'necessary to emphasize that God of the Sikh concept is free of animosity. This was in contradistinction of certain Semitic religious traditions wherein God, along with other attributes, is shown to be revengeful too.'[22]

Guru Arjan gave the Mul Mantar its final form. The Guru Nanak Dev University manuscript, which is an early recension of the Adi Granth, gives the form of the Mul Mantar before its standardization.

Ik Oankar satinamu karta purakhu nirbhau nirvairu akal murati ajuni sabhang satguru parsadi.[23]

There is one supreme being, the eternal reality, the creator, without fear and devoid of enmity, immortal, never incarnated, self-existent, known by grace through the true Guru.[24]

In his final version, however, Guru Arjan replaced the phrase satguru parsadi ('by the grace of the true Guru') with gur prasadi ('by the grace of the Guru'), presumably to provide a more coherent structure to the text of the Mul Mantar. Also, he seems to have indicated that the word gur (principle) in the final phrase stands for the divine principle, functioning behind the free and sovereign act of grace. Thus the word Guru acquires a new meaning in the sense of a divine principle.

Another significant point is that Guru Arjan added the word purakh to the received text of the Mul Mantar. It clearly indicates that by his time the personal (purakh) aspect of the supreme being acquired prominence as compared with Guru Nanak's emphasis on the formless (nirankar) nature of ultimate reality. Moreover, Guru Ram Das had already made this concept popular in his celebrated composition *So Purakh.*[25] It is, important to note however, that Guru Nanak employed both phrases, Karta Purakh and Akal Purakh for the supreme being.[26] He also speaks of a personal God, a God of grace to whom one responds in love.[27] The point that is being made here is that a new emphasis was placed on the concept by Guru Arjan, when he included the word in the Mul Mantar. Piar Singh, however, argues that the fifth Guru employed the word Purakh after

[22]Piar Singh, *Gatha*, p. 134.
[23]GNDU MS 1245, f. 27b.
[24]Translation taken from W.H. McLeod, *Sikhism* (London: Penguin Books, 1997), p. 271.
[25]M4, *Ragu Asa So Purakh*, AG, pp. 10–11, 348.
[26]M1, *Var Majh*, AG, p. 138 and *Maru Solhe 18*, AG, p. 1038.
[27]See McLeod, *Guru Nanak and the Sikh Religion*, p. 165.

Karta to 'emphasize that in the Sikh theological system, God, the Akal Purakh, is the sole creator and not Prakriti and Purusha, both, as certain theological systems of India hold.'[28] Thus the final form of the Mul Mantar was intended to set the Sikh doctrine apart from the theological systems of both Indian and Semitic religious traditions.

Five different forms of the Mul Mantar are used as invocations at the beginning of various sections and sub-sections of the Adi Granth. They range from the mystic formula (*Ik Oankar*) through three short versions (1. *Ik Oankar satigur prasadi*; 2. *Ik Oankar satinamu gur prasadi*; and 3. *Ik Oankar satinamu karta purakh gur prasadi*) to the complete Mul Mantar.[29] It has been suggested that these different forms of invocations are used in the Adi Granth in order to break organizational monotony and to add colourful diversity to the structure of the Sikh scripture.[30] A careful look at this diversity, however, reveals the developmental aspect of the text of the Mul Mantar. The short versions were most conveniently employed for various sub-headings within the raga sections. Moreover, the use of different versions constitutes a departure from a certain classical doctrine of mantra, which holds that a mantra becomes inefficacious if its syllables are changed in any way (or if it is spoken in public).[31]

It is important to note that an invocation at the beginning of a new section or sub-section is always written on the right-hand side of the text in the Kartarpur manuscript. This practice, which is mostly followed in the seventeenth-century manuscripts, was meant to accord a place of honour to the Mul Mantar in the scripture. However, later scribes abandoned that practice and did not pay much attention to the correct order of invocation and raga title. The issue was hotly debated among the Singh Sabha scholars and various sections of the Sikh community led by prominent Sikh sants in the 1950s, and a decision was reached in 1964 to follow the guidelines available in the Kartarpur manuscript. It was further decided that the Damdama version was to be consulted if there was some ambiguity with respect to the position of the invocation in the Kartarpur volume.[32] The

[28]Piar Singh, *Gatha*, p. 134.

[29]For more details on these forms, see my 'The Text and Meaning of the Adi Granth' (Ph.D. thesis, University of Toronto, 1991), pp. 97–8.

[30]Mohinder Kaur Gill, *Guru Granth Sahib di Sampadan–kala* (Amritsar: New Age Book Centre, 2nd edn, 1982; 1st edn, 1974), p. 43.

[31]K.L. Sharma, 'The Classical Concept of Mantra', in Pritam Singh, *Sikh Concept of the Divine*, p. 27.

[32]For details, see Harbhajan Singh, *Gurbani Sampadan Nirnai* (Chandigarh: Satnam Prakashan, 1982), p. 157.

decision, however, reflected the dominance within the Panth of a group of Sikh sants, who followed a canonical mode of interpretation, which takes the linguistic form and arrangement of words of the scripture as literally true. For them, any change in the sequence of the invocation and the raga title would amount to violation of the integrity of the text of the Adi Granth. On the other hand, Sikh scholars who followed the Singh Sabha mode of interpretation, based on the consistent structure of the Adi Granth, continued to maintain their position that the Mul Mantar should always come before the raga title.[33] These Singh Sabha scholars, nevertheless, accepted the decision in good faith and did not try to challenge the authority of the Panth.[34]

More recently, the issue of the Mul Mantar has sparked a world-wide controversy in which my doctoral research on the issue came under fire.[35] Meanwhile, Piar Singh's work on the history of the compilation of the Adi Granth, *Gatha Sri Adi Granth*, was published by the Guru Nanak Dev University (Amritsar) in 1992, and he was also implicated in the vilification campaign that was already on against me. Both of us were faced with the problem of the variant readings of the Mul Mantar, and we tried to explain them in our own ways. However, we agreed on the point that it was Guru Arjan who fixed the final form of the Mul Mantar. I still maintain my academic position on this issue and assert that the minor modifications in spelling and form made no difference to the basic Sikh doctrine.

LITURGICAL TEXTS

1. *Japji:* The Early Morning Prayer

The introductory section of the Adi Granth consists of liturgical texts. It opens with the celebrated *Japji* of Guru Nanak, a work which is regarded as the quintessence of the whole Sikh scripture. Devout Sikhs recite it from memory every morning during the 'ambrosial time' (*amrit vela*) immediately after rising and bathing. According to

---

[33]Sahib Singh, 'Mul Mantar ate Sirlekh', *Sri Guru Granth Sahib Darapan*, Vol. X (Jalandhar: Raj Publishers, 3rd edn, 1971; 1st edn, 1964), pp. 711–30.

[34]ibid., pp. 729–30.

[35]For details on the controversy, see Bachittar Singh Giani, ed., *Planned Attack on Sri Guru Granth Sahib: Academics or Blasphemy* (Chandigarh: International Centre of Sikh Studies, 1994). For rebuttals, see Piar Singh, 'The Mul Mantra Imbroglio,' in *Gatha*, pp. 132–44.

the testimony of Bhai Gurdas, this devotional practice originated during the final period of Guru Nanak's life when he settled down at Kartarpur as the head of a newly emerging religious community: 'The *So Dar* and *arti* were sung [in the evening], while the *Japu* was recited early in the morning during the "ambrosial time"'.[36]

The two available copies of the Goindval volumes do not contain the text of *Japji*. It is believed that there were two other volumes, which have not survived, one of which contained the liturgical texts including the *Japji*. Mohan Singh Diwana claims to have seen the text of *Japji* in one of the Goindval pothis in 1933 at Goindval Sahib, but the description of his discovery appears to be uncertain: 'If I recall correctly, *Jap(u)* was followed by *Siddh Gost(i)*.'[37] It has been claimed that the Guru Har Sahai pothi began with the *Japji*, but its reading has not been made public so far by Giani Gurdit Singh who had taken certain photographs of this manuscript before its loss in 1970.

The Guru Nanak Dev University manuscript, GNDU MS (See photograph on p. 236) 1245, provides an earlier version of the morning prayer before its standardization. It begins as follows:

1k Oankar satinamu karta purakhu nirbhau nirvairu akal murati ajuni sabhang satguru parsadi.

Japu Mahalu //1//
sochai sochi na hovai je sochi lakh var// chupai chup na hovai je lai rahan livatar/ / bhukhia bhukh na utarai je bannha purian bhar// sahans sianapa lakh honi ta ikk na chalai nali// kiu sachiara hoiai kiu kurai tuttai pali// hukam rajai chalana nanak likhia nali//1//[38]

There is one supreme being, the eternal reality, the creator, without fear and devoid of enmity, immortal, never incarnated, self-existent, known by grace through the true Guru.

Japu Mahalu 1
Never can you be known through ritual purity though one cleanse oneself a hundred thousand times. Never can you be revealed by silent reflection though one dwell absorbed in the deepest meditation. Though one gather vast riches the hunger remains, no cunning will help in the hereafter. How then is truth to be attained, how the veil of falsehood torn aside? Nanak, thus it is written: submit to divine order, walk in its way. (1)[39]

[36]*Varan Bhai Gurdas* 1:38.
[37]See Mohan Singh Diwana, 'Discoveries in Sikh Culture (III),' *Journal of Sikh Studies*, Vol. 2, no. 1 (February 1975), p. 60.
[38]GNDU MS 1245, f. 27b.
[39]The translation is taken from McLeod, *Sikhism*, p. 271.

A comparative analysis of this text with the standard version of *Japji* (See photograph on p. 262) reveals the following important differences, which illuminate different stages in the process of its development. First, the Mul Mantar is given in its earlier form, containing the phrase satguru parsadi (by the grace of the true Guru) of the Goindval pothis instead of gur prasadi (by the grace of the Guru) of the Adi Granth. This early form of the Mul Mantar is employed five times only in the GNDU text.[40]

Second, the title of the composition is mentioned as *Japu Mahalu 1*, indicating specifically the authorship of Guru Nanak. Here the use of the term mahalu is very significant, since it reflects an earlier convention followed in the Goindval pothis. In the standard version, however, the symbol mahalu 1 is omitted, perhaps consciously, to assign divine authorship to the text. Guru Arjan seems to have indicated that the ultimate source of all bani is the eternal Guru, who revealed himself through Guru Nanak and his successors. It would be understandable for this fundamental belief to be acknowledged right in the beginning. The entry in the index of the Kartarpur manuscript, however, reads: 'The *Japu* is copied from the manuscript written in Guru Ram Das's hand.'[41] In Guru Ram Das's bani one finds that a number of stanzas of *Japji* have been interpreted for the audience.[42] This is an example of interpretation of the meaning of scripture by means of scripture itself.[43] Evidently Guru Ram Das was the first Guru to attempt to clarify and expound the meaning of certain words, phrases and stanzas of the *Japji* in his works. He must have made a copy of the *Japji* in his hand, which Guru Arjan used at the time of the compilation of the Adi Granth.

The third and the most distinctive difference is that the introductory couplet of the *Japji* is missing in the earlier text. The standard version reads: 'The eternal one, from the beginning, through all time, present now, the everlasting reality.'[44] Three explanations may be offered here. First, the author of this shalok is Guru Nanak himself because of the frequent use of the word sachu in his works. But it was added by Guru Arjan much later when he produced the

---

[40]For details, see Piar Singh, *Gatha* Sri Adi Granth, p. 137.

[41]Kartarpur MS, f. 2/2.

[42]M4, *Var Sarang* (5–12), AG, pp. 1239–42. Also see *Bhairau* 3, AG, p. 1134 and *Kanara* 8, AG, pp. 1296–7.

[43]For details, see Chapter 8, pp. 242–3.

[44]McLeod, *Sikhism*, p. 271.

final text of the *Japji*. Second, this shalok is also repeated with a slight difference as an introductory shalok to the seventeenth octave of the *Sukhmani*. This fact alone makes it the composition of Guru Arjan, who would have expressed Guru Nanak's intention and teachings in his own words.[45] By adding his own shalok at the beginning of the *Japji*, the fifth Guru must have intended to stress the unity of guruship. This may be another reason why he did not write the symbol mahala 1 with the title of the *Japji* in the standard version. Third, Guru Arjan included Guru Nanak's shalok in his *Sukhmani* for the purpose of elaborating upon the theme of the permanence of divine reality in contrast to the impermanence of worldly things.

Finally, the first stanza of the *Japji* that appears here has some linguistic variations. Evidently Guru Arjan modified the language of certain words (*jei/je, utarai/utari, bana/banna, sahans/sahas, honi/hohi, kiu/kiv*), and replaced them with more grammatically and metrically sound constructions in order to standardize the text. For instance, the use of the verb utari (be removed) fits well with the feminine noun bhukh (hunger), whereas the use of its synonymous variant utarai in this case would be regarded as a colloquial expression.[46] Similarly the word jei (even if) with a long syllable was replaced with its short synonym je to fit the metre. It should, be emphasized however, that the meaning of the text remains the same in spite of this revision. There are numerous such examples throughout the text of the *Japji* where Guru Arjan refined the language of certain passages and polished the metre. In this context, Christopher Shackle has aptly pointed out that the language of the Adi Granth allows for great freedom, conferred by the availability of many synonymous variant forms with long and short syllables which may be used to fit the metre and the rhyme.[47]

Traditionally, the concluding shalok of the *Japji* is understood to be Guru Nanak's own composition. There are, however, scholars who regard Guru Angad as its real author.[48] In order to discuss the issue in detail, we must begin with its scriptural position in the earlier recension of the Adi Granth. In the GNDU manuscript the epilogue of the *Japji* is rendered as follows.

---

[45]Guru Arjan's inspiration may well have been based on the following sayings of Guru Nanak: *Japji* 27, AG, p. 6; *Asa Chhant* 3, p. 437 and *Maru Solihe* 2, p. 1022.

[46]For more details, see Piar Singh, *Gatha Sri Adi Granth*, pp. 139–41.

[47]C. Shackle, *An Introduction to the Sacred Language of the Sikhs* (London: School of Oriental and African Studies, University of London, 1983), p. 160.

[48]See W.H. McLeod, trans. and ed., *Textual Sources for the Study of Sikhism* (Manchester: Manchester University Press, 1984), p. 4.

Saloku// paunu Guru pani pita mata dharati mahatu// dinasu rati dui dai daia khelai sagal jagatu// chnagiaian buriaian vachai dharamu haduri// karami apo apani ke nere ke duri// jini namu dhiaia gae masakati ghali// nanak te mukh ujjale hor keti chhuti nali//1//[49]

Shalok. Air is the Guru, water the father, and earth the mighty mother of all. Day and night are the caring guardians, fondly nurturing all creation. In the court of the righteous one, all stand revealed, their deeds declared, both good and ill. As we have acted so we are recompensed, some brought near, others driven away. They who have faithfully followed the name have run their course, their labours done. Freed are they and many others with them. Radiantly, Nanak, they go to glory.[50]

Evidently, this text has minor linguistic variations from the standard version of the concluding shalok of *Japji*. These can be seen in the construction of the following words in both versions: air (*paunu/ pavanu*) day, (*dinasu/divasu*), and near (*nere/nerai*). Further, there is an extra word *hor* (many) in this earlier text. In *Var Majh*, however, this shalok appears in exactly the same form under the symbol of Guru Angad as it is given above.[51] Obviously Guru Arjan revised this shalok in the final version of *Japji*, but retained its earlier form in *Var Majh*.

The inclusion of this shalok in the earlier manuscript clearly indicates that it had already acquired a distinctive liturgical function, perhaps during the Kartarpur period, and that is why it became a part of Guru Nanak's *Japji*. It was perhaps intentionally added to the morning prayer to stress the continuity and unity of guruship. The origin of this shalok, however, may be traced back to the following verse of Guru Nanak's *Maru Solahe*: '[I have] realized thus: air is the Guru and water the father. The earth is the mighty mother of all, who has kept us in her womb. Day and night are the caring guardians fondly nurturing the whole world.'[52] Clearly, the theme of this verse is reflected in the epilogue of the *Japji*, and a considerable degree of verbal correspondence is also to be found in the two texts. Three possible explanations may be offered here for this similarity of language and theme.

First, Guru Nanak must be regarded as the author of the concluding shalok of *Japji*. To support this view, the *Puratan Janam-sakhi* tradition claims that this shalok was recited by Guru

---

[49]GNDU MS 1245, f. 33a.
[50]This translation is slightly adapted from McLeod, *Sikhism*, p. 281.
[51]M2, *Var Majh* 2 (18), AG, p. 146.
[52] M1, *Maru Solihe* 1, AG, p. 1021.

Nanak just before he died at Kartarpur.[53] Presumably it was introduced in Sikh worship as part of the *Japji* by his successor, Guru Angad, who may have made it obligatory that the shalok be recited at the conclusion of all Sikh ceremonies.[54] Thus with the passage of time the shalok became popular under the symbol of Guru Angad. There are other such instances in the Adi Granth, when a composition is repeated at two different places under the symbols of two succeeding Gurus.[55]

Second, Cole has suggested that Guru Nanak may have initiated his successor, Bhai Lehna, into the poetic skill of verse composition in the literary form of a shalok, and this training may have been a part of his designation to the office of guruship at Kartarpur.[56] Thus the two Gurus may have worked together on the text of the epilogue of the *Japji* and, accordingly, both may be regarded as its joint authors. According to the *Miharban Janam-sakhi*, it was Guru Angad who arranged the stanzas of the *Japji* in their present form at the instance of Guru Nanak at Kartarpur. It is also specifically mentioned there that Guru Nanak uttered the concluding shalok of *Japji* while addressing Guru Angad.[57] It might have been Guru Nanak's own instruction to include the shalok in the morning prayer. By doing so, he must have intended to transfer his spiritual authority to Guru Angad through the imprimatur of the bani and to institutionalize the office of guruship to ensure its survival and permanence.

Third, Guru Angad may have drawn inspiration from Guru Nanak's verse when he composed the concluding shalok of *Japji*.[58] The original context of its utterance may very well have been the time when Guru Angad assumed the office of guruship. Being his first utterance in the form of a vak or commandment, it may have acquired its present scriptural position as a part of the morning prayer.

[53]See Central Public Library, Patiala, Photozincograph facsimile of Colebrooke's manuscript of *Puratan Janam-sakhi*, No. 1618, pp. 437–61.

[54]See, W.H. McLeod, trans., *The Chaupa Singh Rahit-nama* (Dunedin: University of Otago Press, 1987), pp. 76 and 163, n. 141.

[55]For instance, Guru Amar Das' shalok 2 (11) in *Var Sri Raga* (AG, p. 86) is repeated under the symbol of Guru Ram Das as shalok 28 in *Salok Varan te Vadhik* (AG, p. 1424).

[56]W. Owen Cole, *Sikhism and its Indian Context 1469–1708* (London: Darton, Longman & Todd, 1984), p. 224.

[57]See *Janam Sakhi Sri Guru Nanak Dev Ji* (*Pothi Harji* and *Pothi Chaturbhuj*), Vol. 2 (Amritsar: Khalsa College, 1969), p. 136.

[58]For other instances of similarities between the compositions of the first two Gurus, see Taran Singh, *Guru Angad Dev Ji* (Patiala: Punjabi University, 1975), pp. 25–32.

Thus, Guru Angad may have affixed the seal on the text of the *Japji* by including his own shalok at the end. By doing so he also could have made the point that he carried the spiritual authority of his predecessor.

In sum, it should be emphasized that it was Guru Arjan who was mainly responsible for the fixing of the text of *Japji*. In the case of thirty-eight stanzas of Guru Nanak, the fifth Guru made some linguistic refinements through the substitution of synonyms for certain words. The basic text and its meaning, however, remain the same despite revision. The earlier reading of the text points towards a strong tradition of oral transmission. It is not surprising that certain changes occurred during the period of oral transmission before it was first written down. The index-note of the Kartarpur bir that 'the *Japu* was copied from the manuscript written in Guru Ram Das's hands', points towards the possibility of other versions circulating within the community. Once the text of *Japji* was fixed in the Kartarpur manuscript, it was faithfully copied in the later manuscripts.

2. *So Dar Rahiras*: The Evening Prayer

The evening prayer of the Sikhs, normally referred to as *So Dar Rahiras* or simply *Rahiras*, is recited at sunset. The specific title *So Dar* (That Door) derives from the first word of Guru Nanak's first hymn in *Asa* raga: 'Where is the place where you dwell, with its door (*so daru*) where you sit keeping watch over all.'[59] The other title *Rahiras* (straight path) stands for supplicatory prayer, which takes its name from the fourth line of the fourth hymn of the fourth Guru: 'O my friend and Guru, grant the light of your glorious name, the support of my life and the guidance which prompts us to sing your praises.'[60] Clearly, the verse is in the form of a petitionary prayer (*binau*, humble submission), which is common to the north Indian devotional literary tradition. Thus the complete title *So Dar Rahiras* means a 'supplicatory prayer offered at that door.'

The most illuminating instance in the standard text of the Adi Granth is the appearance of the *So Dar* hymn in three different versions, one in the *Japu*, the other in *So Dar Rahiras*, and the third at the beginning of *Asa* mode.[61] Originally, only one version appeared in three different places.[62] Indeed, the appearance of the *So Dar* hymn

---

[59] M1, *Sodaru Ragu Asa*, AG, pp. 8–9, 347–8.

[60] M4, *Gujari* 4/1, AG, pp. 10, 492.

[61] M1, *Sodaru*, AG, pp. 6, 8–9, and 347–8.

[62] See GNDU MS 1245, ff. 31a–31b, 33b–34a, 345a.

three times is a unique instance in the Adi Granth. A careful reader can notice the presence of vocatives (*tera, tere, tudhano*) in the *So Dar* and *Raga Asa* hymns, while they do not figure in the standard *Japji* text. In fact, vocatives are considered musical devices that form part of a singing tradition. The morning prayer, *Japuji*, is a contemplative bani and is meant for recitation during the ambrosial hours (amrit vela) of the last watch of the night before dawn. That is why vocatives are not used in the *Japji*. The evening prayer, *So Dar Rahiras*, on the other hand, is meant for congregational worship. The *So Dar* hymn is, therefore, sung in the evening. One can listen to its musical performance during the evening kirtan session, called *So Dar di chaunki* (the 'sitting' of *So Dar*), at the Golden Temple, Amritsar, and appreciate the musicality of this hymn.

In the Kartarpur manuscript, the entry of the title of the evening order reads *sodaru panch sabad*[63] signifying that the title *So Dar* contains a cluster of five shabads (three of them by Guru Nanak and one each by the fourth and the fifth Gurus),[64] which constituted a liturgical order by the time the scripture was compiled in 1604. It is important to note here that the Kartarpur volume does not contain the *So Purakh* text (a collection of four hymns, the first two of them by Guru Ram Das and one each by Guru Nanak and Guru Arjan respectively)[65] in its introductory section. This clearly indicates that it became part of the evening order after the compilation of the scripture. Commenting on its intended usage, W.H. McLeod observes:

The fact that the *So Purakh* group is distinguished in the Adi Granth text from the *Sodar* sequence may conceivably indicate that a separate usage was envisaged by Guru Arjan when he compiled the scripture. If so, there is no indication of what this intention might have been, nor of actual fulfilment of any such intention.[66]

The element of uncertainty with respect to the intended usage of *So Purakh*, as noted by McLeod, becomes clear when we take into account its gradual introduction into Sikh liturgy. For this reason, it

[63] Kartarpur MS, f. 2/2.
[64] The *So Dar* cluster has the following five shabads in the Adi Granth: (1)-(3) M1, *Asa* 1, 2/1 and 3/2, AG, pp. 8–10, 347–9; (4) M4, *Gujari* 4/1, AG, pp. 10, 492; and (5) M5, *Gujari* 5/1, AG, pp. 10, 495.
[65] The *So Purakh* group has the following hymns in the Adi Granth: (1) M4, *Asa* 1/2, AG, pp. 10–11, 348; (2) M4, *Asa* 2/53, AG, pp. 11–12, 365; (3) M1, *Asa* 3/29, AG, pp. 12, 357; and (4) M5, *Asa* 4/29, AG, pp. 12, 378.
[66] W.H. McLeod, *The Chaupa Singh Rahit-nama*, p. 209, n. 18.

was incorporated only later into Sikh scripture. Guru Arjan's decision to include the *So Purakh* text in the introductory section of the Adi Granth would seem to reflect his stress on the personal aspect of the supreme being.[67] That could account for his divergence from the normal pattern of arrangement of hymns of the Gurus according to the chronological sequence of their authors. He placed the two hymns of Guru Ram Das before Guru Nanak's third hymn to bring forward the title of the *So Purakh* text. Moreover, the sequence of the two liturgical texts does have a theological coherence, for if the *So Dar* (that door) is intended for petitionary prayers, then the *So Purakh* (that being) reveals the nature of the supreme being who answers those prayers.

Thus the original form of the Rahiras order contained only the *So Dar* text, which was popular in the Sikh community at the beginning of the seventeenth century. Bhai Gurdas testifies to the tradition of its singing in Sikh worship, which originated during the Kartarpur period.[68] The later addition of the *So Purakh* text to the evening order was done at the instance of Guru Arjan, perhaps during the last days of his life. Traditionally, the oral recitation of *So Dar Rahiras* was followed by the singing of the first five and the last stanzas of the *Anand* in *Ramakali* mode, which commands a particular prominence in Sikh ritual and liturgy.[69] This portion of the *Anand* also became a part of the evening prayer. In the same manner Guru Arjan's *Mundavani* and his shalok *tera kita jato nahin*, with which the Adi Granth concludes, gradually became part of Sikh liturgy and acquired their place at the end of the Rahiras order.

There are other features of *So Dar Rahiras* that developed in response to the needs of the Sikh community in the late seventeenth or early eighteenth century. Let us consider the inclusion of the *benati chaupai* and other compositions of the Dasam Granth (*savayya* and *dohara*) in the evening prayer.[70] For instance, the opening passage reads: 'Extend to me your guiding hand, grant this my heart's desire, [that] at your feet, most gracious lord, accepted I may dwell. Let all my foes be overcome, your hand my sure defence. Let all around me

---

[67]The PUM MS 8, which is the earliest copy of the Kartarpur manuscript, does contain the liturgical text *So Purakh*. See ff. 5b–6a. It was written at a time when *So Purakh* had become part of the evening order, possibly during Guru Arjan's last two years of life. Baba Ram Rai's bir (1659) also contains the text of *So Purakh*.

[68]*Varan Bhai Gurdas* 1:38.

[69]McLeod, *The Chaupa Singh Rahit-nama*, p. 238, n. 359.

[70]Dasam Granth, p. 254.

live in peace, all those within my care.'[71] Surely, the whole theme of the benati chaupai was intended to boost the morale of the community in the face of adverse circumstances, when the Sikhs were fighting battles for survival against the Mughal authorities. The same concern for protection (*rakh* or *tek*) may be seen in the addition of Guru Arjan's pauri from *Var Ramakali* ('You are the mighty one, there where no other is. Even [the unborn child] is under your protection in the fire of the womb'), and of his two shaloks from *Var Gujari* at the end of the extended form of the Rahiras order.[72] It may be stated that the lengthy version of the evening prayer, which includes some extra material that is not to be found in the modern order, appeared in the eighteenth century. This version is still current among the followers of Sikh sants and the Nihang order of the Khalsa.[73] It is no wonder that this lengthy version of Rahiras became popular within the Sikh community after Operation Bluestar of 1984, when the Indian army assaulted the Golden Temple complex at Amritsar. It is important to note, however, that the Singh Sabha scholars were mainly responsible for the fixing of a modern standard form of the Rahiras order.[74]

3. Guru Amar Das's *Anand* or hymn of bliss

It is important for our purpose to understand the evolution of the text of Guru Amar Das's *Anand* in *Ramakali* mode. The second volume of the available Mohan pothis contains only thirty-eight stanzas of its text (ff. 80–92), which clearly indicates that Guru Amar Das was following the pattern of Guru Nanak's *Japji*. Tradition holds that the last two stanzas were added later, one by Guru Ram Das and the other by Guru Arjan.[75] The GNDU MS 1245 contains forty stanzas with some sequential variations on folios 881–6. In particular, two stanzas (nos 26 and 27) do not conform to both, the text of the Goindval pothis and the standard version of the Adi Granth. They even show a marked difference from the Miharban's version of *Anand*, contained in the *Gosti Guru Amar Das Ki* ('Discourse on Guru Amar

---

[71]Dasam Granth, pp. 1386–8. Translation from *Textual Sources*, p. 99.

[72]M5, *Var Ramakali* (9), AG, pp. 961–2 and *Var Gujari* 1–2 (1), AG, p. 517.

[73]For more details on the two different versions of the evening prayer, see McLeod, *The Chaupa Singh Rahit-nama*, pp. 208–9, n. 18.

[74]See *Sikh Rahit Maryada* (Amritsar: S.G.P.C., 15th edn, 1982), p. 8.

[75] See Gursharan Kaur Jaggi, *Babe Mohan valian Pothian*, pp. 16–17. Also see Fauja Singh, *Guru Amar Das: Life and Teachings* (New Delhi: Sterling Publishers, 1979), p. 85, n. 45.

Das'), written by Harji in 1683.[76] Evidently, these stanzas must have come from a different source, perhaps from the oral tradition.[77]

In order to understand the process through which the text of the *Anand* achieved its final form in the Adi Granth, we need to examine the following sequential pattern in the early manuscripts, given in Table 3.1.

Table 3.1 Evolution of the *Anand* from Early Manuscripts

First line of the stanza	Stanza no. in			
	Goindval pothis	MS 1245	Mina text	AG
e rasana tu anarasi	32	32	32	32
e sarira meria har tum mahi	33	33	33	33
mani chau bhaia prabh	X	38	X	34
e sarira meria isu jagg mahi	34	34	34	35
e netaraho meriho	35	35	35	36
e sravanahu merio	36	36	36	37
hari jiu gupha andari	37	37	37	38
ehu sacha sohila	38	40	38	39
anand sunahu vadabhagio	X	39	39	40

A number of interesting points emerge from a comparative analysis of entries in Table 3.1. In the first place, stanza no. 34 of the standard version of the Adi Granth, beginning with the line *mani chau bhaia prabh agam sunia* (My *man* was delighted when I heard of the lord's coming), figures neither in the Goindval pothis nor in Miharban's text. Evidently, it belongs to Guru Arjan, whose composition would scarcely find a place in the Mina document. It is significant, however, that MS 1245 has this composition as stanza no. 38, a fact which points towards the earlier sequence of the *Anand* before standardization. In this context, Piar Singh rightly argues that MS 1245 'conforms more to the accepted version [of the Adi Granth] than to the Mina's Granth,' and that it is 'preposterous to say that MS 1245 is a Mina work.'[78]

Secondly, stanza no. 40 of the Adi Granth, beginning with the line *anand sunahu vadabhagiho sagal manorath pure* (listen to the song

[76]Cited in Raijasbir Singh, ed., *Guru Amar Das Sarot Pustak* (Amritsar: Guru Nanak Dev University, 1986), pp. 196–201.

[77]For the text of these stanzas (nos. 26 and 27), see GNDU MS 1245, f. 884a. Also, see Piar Singh, *Gatha* Sri Adi Granth, pp. 161–2.

[78]Piar Singh, *Gatha*, p. 118–19.

of joy, O blessed souls, the joy of having accomplished all the tasks), appears in both MS 1245 and Miharban's text as stanza no. 39, but does not figure in the Goindval pothis. Clearly, it is Guru Ram Das's composition, which was added to Guru Amar Das's original text of thirty-eight stanzas at the end. The addition was made with the intention of reinforcing the recurring theme of the unity of guruship. It was done in the same way as Guru Angad's shalok was added to the text of Guru Nanak's *Japji*. Guru Ram Das's stanza was available to both Guru Arjan and his brother Prithi Chand, and both of them introduced it in their respective compilations.

Thirdly, the placement of Guru Arjan's stanza (*mani chau bhaia*) at the position of no. 34 in the Kartarpur bir, however, raises an important issue. Both Piar Singh and Gurinder Singh Mann argue that this shift has broken the normal sequence of the composition.[79] For instance, the opening lines of stanzas 32–7 address the various organs of the human body as follows: 'O my tongue!' (*e rasana*); 'O body of mine!' (*e sarira meria*); 'O eyes of mine!' (*e netaraho meriho*); and 'O ears of mine!' (*e sravanahu merio*). The appeal in each case is made to the bodily organs to live in gratitude by remembering the one who has created them. It has been argued that the new stanza at no. 34 'does not thematically fit' in this sequence and has not kept their 'thematic unity and artistic beauty.' Both these arguments are simplistic and their authors do not attempt to understand Guru Arjan's editorial perspective. At times, Guru Arjan consciously breaks the monotony of the normal sequence to provide a deeper insight into the issue at hand.[80] In the present case, Guru Arjan's stanza interjects the theme of a successful body that has achieved spiritual realization and has become the temple (*mandir*) of the divine beloved. In a similar vein, Guru Amar Das likens the human body to *harimandir* (temple of the lord) through which one attains liberation.[81] Thus Guru Arjan's stanza makes perfect sense in the final sequence of the *Anand*, where it stresses the sanctity of human life as envisaged by the third Guru himself.

Finally, from the above analysis it becomes quite clear that Guru

[79]Piar Singh, *Gatha*, pp. 118–9 and Mann, 'The Making of Sikh Scripture,' pp. 88–9, 244, n. 22.

[80]I have noticed at least ten such instances where normal sequence has been consciously broken. For instance, the author-wise sequence of the four hymns of *So Purakh* cluster is as follows: M4, M4, M1, and M5. How can one explain the position of Guru Nanak's hymn here?

[81]M3, *Prabhati* 1, AG, p. 1346.

Arjan was responsible for the final form of the text of Guru Amar Das's *Anand*. He freely used his editorial discretion to add his own stanzas and refine the language of the celebrated works of his predecessors.[82] The basic text and meaning, however, remain intact in each case. Further, any decision about the text of the Adi Granth was taken after careful thought and planning, even after exploring the other alternatives. This is quite obvious from the situation of MS 1245, where the sequence of the *Anand* was still in the process of formation. However, once that sequence was fixed in the Kartarpur bir by Guru Arjan himself, it was not possible for anyone else to introduce any further change in the sequence.

GURU NANAK'S *SUHI* HYMN

One of Guru Nanak's hymns in the *Suhi* mode, beginning with the line *kaun taraji kavan tula tera kavan saraf bulava* (which is the scale, which the weight-measure? which gold-tester may I call in to test you?), has become part of the liturgical text *Shabad Hazare*, which is normally recited as part of the morning order. It appears in the Goindval pothi, Volume I as follows:

Ik Oankar satguru parasadu
Raga Parbhati Lalat

kavanu taraji kavanu tola tera kavanu saraf bulava// kavanu Guru kai pahi dikhia leva kai pahi mullu karava//1// tera baba ant na jana// tun jali thali mahiali bharipur lina tun ape sarab samana//1//rahau// ...

andhula nich jati pardesi khin avai tilu javai// tan ki sangati baba nanak rahata kini bidhi murha pavai//4//1//[83]

There is one supreme being, known by grace through the true Guru.
Raga Parbhati Lalat

Which is the scale, which the weight-measure? Which gold-tester may I call in to test you? Who is the Guru from whom I may receive instruction? Whom do I approach to evaluate you? (1) O Baba! I cannot know your extent. You are all-pervasive on water, land, and on the entire surface of the earth. You are immanent in all creation. (1) rahau ...

My mind, which is fluctuating at each moment, is blind, lowly and alienated.

---

[82]Guru Nanak's *Siddh Gost* in *Ramakali* mode has seventy-three stanzas in the standard version of the Adi Granth. In Volume 2 of the Goindval pothis, however, there are only seventy-two stanzas available. The last stanza must have been added by Guru Arjan himself.

[83]PUL, photocopy of the Jalandhar Volume of the Mohan pothis, f. 83b.

Baba Nanak continuously abides in its company: how may this foolish mind attain enlightenment? (4.1)

It is important to note that this reading of the Goindval pothis is closer to the reading of MS 1245.[84] In particular, the use of the common word *tola* (weight-measure) in both cases establishes a clear textual relationship between the two documents. A comparison of these readings with the standard version of Guru Nanak's hymn in the Adi Granth[85] reveals certain linguistic variations. The most significant points that emerge from this analysis are discussed below.

First, the symbol mahala 1 is missing from the title of the hymn in the above reading. This conventional symbol is not to be found at the beginning of every hymn in the Goindval pothis, as is the case in the Adi Granth. Sometimes there is a special heading, such as *Raga Suhi Guru Babe ki*, which signifies that the hymn in the *Suhi* mode is by Guru Baba (Nanak). Elsewhere, we also encounter other titles, such as *Raga Tilang Babe Patishah ka*, which suggests the use of the term patishah (king) for the Gurus.[86] It is important to note, however, that the use of the symbol mahala had also come into vogue by the time the extant Goindval pothis were written. Regarding the usage of the code-word mahala W.H. McLeod raises the following question:

The word mahala defies a single meaning. In its literal sense it means either 'woman' (from the Skt. *mahila*) or 'place of alighting' (from the Arabic *mahal*). The meaning of the latter has been extended to cover abode, residence, mansion, place, and queen (i.e., the occupant of the mahal); also *mahalla*, 'section of the town'. None of these, however, seems appropriate and the reason why the word was chosen accordingly remains a mystery.[87]

To understand this mystery we need to examine its contemporary usage in the Mughal empire of Akbar, where the term mahal was employed for a principality held by a chieftain.[88] The term mahala could thus have been adapted in the spiritual domain to refer to the Sikh Gurus, who held the office of guruship. It should also be noted that the Gurus were looked upon as true kings (*sacha patishah*) by

[84]See GNDU MS 1245, ff. 702a–702b.

[85]M1, *Suhi* 2, AG, pp. 730–1.

[86]Jalandhar pothi, f. 182a.

[87]W.H. McLeod, *The B40 Janam-Sakhi* (Amritsar: Guru Nanak Dev University, 1980), p. 3, n. 2. For an intersting discussion on the correct pronunciation of the word mahala, see Piar Singh, *Gatha Sri Adi Granth*, pp. 489–94.

[88]See the list of mahals in tabular form, given in *Ain-i Akbari*, the manuscripts of which are kept at the British Library, MSS Additional 7652 and 6552.

the Sikh community, since by that time the status of Guru was sup-
plemented by the attributes of royalty. The Sikhs started venerating
the Gurus in a most dignified way, a way which was marked by the
symbols of royalty such as the use of a canopy, a throne and the
waving of a whisk over their heads.[89] The conventional use of the
symbol mahala in the title of Gurus' hymns, therefore, may even
signal a new development in Sikh self-understanding with respect
to the status of the Guru.

Secondly, the hymn was originally meant to be sung in the
measure *Parbhati Lalat* in the worship daily. But Guru Arjan placed
this hymn under the *Suhi* mode, which suggests that he had a more
pressing thematic concern in mind. What could that concern be?
It is noteworthy that a great deal of marital imagery and themes
are to be found in the *Suhi* raga. This raga, in particular places
much emphasis on the themes of husband-wife relationship, where
husband (*sahu* or *pir*) stands for the supreme being and wife (*dhanu*
or *suhaganu*) stands for the soul.[90] Guru Ram Das's wedding hymn
(*lavan*) is also to be found in the *Suhi* mode in the Adi Granth.[91]
The central theme in Guru Nanak's hymn is also focused on the
word sahu (husband), which fits very well in the total context of
Suhi raga.

Thirdly, there are certain linguistic variations in the hymn which
are different from their synonyms in the standard text. For instance,
the word *kaun* is written as *kavanu* (which), *tula* as tola
(weight-measure), *dekhai* as *vekhai* (to view) and *kiumkari* as *kin bidhi*
(how or by which means?). Similarly the first line in the refrain of
the standard version, *mere lal jiu tera antu na jana* (I cannot know
your extent, my dear beloved) is written in the earlier version as *tera
baba antu na jana* (O Baba! I cannot know your extent). The
replacement of the word baba (father) with *mere lal* (my dear
beloved) is quite significant since its tone fits very well in the context
of the *Suhi* mode. The use of honorific particle *jiu* in referring to the
divine beloved (my dear beloved) acts as a singing device, which
makes the hymn more musical. Evidently Guru Arjan's literary talent
was at work behind this whole process of refinement.

[89]See, for instance, panegyrics by the bards in praise of Gurus, particularly by
bard Haribans, *Savayye Mahale Pañjaven Ke 1–2*, AG, p. 1409. The later usage of *Patishahi
10* for the compositions of Guru Gobind Singh in the Dasam Granth confirms our
interpretation.

[90]Taran Singh, *Sri Guru Granth Sahib Ji da Sahitak Itihas* (Amritsar: Fakir Singh
and Sons, 1963), pp. 264–6.

[91]M4, *Suhi Chhant 2*, AG, pp. 773–4.

Finally, the signature line of the earlier version of the hymn contains the personal name Baba Nanak. The title Baba (father) is suggestive of a most revered figure in the Punjabi society of the time. Because of his piety and humility, Guru Nanak was known as Baba Nanak during his lifetime, and the same epithet is widely used in the janam-sakhis. In the standard text, however, Guru Arjan omitted the personal title Baba and retained the name Nanak [for the sake of uniformity]. By his time the name Nanak had become a symbol of authority in the compositions of all Sikh Gurus. This point may be further elaborated with the help of the following citation:

When one looks at the Sikh scriptures one finds that the name Nanak denotes not just one man but a class: all the Gurus in his lineage who composed poetry that was collected in the Adi Granth. They all sign their poems, as is characteristic in the *pad* genre that is the backbone of the Adi Granth and most medieval north Indian devotional poetry, and remarkably, they all sign their poems with a single name—Nanak's. (Divisions in the text indicate which 'Nanak' is which.) So Nanak, the Guru, is not just a person but a principle.[92]

Thus the name Nanak stands for a principle rather than a person. Throughout the Adi Granth it serves as a symbol of authority rather than an individual Guru's personal identity, which is marked by the symbol mahala in the title of the composition. In this context, J.S. Grewal aptly remarks: 'The use of the epithet Nanak by the successors of Guru Nanak in their compositions is no mere imitation of the founder. The continuity of the mission as well as the supreme position of Guru Nanak is implied in a most effective way in the use of this epithet.'[93] J.S. Hawley argues in a similar vein as follows:

The author's name is no mere footnote. It anchors the poem to life, a personality, even a divinity that gives the poem its proper weight and tone ... By providing this tie, the signatures in bhakti poems communicate more than authorship. They lend these poems authority and conviction, and they establish an aura in which the act of listening can be as intense as the speech.[94]

Here, Hawley maintains that the signature at the end of bhakti poems

---

[92]John Stratton Hawley and Mark Juergensmeyer, *Songs of the Saints of India* (New York: Oxford University Press, 1988), p. 75.

[93]J.S. Grewal, *Guru Nanak in History* (Chandigarh: Panjab University, 1969), p. 290.

[94]See John Hawley, 'Author and Authority in Bhakti Poetry,' *The Journal of Asian Studies* 47(2) (1988): 275–6 and 287–8.

signifies primarily authority rather than simply authorhsip. Thus the name Nanak in the hymns of the Adi Granth implies the continuity and unity of guruship in Sikh tradition.

GURU ARJAN'S *TILANG* HYMNS

It has been suggested that the *Tilang* raga has a special appropriateness for the hymns associated with Islam. A great deal of Persian and Islamic loan-words are to be found in this raga.[95] It appears that the *Tilang* raga was quite popular among the Muslim singers (particularly the sufis or dervishes) of the Punjab in the sixteenth century.[96] There are only five hymns of Guru Arjan in this mode in the standard version of the Adi Granth.[97] It is interesting to note that MS 1245 provides earlier forms of these hymns, all of which were revised in the final version of the Kartarpur volume. They illuminate the process of their standardization in the final text. The following concerns are noteworthy in the *rédaction* process at work in the revision of these hymns.

1. Fixing of the Sequence of Verses in a Hymn

In the standard version of the Adi Granth, the second shabad of Guru Arjan in the *Tilang* mode begins with the line: 'There is no other apart from you.'[98] Although the same line is mentioned in the index of MS 1245, the main text begins as follows:

Tilang Mahala 5//
sabh upari parbraham dataru// teri tek tera adharu//1//rahau// tudhu binu duja nahin koi// tun kartar karahi so hoi// tera joru teri mani tek// sada sada japi nanak eku//1//[99]

Tilang Mahala 5
Surpassing all, O supreme lord, is your support and succour. (1) rahau. There is no other apart from you. Whatever you will, O creator, comes to pass. Your power is the *man's* only support. Contemplate ever and ever, Nanak, the one [and the only lord]. (1)

The comparison of this text with its standard form clearly indicates that Guru Arjan changed the order of verse in the rahau (pause or

[95]C. Shackle, 'Approaches to Persian Loans in the Adi Granth', *Bulletin of the School of Oriental and African Studies* (1978), 41(1): 81–3.
[96]Piara Singh Padam, *Sri Guru Granth Prakash* (Patiala, 1990), p. 278.
[97]M5, *Tilang* 1–5, AG, pp. 723–4.
[98]M5, *Tilang* 2, AG, p. 723–4.
[99]GNDU MS 1245, f. 681b.

stop), which normally represents the central idea of the hymn, and which is used as a refrain (*sathai*) in a musical performance. In this instance, he fixed it after the first verse (*antara*) of the hymn. It may also indicate that each verse of a hymn must be understood as an independent unit in itself. This seems to be the case, especially in instances where there is no thematic development of an idea over the different verses of a hymn.[100] It should also be emphasized here that the earlier form of Guru Arjan's *Tilang* hymn confirms an important fact concerning the oral transmission of bani in the Sikh community. The hymns of the Gurus were primarily intended to be sung in a congregational setting. Thus, this earlier text was certainly popular in the kirtan (devotional singing) sessions during Sikh worship.

Although the rahau-verse normally comes after the first verse of a hymn, this convention is not followed universally in the Adi Granth. For instance, the opening verse of Guru Arjan's fifth hymn in *Tilang* mode reads: 'O wise nobleman! contemplate in your heart how the true king, the liberator, comes to abide in the *man* and body through love.'[101] Guru Arjan fixed this rahau-verse at the beginning in the standard text. It had been written after the first verse in the GNDU text. The following is the earlier reading.

Tilang Mahala 5//
didane didar sahib kachhu nahin iska molu// pak paravadagar tun khudu khasam vadda atolu//1// mira dana dil sochu// muhabate mani tani basai sachu sahib bandi mochu// rahau//[102]

Tilang Mahala 5
There can be no price on beholding the lord. You yourself are the holy nourisher, vastly beyond all measuring. (1) O wise nobleman! contemplate in your heart how the true lord, the liberator, comes to abide in the *man* and body through love. rahau

The hymn appears to have been addressed to a Muslim nobleman, probably a Nawab of Lahore,[103] who was invited to follow the path of love as enunciated by the Guru. Apart from the position of the rahau-verse, this text contains the word *sahibu* (lord) instead of *shah* (king) of the final form, which was introduced by Guru Arjan for metrical purposes. These minor textual variations, which do not alter

---

[100]Mukund Lath, 'Bhajan as Song: Towards an Oral Stemma of Namdev's padas', in Monika Thiel-Horstmann, ed., *Bhakti in Current Research, 1979–1982* (Berlin, 1983), pp. 231–2.
[101]M5, *Tilang* 5, AG, p. 724.
[102]GNDU MS 1245, f. 682b.
[103]See *Shabadarath Sri Guru Granth Sahib Ji*, Vol. II (Amritsar: 1979), p. 724.

the original meaning at all, can best be explained as the result of liberty taken by the Sikh musicians in singing.[104]

2. Linguistic Modifications of Certain Words in a Hymn

In the standard version, Guru Arjan's third hymn in *Tilang* raga begins with the rahau-verse: 'Gracious, gracious is the lord. My lord is gracious indeed. He bestows bounties on all creatures.'[105] Its earlier form, however, reads as follows:

Tilang Mahala 5//
miharvanu piara miharvanu// haum kurbanu sagal jian kaum dehiga danu//rahau/
/ kahe re dolahi prania tao nao rakhaiga rakhanhara// jini paidaish tun kia soi dei
adhara//1// jini upai medani soi karaiga sara// ghati ghati malaku dilan da sacha
parvadgara//2// ... [106]

Tilang Mahala 5
Gracious, gracious is the [divine] beloved. I sacrifice myself to him who bestows bounties on all creatures. rahau. O creature! why do you waver? The protector shall protect you. He who has created you, shall preserve you too. (1) He who has created the whole world, looks after it as well. Present in every heart, the lord is the heart's [only] true guardian. (2) ...

A comparative examination of this text with its standard version reveals certain linguistic variations. For instance, the first line in the standard version, *miharvanu sahibu miharvanu*, is written in the earlier text as *miharvanu piara miharvanu*. That is, in the final text the word sahibu (lord) replaces *piara* (beloved). The phrase *haum kurbanu* (I sacrifice myself) is dropped from the second line. Instead a new line, *sahibu mera miharvanu* (my lord is gracious), is added, emphasizing the divine nature of graciousness. The remainder of the rahau-verse is recast as *jia sagal kau dehi danu* (he bestows bounties on all creatures) to create better metrical and rhyming effect.

The language of the first verse of the hymn is modified in the final text (*tun kahe dolahi prania tudhu rakhaiga sirjanharu// jini paidaish tun kia soi dei adharu//1//*) without changing the original meaning. In the first place, the musical filler *re* (O) is replaced with the personal pronoun tun (you) in order to establish personal contact with the audience. Secondly, the short phrase *tao nao* (to you) is replaced with a singular oblique pronoun tudhu (you) to shorten the syllables for metrical purposes. Thirdly, the word rakhanahara (Protector) is

[104]M. Lath, 'Bhajan as Song', p. 230.
[105]M5, *Tilang* 3, AG, p. 724.
[106]GNDU MS 1245, ff. 681b–682a.

replaced with sirjanaharu (creator) to change the end-rhyme. Similarly, minor linguistic modifications were made in other verses of the hymn to standardize the text. It should be emphasized here, however, that this revision is in keeping with both the rhythm and the meaning of the hymn.

The fourth hymn of Guru Arjan in the *Tilang* raga begins with the line: 'O Creator! [I am] yearning [for you] through [my love for your] creation' (*karate kudaratim musatak*).[107] Although the same line appears in the index of the GNDU volume, the complete hymn in the main text reads as follows:

Tilang Mahala 5//
karata kudarate musataku// din dunia eku tun sabh khalak hi te paku// rahau//
khin mahi thapi uthapada acharaju tera rupu// kavanu janai chalat tere andhiare
mahi dipu//1// khudu khasam khalak jahanu alahu miharvan khudai// dinu raini
tujhai aradate se kium dojaki jahi//2// ajaraiairu bande jisu tera adharu// gunaha
on ke sagal aphu jo jan dekhate didaru//3// dunia chij philahal sagali sachu sukh
tera nau// mili pir nanak bujhia sada ekasu gau//4//4[108]

Tilang Mahala 5
Creator! [I am] yearning [for you] through [my love for your] creation. You are the only one [who is my true support] in both this world and the next, [even though] you remain apart from all your creation. rahau. You have the power to create and destroy in an instant! Wondrous is your form! Who can know your wonders? You are like a lamp in the darkness. (1) You yourself are the master of creation, the gracious Allah, the lord (khuda'i). How can they who remember you day and night go to hell? (2) The people who take shelter with you shall find the angel of death (Azrael) friendly. Those servants who crave for your vision (didar) will have their sins forgiven. (3) All the objects of the world are short-lived. Your name [brings] to all true joy. By meeting with the pir, Nanak, this realization has come: that one should ever sing [the glory of] the one lord. (4)

Evidently, Guru Arjan made an exceptionally free use of Persian and Islamic words in this hymn. The use of such poetic words as musataku (*mushtaq*, 'yearning') and didar ('vision of the beloved') particularly reminds one of the typical vocabulary of Muslim lyrical poetry, with its extensive debt to the language of the courtly (and mystical) *ghazal*.[109] The major points that emerge from the discussion of this hymn are as follows.

First, Guru Arjan modified the language of the rahau-verse

[107]M5, *Tilang* 5, AG, p. 724.
[108]GNDU MS 1245, f. 682a.
[109]C. Shackle, 'Approaches to Persian Loans in the Adi Granth,' pp. 86–7.

through the substitution of the words karate (O creator!) and kudartim (with the creation) for karata (creator) and kudarate (in the creation), in order to recast the Persian words into Punjabi constructions. For instance, the Punjabi word karate is used as a noun in the vocative case when addressing Akal Purakh directly, which shows an intimate relationship with the divine. Similarly the word kudartim is employed to express an intimate relationship with the creation. The phrase *acharaju tera rupu* (wondrous is your form) in the first verse is replaced with the plurals *acharaj tere rup* ('wondrous are your forms') to stress the nature of divine immanence. The interrogative pronoun kavanu (who?) is replaced with kaunu to fit the metre. Similarly, the phrase *dinu raini tujhai aradate* ([they who] remember you day and night) is replaced with *dinasu raini ji tudhu aradhe* ([he who] remembers you day and night) to create a singular form of the expression.

Second, Guru Arjan employed the Islamic words for the supreme being, such as the Arabic *alahu* (Allah) and Persian khudai (khuda'i) to address his Muslim audience. He also refers to *ajarailu* (Azrael), the angel of death from the Islamic celestial hierarchy. The obscure phrase *ajaraiairu bande* in the early text must have been popular in the village communities. If the canon of unusual readings (*lectiones arduae*) is applied to this phrase to determine the age of the document, then MS 1245 will certainly prove to be much older than the Kartarpur manuscript. It was replaced with *ajarailu yaru bande* ('Azrael is that person's friend') in the standard text which is more intelligible in the present context. Further, the use of such words as aphu (*afu*, 'be forgiven'), gunaha (gunah, 'sins') and dojaki (*dozakh*, 'hell') reflects the preoccupation of contemporary Islam with hell-fire eschatology. Guru Arjan addressed this theme because his Muslim audience must have been deeply concerned with the forgiveness of 'sins' to escape the punishment of hell. He offered them a way out of their predicament in the prescription of nam simaran (How can he who remembers you day and night go to hell?). In fact, he was inviting them to follow the path of the Guru by addressing them in their own terms.

Third, the Persian word philahal (*fi'l-hal*, transitory) links the meaning of the hymn to the *memento mori* theme of the Punjabi sufi literature, which emphasizes the transitoriness of worldly things.[110] The most significant revision of this hymn by Guru Arjan is, however,

---

[110]For more details, see ibid., pp. 83 and 89.

in the substitution of the phrase *gur mili nanak bujhia* (by meeting with the Guru, Nanak, this realization has come) for *mili pir nanak bujhia* (by meeting with the pir, Nanak, this realization has come) in the final text. It suggests that the hymn was originally directed at a Muslim audience, for whom the role of the pir would be a relevant feature of spiritual development.

Finally, the language and style of the *Tilang* hymns clearly presuppose Muslim audiences, and it is quite possible that a significant number of Muslims were attracted to the Sikh faith due to its universal appeal.[111] Like Guru Nanak, Guru Arjan frequently employed Persian and Islamic loan-words to reach out to his Muslim audience of the countryside, but the truth which he wished to express was his own. In this context, Christopher Shackle mentions a class of Muslim poets (*sha'ir*), drawn from sufi circles, which constituted the elite of the countryside. The Guru's appeal was naturally directed at the Muslim audience of the sha'ir.[112] It is no wonder that some of those Muslim poets may have felt threatened by his growing popularity.

3. Fixing of the Musical Mode of a Hymn

The GNDU manuscript contains a hymn in the *Tilang* raga, the revised text of which is to be found in the *Suhi* mode in the standard version of the Adi Granth.[113] The earlier reading is as follows:

Tilang Mahala 5//
jo gur disai sikkhara nivi nivi lagaum pai// akhan biratha jia ki Guru sajanu dehi milai// soi dassi upadesara mera manu anat na kahu jai// haum ehu manu taim kum devasa mai marag dei batai// haum aia durahum chali kai mai takki tau saranai// mai asa rakhi chitu mai mera sabho dukkhu gamvai// itu maragi challe bhaiare Guru kahai so kar kamai// tiag man ki matari visari duja bhau// ium pavahi hari darasara namha laggai tati vau// haum apahum boli na janada mai kahia sabhu hukamau// hari bhagati khajana bakhasia jan nanak kia pasau// bahuri na tisana bhukhari haum rajja tipati agghai//1//5//[114]

---

[111]The conversion of Muslims to the Sikh faith was one of the charges laid against Guru Arjan by Emperor Jahangir in his *Tuzuk-i-Jahangiri*. See Ganda Singh, *Guru Arjan's Martyrdom: Reinterpreted* (Patiala: Guru Nanak Mission, 1969), pp. 10–15.

[112]See Christopher Shackle, 'Early Muslim Vernacular Poetry in the Indus Valley: Its Contexts and its Character,' in Anna Libera Dallapiccola and Stephanie Zingel-Ave Lallemant, eds, *Islam and Indian Regions* (Stuttgart: Franz Steiner Verlag, 1993), pp. 276–7.

[113]M5, *Suhi* 3, AG, p. 763.

[114]GNDU MS 1245, ff. 682a–682b.

Tilang Mahala 5.
Whichever disciple of the Guru I meet I bow low to touch his feet. I state my heart's agony to him so that he may help me meet my Guru and friend. I seek instructions from him to control my endlessly straying mind. I will sacrifice my *man* to you, if you show me the true path. I have come from far to seek your protection. I cherish the hope in my heart that you will remove all my sufferings. Follow this true path, my brother, and do the bidding of the Guru. Renounce the [evil] inclinations of your mind and refrain from loving the other. In this way you will have the holy vision of the lord, and no calamity will come to you. I myself do not know how to speak, I have only conveyed the order [of the lord]. The lord has blessed me with the treasure of devotion, and it is this which the servant Nanak celebrates. I am now completely satiated and my craving no longer exists.

A comparative analysis of this text with its standard form in the *Suhi* mode reveals a number of interesting points. First, there is a marginal note in a different hand on folio 682a of the GNDU manuscript (*suhi vichi lia hai*, It is taken to the *Suhi* mode) to clarify that this hymn is repeated in the *Suhi* mode on folio 729b, with the addition of the first line appearing at the end as well. This editorial comment clearly indicates that the decision to place this hymn in the *Suhi* raga was taken at the time of the composition of this earlier recension.

Second, the reason for arranging this hymn in the *Suhi* raga is based on thematic consideration. Even in the GNDU manuscript, its second appearance is entitled *Gunavanti* (virtuous woman), which fits very well in the sequence of the preceding two hymns of Guru Nanak entitled *Kuchajji* (slovenly or uncultured woman) and *Suchajji* (skilful or cultured woman) respectively.[115] Here, one can discern the step-wise progression of the theme of spiritual development of a woman's soul yearning for union with her divine husband, which is a characteristic feature of the *Suhi* raga.

Third, a linguistic examination of the cluster of three hymns (that is, two hymns by Guru Nanak and one by Guru Arjan) clearly suggests that Guru Arjan had very carefully reworked the poetic genre of *kafi* and the south-western style (*dakkhani*), which was given definitive form by Guru Nanak himself. It is important to note that the label *dakkhana* (in place of the usual shalok) in the Adi Granth is not a separate metrical category, but rather an indication that the verse is written in a language reflecting languages of the south (as defined from the Amritsar area, particularly the Multan area). It is therefore

---

[115]GNDU MS 1245, ff. 728b–729b. Also see AG,762–3.

quite appropriate to call this idiom the dakkhani style.[116] The expression *haum ehu manu taim kum devasam* (I will sacrifice my *man* to you) clearly points towards the dakkhani style, although the language is not used throughout Guru Arjan's hymn. It is quite possible that the hymn was originally intended for the south-western audience of the Multan area.

Fourth, in the first line of the final reading (whichever disciple of the Guru I meet I bow to him to touch his feet) one can see the addition of an oblique pronoun *tisu* (him) and an honorific particle *jiu* (which may refer to a highly respected person in this context) at the end. Here the word *jiu* is intended as a musical device. There is also the re-positioning of words in the phrase *jo gur disai sikkhara*. Similarly, there are some minor linguistic improvisations to be found in other lines of the final reading. Three following stages may be discerned in this process of linguistic revision:

1. *tiagi man ki matari visari duja bhau// ium pavahi hari darasara namha laggai tati vau//*[117]
2. *tiage man ki matari visare duja bhau// ium pavahi hari darasavara namha laggai tati vau//*[118]
3. *tiage man ki matari visare duja bhau jiu// ium pavahi hari darasavara namha laggai tati vau jiu//*[119]

Clearly, these linguistic modifications at different stages of textual transmission are meant to provide grammatically sound constructions and to create better metrical and rhythmic effects. For instance, the addition of jiu in the final text adds sweetness and music to its tonal effect.[120] It should be emphasized, however, that the original meaning of the text remains intact in this linguistic revision.

Finally, the most significant point about the standard version is that the first line is repeated at the end. This is clearly intended to venerate the worthy Sikh of the Guru (*gur sikkhara*), who must have been responsible for bringing people into the Sikh fold.[121] In

---

[116]See Shackle, 'Early Muslim Vernacular Poetry in the Indus Valley', pp. 276–8. For more details on this style, see his 'The South-Western Style in the Guru Granth Sahib', *Journal of Sikh Studies*, V, 1 (Amritsar: Guru Nanak Dev University, 1978), pp. 69–87.

[117]GNDU MS 1245, f. 682b.

[118]GNDU MS 1245, f. 729b.

[119]*Shabadarath*, Vol. III, 763.

[120]The word jiu was also added to Guru Nanak's two preceding hymns in order to achieve uniformity in rhyme and metre. Earlier readings of these hymns do not contain this word in the end-rhyme. See GNDU MS 1245, ff. 729a–729b.

[121]See Surjit Hans, *A Reconstruction of Sikh History*, p. 145: 'In the compositions of

particular, the original form of the line (*jo gur disai sikkhara tisu nivi nivi lagaum pai jiu*) is retained in this case to emphasize the role of the Guru and the devout Sikh.

GURU ARJAN'S *RAMAKALI* HYMN

One of the main issues that has drawn scholarly attention in the Kartarpur–Banno debate is related to a hymn by Guru Arjan in the *Ramakali* mode. A single couplet stands recorded in the standard version of the Adi Granth after chhant 4, before Guru Arjan's composition on the six seasons (*ruti*) of the Indian calendar.[122] In order to address the incomplete nature of this hymn, W.H. McLeod argues that there should apparently be a complete hymn in the section assigned to the longer chhant compositions. The organization of hymns in this section indicates that the couplet must be either the first two lines of a chhant, or a shalok introducing a chhant.[123] The academic issue raised by McLeod drew a great many polemic responses from Sikh scholars, which generated more heat than light on the Kartarpur–Banno debate.[124]

It is important to note that only two lines of this hymn are to be found in the manuscripts of both the Kartarpur and the Lahore traditions.[125] Even in the Kanpur manuscript (1642), which is claimed to be the first copy of the Adi bir prepared by Bhai Banno (and hence popularly known as Banno bir), the additional twenty-two lines of the hymn were added later in a smaller hand.[126] One can argue that the scribe had originally written a single couplet since the remainder of the hymn was not available at that time. When the additional portion became available, he completed the hymn in the Banno version of the Adi Granth. This explanation may be supported by the scribal practice of writing the opening verse first and completing the text later. But this simple explanation does not solve the textual puzzle. I shall argue that the completion of this hymn

---

Guru Arjan, we come across the figure of worshippable Sikh who converted men to Sikhism.'

[122]M5, *Ramakali*, AG, p. 927.

[123]W.H. McLeod, *The Evolution of the Sikh Community* (Delhi: Oxford University Press, 1975), p. 76.

[124]For instance, see Daljeet Singh, *Essays on the Authenticity of the Kartarpuri Bir* (Patiala: Punjabi University, 1987) and other works originating from the Institute of Sikh Studies, Chandigarh.

[125]See my 'The Text and Meaning of the Adi Granth,' pp. 45, 49, 53, 55, 58 and 60.

[126]ibid., pp. 62–3.

was intentionally done at a time when the volume was converted into the Banno text.

In order to understand the problem of the Banno recension, we must examine Guru Arjan's *Ramakali* hymn in its original context. In folio 703/1 of the Kartarpur manuscript the two lines read as follows:

Raga Ramakali Mahala 5
ran jhunjjhanara gau sakhi hari ek dhiavahu// satgur tum sev sakhi mani chindiara
phalu pavahu//

Ramakali Mahala 5
Sing the trilling tunes in the [dance]-field, my sister-friends, by meditating on the one lord. By serving the true Guru, my sister-friends, accomplish your heart's desires.

The opening words, *ran jhunjjhanara* (trilling tunes [sung in the dance]-field), indicate a wedding scene at which Punjabi girls were accustomed to gather together in a circle to sing wedding songs. Guru Arjan may have uttered these aphoristic sayings on the happy occasion of a marriage, intending that these be developed into a complete hymn later. As the opportunity for its completion never came, only two lines, followed by a blank space, stand recorded in the Kartarpur manuscript. Because there is no mention of this hymn in the index of this volume, and because the entry of the couplet (though made by the same scribe) was done with a different pen, we may conclude that the couplet was introduced some time after the compilation of the Adi Granth in 1604 and before Guru Arjan's death in 1606. This is also confirmed by the fact that this couplet (or complete hymn) is not to be found in an earlier Sikh scriptural tradition, popularly known as MS 1245 preserved at the Guru Nanak Dev University library.[127]

The complete hymn, along with the additional lines, is to be found in the Banno version of the Adi Granth. It reads as follows:

Raga Ramakali Mahala 5
Sing the trilling tunes in the [dance]-field, my sister-friends, by meditating on the one lord. By serving the true Guru, my sister-friends, accomplish your heart's desires. Through the contemplation of the true Guru a unique son is born by destiny. The true Guru has sent the long-lived child to enjoy great fortune. Immense joy abounds by singing blissful songs of praise on

---

[127]GNDU MS 1245, f. 861a. The last line of the Ramakali chhant (*bali jae nanak sada karate sabh mahi rahia samai jiu. 4.4*) is followed by Guru Arjan's composition on the six seasons (*ruti chhia*). There is no blank space here.

the lord. Says Nanak, the journey [of life] has borne fruit through contemplation of the person of the true Guru. (1) By collecting the nectar-like food the whole family was called [into the Guru's presence]. Let the immortal divine Name be distributed (*vandiahu*) to all so that everyone is completely satisfied. The true Guru made the distribution [of the divine name] to everyone while sitting [on the throne] and all were blessed with the gift of love. Everyone received a share (*vand*) according to his destiny, and no one went empty-handed [from the house of the Guru]. The whole Sikh sangat gathered together [in the Guru's presence] and each person was absorbed in great joy. Says Nanak, 'By seeking the lord's protection I have attained all comforts.' (2) All the rites (*riti*) were performed by meditating deeply on the lord. The tonsure ceremony (*bhaddanu unet*) was conducted by repeating the divine knowledge of the Guru. Repeating the Guru's knowledge provided all comforts, and thus the boy was sent to school. The child received a perfect education by obeying the lord in his heart. All were feasted (*jevanavaru*) lavishly at the time of the name-giving (*namukaran*) ceremony [of the child], and no one went away empty-handed. Nanak, the humble servant of God, pleads: 'My lord is [my] friend at death.' (3) The saintly people who gathered together [in the Guru's presence] suggested that the boy should now be betrothed (*mangeva*). By good fortune, those of rectitude and wisdom were found as parents of the bride. Let the gift of amrit (divine name) be distributed among all. The mystical state of union with the immortal name was attained when the Guru established the divine knowledge (in the *man*) and removed all kinds of suffering. The auspicious moment, which was written [by destiny] from the very beginning, came and the marriage was affirmed by the parents of the bride. The lord arranged the marriage-party in such a way that all kinds of sages, devotees and godly men participated in it. Says Nanak, the task of [marriage] was accomplished and the unstruck music sounded forth. (4)[128]

Evidently, the hymn describes the rituals in the life-cycle of an individual in Punjabi society in the seventeenth century which included the birth of a male child, the name-giving ceremony, the puberty rite, the first admission in a school, the betrothal rite and the marriage ceremony. A further symbolic meaning gets attached to these rituals since they are used as occasions for the distribution of the gift of amrit (the divine name) among the devotees of the Guru.

The real issue, however, is related to the authorship of the Banno hymn. Did Guru Arjan compose the *Ramakali* hymn? If he did not do so, who else could have been responsible for completing this hymn, and why? To find answers to these questions, we must examine

---

[128]Patiala, Tikana Bhai Ramkishan, Gurdita Sekhon MS (1653), f. 478a.

the poetic style of this hymn and other linguistic features with reference to other works of Guru Arjan. This method of enquiry reveals the following significant points.

The fourth line in the first stanza (*satguru sachai bheji dia char jivan vaddu punnia,* the true Guru has sent the long-lived child to enjoy great fortune) alludes to the opening lines of Guru Arjan's hymn in *Asa* raga, which he composed to celebrate the birth of his only child, Hargobind, the sixth Guru: The true Guru has sent the child. The long-lived child has been born by destiny (*satguru sachai dia bheji// chir jivan upajia sanjogi*).[129] This allusion has been largely responsible for the assumption that the Banno hymn concerns the life-cycle rituals relating to Guru Hargobind's early life. For instance, G.B. Singh's manuscript note on the copy of a Banno recension in the India Office Library reads: 'The hymn (chhant) about the early life of the sixth Guru is given complete[ly] (24 lines); and not only the first two lines.[130] It is important to note, however, that apart from this indirect association, there is no explicit reference to the sixth Guru in the text itself. Rather, the author of the Banno hymn employs the metaphor of a unique son (*anup balak*) as a poetic convention to describe the life-cycle rituals of Punjabi society in general.[131]

Secondly, there are certain linguistic expressions in the hymn which cannot be the work of Guru Arjan. For instance, for him to have used the phrase *satgur bahi kai vand kini* (the true Guru made the distribution while sitting) for himself is totally alien to the humble nature of Guru Arjan.[132] He never directly refers to himself as the true Guru in his compositions. The hymn was definitely composed by a scribe who was highly motivated by the idea of completing the incomplete text in the name of the Guru. A recent example of a somewhat similar sort may be seen in Jodh Singh's addition of his own interpretation to his description of the Kartarpur bir to solve the textual problem of this hymn. His note on the description of folio 703/1 reads as follows:

[129]M5, *Asa* 7, AG, p. 396.

[130]India Office library, MSS Panj. F1. The Manuscript note 4 (d). Also see McLeod, *Evolution of the Sikh Community*, p. 77.

[131]See *Shabadarath* Vol. III, p. 927. Here Teja Singh provides allegorical interpretation of this hymn in the footnote. However, he does not say that he accepts the authorship of Guru Arjan. Gurinder Mann's claim that Teja Singh 'accepts Guru Arjan's authorship of this hymn' (see 'The Making of Sikh Scripture,' p. 218) is misleading. One must use extreme caution in assessing his arguments.

[132]Piar Singh, *Gatha Sri Adi Granth*, p. 480.

Raga Ramakali Mahala 5 Salok
ran jhunjjhanara gau sakhi hari ek dhiavahu// satgur tum sev sakhi mani
chindiara phalu pavahu//1//[133]

The word salok in the title and the numeral 1 at the end of the couplet do not occur in the original text of the Kartarpur volume. This is an example of making an incomplete text look like a complete text. Further, there are other examples in the Adi Granth where Gurus employ single-line aphoristic sayings instead of shaloks. These single lines may be seen in the section assigned to Gurus' shaloks, surplus to the vars.[134]

Thirdly, the most significant point is that Guru Arjan never employed such words as vand (distribution) or vandiahu (distribute!) anywhere in his compositions in the Adi Granth.[135] These words did not form part of his usual lexicon. This fact alone makes improbable his authorship of the additional material of the hymn. Similarly, other words such as riti (rites), *bhaddanu unetu* (the tonsure rite), jevanavaru (the ritual feast associated with the sacred thread ceremony), namukaran (the name-giving ceremony) and mangeva ('the betrothal rite') only appear in the Banno version of the Adi Granth in this disputed hymn.[136] Thus they were intentionally employed to give legitimacy to brahminical rituals in Sikh society, which were otherwise strongly repudiated by the Sikh Gurus, particularly by Guru Arjan himself. On a number of occasions Guru Nanak criticized the sacred thread (*janeu*), and other rituals associated with death (like *pind*, *patal*, *kiria*, and *diva*).[137] Guru Arjan referred to the celebration of Guru Hargobind's birth by the sangat in the form of the singing of gurbani, particularly the *Ramakali Anandu* of

[133]Bhai Jodh Singh, *Kartarpuri Bir*, p. 97.

[134]See M1, *Salok Varan Te Vadhik*, 12, 27 and 28, AG, pp. 1411–12. Shalok 28 is by Guru Amar Das, who responded to Guru Nanak's reflection on the city of Lahore.

[135]For instance, see Gurcharan Singh, *Adi Granth Shabad-Anukramanika*, Vol. II: pp. 2290, 2293, 2294 and 2296.

[136]In another context, however, Guru Nanak employs the word *bhaddu* (shaving the head) to criticize the Jains 'who pluck their heads with their hands, refusing to use a razor.' See M1, *Var Malhar* (16), AG, p. 1285.

[137]M1, *Var Asa 1* (15), AG, p. 471 and *Asa 32*, AG, p. 358. Also see Sundar's *Ramakali Saddu*, AG, pp. 923–4. Five balls of rice and flour called pinda are usually placed on leaves (patal) to perform the death rite (kiria) at the time of cremation. Then an earthenware lamp (diva) is lighted in the evening for eleven days. During this period of mourning, balls of rice, ghee and sugar (termed *pinda dan*) are either fed to a crow or thrown in water. For details see Harjot Oberoi, 'From Ritual to Counter-Ritual: Rethinking the Hindu-Sikh Question, 1884–1915,' in *Sikh History and Religion in the Twentieth Century*, ed. Joseph T. O'Connell et al. (Toronto: University of Toronto, Center for South Asian Studies, 1988), pp. 144–6.

Guru Amar Das (*gurbani sakhi anandu gavai*).[138] Evidently this latter tradition was the one in vogue among Sikhs at that time.

Fourthly, it is the fifth Guru who, like Guru Nanak, criticizes both Hindu and Muslim beliefs, practices and texts. In one of his comments on Kabir's hymns, he explicitly says: 'We are neither Hindu nor Musalman.' He further states that he has settled the difference between Hindu and Muslim (as Kabir did), not by working out some kind of synthesis of the two, nor by keeping the observances of both, such as fasts, pilgrimage, prayers and worship, but by cultivating the remembrance of Akal Purakh within the heart.[139] Although there is no direct reference to life-cycle rituals as such, it is implied in the general category of Hindu practices.[140] One can then raise the question as to how Guru Arjan could have been the author of such a hymn, which sanctifies Hindu rituals, when he himself was a strong critic of them. It is much more likely that the real author of the extra material in the *Ramakali* hymn was a person who was under a strong brahminical influence. In this context, Piar Singh has suggested that either a *bhat* (bard) or a *pandit* (a brahmin family priest) composed this hymn on the occasion of the marriage to receive *jajamani* (gift or stipend) from his patrons.[141] This hymn, he argues, became current under the signatures of Nanak and was then incorporated into the Banno version of the Adi Granth. Gurinder Mann, on the other hand, unconvincingly uses the argument of signatures to prove Guru Arjan's authorship of this hymn.[142] Two signatures *binvanti nanak* (Nanak begs) and *janu kahai nanak* (Nanak the servant says) that appear in this hymn, also appear in certain hymns of Guru Arjan. But this sole convention cannot be used to attribute the hymn to the fifth Guru. It seems likely that anybody (a pandit or a bhat) could have picked up such expressions and composed the hymn in the name of Guru Arjan.

Fifthly, the poetic style of the hymn is flattering and plodding, unlike what we encounter in the authentic bani of Guru Arjan. In the first two lines following the original couplet, for instance, one

[138]M5, *Asa* 7, AG, p. 396.

[139]M5, *Bhairau* 3, AG, p. 1136. This hymn is a comment on Kabir.

[140]For the explicit rejection of Hindu life-cycle rituals by the Gurus, see Dalbir Singh Dhillon, *Sikhism: Origin and Development* (New Delhi: Oriental Publishers, 1988), pp. 275–9.

[141]Piar Singh, *Gatha Sri Adi Granth*, p. 481. The jajamani system requires that a patron pay a gift or stipend for the services provided by brahmins, bards, barbers and others.

[142]See Mann, 'The Making of Sikh Scripture', p. 217.

can easily sense how the author is at pains to create a tortured rhyme (*jammiā/punniā*), and similar is the case with the last two lines of the hymn (*surā/tūrā*). The use of the clumsy phrase *char jivan* in contrast to Guru Arjan's *chir jivan* is another indication that the author of the additional part was not a good poet. More importantly, it is lacking in the structural unity that is usually achieved by Guru Arjan in his hymns. The overall tone of reading in the original scarcely matches the rhythmic beauty of Guru Arjan's poetic style.

Finally, the theory of the origin of the Banno recension (that I have discussed in detail in my doctoral work[143]) needs to be further qualified in view of the above analysis. The issue of brahminical influence must be considered in the union of Hindali, Udasi and Bhatra interests. We shall return to this issue in Chapter Seven. This Banno interest group, it seems, had a hidden agenda to arrest the process of crystallization of the Sikh tradition. Whereas the elite group of the Panth had developed a strong sense of distinctive identity, a large body of believers was still following brahminical traditions.[144] The Banno group had started to exert its influence within the Panth in the area of Khara Mangat in Gujrat district, while the main centre of Sikh activities under Guru Hargobind had already shifted to Kiratpur. Even the Amritsar area was under the control of Minas, Prithichand's descendants, and their followers. This was a time when apocryphal literature was proliferating under brahminical influence. This is evident from a manuscript containing the text *Sukhamani Sahansarnama* written by Miharban's successor under the symbol of mahalu 8 in 1646 (sambat 1703 manghar sudi 1).[145] This composition is based on the model of Guru Arjan's *Sukhamani* and praises the Vaishnava *avatar*s and other figures from Hindu mythology. It clearly indicates that the process of Hinduization of Sikh tradition had already begun. It was during this period that the Banno bir was copied from the original volume in 1642, although the additional material was interpolated into it some time later. This was an intentional tampering with the Adi Granth text, which was done to legitimize the Hindu life-cycle rituals in the Sikh community by putting words into the mouth of Guru Arjan.[146]

[143]See my 'The Text and Meaning of the Adi Granth,' Chap. 3.

[144]W.H. McLeod, *Who is a Sikh?* p. 18.

[145]See Punjabi University Library, MS # 115600. Also see Piar Singh, *Adi Sakhian*, 3rd edn (Ludhiana: Lahore Book Shop, 1983; 1st edn, 1969), p. 54 for the accretion of the material relating to brahminical rituals in the janam-sakhis.

[146]In this context, Harjot Oberoi's thesis that Sikh life-cycle rituals were introduced

In the light of the textual analysis of the *Ramakali* hymn, let us examine W.H. McLeod's views on the Kartarpur–Banno debate. The following excerpts from his article may prove useful in our analysis:

The nature of these points as recorded in the Banno version suggests an obvious reason for their deletion from the Kartarpur manuscript. They incorporate concepts which would be unacceptable in the light of later [Khalsa] ideals. This particularly applies to a *Ramakali* hymn attributed to Guru Arjan which, in its Banno form, refers to the shaving of child Hargobind's head....

If the additional portions supplied by Banno version correspond to deletions in the Kartarpur manuscript there could conceivably be justification for concluding that Banno represents an earlier recension than Kartarpur....

Let it not be supposed that at this stage I am arguing this case as one which I am personally prepared to affirm. This I am certainly not prepared to do....

There is thus no suggestion that the Kartarpur claims are on the brink of refutation. The point which I am endeavouring to make is simply that we need a sustained campaign of textual analysis if we are to establish a sure and certain text.[147]

Here McLeod argues that the Khalsa ideals could have provided the motive for the deletion (though upon close examination we now know that there is no actual deletion) of the additional portions of the *Ramakali* hymn in the Kartarpur manuscript. I have personally examined folio 703/1 of the Kartarpur manuscript and can therefore affirm that while there is a blank space of more than two folios after the opening verse of the *Ramakali* hymn, there is no evidence of any erasure or any other kind of deletion. If there were such a deletion, it would support the claim that the Banno text may actually represent an earlier recension than the Kartarpur text.

Thus McLeod's hypothesis is a clear case of retrospective interpretation which cannot be convincingly applied to explain the early seventeenth-century Sikh situation. The question of later deletion in this instance cannot be taken seriously since there are a number of seventeenth-century manuscripts of the Adi Granth that do not contain the extra material of the Banno version. Also, the assumption

---

in the Sikh community for the first time as a result of Tat Khalsa reforms in the late nineteenth century, is questionable. Although it reflects the nineteenth-century Sikh situation and is based on the data of that period, it does not take into account the Sikh Gurus' attitude towards Hindu rituals as found in the Adi Granth. See his 'From Ritual to Counter-Ritual,' pp. 136–58.

[147]McLeod, 'The Sikh Scriptures: Some Issues,' pp. 101–3.

that the hymn is somehow related to the puberty rites of Guru Hargobind cannot be sustained. It should be emphasized here, however, that McLeod suspends his final judgement on the Kartarpur–Banno issue and, instead, urges that there be a sustained campaign of textual analysis to establish a sure and certain text. Recently, however, McLeod has revised his position on the issue of Guru Arjan's *Ramakali* hymn.[148]

In concluding the argument of this section it may be stated that the *Ramakali* hymn, as found in the Kartarpur manuscript, never consisted of more than two aphoristic sayings, which may have been uttered by Guru Arjan on the occasion of a marriage. These sayings, which stand recorded in the Kartarpur volume, were perhaps intended to be developed into a complete hymn later. There is another such instance provided by *Var Basant* in the Adi Granth, which, unlike other vars of the Gurus, has only three stanzas.[149] According to tradition, when Guru Arjan had just completed three stanzas of this var, he was informed by a Sikh that *langar* ('communal meal') was ready. He left the work unfinished and joined the congregation for meals.[150] This incomplete composition was recorded in the Kartarpur manuscript much later. Unfortunately Guru Arjan was executed by the Mughal authorities in 1606, before he could complete these compositions. It is my contention that it was the Banno group that completed the *Ramakali* hymn in their version of the Adi Granth in order to legitimize the brahminical life-cycle rituals in the Sikh community. This is my answer to the academic question raised in the Kartarpur–Banno debate that has been going on for the last two decades.

CONCLUSION

It is evident from the textual variations as they appear in the two extant volumes of the Goindval pothis and in the early manuscripts of the Adi Granth that Guru Arjan frequently revised the received

---

[148]In a personal communication, W.H. McLeod writes: 'It provides what I have so long sought, namely a thorough competent textual analysis of certain portions of Sikh scriptures. In the course of so doing you have at last answered the question which I was raising (all of sixteen years ago) of Guru Arjan's two lines in *Ramakali* raga. Prior to this no one had provided me with a satisfactory answer to my concerns. Now, however, that answer has been provided' (personal letter, 1 May 1991).

[149]M5, *Var Basant* AG, p. 1193.

[150]See *Shabadarath*, IV: 1193.

texts in the interest of establishing a canonical scripture.[151] The use of the word sudh ('correct') in the margins of the Kartarpur manuscript in a different hand acquires a new significance in the light of the findings of the present study. Clearly, Guru Arjan would employ it only when he had approved the content, form and organization of the bani in a particular raga section in the first canonical text. He applied meticulous standards to give the scripture its unique form. He used the best possible words to crystallize the divine message. As fifth 'Nanak' he had the spiritual authority to do so. Thus, any decision taken by him with respect to the content and style of the works of his predecessors and of his own composition, would be regarded as final.

During the editorial process, Guru Arjan achieved linguistic refinement through the substitution of synonyms for certain words, and other minor modifications of the text. He took extraordinary care to maintain the original meaning and rhythm of those hymns, which were revised in the final text. Thus no theological change was introduced in the revision of the received texts. His editorial achievement can be seen from the remarkably consistent structure of the Adi Granth. This should, however, be added that there are certain instances where he consciously diverged from consistency. It was meant to provide a deeper theological coherence to the text, a coherence which is not visible on the surface. For this purpose, he sometimes added his own couplet or stanza to the celebrated works of his predecessors.

Variations in the early manuscripts must not be regarded simply as scribal errors in the usual sense, but rather as examples of regional or dialectal forms used in the oral transmission of a singing tradition.[152] This point is generally missed in some of the studies on the manuscripts of the Adi Granth. For instance, G.B. Singh, who did pioneering work on the manuscripts of the Adi Granth, failed to understand the issue of variant readings.[153] Moreover, it should be kept in mind that the Gurmukhi script was not fully developed even at the time when the two extant copies of the Goindval pothis were

---

[151]Bill Readings, 'Canon and On: From Concept to Figure,' *Journal of the American Academy of Religion*, LVII/1 (Chico: Scholars Press, Spring 1989), p. 159.

[152]K.E. Bryant, 'Towards a Critical Edition of the *Surasagar*,' in Winand M. Callewaert, ed., *Early Hindi Devotional Literature in Current Research* (Leuven: Katholieke Universiteit, 1980), p. 12. Also see Winand M. Callewaert, 'Text Analysis with Computer in Devanagari,' in Thiel-Horstmann, ed., *Bhakti in Current Research*, p. 65.

[153]See G.B. Singh, *Prachin Biran*, pp. 80–8.

written. It was during Guru Arjan's period that the Gurmukhi script was standardized with the introduction of proper vowel-signs. As the writing system developed so did the use of proper grammatical constructions.

In order to appreciate the project of canon formation, however, we must not forget other human actors who were involved in the process. In this context, Bhai Gurdas is universally regarded as Guru Arjan's amanuensis in the making of the scripture. His extended visits to Varanasi and Agra were presumably intended to learn the various conventions of Sanskritic learning.[154] His own thirty-nine vars and a series of Braj poems in the *kabitt* style clearly indicate his knowledge of Indian scriptural traditions and philosophical systems. Moreover, there was Jagana Brahman, a resident of Agra, who must have had his own training in the studies of Sanskrit and Hindu scriptures.[155] He was a devout follower of Guru Arjan and a scribe of repute of the correct (sudh) copies of the Adi Granth. The presence of certain Sanskritic conventions in the Kartarpur manuscript clearly points in the direction of this training of the scribes. Incidentally, there are at least four different handwritings discernible at different places, although the major portion of the Kartarpur bir is written by the primary scribe. Thus the preparation of the scripture was the result of teamwork under direct supervision of Guru Arjan.

[154]Harbans Singh, *The Encyclopaedia of Sikhism*, Vol. II, p. 138.
[155]ibid., p. 315.

4

RAGA ORGANIZATION OF
THE ADI GRANTH

> Guru Nanak wished his hymns to be sung to *ragas* that express
> the spirit of the text and performance style to be compatible
> with the meaning of the hymn. The succeeding Gurus
> followed his example. The *ragas* named in the Holy Book
> were selected probably because of their suitability for
> expressing the ideals represented in the texts for which they
> were to be used. Over the centuries *raga* names and the exact
> pitch of tones may have varied. Lack of a precise national
> system for Indian music indicates that the preservation of
> *ragas* has been dependent upon oral tradition.[1]

The creation of the Sikh scripture may be seen as passing through
four main formative stages. First of all, there was the primary
experience of Guru Nanak, reflecting upon his own situation
and that of his society and seeking some intimation of the divine
truth. The verbal expression of that experience was in the form of
poetic compositions of surpassing beauty referred to as the bani of
Guru Nanak. This may be called the stage of primary experience.
This stage must, of course, remain inaccessible to us for scholarly
analysis except by inference from later stages. The second stage began
when Guru Nanak's compositions were used in Sikh liturgy, thereby
passing into oral tradition through memorization, in forms which
became stylized and systematized and developed rich patterns of
symbolic association. In particular, Guru Nanak's bani was used in
devotional singing in the congregational setting at Kartarpur. Even
if it was written down during that period, this must have been simply
a device to facilitate its being memorized by the singers and the
newly emergent Sikh community. It is in the absence of any

[1]Harbans Singh, ed., *The Encyclopaedia of Sikhism*, Vol. II, p. 166.

manuscript of Guru Nanak's original pothi that we must consider its possible features. One can safely argue that at first writing was perceived as simply a mnemonic device to ensure that the oral rendering of gurbani be accurate. It was also meant to preserve Guru Nanak's hymns in the takari or lande forms without any vowel-signs, and the initial impetus must have been to pass on the bani as a legacy for future generations. One should not expect perfection in the earlier written forms by comparing them with modern standards. In its basic sense, however, the bani remained functional as an oral text. This might be called the stage of primary witness.

The third stage began when later generations professed loyalty to the original tradition, adopting its basic message and developing it further in the light of new experiences. In other words, Guru Nanak's successors drew inspiration from his bani and added their own compositions to the evolving corpus of Sikh scriptural tradition. Thus they reinterpreted the message of Guru Nanak in new contexts and laid the foundation for its living survival. The compilation of the Goindval pothis by the third Guru, and then the compilation of the first canonical text by the fifth Guru, were the two most significant developments in the process of consolidation of the Sikh tradition. During this phase, the main effort was to achieve theological coherence. This might be called the stage of theological *rédaction*. Finally, a canon of scripture was defined by the tenth Guru, Gobind Singh, marking a significant completion of a matrix of revelation for the Sikh community. It was believed that the core truths of the tradition had been established irrevocably, and the documents included in the canon were witnesses to these truths in an authoritative way. This might be called the stage of canonical definition.[2]

In this chapter our main concern is to understand how the bani was transmitted orally in the early Sikh community and how that oral transmission played a significant role in the formation of the Sikh canon. The divisions in the middle section of the Adi Granth have been made on the basis of ragas or melodic patterns. The fundamental question that arises is the rationale behind this key organizational principle in the Sikh scripture. In order to find the answer to this question, however, we need to define the key terms and then put this enquiry briefly into the theoretical perspective of

---

[2]These four points of the 'Development of the Canon of Scripture' have been adapted from Keith Ward's work, *Religion and Revelation* (Oxford: Clarendon Press, 1994), pp. 218–21.

the musical tradition of north India. The term raga is derived from a Sanskrit root, *ranj*, which means to colour with emotion; thus the name implies many features beyond those of actual pitches. A raga may be defined as 'a melodic formula that includes particular embellishments and tone colors.'[3] In actual musical performance, any given raga specifies particular combinations of grace notes and microtonal ornaments. In theory, the ragas are composed to suit various moods, intervals of time and specific seasons. Moreover, each raga has acquired a particular spiritual significance of its own on the basis of tradition and usage. That is why great care has been taken in the past centuries as well in modern times with regard to the preservation of exact pitch relationship between the tones of any established raga. Thus in any musical performance one must maintain the exact number of vibrations in order to produce the mood ascribed to a given raga.[4] According to the metaphysical theory of ancient Indian music, the physical vibrations of musical sound (*nada*) were inextricably connected with the spiritual world, so that the validity of a ritual and the stability of the universe were believed to be adversely affected by a faulty intonation of sacred texts.[5]

In Hindustani musical theory there are two important tones (*amsa*) that dominate each raga: the vadi (sonant) and the *samvadi* (co-sonant). The vadi is often considered to be the most important pitch, melodically, in a raga; the samvadi may be secondary in importance. The vadi is often not the ground tone of the raga. The samvadi is usually fourth or fifth above vadi, although like the reciting tones of other musical traditions (such as Christian chant), there are various distributions of fundamental tones.[6] Given the large number of melodic possibilities of various ragas, it is quite logical that music theorists should organize them into related groups. Perhaps the most controversial theory about their arrangements is the one that attempts to determine the times of the day at which specific ragas are most suitable.[7] In describing the relationship

[3] Barbara Stoler Miller, ed. and trans., *Love Song of the Dark Lord: Jayadeva's Gitagovinda* (New York: Columbia University Press, 1977), p. 13.

[4] See Harbans Singh, *The Encyclopaedia of Sikhism*, Vol. II, p. 160.

[5] William P. Malm, *Music Cultures of the Pacific, the Near East, and Asia* (Upper Saddle River, NJ: Prentice-Hall History of Music Series, 3rd edn, 1996; 1st edn, 1967), pp. 115–27.

[6] ibid., p. 119.

[7] O.C. Gangoly, *Ragas and Raginis* (Bombay: Nalanda Publications, 1958; 1st edn, 1935), pp. 90–2 and Walter Kaufmann, *The Ragas of North India* (Bloomington: Indiana University Press, 1968), pp. 14–20.

between ragas and the time of their performance, for instance, Danielou makes the following observation.

The cycle of the day corresponds to the cycle of life which has its dawn, its noon, its evening. Each hour represents a different stage of development and is connected to a certain kind of emotion. The cycle of sounds is ruled by the same laws as all other cycles. This is why there are natural relationships between particular hours and the moods evoked by musical modes.[8]

According to this time theory musicians put emphasis on the *purvang* (first portion, in which the vadi is in the lower tetrachord) in the performance of all ragas between noon and midnight. Similarly, in the ragas performed between midnight and noon the *uttrang* is prominent, that is, the vadi is in the upper tetrachord.[9] In light of this time theory, all the ragas of the Adi Granth are assigned particular time-intervals for their musical performance.[10]

DEVOTIONAL MUSIC IN THE SIKH TRADITION

We need to examine the place of devotional music in the Sikh tradition in the historical context of the sixteenth century. The term kirtan is derived from the Sanskrit root *kirti*, which means singing a devotional song in praise of the lord of the universe. The form of the kirtan was derived from old *prabandha* style of singing, a style which was characterized by the rigour of its rules leaving no place for improvisation. It was a rich and flourishing musical genre from, at least the Gupta age, down to the thirteenth or fourteenth centuries.[11] These early classical songs, commonly known as pada-prabandhas, led to the dhrupad (fixed word) style of music which became popular in north India during the fifteenth and sixteenth centuries. The dhrupad style is slower, much less ornamented and more sedate than the *khayal* style with its allowable freedom.[12] With this transition from

---

[8]Alain Danielou, *The Ragas of Northern Indian Music* (London: Barrie and Rockliff, 1968), p. 95.

[9]N.A. Jairazbhoy, *The Ragas of North Indian Music: Their Structure and Evolution* (London: Faber and Faber, 1971), p. 43.

[10]For more details, see *The Encyclopaedia of Sikhism*, Vol. II, pp. 170–8.

[11]Winand M. Callewaert and Mukand Lath, *The Hindi Padavali of Namdev* (Delhi: Motilal Banarsidass, 1989), p. 56.

[12]See *The Encyclopaedia of Sikhism*, Vol. II, p. 162. Although Amir Khusrau is credited with the invention of the khyal style in the thirteenth century, its popularity did not spread until some centuries later. This style dominates north Indian classical music today.

classical prabandha to dhrupad style, we enter into what Donna Wulff calls the bhakti conception of music, in which 'it is for God and not for an earthly audience that the devotee plays and sings.'[13] It is no wonder that most of the songs of medieval poet-saints were sung in the dhrupad style by the professional singers. Indeed, this style was most suitable to the medieval devotional poetry written in the pad genre in north India. This was one of the styles which became the model for shabad kirtan (hymn-singing) in early Sikh tradition. Apart from the dhrupad style there were other styles of singing such as kafi, dhamar, chhant, and var based on the folk tunes which were quite popular in the Punjab during the period of the Gurus.[14] In this context, Ajit Singh Paintal aptly observes:

The Sikh Gurus adopted only the more vital elements of music in their *kirtan*, but they completely eschewed the dance performed by Vaishnava and Shaiva devotees and by the Sufis in their *sama* gatherings. The Sikh Gurus also rejected the rhythmical clapping with hands with which the Sufis accompanied their singing.[15]

It must be stated here that the discussion of musical styles of north India is as lifeless as the word sonata unless we imagine each in terms of a live musical performance.

It should be emphasized that shabad kirtan has always been an integral part of Sikh worship from the very beginning. According to the janam-sakhis, Guru Nanak kept with him, as life-long companion, a Muslim musician, Mardana, who used to play the *rabab* (rebeck) while he sang the praises of Akal Purakh. All the old murals and paintings show the two of them sitting together in a musical performance. Bhai Gurdas acknowledges Mardana as the professional *rababi* (rebeck-player) who accompanied Guru Nanak on his missionary tours.[16] A careful analysis of Guru Nanak's works reveals that he stressed on the mode of devotional singing as the only efficacious means of liberation: 'It is through singing of divine praises that we find a place in the lord's court.'[17] Further, he describes

[13]Donna Marie Wulff, 'On Practising Religiously: Music as Sacred in India', in Joyce Irwin, ed., *Sacred Sound: Music in Religious Thought and Practice* (Chico: Scholars Press, 1983), p. 157.

[14]D.S. Narula, 'Guru-Sahiban di Samakalin Bharti-Sangit-Parampara', in Satbir Singh and Gurnam Singh, eds, *Simriti Granth: Aduti Gurmat Sangit Samelan 1991* (Ludhiana: Gurdwara Gur Gian Prakash, 1991), pp. 4–7.

[15]Ajit Singh Paintal, 'The Traditions of Sikh Devotional Music', in ibid., p. 50.

[16]*Varan Bhai Gurdas* 1: 35.

[17]M1, *Var Majh* 2 (12), AG, p. 143.

the ecstasy that devotional music evokes in the *Asa* mode:

The jewel-like ragas along with their fairy families (wives and sons), are the source of the essence of the 'nectar of immortality' (amrit). This wealth belongs to the creator—Few they be who realize this.

(M1, *Asa* 9, AG, p. 351)

Here, the expression *raga ratan parian parivar* (the jewel-like ragas along with their fairy wives and sons) clearly indicates Guru Nanak's familiarity with the gender-based raga–ragini system which was prevalent at that time. This complex system originated, it seems, when Narda, the author of *Panchama-Sara-Samhita* (*c.* 600–900), called subordinate ragas as raginis for the first time. Another famous music theorist, Mesha Karana, a contemporary of Guru Nanak, wrote his *Raga-mala* (1509) in which he classified his material into six head ragas, each having five female ragas (raginis) and eight sons (putra), for a total of eighty-four ragas.[18] In fact, this classification corresponds closely to the one found in the *Raga-mala* at the end of the Adi Granth. We shall return to this issue in the final section.

For Guru Nanak, the ethical aspects of devotional music must always take precedence over its technical performance. Mere singing of devotional songs in melodic patterns is of no good if one's heart is full of hypocrisy (*kapat*).[19] That is why devotional music must always be seen as a means of spiritual development rather than as a source of entertainment. Moreover, Guru Nanak strongly criticized the voluptuous indulgence in secular music popular among the upper classes at that time.

False are those songs, musical measures and reverberating accompaniments, which arouse the three qualities (of maya) and, destroying devotion, draw people away from the divine. Suffering cannot be removed by duality and evil thinking. Liberation is achieved through the teachings of the Guru, and the singing of the divine praises is the true remedy for life's ills.

(M1, *Bilavalu Astapadian* 2, AG, p. 832)

Clearly, any musical performance that takes people away from Akal Purakh does not find approval in Guru Nanak's bani. At the same time, singing of the divine praises is acknowledged as the panacea for all the sufferings of the world. For the sake of convenience, therefore, we must distinguish between the secular and sacred contexts in which particular musical performances take place. Similarly, it is crucial to

---

[18]See *The Encyclopaedia of Sikhism*, Vol. II, p. 158.
[19]M1, *Prabhati Astapadian* 1, AG, p. 1342.

understand the actual context of Guru Nanak's bani to see his attitude towards those performances.

Guru Nanak employed nineteen major ragas for his bani, whereas Guru Amar Das used seventeen of them for his own compositions. It is worth noting that the first major collection of bani was arranged, keeping in mind the needs of the singers. This is evident from the two available copies of the Goindval pothis, which are arranged according to ragas. This tradition of organizing collections of devotional songs in accordance with ragas may be seen in the eleventh century *Gorakh-bani*, Jayadeva's *Gita Govinda* (1200) and other medieval collections of religious songs.[20] In fact, this tradition was well established during the sixteenth century. The newly found Fatehpur manuscript of the padas of Surdas, compiled in 1582, was based on this tradition of raga division as a principle of organization.[21] Guru Amar Das continued this tradition when he compiled the Goindval volumes. In order to understand this key principle of organization, however, we need to examine the structure of the two available copies of the Goindval pothis more thoroughly.

In the context of the present discussion, Gurinder Singh Mann has offered a preliminary analysis of the raga structure of the Goindval pothis from two angles.[22] First, the raga titles of the two volumes indicate a clear acceptance of gender distinction which is evident from such titles as *Suhi Babe Di* ([hymn] by Guru Nanak in *Suhi* mode, which is a female raga), *Basant Babe Da* ([hymn] by Guru Nanak in *Basant* mode, which is a male raga) and so on. Although the name ragini is not used in the extant volumes, the Punjabi postpositions di and da refer to feminine and masculine genders respectively. Obviously, the compiler of the two available copies of the Goindval pothis was aware of the contemporary gender-based categorization in the musical tradition of north India. Mann's argument of 'an interesting balance' of female and male ragas in the manuscripts, however, becomes strained when he fails to fit the [male] *Tilang* mode in the Jalandhar pothi. Nevertheless, his

---

[20]P.D. Barthwal, ed., *Gorakh-bani* (Allahabad: Hindi Sahitya Sammelan, 2nd edn, 1946) and Miller, *Love Song of the Dark Lord*. The twenty-four songs of *Gita Govinda* have been associated with eleven different ragas.

[21]Gopal Narayan Bahura, ed., *The Padas of Surdas* (Jaipur: Maharaja Swami Man Singh II Museum Trust, 1982). The structure of the later part of the manuscript has the following raga sections: *Bilaval, Asavari, Dhanasari, Gujari, Gauri, Kalayan, Kanara,* and *Kedara* with one hymn of *Malhar* at the beginning and two at the end.

[22]Gurinder Singh Mann, 'The Making of Sikh Scripture', pp. 134–7.

argument that female ragas precede the male ragas in the structure of the extant pothis reflects his concern to present the textual evidence from a modern feminist perspective.

Second, Mann argues that the raga sequence of the Goindval pothis may be seen to fit in the raga scheme of the writings of Pundarika Vitthala, a sixteenth-century south Indian commentator on the music of north India. Accordingly, the ragas *Suhi, Prabhati, Dhanasari, Basant* and *Bhairau* of the Jalandhar volume are recorded as morning ragas in Vitthala's scheme. Once again, the *Tilang* raga which is normally sung at night creates difficulties in Mann's analysis. The Pinjore volume includes ragas *Ramakali, Sorathi, Malhar* and *Sarang*. The opening raga *Ramakali* could be sung at all times, according to Vitthala, although it is normally sung in the morning. Both *Malhar* and *Sarang* are associated with the uncertainty of rainy season, and thus they could be assigned to various times of the day. However, raga *Sorathi*, which is sung in the first quarter of the night, fails to fit the 'neat scheme' of Mann's arguments. He acknowledges that 'with the exception of *rag vadhansu* in the pothi that Gian Singh saw at Patiala, *rag sorathi* in the pothi at Pinjore, and *rag majh* in the fourth pothi, all of which do not appear in the scheme of Vitthal, the *rag* affinity based on time seems to be the rationale for *rag* combinations in all of the Goindval *pothis*.'[23] Further, Mann argues that the pothi at Jalandhar (Volume I) and the pothi seen by Gian Singh (Volume III) contain the *Purba* and the pothi at Pinjore (Volume II) and the fourth one (Volume IV) the *Uttra* ragas.[24] That is, the first set of Volumes I and III employ the purvang in the performance of all ragas between noon and midnight. Similarly, the second set of Volumes II and IV employ the uttrang in the performance of all ragas between midnight and noon. As we have already noticed, there are certain difficulties with this scheme. Moreover, six major ragas out of the nineteen ragas of the Goindval pothis such as *Majh, Asa, Vadahansu, Sorathi, Tilang,* and *Tukhari* do not occur in any work of Pundarika Vitthala.[25] Thus Mann's hypothesis cannot be convincingly applied to explain the raga structure of the Goindval pothis, even though it may initially seem plausible.

[23]ibid., p. 136.

[24]ibid., p. 137.

[25]See the list of ragas in Vitthala's works in V.N. Bhatkhande, *A Comparative Study of Some of the Leading Music Systems of the 15th, 16th, 17th, & 18th Centuries* (Delhi: Low Price Publications, reprint, 1990), pp. 50, 54, 59.

Instead of imposing fixed categories from classical musical tradition of north India on the structure of the Goindval pothis, we need to look at the actual data of the two extant volumes more closely. For instance, there are certain musical directions inserted in the text at a number of places. Note the following examples:

Mahalu 3 Suhi: 'Loved friends have arrived at my home' (*Mahalu 3 Suhi: ham ghari sajan ae*).

Suhi Chhand Mahalu 3: According [to the tune] of 'Come, beloved friend' (*prathai Suhi Chhand Mahalu 3: avahu sajana ham*).

'Come, beloved friend, that I may behold your sight!' These lyrics are to be sung to the tune of the above hymn (*avahu sajana darasanu dekhahu tera ram chhand etu dhuni gavan parathai hoe*).[26]

In the first instance, it is stated that Guru Amar Das's lyrical hymn *sukh sohilara hari dhiavahu* (meditate on the lord by chanting the joyous song) must be sung to the tune of Guru Nanak's lyrical hymn *ham ghari sajan ae* (loved friends have arrived at my home). In the second and third instances, the two musical directions explicitly state that Guru Amar Das's lyrical hymns (chhand) must be sung to the tune of Guru Nanak's lyrical hymn *avahu sajana darasanu dekhahu tera ram* (come, beloved friend, that I may behold your sight). All these musical directions concerning the chhants reveal an important fact that they were sung in the popular folk tunes used at the time of weddings or other happy occasions. Further, the oral transmission of popular tunes in a fixed form was ensured through these directions in the early Sikh community.

There is another striking instance on folio 124 of the Jalandhar pothi with the following musical instruction: 'Raga *Dhanasari* should be sung first at the balcony' (*chaubarai gavai pahila ragu dhanasari*).[27] If this was indeed the case, then the two available volumes are definitely not the original Goindval pothis. The reason for this is as follows. According to Bhai Gurdas, when Guru Amar Das bypassed his own two sons and appointed Guru Ram Das as the fourth Guru, Mohan became crazy (*kamala*) and Mohri got the *chaubara* (balcony) built for him to establish the seat of parallel guruship.[28] The two available copies of the Goindval pothis were prepared much later, and the reference to chaubara in the above musical instruction

---

[26]Piar Singh, *Gatha*, p. 100.

[27]Gurinder Singh Mann, *The Goindval Pothis: The Earliest Extant Sources of the Sikh Canon*, p. 175, n. 53.

[28]*Varan Bhai Gurdas* 26: 33.

clearly points in this direction. In fact, there was no need for Guru Amar Das to write this kind of strange instruction in the original Goindval pothis. The tradition of singing raga *Dhanasari* in the balcony began only after Mohan had fully established his parallel guruship. The real worth of the two extant volumes emerges only when we identify the circles as well as the circumstances in which they originated.

Further, there is frequent use of dakkhani (southern) forms of ragas in the two available pothis, the forms of popular regional varieties that were employed in the south (*dakkhan*) as defined from the Goindval area. These forms must have been employed by the Sikh community from the Multan and Sindh areas. This is obvious from such titles as *Ragu Suhi Chhand Dakhani* (I, f. 31), *Ragu Suhi Dakkhani* (I, f. 52), *Ragu Parabhati Dakkhani* (I, f. 70), *Ragu Parabhati Dakkhani Astapadian* (I, f. 86), *Ragu Dhanasari Dakkhani* (I, f. 148), *Ragu Basant Dakkhani* (I, f. 203), *Ragu Bhairau Dakkhani* (I, f. 231), *Ragu Ramakali Dakkhani* (II, f. 12), *Ragu Ramakali Dakkhani* (II, f. 24), *Ragu Ramakali Dakkhani Siddhi Gosti* (II, f. 55), *Ragu Malhar Dakkhani* (II, f. 188), *Ragu Malhar Dakkhani* (II, f. 204), *Ragu Malhar Astapadian Dakkhani* (II, f. 205), *Ragu Sarang Dakkhani* (II, f. 216), and *Ragu Sarang Astapadian Dakkhani* (II, f. 218). Interestingly, all these titles appear only at the beginning of Guru Nanak's hymns. Nowhere do they appear as the titles of Guru Amar Das's hymns (or even any bhagat's compositions). This surprising number of instances cannot be considered as just accidental.[29] They throw considerable light on the popularity of Guru Nanak's bani among the southern audiences who employed the tunes of ragas from the south Indian (or Karnatak) musical tradition. Thus any attempt to superimpose a particular theory from the north Indian tradition of music will not do justice to the raga organization of the Sikh scriptural tradition.

Guru Ram Das introduced another musical dimension to the Sikh tradition by adding eleven new major ragas to the set of nineteen ragas that he inherited from his predecessors.[30] He employed technical terms to provide direction in the musical performance of

---

[29]This significant point escaped the attention of Gurinder Singh Mann, who simply writes: 'The frequent use of *dakhani* (southern) forms of *ragas* available in the Goindval *pothis* is considerably trimmed in the Kartarpur *pothi*.' See 'The Making of Sikh Scripture', p. 139.

[30]For details on Guru Ram Das' knowledge of music, see Surjit Hans, *A Reconstruction of Sikh History from Sikh Literature* (Jalandhar: ABS Publications, 1988), pp. 91–4.

his hymns. For instance, the use of the word *sudhang* (pure note) in the title of *Asavari* mode clearly indicates that his hymns must be sung by using the pure notes of that raga.[31] Callewaert and Lath did not understand the significance of this word sudhang in their brief analysis of the pattern of arrangement within the *Asa* mode, and they simply put a question mark after this title.[32] Indeed, Guru Ram Das himself used to sing kirtan in classical ragas. Note the following reference in which he expresses the joy of having performed in the mode of *Bilaval*:

I have lauded the exalted lord, the supreme master, in the tune of *Bilaval*. I have faithfully followed the Guru's teachings, by great fortune, ordained from the beginning. All recite lord's praises day and night with constant devotion in their hearts. My mind and body are in bloom like a fresh garden. The gloom of ignorance is lifted by the lamp of enlightenment lit by the Guru. Says Nanak: the servant finds life from beholding the lord's face, even though it be for a short span of time.

(M4, *Var Bilaval* 1 (1), AG, p. 849)

Clearly, this shalok highlights the fact that *Bilaval* is a raga expressive of joy. Through his personal experience Guru Ram Das explicitly states that true joy comes not from melody but from constancy of devotion. That is, even in his praise of the ecstatic performance of *Bilaval* raga, it is devotion (bhakti) to the Guru that takes precedence over music.

There is another significant instance in the *Nat-narayan* raga, where Guru Ram Das prescribes a change of drum-rhythms (*paratal*) after each verse while singing those particular hymns.[33] Here Guru Ram Das must be referring to the rhythms of *pakhavaj* (a two-ended barrel-shaped drum), since *tabla* (a pair of small kettle drums) was invented in 1725.[34] In fact, the tabla is not mentioned in the *Ain-i-Akbari* catalogue of musical instruments which Abul Fazl compiled for the Emperor Akbar.[35] There are different theories about the invention of the tabla. According to one account, the invention of tabla is attributed to a different Amir Khusrau who lived in the

---

[31]M4, *Asavari Sudhang* 14–15, AG, pp. 369–70. For more dtails on *Sudh Asavari*, see Jairazbhoy, *The Ragas of North Indian Music*, pp. 165–6.

[32]Callewaert and Lath, *The Hindi Padavali of Namdev*, p. 96.

[33]M4, *Nat-narayan Paratal* 7–9, AG, pp. 977–8.

[34]Stewart Rebecca, 'The Tabla in Perspective' (Ph.D. dissertation, University of California, Los Angeles, 1974), pp. 6–7.

[35]Cited in Robert S. Gottlieb, *Solo Tabla Drumming of North India: Its Repertoire, Styles, and Performance Practices*, Vol. I (Delhi: Motilal Banarsidass, 1993), p. 2.

eighteenth century. It is further suggested that the pakhavaj was cut into two halves to form the tabla. Another explanation traces the origin of tabla from the puskara drums such as are depicted in the temple carvings at Muktesvara and Bhuvanesvara (*c.* 6th–7th centuries). The drummers are shown seated, playing on sets of two or three small drums with their hands. Indian musicologists support this theory that the puskara drums were forerunners of tabla. Given the varying accounts, however, it may be safely argued that although different drums—the *naqqara, dukkar,* pakhavaj, and the ancient puskara— may have contributed to the development of the tabla, it was only in the eighteenth century that the modern tabla performance became popular.[36]

Our main concern here is about the *paratal gayaki,* a musical style based on the changing of drum-rhythms, which was introduced in the Sikh tradition by Guru Ram Das. This style was further developed by Guru Arjan. There are fifty-five hymns of both Guru Ram Das and Guru Arjan in *Asa, Dhanasari, Suhi, Bilaval, Ramakali, Nat-narayan, Bhairau, Sarang, Malhar, Kanara,* and *Prabhati* ragas which must be sung in paratal style.[37] In this style, different parts of the same shabad are sung in different *tala* (drum rhythms) such as *tintal, chautal, dhamar, sulphakte, jhaptal, chanchal, dipchandi, ada* (*ara-chautal*), *kahirava, dadara,* and so on. In this context, Ajit Singh Paintal observes: 'While singing Partal composition, Ragis enjoyed complete freedom to create variety by employing different Talas for various parts of the shabad. Such composition can only be rendered by well-versed Ragis.'[38] It is important to note that the ministry of Guru Ram Das and Guru Arjan was during the period of the reign of Emperor Akbar, which was certainly the peak time of north Indian music. It is no wonder that professional musicians frequently performed in the court of the Gurus.

FINAL SEQUENCE OF THE RAGAS IN THE ADI GRANTH

Guru Arjan evidently inherited a rich musical tradition from his father. He employed the same thirty major ragas for his own bani as were used by his father. At the time of preparing the first canonical text of the Adi Granth, he established the sequence of the ragas after working on a number of early traditions. This is evident from

[36]ibid., pp. 1–8.
[37]Amritpal Kaur, 'Paratal Gayan Shaili', in *Simriti Granth –1991*, pp. 26–9.
[38]See Paintal, 'The Traditions of Sikh Devotional Music', p. 51.

comparing the arrangement of ragas in the two available Goindval pothis, GNDU MS 1245 and in the Kartarpur manuscript. He did not accept the gender-based classification of the ragas of the Goindval pothis. He also shifted certain hymns from one raga to another to locate them on the basis of themes. Obviously, he had intended to compile a scripture with theological as well as musicological coherence in mind. For instance, the combined title of *Maru-Kedara* in the Goindval pothis is not allowed in the Kartarpur volume, and the hymns of the two ragas are recorded under each raga separately. Moreover, raga *Tukhari* has been inserted between the sequence of these two ragas. The reason for this change may be stated as follows.

Traditionally, *Maru* raga is associated with the setting of goals at the time of 'blowing of a bugle' before battle: 'The coward cannot stand [the scene of the battlefield] when the bugle of *Maru* is blown.'[39] Its main theme is related to the battle which is fought within oneself against the five evil impulses of lust, anger, covetousness, attachment to worldly things and pride.

One should meditate through the Guru's word and become detached through the love of the divine name. Thus one should win over five enemies [of evil impulses], Nanak, this is indeed the successful performance of the *Maru* raga.   (M5, *Salok Varan Te Vadhik* 3, AG, p. 1425)

Clearly, *Maru* raga is linked with the burning heat of the war. There was a need to introduce the cooling effect of *Tukhari* (Sanskrit *tushar*, 'winter frost') raga. In this context, Guru Amar Das's assertion that the divine name 'makes the burning heat of sand cold' (*maru te sital kare*) seems valid.[40] After the *Tukhari* raga comes *Kedara*, which is associated with the raising of the flag of victory: 'The tune of *Kedara* is taken from the flapping of the flag in the wind.'[41] Again, the successful performance of the *Kedara* raga depends upon 'one's love for the Guru's word.'[42] Thus the introduction of the *Tukhari* raga between *Maru* and *Kedara* was intended to create a balanced effect in one's mind so that one keeps one's cool even in victory.

There are thirty-one major ragas and twenty-nine regional varieties of certain ragas, which are used in the final version of the Adi Granth. It has been claimed that out of these, five major ragas, namely *Majh*,

---

[39]Satbir Singh, 'Sri Guru Granth Sahib vich Ragan di Taratib', in *Simriti Granth—1991*, p. 7.

[40]M3, *Maru* 5, AG, p. 994.

[41]See Satbir Singh, 'Sri Guru Granth Sahib de Ragan di Taratib', p. 7.

[42]M3, *Var Maru* 1 (2), AG, p. 1087.

Asa, Vadahans, Maru, and *Tukhari* are unique to the Sikh tradition. Similarly, there are seventeen regional varieties that are to be found only in the Adi Granth. These are: *Gauri-guareri, Gauri-bairagan, Gauri-dipaki, Gauri-purabi-dipaki, Gauri-majh, Gauri-malava, Gauri-mala, Gauri-sorathi, Asa-kafi, Tilang-kafi, Suhi-kafi, Suhi-lalit, Bilaval-gaund, Maru-kafi, Basant-hindol, Prabhati-bibhas* and *Bibhas-prabhati*.[43] Apart from these exceptions, all other musical modes used in the Adi Granth may be traced back to the musical tradition of north India at that time. It is important to note that the *Asa* raga was employed by Guru Nanak for most of his compositions. It was his favourite raga, and that is why it has always been a part of early morning Sikh kirtan. The early morning singing of *Var Asa* at the Golden Temple and other gurdwaras is a particularly major Sikh tradition.[44] Apart from the Sikh tradition the *Asa* raga is now found only in the musical tradition of Afghanistan, not in the musical tradition of north India.[45] Further, ragas *Maru* and *Vadahans* are found in the list of the *Raga Trangini* (*c.* fourteenth century) of Lochana Pandit.[46] Thus the claim that certain ragas and their varieties are unique to the Adi Granth needs to be further explored in the light of other contemporary musical traditions (both Indian and Islamic) prevalent in the Punjab of those days.

The main concern at this point is not to study the technical nature of the ragas of the Adi Granth, but rather to explore the reasons for the Gurus' choice of particular modes and their organization in the final text. The division of the first canonical text into thirty ragas by Guru Arjan may have been inspired by the system of thirty *gramaragas* developed in the musical treatise *Brhaddesi* (late first millennium) attributed to sage Matanga.[47] In particular, the use of *Prabhati bibhas* was certainly based on *gramaraga-bhasa* system, since bhasa gave rise to variants called *vibhasas*.[48] Here, we begin with the question why Guru Arjan placed

---

[43]Devinder Singh Vidiarthi, 'Gurbani ate Raga', *Khoj Patrika*, No. 26 (Patiala: Punjabi University, September 1985), pp. 248–9.

[44]See Madanjit Kaur, *The Golden Temple: Past and Present* (Amritsar: Guru Nanak Dev University, 1983), p. 121.

[45]Personal interview with Professor James Kippen, Faculty of Music, University of Toronto.

[46]Bhatkhande, *Leading Musical Systems*, p. 21.

[47]See Richard Widdess, *The Ragas of Early Indian Music: Modes, Melodies and Musical Notations from the Gupta Period to c.1250* (Oxford: Clarendon Press, 1995), pp. 10–12.

[48]ibid.

Siri raga at the beginning and *Prabhati* at the end. The following answers may be offered for the placement of *Siri* raga at the beginning. First, it is linked with Guru Amar Das's assertion that 'the *Siri* raga is chief among the ragas.'[49] Second, the *Raga-mala* also makes the same assertion that 'all [ragas] sing the praise of *Siri* raga.' Third, Bhai Gurdas describes the understanding of his times when the *Siri* raga was acknowledged as 'chief' among the ragas.[50]

Finally, in two other contemporary musical traditions of Shaiva and Kali Nath schools, the position of *Siri* raga was regarded as number one.[51] Moreover, the character of *Siri* raga is mysterious, gentle, and often depicts the meditative aspect of love and the nostalgic prayerful mood of early evening.[52] For instance, Guru Nanak's opening hymn in *Siri* raga sets the tone of the Adi Granth by focusing on the meditation of the divine name in contrast to worldly powers, represented by palaces adorned with pearls and gems, fragrant scents, the dalliance of attractive women, the miraculous powers of the Siddhas and the temporal power of the kings.[53]

Similarly, the position of *Prabhati* raga at the end of the first canonical text of the Adi Granth appears to be based on the following reasons. First, the message of the divine name is reinforced in the *Prabhati* raga. The most striking example is the correspondence between the rahau-verses of Guru Nanak's first hymn in the *Siri* raga and his last hymn in the *Prabhati* mode.

1. May my heart burn in flames should I live without the Lord![54]
2. May my life burn in flames without the divine Name![55]

The emphasis in both cases is placed upon the divine name as the ultimate solution to one's problems. Guru Arjan may have adopted

---

[49]M3, *Var Siri Raga* 1 (1), AG, p. 83.

[50]*Kabitt Bhai Gurdas*: 376.

[51]See Charan Singh's article, 'Gurmat Sangit', included as Appendix I in Vir Singh (*samp.*), *Sri Guru Granth Kosh*, Vol. III (Amritsar: Khalsa Tract Society, 4th edn, 1954), p. 1184.

[52]Kaufmann, *The Ragas of North India*, p. 226.

[53]M1, *Siri Ragu* 1, AG, p. 14. All the thirty-three hymns of Guru Nanak (AG, pp. 14–26) stress the same theme, that is, the supremacy of the divine name over worldly powers.

[54]ibid., p. 14.

[55]M1, *Prabhati* 17, AG, p. 1332. All the seventeen hymns of Guru Nanak in this raga (AG, pp. 1327–32) stress the message of the divine name.

the ancient rule of *upakram-upasanhar* of Indian scriptural tradition, which states that a scripture or any of its sections must begin and end with the same letter or theme.[56]

Secondly, the *Prabhati* raga is sung at sunrise. The word *prabhati* is derived from *prabhat*, which means dawn. Thus the singing of this raga is meant to inspire optimism in one at the beginning of a new day. Thirdly, it is commonly held in Indian musical tradition that the most important periods of the twenty-four hours of day and night are sunrise and sunset.[57] In this context, one may understand why Guru Arjan placed the *Siri* raga, which is performed at sunset, at the beginning of the Adi Granth, and why he placed the *Prabhati* raga, which is performed at sunrise, at the end of the Sikh scripture. In this way, Guru Arjan may have reiterated the spirit of optimism at the end of the Adi Granth. In other words, the performance of *Siri* raga in the evening prepares one for the dark night of *Sorathi* raga representing the worldly powers in life, whereas the *Prabhati* raga shows the light at the end of the tunnel. All other ragas are assigned other time intervals between sunrise and sunset.[58]

It should be emphasized, however, that *Prabhati* is not the last raga in the text which eventually came to be regarded as the Adi Granth. The final version of the Sikh scripture ends with *Jaijavanti* raga. This raga, in which his four hymns on the *memento mori* theme are composed, is the contribution of Guru Tegh Bahadur. No other Guru has employed this raga for his compositions. The final position of the *Jaijavanti* raga was fixed only after experimentation with two different positions in the raga sequence of the Adi Granth. In certain manuscripts, *Jaijavanti* comes after the *Jaitsari* mode,[59] while in some other instances it comes after the *Gauri* mode.[60] *Jaijavanti* is a highly majestic raga which is assigned to the night hours. Its performance is associated with the feeling of victory (*jai jai*) over worldly temptations. With its final position in the raga sequence, the cycle of time is complete.

[56]Mohinder Kaur Gill, *Guru Granth Sahib di Sampadan-kala* (Amritsar: New Age Book Centre, 2nd edn, 1982), p. 38.

[57]Kaufmann, *The Ragas of North India*, p. 16.

[58]For details, see *The Encyclopaedia of Sikhism*, Vol. II, pp. 170–8.

[59]See Harjas MS (late seventeenth century), ff. 283b–284a, where *Jaijavanti* comes after *Jaitsari* raga. In Jograj MS (1667), raga *Jaijavanti* was inserted in the margins after *Jaitsari* on folio 315a. Also see IOL MSS Panj. D 1 (1848), f. 342a.

[60]See IOL, MSS Panj F. 1 (1758), f. 188a where *Jaijavanti* was first written after the *Gauri* raga, but it was deleted with the use of hartal. The text is still visible. Then *Jaijavanti* was written after the *Jaitsari* raga on folio 357b.

There is an interesting entry of the 'index of indices' in the Kartarpur manuscript which divides the thirty ragas into eight groups as given in Table 4.1.

Table 4.1 'Index of Indices' in the Kartarpur Manuscript

Group	Folio	Raga
I.	3	*siriraga tatha majh tatha gauri*
II.	6	*asa tatha gujari dev gandhari*
III.	9	*bihagara vadahans sorathi*
IV.	10	*dhanasari jaitsari todi bairari tilang*
V.	12	*suhi bilavalu gond ramakali*
VI.	15	*nat mali gaura maru tukhari kedara*
VII.	17	*bhairau basant sarang malhar kanara*
VIII.	20	*kalyan tatha bibhas prabhati*[61]

The folio number for each group indicates that all the hymns of the ragas are written in their respective folios, beginning with the first group in folio 3 and ending with the last group in folio 20. Thus the index of all the hymns of the Adi Granth ragas is completed on folio 20. Our primary concern here is to examine these eight groups and assess whether there is any rationale behind these groups that could explain the raga organization of the Adi Granth.

It may be suggested that these eight groups were originally related to eight *chaunki*s (sittings) of kirtan that were established as part of the daily routine at Harimandir Sahib during the period of Guru Arjan. This tradition of eight chaunkis of *ragis* (Sikh musicians) and seven chaunkis of rababis was well alive when the British took control of Darbar Sahib after the annexation of the Punjab in 1849. This is evident from the *Dastur al-'Aml Sri Darbar Sahib*, a document which was prepared and signed by a large number of Sardars and the functionaries of the Golden Temple in the presence of the Deputy Commissioner of Amritsar in 1859.[62] The author of *Sri Gurbilas Patashahi 6* (early nineteenth century), however, describes the following five chaunkis: (1) *Asa di Var di chaunki* (early morning); (2) *Anand di chaunki* (one and a half hour after sunrise); (3) *Charan Kanval di chaunki* (four hour after sunrise); (4) *So Dar di chaunki* (evening); and (5) *Kanare di chaunki* (late

[61]Kartarpur MS, f. 2/2.
[62]Giani Kirpal Singh, 'Sri Harimandir Sahib dian Kirtan Chaunkian', in *Simriti Granth—1991*, pp. 17–19. Also See Ian J. Kerr, 'The British and the Administration of the Golden Temple in 1859', in *The Punjab Past and Present*, Vol. 10, Part 2 (October 1976), pp. 306–21.

night).[63] The Persian work *Sair-i-Punjab* gives the number of chaunkis as six: (1) *Asa di chaunki* (before sunrise); (2) *Ramkali di chaunki* (one and a half hour after sunrise); (3) *Bilaval di chaunki* (four hours after sunrise); (4) *Sarang di chaunki* (afternoon); (5) *Rahiras di chaunki* (evening); and (6) *Kanare di chaunki* (three hours after sunset).[64] Sant Sham Singh (*c*. 1800–1923) who performed kirtan at the Golden Temple early in the morning with his *siranda* (a specially designed string instrument) for nearly half a century, mentioned in his *Hari Bhagati Premakar Granth* (1913) the tradition of eight chaunkis of ragis and several chaunkis of rababis by their names.[65]

The number of the chaunkis have, however, been variously described by twentieth-century scholars. For instance, W.H. McLeod gives their number as four, as follows: *Asa di Var di chaunki* (early morning); *Bilaval di chaunki* (four hours after sunrise); *Raharasi di chaunki* (immediately before the recitation of raharas); and *Kalyan di chaunki* (immediately before kirtan sohila).[66] McLeod seems to have followed Kahn Singh Nabha's description with a slight change in the name of *Charan Kanval di chauki* which he writes as *Bilaval di chauki*.[67] Currently there are five acknowledged chaunkis of devotional singing at the Golden Temple. These are: *Asa di Var di chaunki, Anand di chaunki, Charan Kanval di chaunki, So Dar di chaunki,* and *Kirtan Sohile di chaunki*.[68] The point that I am trying to make here is that the numbers and names of the chaunkis have been changing from time to time. More importantly, we need to assess whether the original classification of the ragas into eight groups is valid or not.

The first set of three groups of ragas I, III and VI belong to the purvang and all the ragas in these groups are sung between noon and midnight, particularly in the evening and the first quarter of the

[63]Giani Inder Singh Gill (*samp.*, i.e. editor), *Sri Guru Bilas Patashahi 6* (Amritsar: Vazir Hind Press, 1977), pp. 153–4.

[64]Cited in Devinder Singh Vidiarathi, *Kirtan: Sandarabh ate Sarup* (Patiala: Punjabi University, 1992), p. 138.

[65]ibid., pp. 138–9. A cyclostyled copy of *Hari Bhagati Premakar Granth* (1913) is preserved in the Sikh History Research Department at Khalsa College, Amritsar. The description of chaunkis is given on folio 286a.

[66]W.H. McLeod, *Historical Dictionary of Sikhism* (Lanham, Md., & London: The Scarecrow Press, 1995), p. 61.

[67]Kahn Singh Nabha, *Gurshabad Ratanakar Mahan Kosh* (Patiala: Bhasha Vibhag, 4th edn 1981; originally published in 1930), p. 463.

[68]Giani Kirpal Singh, 'Sri Harimandir Sahib dian Kirtan Chaunkian', pp. 17–18.

night. The second set of two groups II and V belong to uttrang and all the ragas in these groups are sung between midnight and noon, particularly early in the morning and before noon. The last set of three groups IV, VII and VIII cannot be rigidly categorized according to these two methods. For instance, the two ragas in group VIII are *Kalyan* and *Prabhati*, one of which is sung in the first part of the night while the other is sung at sunrise. In other words, *Kalyan* belongs to the purvang while *Prabhati* belongs to the uttrang. Similarly, the ragas of group IV have their own time-intervals of the day and night and belong to both purvang and uttrang categories. The ragas of group VII are, however, organized according to a different criterion in mind, a criterion which is based upon a seasonal setting. For instance, the four ragas *Bhairau, Basant, Sarang,* and *Malhar* are appropriate to autumn, spring, summer, and the rains respectively.[69] These ragas can be sung and played any time of the day and night during the season allotted to them. The specificity of time in the case of seasonal ragas is relaxed. The singing of *Basant* raga at the Golden Temple, for instance, begins on the first day of the month of magh at the time of Maghi festival in the middle of January and continues for the next two months till the festival of Hola Mahalla which usually falls in March.

Further, some ragas are linked with particular regions. For instance, the *Majh* raga is unique to the Punjabi culture because of its association with the Majha region. There are eleven regional varieties of *Gauri* raga alone, which are used in the Adi Granth. Some of these melodies are associated with certain social groups. For instance, *Gauri-guareri* was sung by milkmen and milkwomen while *Gauri-bairagan* was usually performed by *bairagis* or ascetics.[70] Further, there are certain regional varieties such as *Gauri-dakkhani, Vadahans-dakkhani, Bilaval-dakkhani, Ramakali-dakkhani, Maru-dakkhani* and *Prabhati- dakkhani,* which were influenced by the musical tradition of the Deccan in south India. Their use in the Adi Granth may perhaps be seen as a symbolic expression of the Sikh claim to universality, which would embrace a southern audience.

Moreover, there are many regional and folk traditions that maintain independent styles. One should never underestimate the

---

[69]See Frederic Pincott, 'The Arrangement of the Hymns of the Adi Granth', *Journal of the Royal Asiatic Society*, Vol. XVIII (Calcutta, 1878), p. 442.

[70]Callewaert and Lath, *The Hindi Padavali of Namdev*, p. 95.

sociological significance of this medium and its message. For instance, there are twenty-two vars (ballads) in the Adi Granth. They are sung by performing groups of three or four dhadis (minstrels) in popular folk tunes to the accompaniment of *dhadds,* small two-faced drums held in one hand and played with the fingers of the other, and a *sarangi.* Similarly, there are popular genres like chhands (lyrical songs), *ghorian* (wedding songs), *alahanian* (laments), *birahare* (songs of separation), arti (prayer), saddu (call), sohila (song of happiness), *karahale* (camel tunes), *vanajara* (song of trader), *pahare* (songs of quarters of life), *mangal* (songs of celebration), chaubole ('songs of four listeners'), dakkhane (songs of southern people), *baraha mahan* (song of twelve months), ruti (song of seasons), *din raini* (song of day and night), *patti* (acrostic song), and so on.[71] There is another genre kafi associated with the sufis of the Punjab. Four major ragas of the Adi Granth employ this genre in the mixed form such as *Asa-kafi, Tilang-kafi, Suhi-kafi,* and *Maru-kafi.* All these popular folk tunes balance the classical tradition of ragas. In this context, Gurnam Singh argues that 'a scientific use of the popular and not so common means and organs of both the Hindustani and Karnataki Indian music was made apart from the different parts of classical and folk music.'[72]

It is instructive to note that in any given raga the hymns of the Gurus are divided into subsections of chaupadas, astapadis, chhants, longer compositions and vars. This sequence is different from that of the two available Goindval pothis where chhants come before the astapadis. The reason for this change seems to be linked with the concern to create a balance between classical and folk traditions. Since chaupadas and astapadis are sung in the classical ragas they are put together in the beginning of the raga. The last part belongs to the folk tradition in which chhants and vars are put together along with longer works (like *Sukhmani, Anand* and *Siddh Gost*) which are meant to be recited. It is not simply the criterion of the increasing length of compositions that is followed in the structure of the Adi Granth. Rather, it is the question of creating a theological and musicological coherence in the final sequence. Moreover, there is a separate musical category of *ghar* which is not to be found in the Goindval pothis. Although it appears in the GNDU MS 1245 at

[71]For more details, see Piara Singh Padam, 'Gurbani te Lok Sangit', *Vismadu Nad,* no. 1 (October 1992), pp. 83–6.

[72]Gurnam Singh, 'Sangeet Prabandh of Gurbani', in *Simriti Granth—1991,* p. 47.

certain points, it is employed in its fully developed forms of seventeen ghars only in the Kartarpur manuscript. There is, however, no consensus among the scholars about its exact meaning. It seems to have been adapted from the seventeen different rhythms (*graha+tals*) within various melodic patterns, which Ameer Khusrau is credited with inventing in Indian music on the pattern of Iranian music.[73] It should be emphasized, however, that in the structure of the Adi Granth ghars are mentioned as melodic variations within the same raga pattern. They are in fact 'musical clefs' according to which various padas are organized in the raga sections.[74] They play an important role in the actual musical performance.

SELECTION OF RAGAS AND THE *RAGA-MALA*

The most important issue at this point, however, is related to the choice of ragas. Guru Nanak and the succeeding Gurus seem to have selected the ragas very carefully. For instance, Guru Nanak describes his own understanding of *Sorathi* raga as follows.

The performance of the *Sorath* raga shall have a lovely affect, if the true one is borne in the *man*. The teeth should not be soiled [with biting food, which is immorally obtained], the *man* should be free of hostility, and the tongue should sing the praise of the true one.

(M1, *Var Sorathi* 1 (1), AG, p. 642)

Similarly, there are other such shaloks by the succeeding Gurus, which state that only those ragas should be used which produce a balanced effect on the minds of both listeners and performers.[75] Any raga that arouses passion of any kind must *ipso facto* be omitted. For instance, there are still some musicians who believe that *Dipak* raga generates fire if correctly performed.[76] Whether it is true or not, this raga is not used independently in the Adi Granth. It is, however, used as *Gauri-dipaki* in the mixed form (*Sankar raga*), so that its extreme effect is toned down. The resulting form is most suitable for the creation of a reflected mood.

[73]Jasbir Singh Sabar, 'Sri Guru Granth Sahib vich Sangit Suchak Sanket', in *Simriti Granth—1991*, p. 33.

[74]Taran Singh, *Guru Nanak: His Mind and Art* (New Delhi: Bahri Publications, 1992), pp. 19 and 154–5.

[75]See M3 (AG, pp. 83, 311, 516, 585, 950, 1087, 1419), M4 (AG, p. 849) and M5 (AG, 1425). Also see Jagir Singh, 'Gurmat Kavi vich Sangit da Mahatav', *Khoj Patrika*, no. 26 (Patiala: Punjabi University, September 1985), pp. 256–65.

[76]Kaufmann, *The Ragas of North India*, pp. 12–13.

The issue of selection of particular ragas may be further elaborated with a comparative examination of the ragas used in the Adi Granth and the list given in the *Raga-mala* at the end. For instance, a verse introducing the raga-family of *Hindol* reads as follows: 'Then comes the turn of *Hindol* with five consorts and eight sons. Passionate waves of melodic figurations rise when the musicians sing by strumming the strings.'[77] The technical word *tan* (melodic figuration) stands for a sequence of notes performed at a fast speed near the end of the performance.[78] In the case of the performance of *Hindol* raga, the tans create a jubilant atmosphere. The word hindol literally means swing and refers to the swing of Krishna. In the musical setting of this raga, the *gopis* (cowherd-girls) move the swing with passion, while Krishna plays a transverse flute to create a mood of amorous love.[79] Like *Dipak*, this raga is not used independently in the Adi Granth. It is, however, employed in the mixed form as *Basant-hindol* to create a gentle tonal effect in one's mind. In this context, Khushwant Singh aptly remarks: '*Megh* and *Hindol* were not used because of their jubilant tone; *Jog* and *Dipak* were likewise rejected for their melancholy.'[80]

On the issue of the popularity of various ragas among different religious groups of Indian society, Taran Singh makes an important observation.

Guru Nanak wrote a large number of lyrics to suit all climes, cultures, seasons and times. When he made innovations in combining certain measures like Basant and Hindol, he aimed at sobriety and avoided extremes. By this device, he brought together various sections and sects of India. His poetry served as a bridge between the Muslims and the Hindus. The former were fond of Asa, Suhi and Tilang and the latter of the remaining rags. Yogis were devoted to Ramkali. Majh was a local rag of the Punjab. Gujari belonged to the Gujar tribe. Seasonal rags of Basant, Malar, Sarang, Suhi, Bilawal and Ramkali were sung in national gatherings which consisted of the Hindus and Muslims. They are expressive of joyous moods. Such congregational singing brought the community closer.[81]

Here, Taran Singh presents a non-sectarian interpretation of Guru Nanak's message and correctly associates certain ragas with different

---

[77]*Raga Mala*, AG, p. 1430.

[78]For more details, see Kaufmann, *The Ragas of North India*, p. 29.

[79]ibid., p. 114.

[80]Khushwant Singh, *A History of the Sikhs*, Vol. 1 (Delhi: Oxford University Press, 5th impr., 1984; 1st published, Princeton University Press, 1963), p. 307.

[81]Taran Singh, *Guru Nanak*, p. 137.

social groups. He argues that in combining *Basant* and *Hindol* ragas Guru Nanak's aim was to create a mood of sobriety and avoid extremes. The Guru employed only those ragas which produced a balancing effect on the minds of his audience. Taran Singh's approach certainly reflects the spirit of his age in which the overall stance of Indian scholarship was to discourage sectarianism and communalism. Nevertheless, this view is in complete agreement with the inclusive ideal of the Adi Granth.

The issue of *Raga-mala* has puzzled both scholars and Sikhs throughout its history.[82] It is recorded in the Kartarpur volume in the same hand as the rest of the text. Winand Callewaert and Mukund Lath remark that the role that music plays in the Adi Granth is also reflected in the fact that the Granth ends with a *Raga-mala*. They further argue that the *Raga-mala* has 'no relevance in the Granth, except as a kind of tribute to the importance of music for it.'[83] The *Raga-mala* issue must be approached in the context of the musical tradition of north India during the sixteenth century. Many of the treatises on north Indian music dating from about the eleventh century describe ragas in terms of hierarchy, raga (male) and ragini (female), a fanciful classificatory scheme which was extended to include putra (son) as the number of the ragas increased.[84] This kind of classification is to be found in the Adi Granth *Raga-mala*.

The first known text of *Raga-mala* was written in 1509 by Kshema Karna, who lived in the state of Rewa.[85] The manuscript recording is preserved in the Government Collection of the Asiatic Society of Bengal, Calcutta. Another copy of this manuscript is kept in the India Office library, which is ascribed to an author named Kshema Karna Pathaka. Kshema Karna groups his material into six head ragas, each having five raginis and eight sons, for a total of eighty-four ragas.[86] During the sixteenth century there appears to have been an increase in the number of works dealing with the pictorial representation of ragas. Each school of musical thought had its own collection of

[82]For details, see Surinder Singh Kohli, *A Critical Study of the Adi Granth* (Delhi: Motilal Banarsidass, reprint 1976; 1st edn, 1961), pp. 100–12. Also see Balbir Singh, *Raga-mala da saval te Jodh Kavi ate Alam* (Amritsar: Khalsa Samachar, 3rd impr., 1969) and Shamsher Singh Ashok, *Madhav Nal Kam Kandala te Raga-mala Nirne* (Amritsar: Singh Brothers, 1981).

[83]Callewaert and Lath, *The Hindi Padavali of Namdev*, p. 97.

[84]Jairazbhoy, *The Rags of North Indian Music*, p. 91.

[85]Kaufmann, *The Ragas of North India*, pp. 47–8.

[86]ibid.

Raga-mala. There was another author, Pundarika Vitthala, who wrote his *Raga-mala* in 1576, during the reign of Emperor Akbar.[87] Pundarika groups his ragas into six male ragas, each of which possesses five female ragas and five sons, making a total of sixty-six ragas. He claims that his classification of ragas is the only correct one in the north. Yet another text of *Raga-mala* in Hindi appeared from the school of the famous musician Tansen.[88]

It appears that the *Raga-mala* of the Adi Granth was quite popular in the musical tradition of the Punjab. Guru Arjan may have included it in the scripture with the intention of highlighting the distinctiveness of the ragas of the Adi Granth in the context of the prevailing musical tradition. It certainly helps to illuminate certain characteristic features of the Sikh approach towards the ragas. For instance, its text follows the raga-ragini-putra classification of six-five-eight, giving rise to a total number of eighty-four ragas. There is no such system in the Adi Granth, where all the major ragas appear under the same title of Raga, not under the title of Ragini.[89] Only one-fourth of the Raga-mala list is accepted in the Sikh tradition. Moreover, the exclusion of sixty-three ragas of the *Raga-mala* that are not employed in the Adi Granth may reveal the choices made by the Gurus.

A thorough comparison of the ragas of the Adi Granth and the list of the ragas given in the *Raga-mala* is required to understand the systematic preferences of the Sikh Gurus. It might be possible to deduce from such systematic preferences the implicit principles guiding their choices. Such a musicological and theological analysis would entail a major study in itself. Here I have offered but a few probes that may stimulate further research in this area. This kind of research must be taken up by a person who is trained in the musical tradition of north India. It may involve field study in the oral performance of the ragas of the Adi Granth by different ragis belonging to old family traditions (*gharanas*), since sacred music is generally passed on to different generations without any change. Through this research it will soon become obvious that the whole debate on the controversy of *Raga-mala* has been totally misdirected.

[87]ibid., pp. 49–50.

[88]ibid., pp. 48–9.

[89]Kaufmann cites the Persian work *Naqmat-e-Asaphi* (1813) of Muhammed Rezza Khan, who declares for the first time the raga-ragini (husband-wife) system absurd. See ibid., pp. 55–6. Kaufmann appears to be unaware of the Adi Granth system of ragas.

A few years ago, Callewaert and Lath had raised the concern that the Sikhs do not 'seem to have devoted much attention to preserving a fixed form or character for their music, being open to the influence of what was popular or current at different times'.[90] That concern is being addressed now with great enthusiasm. Indeed, an attempt in this direction was made when the first Aduti Gurmat Sangit Samelan was organized in 1991 at Gurdwara Gur Gian Prakash, Jawaddi Kalan, Ludhiana, in which all the classical ragas of the Adi Granth were performed by various professional musicians. Ancient tunes of various ragas were discussed by a panel of judges who tried to identify the original tradition of singing. There were, of course, some disagreements on the character of *Maru* raga. Nevertheless, the performance of the ragas of the Adi Granth, along with ancient folk tunes, has been given a new lease of life within the Sikh Panth.

CONCLUSION

Devotional music has always been part and parcel of the Sikh tradition. Guru Nanak and the succeeding Gurus laid great emphasis on the performance of those ragas which produced a balancing effect on the minds of listeners and performers. The gender-based classification of the Mohan pothis was not accepted in the first canonical text of the Adi Granth. The final sequence of ragas in the Adi Granth was a blend of a number of popular and regional music systems of north India at that time. In doing so, Guru Arjan created a theological and musicological coherence in the very structure of the Adi Granth.

Furthermore, the classical and folk tunes were simultaneously employed keeping in mind the sociological significance of the folk tradition. The primary intention of the Gurus was to reach out to various audiences from different parts of India through the medium of musical styles. For instance, if they wanted to address the sufi audience they would employ the kafi genre of singing. Similarly, they would employ folk tunes to address the rural people. If the performance of *Ramakali* raga was best suited for an audience of nath yogis, then *Siri* raga was mostly addressed to Vaishnava audience. Thus the Gurus employed all the popular styles of singing for their compositions.

In sum, the raga organization of the Adi Granth presents an excellent combination of lyrical and rational elements. It is far more

---

[90]Callewaert and Lath, *The Hindi Padavali of Namdev*, p. 97.

complex than any simple explanation would describe it. It may be added here that understanding the ragas of the Adi Granth and their organization solely in terms of the modern north Indian musical tradition is inadequate. Modern music is unlikely to go back to traditions before Tansen (late sixteenth century), and it is probably traceable to the eighteenth or nineteenth centuries. Perhaps scholars would be interested in examining both the Adi Granth raga system and contemporary treatises on the classical north Indian musical tradition since the former may be crucial in understanding the latter.[91]

---

[91] I owe this suggestion to Professor James Kippen.

5

GURU ARJAN'S EDITORIAL PERSPECTIVE

> The Adi Granth is both one and many. On the one hand
> there is little that fails to fit a single, consistent doctrinal
> pattern. On the other there is a variety which serves to stress
> and illuminate different aspects of the pattern.... The doctrinal
> consistency of the Adi Granth is, like the beauty of so much
> of its poetry, something that neither the textual problems
> nor neglect can destroy.[1]

W.H. McLeod makes a perceptive observation on the
fundamental importance of the doctrinal pattern of the
Adi Granth in the above citation. On the variety of styles,
he adds: 'The diverse styles offered by Nanak's successors range from
Guru Angad's pithy couplets and the eminently simple declarations
of Guru Amar Das to the music of Guru Ram Das. Most prolific of
all the Gurus, Arjan covers a wide span of human experience and
related doctrine.'[2] Indeed, the argument of this study is centred upon
Guru Arjan's editorial insights by means of which he was able to
produce the first canonical text of the Adi Granth in 1604. Even a
lay reader of the Sikh scripture cannot fail to acknowledge that it is
a masterpiece of organization. Harbans Singh, a distinguished
interpreter of Sikh history and tradition, makes the following
observation on Guru Arjan's achievement: 'A genius unique in
spiritual insight and not unconcerned with methodological design
had created a scripture with an exalted mystical tone and a high
degree of organization.'[3] In this section, therefore, we shall make an

[1] W.H. McLeod, *The Sikhs: History, Religion, and Society* (New York: Columbia
University Press, 1989), p. 87.
[2] ibid.
[3] Harbans Singh, *Sri Guru Granth Sahib: Guru Eternal for the Sikhs* (Patiala: Academy
of Sikh Religion and Culture, 1988), p. 6.

attempt to discern various principles that were at work in the creation of a new scripture at the beginning of the seventeenth century.

It is evident from the systematic arrangement of the Adi Granth that Guru Arjan followed a well-defined pattern of organization which was seldom breached.[4] The Adi Granth is divided into three major sections. It begins with an introductory section containing the liturgical texts, and concludes with an epilogue comprising a group of miscellaneous works which could not be accommodated in the middle section. The bulk of the material, however, is arranged in the middle section of the Adi Granth, the distinctive structure of which is our main concern here. The primary division of the middle section is based on ragas or musical modes which number thirty-one in the standard version of the Adi Granth. Each raga has further subdivisions based on the length of the compositions, beginning with the shorter pad genre, followed by other poetic forms (astapadi, chhant, and other longer works such as Guru Nanak's *Siddh Gost*, Guru Amar Das's *Anandu* and Guru Arjan's *Sukhmani*), and ending with the longer var or ballad. The hymns in each of these classifications are arranged in such a way that the works of Guru Nanak are placed first and are followed by those of the later Gurus in the order of their succession. Similarly the bhagat bani is arranged at the end of each raga. In order to understand the structure of the Adi Granth fully we must try to find clues to Guru Arjan's primary concerns with respect to his editorial insights.

DOCTRINAL CONSISTENCY

The compilation of the Adi Granth is based on a single, consistent doctrinal pattern that we encounter in the works of the Gurus. This must be regarded as one of the fundamental criteria for the creation of the scripture, which owes much to the enormous energies of Guru Arjan. Here, we intend to examine the issue of doctrinal consistency behind the diversity of styles offered by Guru Nanak's successors as it appears in the actual process of compilation of the Adi Granth.

---

[4]For an earlier treatment of the subject, see Frederic Pincott, 'The Arrangement of the Hymns of the Adi Granth,' *Journal of the Royal Asiatic Society*, XVIII (Calcutta, 1885), pp. 437–61. This article was a rebuttal of Trumpp's assertion: 'By thus jumbling together [of] whatever came to hand, without any judicious selection, the Granth has become an exceedingly incoherent and wearisome book.' See Ernest Trumpp, *The Adi Granth* (New Delhi, reprint, 1970; 1st edn, London, 1877), p. CXX.

1. Unity of Guruship

In order to stress the theme of the unity of guruship, Guru Arjan intentionally incorporated in certain instances his own shaloks in the works of Guru Nanak. In doing so, he was following a convention that had originated with Guru Angad, a disciple as well as the immediate successor of Guru Nanak. For instance, three shaloks of Guru Angad, which appear under his distinctive symbol in *Var Asa* and *Var Majh* are repeated in *Sahaskriti* shaloks under the symbol of Guru Nanak. In this case, there is a certain blurring of boundaries between the compositions attributed to the first two Gurus, which poses important textual problems. The issue will receive further treatment in the third part of this section.[5]

Here, we shall focus on a unique example where Guru Arjan consciously inserted his couplet at the beginning of Guru Nanak's hymn. In an earlier recension of the Adi Granth, for instance, the *Maru* raga begins as follows:

There is one supreme being, known by grace through the true Guru (*IK Oankar satgur parasadi*)

Raga Maru Mahala 1 Chaupade

They who listen to the [divine] call in the later part of the night, repeat the name of the lord. They are provided with the symbols of royal authority and dignity such as pavilions, canopies, tents and equipped chariots at their disposal. They who have meditated on your name, receive direct communication from you. (1) Baba! Devoid of good actions I am untruthful at heart. I have not yet attained your name. My *man* is blind and lost in illusion. (1) rahau.[6]

This passage explicitly states that the practice of meditation on the divine name in the last watch of the night is the inevitable result of divine grace, which functions in the form of a call (*sadara*). Those devotees who listen to the divine summons and who act accordingly, receive the highest honours in the world. They are the ones to whom Akal Purakh reveals himself through direct communication. All others who have not yet realized the divine name remain deluded in falsehood. This is a clear statement of Guru Nanak's understanding of divine revelation.

In the final text, Guru Arjan replaced the abbreviated form of the invocation with the complete Mul Mantar, added his own shalok in

---

[5]See M2, *Var Asa* 2–3 (12), AG, p. 469 and *Var Majh* 2 (23), p. 148. Also see M1, *Salok Sahaskriti* 1–4, AG, p. 1353).
[6]GNDU MS 1245, f. 922a..

the beginning and gave a new title shabad (Word) to Guru Nanak's hymn for the first time in the Adi Granth. Mohan Singh Diwana is baffled by this unique instance in the Adi Granth:

Where in the world is this tradition-pattern of two-line four stanzas, each stanza with its separate rhyme, but prefaced by a salok, three lines before *rahau* (very significant in this case), long and short, or almost equal, with language differences and interesting *qafias* and rhyme-schemes and strange measures and flows and no superfluous vowel signs ... (i) or ... (u).[7]

Clearly, Diwana's remark about the vowel-signs reflects his inadequate understanding of the grammatical conventions of the Adi Granth language.[8] The final reading of the first *Maru* hymn with certain linguistic modifications appears as follows:

There is one supreme being, the eternal reality, the creator, without fear and devoid of enmity, immortal, never incarnated, self-existent, known by grace through the Guru.

Raga Maru Mahala 1 Gharu 1 Chaupade ('four-verse composition')
Shalok
Divine Friend, may I ever live as the dust of your feet! Seeking your shelter, Nanak, may I ever behold you present by my side. (1)[9]
Shabad ('word')
Those who listen to the [divine] call in the later part of the night, repeat the name of the lord. They are provided with the symbols of royal authority and dignity such as pavilions, canopies, tents and equipped chariots at their disposal. They who have meditated on your name, receive direct communication from you. (1) Baba! Devoid of good actions I am untruthful at heart. I have not yet attained your name. My *man* is blind and lost in illusion. (1) rahau ...

(M1, *Maru* 1, AG, p. 989)

Here the opening shalok indicates the reflective and mystical setting of Guru Nanak's hymn. By assigning a new title to the hymn, Guru Arjan meant that any individual hymn from the Adi Granth must be invariably understood as a shabad. It should be noted that Guru

[7]See his article, 'Discoveries in Sikh Culture (III),' *Journal of Sikh Studies*, Vol. ii, no. 1 (Amritsar: GNDU, February, 1975), p. 87.

[8]For a useful study on the grammatical conventions of the language of the Adi Granth, see Christopher Shackle, *An Introduction to the Sacred Language of the Sikhs* (London: School of Oriental and African Studies, University of London, 1983).

[9]This shalok appears under Guru Arjan's distinctive symbol in *Var Gujari* (M5, 1 (4), AG, p. 518). Another such instance is Guru Nanak's *Japji* where Guru Arjan's shalok is placed at the beginning of the composition (AG, p. 1).

Arjan repeated this title in a second instance in the *Maru* raga only.[10] The meaning of the passage itself points out that shabad is the vehicle of communication between Akal Purakh and an individual. McLeod defines shabad as follows: 'The Word embraces all that is Truth, all that expresses the nature of God and the means of attaining Him, and this may be perceived in divine laws governing the universe as well as in the ineffable mystical experience.'[11] This unique title in the *Maru* raga, therefore, reflects a new awareness in Sikh self-understanding with respect to the divine status of the Gurus' compositions. It appears that the tradition of conferring royal honour upon the volume containing gurbani must have come into vogue by this time. Indeed, the installation of the Adi Granth in the newly-built Harimandir was under way when Guru Arjan declared: 'The scripture is the Lord's dwelling-place.'[12]

The addition of Guru Arjan's shalok at the beginning of Guru Nanak's hymn further highlights the issue of doctrinal consistency in guruship. It serves to underline Guru Arjan's claim that he carries the spiritual authority of Guru Nanak. The meaning of the shalok conveys the idea that when one awakens to the reality of the divine name through humble submission, one feels the presence of the lord within and all around ('I ever behold you present by my side'). Thus the fundamental message of all the Gurus remains consistently the same: that liberation can be achieved only through meditation on the divine name.[13] The declaration of this message is made in the *Maru* raga, which is traditionally associated with the setting of goals at the time of blowing of a bugle in the wake of some undertaking.[14]

There is yet another striking instance relating to a hymn (*kudarat karanaiharu apara*) in Guru Nanak's *Maru Solahe* in the standard version of the Adi Granth. Interestingly, this hymn appears under the symbol of Guru Arjan in the GNDU MS 1245 as follows:

Maru Solahe Mahala 5
The creator is limitless in his power. No creature has any recourse against

---

[10]M1, *Maru* 5, AG, p. 990. Here Guru Nanak's sabad is preceded by Guru Arjan's shalok, which appears under his symbol in *Var Gujari* (M5, 2 (4), AG, p. 518).

[11]See McLeod, *Guru Nanak and the Sikh Religion*, p. 193.

[12]M5, *Sarang* 90, AG, p. 1226. For the contemporary practice of installation of the Guru Granth Sahib ceremonially each morning in the Golden Temple, see Patwant Singh, *The Golden Temple* (New Delhi: Time Books International, 1988), pp. 145–64.

[13]McLeod, *The Sikhs*, p. 87.

[14]Satbir Singh, *Sri Guru Granth Sahib da Sar-Visthar*, Vol. I (Jalandhar: New Book Company, 1985), pp. 71–5.

him. He himself provides sustenance to his creatures and his order is operative over one and all ... (1)

[If] one meets the true Guru, then one is invited to the [divine] palace. One receives honour and liberation in the true court. One devoted to the world (sakat) will not find place in the divine temple (harimandir), and one will continue to suffer in the [cycle of] birth and death. (7) Serve the true Guru [who is like a] deep ocean. Obtain the profit of jewels of divine name. Bathe in the pool of nectar (amritsar) to shed the impurity of evil. Thus one attains contentment in the holy pool of the Guru ... (8)[15]

Here, the use of two significant words Harimandir and Amritsar clearly indicates that the hymn was composed by Guru Arjan after he had already constructed the temple in the midst of the pool of water at Amritsar. It was the historical context that gave rise to the use of this particular vocabulary. Now the question arises: Why did Guru Arjan want to add this hymn in the section of Guru Nanak's compositions? In order to find an answer to this question we need to examine the actual position of this hymn in the Kartarpur manuscript.

It is important to note that there are specific editorial instructions in the margins about the new position of this hymn. There is a marginal note on folio 778/2, indicating that 'the right place of twenty-second solaha belongs to Guru Nanak's hymn which is currently located on folio 800' (*22 baihavan solaha pati 800 sahi hai/ mahale 1/ pahile ka*). The editorial comment in the index in folio 16/ 1 further clarifies that the 'hymn (*kudarati karnaiharu apara*) of folio 799 should come at number 22.' In my own examination of the Kartarpur bir I found out that a new thick pen had been used to write this hymn under the new title as follows:

Maru Mahala 1
By the grace of the eternal one, the true Guru.

The creator is limitless in his power. No creature has any recourse against him. He himself provides sustenance to his creatures and his order is operative over one and all ... (1)

[If] one meets the true Guru, then one is invited to the [divine] palace. One receives honour and liberation in the true court. One devoted to the world (sakat) will not find place in the divine temple (harimandir), and one will continue to suffer in the [cycle of] birth and death. (7) Serve the true Guru [who is like a] deep ocean. Obtain the profit of jewels of divine name. Bathe in the pool of nectar (amritsar) to shed the impurity of evil. Thus one attains contentment in the holy pool of the Guru ... (8)[16]

---

[15]GNDU MS, f. 1001a.
[16]Kartarpur MS, f. 800a.

The second reading, it may be noted, does not have the musical device (*he*) at the end of the original verse. Further, the position of this hymn is in the section of Guru Arjan's *Maru Solahe*. Bhai Jodh Singh accepted Guru Nanak's authorship of this hymn and suggested that it was written here because there was no space for it on folio 778. In his description he has given the position of this hymn on folio 799/2 instead of folio 800a. He was apparently trying to resolve the discrepancy between the index note (f. 799) and the text note (f. 800) through his method of folio numbering.[17] Guru Arjan's decision of shifting this hymn to Guru Nanak's cluster of *Maru* solahe, however, may be explained in two different ways. First, the rhyme-scheme of this hymn fits very well in the sequence of the last four hymns (Solahe 18-21) of Guru Nanak. Second, Guru Arjan may have intended to stress the unity of guruship by inserting his own hymn at the end of Guru Nanak's solahe. By doing so he may have also intended to show that the construction of Harimandir was in fact the fulfilment of Guru Nanak's own intentions.

2. The Continuity of a Theme

The most significant factor in deciding the proper place of certain hymns in various sections of the Adi Granth was based on the continuity of a particular theme. For instance, a careful reader of the Adi Granth will be struck by the closeness with which the compositions of Guru Amar Das are modelled in language, style and form on those of Guru Nanak. Guru Amar Das composed all his bani in seventeen of the nineteen ragas employed by Guru Nanak, and his hymns follow those of Guru Nanak even section by section. Both wrote their pattis in *Asa* mode, their alahanian in *Vadahansu* raga and their solahe in *Maru* raga. Evidently Guru Amar Das had a particular composition in mind when writing his own bani. There is a particularly striking example in the *Majh* raga where Guru Nanak's single astapadi ('octave'), which stresses the theme of the meditative exaltation of the shabad (*haum vari jiu vari sabadi suhavania*, 'I devote myself to the glorious word'), is followed by Guru Amar Das's thirty-two octaves on the same theme.[18] Evidently Guru Amar Das was so inspired by the meaning of this particular astapadi of Guru Nanak that he was impelled to produce a cycle of octaves around it

[17]See Bhai Jodh Singh, *Kartarpuri Bir*, p. 105.
[18]M1, *Astapadi* 1, AG, p. 109 and M3, *Astapadian* 1-32, AG, pp. 110-29. For more details, see C. Shackle, 'The First Restatement of the Bani,' *The Sikh Courier* (Sikh Cultural Society of Great Britain, Autumn-Winter, 1985): 72-3.

in the same metrical pattern and rhyme-scheme. Even Guru Nanak's phrase *haum vari jiu vari* (I devote myself) is repeated in all the refrains of Guru Amar Das's hymns. This phrase may have been adapted from the folklore of Punjabi girls, who still sing such songs with a constant refrain *haum vari ve biba vari* (I devote myself to you, O beloved!) on the occasions of betrothal, marriage and other such events. To mark the celebration of the forthcoming marriage they usually start the singing of these songs during the night at least one or two weeks before the actual event. The Gurus also used this phrase in the hymns of *Majh* raga, which is associated with the Majha region of the Punjab. Christopher Shackle has aptly remarked that 'there is a triangle of forces underlying the bani of Guru Amar Das: the bani of Guru Nanak, his own Guruship, and the established existence of the community of the Sikhs.'[19]

There is another striking instance in the *Dhanasari* mode, where Guru Nanak's hymn inspired a response from Guru Amar Das. The hymn by the first Guru reflects the theme of human forgetfulness of the divine name. It reads:

Dhanasari Mahala 1.
How can I remember [the lord]? It is hard to achieve remembrance [through cunning]. The heart burns [inside] and the spirit wails. The true one himself creates and exalts in his creation. Forgetting him how can one be good? (1) He is not attained by clever device or command. My mother! How can I attain the truth? (1) rahau

(M1, *Dhanasari 3*, AG, p. 661)

Clearly, this hymn is the direct product of Guru Nanak's deep understanding of human nature based on what Shackle calls 'the dialectic between the most profound inward experience and a life rich in outward adventure.'[20] Guru Nanak raises important issues related to the condition of separation from the divine truth: How can one remember the divine name when one is burning inside with the fire of anguish? How can one attain the divine truth?

In order to respond to the questions raised by Guru Nanak, Guru Amar Das composed a hymn in the same raga and metrical pattern.[21] He carried forward the theme of divine grace, which was

[19]Shackle, 'First Restatement of the Bani,' p. 73.
[20]ibid., p. 72.
[21]For other such instances of Guru Amar Das's direct responses to Guru Nanak's shaloks, see *Var Majh*, 1–2 (16), AG, p. 145 and *Salok Varan Te vadhik*, 27–8, AG, p. 1412.

the only solution offered for the human predicament in the last line of Guru Nanak's hymn (As is the [lord's] glance [of grace], so is the state [of the creature]). In the Kartarpur manuscript the hymn reads:

Dhanasari Mahala 3
By the gracious glance comes remembrance of him. Then [the hardness of the] soul is melted and [the heart] absorbed in meditation. Thus one attains identity between self and supreme self. The duality [of the self] is effaced within. (1) By the Guru's grace is [he] attained. Death cannot destroy, should the mind be absorbed in the lord. (1) rahau[22]

Obviously Guru Amar Das draws his inspiration from the hymn of Guru Nanak, which he uses in consciously re-creating his style and theme while keeping in mind the needs of the growing Sikh community. He offers to his own audience a path of divine grace which can be attained through the Guru.

Guru Arjan consciously diverged from the sequence but maintained the continuity of the theme. He fixed Guru Amar Das's hymn in the section marked for the hymns of Guru Nanak in the *Dhanasari* mode. He even entered two editorial notes in the index on folio 10/2 of the Kartarpur manuscript to specify the authorship of Guru Amar Das's hymn, which was assigned a place in the section devoted to Guru Nanak's hymns.[23] Guru Arjan was in fact following the editorial direction of Guru Amar Das, who had already entered his own hymn alongside Guru Nanak's hymn in the Goindval pothis.[24] In spite of Guru Arjan's clear editorial directions, later scribes failed to recognize that Guru Amar Das authored this hymn, and hence replaced the symbol mahala 3 with mahala 1 in their copies of the Adi Granth.[25] This confusion lasted throughout the eighteenth-century manuscript tradition. Even in the modern standard printed edition of the Sikh scripture, which purports to be an exact copy of the Kartarpur volume, the hymn is attributed to Guru Nanak.[26]

---

[22]Kartarpur MS, ff. 499/2–500/1.

[23]For details, see Chapter 2, p. 55.

[24]PUL, photocopy of volume I, ff. 122b–123a. In the GNDU MS 1245, f. 565b, the title of Guru Amar Das's hymn reads: *Dhanasari Mahala 1. 3.*, which indicates that the hymn of the third Guru is in response to Guru Nanak's.

[25]The seventeenth-century manuscripts that do not attribute the hymn to Guru Amar Das are: (1) PUM MS 6, f. 301a; (2) Una Sahib MS 2, f. 255a; (3) PUM MS 1, f. 327b (number 3 of M3 is deleted and 1 is written in its place); (4) MS copy of Ram Rai's bir, f. 338b.

[26]M1, *Dhanasari* 4, AG, pp. 661.

3. Ascription of Dual Authorship to Identical Compositions

There is a particularly illuminating instance in *Var Gauri*, where a stanza of Guru Ram Das is repeated by Guru Arjan with a slight variation under his own distinctive symbol. It reads:

Pauri M5.
The four Vedas declare, Nanak, what the sants and sages contemplate. Those words which the devotees [of Akal Purakh] utter from their lips, find fulfilment. Theirs are open and luminously clear statements, heard by all the people. The foolish ones, who enter into strife with sants, shall find no joy in life. They [the sants] long for virtues, while they [the foolish ones] burn [in the fire of] pride. What can these poor wretches do when they are cursed with misfortune from the beginning? They who are cursed by Akal Purakh, do no good to any one. They show malice towards the one who is free from malice (nirvair), [and hence] they are destroyed by the law of dharam. Those who are cursed by sants, wander about in agony. The tree which is cut off from the roots, shall only bear withered branches. (31)

(M4, *Var Gauri*, Pauri M5 (31), pp. 316–17)

This stanza, (appearing at number twelve) is ascribed to Guru Ram Das, since the actual var belongs to him.[27] Here one may raise the following questions: Why would Guru Arjan use his father's composition under his own symbol? What is so significant about this stanza that he repeated it?

In the first place, Guru Ram Das's *Var Gauri* focuses on the issue of dealing with the problems created by detractors. In fact, those detractors were rival claimants to the office of guruship. Their rivalry was heightened when Guru Arjan was designated for the *gaddi* (throne) of Guru Nanak in preference to his elder brother, Prithi Chand.[28] One strategy that Guru Arjan adopted to consolidate his position was to claim that he carried the spiritual authority of his father in every sense, so that he could even use his composition under his own distinctive symbol. Further, by repeating the stanza he could also make the point that he intended to deal with the detractors in the manner of his father.[29]

Secondly, it is quite possible that Guru Ram Das transferred his

[27]M4, *Var Gauri* (12), AG, p. 306. For another instance, see Guru Amar Das' shalok 2 (11) in *Var Sri Raga* (AG, p. 86), which is repeated under the symbol of Guru Ram Das as shalok 28 in *Salok Varan Te Vadhik* (AG, p. 1424).

[28]Surjit Hans, *A Reconstruction of Sikh History* (Jalandhar: ABS Publications, 1988), pp. 106–8, 137–41.

[29]G.B. Singh failed to understand Guru Arjan's intention in repeating this stanza. See his *Prachin Biran*, p. 87.

spiritual authority to his son through the imprimatur of this pauri containing a piece of advice on how to deal with the detractors. After assuming the office of guruship, Guru Arjan may have then proclaimed this stanza in the form of a vak or commandment. The dominant theme of this stanza is certainly related firstly, to the proclamation of the divine word by saintly people; and secondly, to the condemnation of those who do not accept their authority. The last line in particular provides a warning to detractors.

Finally, it is worth noting that the second appearance of the pauri has some minor linguistic variations (*nanak vicharahi sant jan/ nanak vicharahi sant muni jana; paragat pahara japada/ paragat paharai japade;* and *vairu karahi nirvair nali/ vairu karani nirvair nali*), which were deliberately done by Guru Arjan to avoid repeating the exact wording of the hymn.[30] This point explains a great deal about the meticulous care with which the scripture was compiled by the Guru. There are a number of marginal notes in the Kartarpur volume where he directs the scribe to delete particular hymns, which are repeated at two different places.[31] Thus, whenever a composition is repeated in the Adi Granth, we may assume that there is always a significant reason behind it.

THE IDEAL OF THE BALANCED LIFE

The second major concern reflected in Guru Arjan's editorial insights appears to be linked with the ideal of the balanced life. This ideal is well reflected in his scheme of arrangement, where Guru Arjan clearly indicates that faith should produce a balanced outlook, tempering both happiness and sadness. Throughout the lyrical bani of the Gurus, the sad and the joyous are subtly interwoven with moods of yearning and rejoicing.[32] In this context Niharranjan Ray makes the following observation:

To maintain a harmonized balance between attachment and detachment, between worldliness and other-worldliness, between the temporal and the spiritual, has never been very easy in human society; yet this was the task which Guru Nanak set himself to, and as one goes through the life and activities of the Gurus and the history of Sikh society one feels that they carried out this task admirably and well.[33]

[30]The most illuminating instance is the appearance of the *So Dar* in three different versions (M1, AG, pp. 6, 8–9, 347–8).

[31]Kartarpur MS, ff. 511/1, 550/2, 836/1.

[32]Patwant Singh, *The Golden Temple*, p. 47.

[33]Niharranjan Ray, *The Sikh Gurus and the Sikh Society* (New Delhi: Munshiram Manoharlal, 1975), p. 45.

The ideal of the balanced life was the main reason why Guru Arjan changed the sequence of certain longer works in the *Ramakali* raga, in the earlier manuscripts. For instance, Guru Amar Das's liturgical text *Anandu* follows the longer works of Guru Nanak and comes after the *Siddh Gost* in the second volume of the Goindval pothis.[34] The same sequence is followed in the earlier recension of the Adi Granth, GNDU MS 1245, where the *Anandu* is located after the *Siddh Gost* of Guru Nanak and before *Var Ramakali* of the third Guru.[35] In the final text, however, Guru Arjan juxtaposes the *Anandu*, Guru Amar Das's hymn of joy, and the *Saddu* (call), Sunder's dirge on the Guru's death. Another such example is the inclusion of the ghorian (songs sung by women at wedding parties) and the alahanian (laments) put on adjacent pages under *Vadahansu* raga.[36] These two are the most striking examples of Guru Arjan's editorial stance that one should accept joys and sorrows with equanimity.

The concern for a 'balanced approach' towards sinners is revealed in Guru Arjan's comments on Kabir. Kabir repeatedly stressed the value of associating with righteous and saintly people for the cultivation of proper devotional conduct.[37] This is in line with the Sikh concept of spiritual fellowship (*sadh sangat*), in which the eternal Guru is mystically present. This concept is fundamental to the teachings of the Gurus. Guru Arjan spells it out in detail in the seventh octave of *Sukhmani*.[38] However, Kabir is strongly opposed to any kind of association with sinners. He describes them with loathsomeness as the meat-eating, liquor-drinking, Devi-worshipping sakta: 'Do not associate with sinners (saktas), flee from them. By touching a blackened vessel, one is sure to get stained!'[39] For Kabir, sinners are totally lost and for them the door of liberation is closed. Hence one must stay away from the bad moral influence of sinners.

On the issue of dealing with sinners Guru Arjan makes two comments on Kabir, which are inserted in his *Var Ramakali* and which are repeated in Kabir's shaloks in the epilogue of the Adi Granth.

[34]Gursharan Kaur Jaggi (*samp.*), *Babe Mohan valian Pothian*, p. 20.

[35]GNDU MS 1245, f. 881a. The close correspondence suggests that the preparation of this earlier recension was based upon the Goindval volumes.

[36]M4, *Vadahansu Ghorian*, AG, p. 575 and M1, *Alahanian*, AG, p. 578.

[37]Kabir, shalok 130, AG, p. 1371: 'Do not leave the way of the sants, follow in their path. Just seeing them one is purified. Meeting them one invokes the divine name.'

[38]For details, see W.H. McLeod, trans. and ed., *Textual Sources for the Study of Sikhism* (Manchester: University of Manchester Press, 1984), p. 112.

[39]Kabir, Shalok 131, AG, p. 1371.

Salok Mahala 5
Kabir, though the earth belongs to the sants, thieves have taken possession of it. Yet the earth feels not their weight, and for them (the thieves) it is all gain! (1)

Mahala 5.
Kabir, on account of the husk rice is beaten with a pestle. If one sits in the company of the wicked the god of death (Dharamrai) will take one to task! (2)[40]

Pauri
You yourself are the great family [of the world's saintly people], although you yourself remain aloof. You yourself alone know your own worth. You yourself are all in all [in the creation] which you yourself have created. You yourself have the power to expound your own doings. Blessed is the place where you dwell! Blessed are the devotees who have beheld you, O true lord! Only the one who has your grace praises you. One who has the company of the Guru, Nanak, becomes pure and holy. (20)

(M5, *Var Ramakali*, 1–2 (20), AG. pp. 965–6)[41]

In the first shalok Guru Arjan suggests that the presence of sinners (*tasakar*, thieves) in the company of the holy can in no way affect the saintly people (sadh), for they look on all things with equanimity. Moreover, the company of the holy is all gain for the sinners because they may turn towards Akal Purakh by accepting the sound moral influence of the sants. In contrast with Kabir, Guru Arjan seems to keep the company of the sants open for sinners. This serves to underline the optimistic Sikh view that it is never too late to turn towards Akal Purakh and that every sinner is a potential sant. Kabir remains a solitary spiritual seeker who does not seem to have a sense of social mission or the idea of an organized religious community.[42] By contrast, the Sikh Gurus have a strong sense of mission which compels them to proclaim their message for the ultimate benefit of their audience and to promote socially responsible living. While as a mystic Kabir can afford to stay away from the sinners (saktas) the Sikh Gurus cannot do so, and they keep their doors open for them principally because of their sense of mission.

However, in his second comment Guru Arjan seems to warn

[40]The translations are adapted from Charlotte Vaudeville, *Kabir*, Vol. I (Oxford: Clarendon Press, 1974), p. 322.

[41]The two shaloks which precede the pauri are also incorporated in Kabir's shaloks (nos. 210–11, AG, p. 1375) along with other comments on the bhagat.

[42]Karine Schomer, 'Kabir in the Guru Granth Sahib: An Exploratory Essay,' in Mark Juergensmeyer and N. Gerald Barrier, eds, *Sikh Studies: Comparative Perspective on a Changing Tradition*, pp. 75–86.

against the dangers of keeping bad company. He employs the symbol of edible rice (*chavala*) to make the point. The edible rice is obtained by beating the unhusked grains with a long pestle. The husk (*tukh*) here symbolizes the wicked. On account of its association with the husk, 'good' rice undergoes the punishment of being pounded with the pestle.[43] Guru Arjan shares Kabir's view to the extent that one must stay away from the sinners. He clearly implies that when one starts to accept evil moral influence in the company of the wicked, one is sure to suffer the consequences of such association. He wants to apprise his audience that one should keep company with discernment and should associate with saintly people in order to cultivate virtues in life. In his comments on Kabir, Guru Arjan seems to move toward a 'balanced approach' with regard to the company of sinners. That is, one should neither flee from them nor indulge excessively in their company.

In the pauri, Guru Arjan adds a further note on his own comments regarding Kabir. He says that ultimately this spiritual fellowship represents the mystical presence of the eternal Guru. All the saintly people become part of a big divine family (*badd parvaru*), each glowing with the spirit of holiness. By stressing the spiritual power of the holy congregation Guru Arjan was inviting people from all walks of life to join his fast-growing religious movement. Bhai Gurdas testifies to the ever-growing strength of the Sikh sangat at the court of Guru Arjan: 'Innumerable Sikhs come to the sangat from four directions to pay their homage [to the Guru]'.[44] One can corroborate this claim with the following evidence from the Persian source, *Dabistan-i-Mazahib*: 'In short, during the time of each *Mahal* (Guru), the Sikhs increased till in the reign of Guru Arjan Mal they became numerous, and there were not many cities in the inhabited countries where some Sikhs were not to be found.'[45]

There are other such instances of the Gurus' comments on Shaikh Farid, which stress the ideal of the balanced life. In one of his shaloks, for example, Shaikh Farid stresses that one must adopt the sectarian sufi dress (*kambalari*, blanket) and renounce the world to follow the mystic path of love.[46] In his comment, Guru Amar Das provides a corrective to Shaikh Farid's view of renunciation by stressing the

---

[43]Vaudeville, *Kabir*, p. 328.

[44]*Varan Bhai Gurdas* 24: 20.

[45]See 'Nanak-Panthis', Ganda Singh, ed., *The Punjab Past and Present*, Vol. I. no. 1 (April 1967), p. 57.

[46]Shaikh Farid, Shalok 103, AG, p. 1383.

ideal of the life of the householder.[47] However, in order to guard against the temptation to become too worldly, Guru Arjan adds a further comment to assert that one must create a balance between renunciation and worldliness.[48] Thus in responding to Shaikh Farid, the Gurus reject not only the extremes of asceticism and self-mortification, but also of indulgence and love of worldly attractions. Emphasis is placed upon moderate living and disciplined worldliness.

OPTIMISTIC SIKH VIEW

The third major doctrinal concern reflected in Guru Arjan's editorial stance seems to be associated with the spirit of optimism. A careful examination of Shaikh Farid's bani in the Adi Granth suggests that its dominant theme is linked with the 'gloomy view' of life in the world.[49] In fact, Guru Arjan took special pains to 'restore social sanity to the views of Shaikh Farid where they touch borders of nihilism and total denial of life here and now.'[50] In his comments on Shaikh Farid, for instance, Guru Arjan's major concern is related to the pessimistic tone which finds its highest expression in the following shaloks.

Farid, if my throat had been cut on the same day as my navel string, I should not have fallen into such trouble nor undergone such hardship. (76)
    Farid, I thought I alone was in pain, but actually the whole world is in pain. I went up on the roof and looked on every house in flames. (81)
    (Shaikh Farid, Shaloks 76 and 81, AG, pp. 1381–2)

Here Shaikh Farid seems to be cursing human life as worthless. His attitude towards it is comprehensively negative. For him the life in this world is devoid of joy, containing and terminating in suffering (*dukkh*). This is contrary to the life-affirming principles of the Sikh faith.

    In responding to the issues raised by Shaikh Farid, Guru Arjan offers solutions from the Sikh perspective. His comments are

[47]M3, Shalok 104, AG, p. 1383.
[48]M5, Shalok 105, AG, p. 1383. The Gurus' comments on Shaikh Farid are examined in detail in my 'Sikh Self-Definition,' pp. 49–51.
[49]For details, see Christopher Shackle, 'Early Muslim Vernacular Poetry in the Indus Valley: Its Contexts and its Character,' in Anna Libera Dallapiccola and Stephanie Zingel-Ave Lallemant, eds, *Islam and Indian Religions*, pp. 268–74.
[50]Attar Singh, ed., *Socio-Cultural Impact of Islam* (Chandigarh: Panjab University, 1976), p. 10.

interjected into his own *Var Ramakali* and then repeated in Shaikh Farid's shaloks in the epilogue of the Adi Granth to reiterate the Sikh viewpoint.

Salok Mahala 5
This lovely world is like a garden, Farid, in which some poison-bearing plants also grow. But they for whom the master cares do not suffer at all. (1)

Mahala 5
How sweet is life, Farid, with health the body blooms! Yet those who love their dear, sweet [lord], are rarely ever found! (2)

Pauri
Contemplation, austerity, self-restraint, compassion and righteousness come to whom they are granted. He, who has his fire (of desire) assuaged by the lord himself meditates on the divine name. The inner-controller, the inscrutable supreme being, grants his unique vision to him. Sustained by the holy fellowship (sadh sangat) he is dyed in the lord's love. The vices of such a one are annulled, his face shines radiantly and he is saved by the divine name. His fear of the cycle of birth and death dissolves and he is never born again. By holding out his sash [the lord] pulls him from the dark well [of ignorance]. By grace, Nanak, he is clasped [to you]. (21)

(M5, Var Ramakali 1–2 (21), AG, p. 966)[51]

Christopher Shackle aptly maintains that this extraordinary passage, in which reference to Farid is carefully worked out, provides the most revealing clues to Guru Arjan's intentions in the compilation of the Adi Granth.[52] In his first comment, Guru Arjan asserts that just as poison-bearing plants also grow in a beautiful garden, so suffering is an inevitable part of life. Joy and suffering are two aspects of worldly life which make life worth living. The Guru further provides the hope that one may find the way through the grace of the master (pir) to accept pain and pleasure with equanimity. Whereas Shaikh Farid regards the world with indifference or as a place of suffering, Guru Arjan likens it to a beautiful garden (*bhum rangavali,* colourful earth), thus emphasizing a positive attitude towards life in the world.

In his second comment, Guru Arjan maintains that human life is the most delightful (*suhavari*) experience that one can have with

---

[51]The two shaloks are also to be found among Shaikh Farid's shaloks (nos 82–3, AG, p. 1382).

[52]See C. Shackle, 'The South-Western Style in the Guru Granth Sahib,' *Journal of Sikh Studies,* Vol. V, no. 1 (February 1978), p. 85, n. 38. This note also mentions the references to Kabir (discussed in the preceding section) and to Guru Nanak as in stanza (18) of *Var Ramakali.*

the gift of this beautiful body (*suvannari deh*). Elsewhere the human being has been called the epitome of creation: 'All other creation is subject to man; man reigns supreme on this earth.'[53] The Guru further proclaims that human life provides an individual with the opportunity to remember the divine name and ultimately to join with the lord.[54] But rare (*virle*) are the ones who seek the divine beloved while participating in worldly actions and delights. Thus in contrast with Shaikh Farid, Guru Arjan places a positive value on human life and seeks to ignite a spirit of optimism among his followers.

In the pauri, Guru Arjan adds a further comment on Shaikh Farid, that human life becomes fruitful only if one joins the spiritual fellowship (sadh sangat) to cultivate virtues in life. Here again his intention is to extend an invitation to the contemporary followers of the sufi poet in the Punjab to join the Sikh movement. It is important to note here that Guru Arjan's comments on Shaikh Farid facilitate the integration of his verses into the Sikh scriptural tradition. Also, by providing a corrective to sufi ideas Guru Arjan seeks to show which of the two traditions possesses truer insights.

THE INCLUSIVE IDEAL

The inclusive ideal of the Adi Granth is the culmination of its effort to transcend conventional forms of Hindu tradition and Islam. Its message is open to all people regardless of their caste status, vocation or religious affiliation. The fundamental aspect of this message is the claim that liberation can be achieved only through inward meditation on the divine name, not through any external religious observances. Evidence for this inclusive claim may be seen in the Adi Granth itself from two different angles. First, the linguistic structure of the Adi Granth is such that it can be seen to be intended for a wide, popular audience from different regions of India. Second, it includes the works of bhagats of Hindu and Muslim backgrounds. In this context, W.H. McLeod aptly observes: 'The result is a scripture which testifies in its actual composition to its concept of religious toleration. Hindu and Muslim belief interpreted in terms of interior devotion deserved and received a place within a scripture dedicated

[53]M5, *Asa* 12, AG, p. 374.
[54]M5, *Asa* 4, AG, p. 15: 'Precious this life you receive as a human, with it the chance to find the lord (*Gobind*).'

to the practice of interior devotion.'[55] These two points need to be examined thoroughly to understand the implications of Guru Arjan's editorial insights.

In fact, the linguistic structure of the Adi Granth has been the focus of scholarly attention since the last century. For instance, Ernest Trumpp, the controversial nineteenth-century German philologist, was the first scholar to take notice of the richness of the language of the Adi Granth. He suggested that, 'Nanak and his successors employed in their writings purposely the Hindui idiom, following the example of Kabir and the other saints, who had raised the Hindui to a kind of standard for religious compositions, and by employing which they could make themselves understood to nearly all the devotees of India, while Punjabi was only intelligible to the people of Punjab.'[56] To a certain extent, his argument of Hindui as 'a kind of standard for religious compositions' is in the context of the medieval situation in which the sants and bhagats were appealing to popular audiences in north India. However, the simple label 'Hindui' cannot be applied to the complexity of the linguistic structure of the Adi Granth.

Christopher Shackle cautiously labels the linguistic pattern of the Adi Granth with a single collective expression 'the Sacred Language of the Sikhs' (SLS). He further stresses the 'mixed character' of SLS, which is the result of drawing upon 'a variety of local languages and dialects, as well as incorporating a good many archaic forms and words.'[57] In this context, Michael Shapiro argues that it is an anachronism to categorize the language of the Adi Granth as either Punjabi, Hindi or Braj, since these languages attained recognizably distinct forms only somewhat later.[58] W.H. McLeod, on the other hand, maintains that the Adi Granth language represents a Punjabi/western Hindi version of Sant Bhasa, the 'language of the sants,' which served as a lingua franca for the sant tradition.[59]

In his analysis of the linguistic pattern of the Adi Granth, which contains various local styles and usages, but which nevertheless sustains a sufficient degree of uniformity, Christopher Shackle concludes

[55]See his article 'Religious Tolerance in Sikh Scriptural Writings,' in Gurbachan Singh Talib, ed., *Guru Tegh Bahadur: Background and the Supreme Sacrifice* (Patiala: Punjabi University, 1976), pp. 239–40.

[56]Trumpp, *The Adi Granth*, p. cxxv.

[57]C. Shackle, *An Introduction to the Sacred Language of the Sikhs*, p. ii.

[58]Michael C. Shapiro, 'Observations on the Core Language of the *Adigranth*,' BIS 3 (1987): 181–93.

[59]See McLeod, *The Sikhs*, pp. 85–6.

the discussion of the 'South-Western Style' with the following observation.

This brief survey will, however, have fulfilled its aim if it encourages speculations as to how it was that so many elements drawn from local traditions were made to serve as the perfectly blended instruments for the expression of great religious poetry by the magical touch of the founder of Sikhism, and how it then was that, in a still richer mixture, such elements were carefully ordered and arranged by the compiler of its holy book, deliberately to underline the new religion's claims to universality.[60]

Indeed, one of Guru Arjan's primary concerns with respect to the inclusion of various linguistic elements in his arrangement of the Adi Granth was to underscore the inclusive ideal of the Sikh religion. Elsewhere, Shackle has reiterated that the very requirements of the universality of Guru Nanak's teachings required that he draw upon a wide range of linguistic resources.[61] One may argue that the variety of the SLS was simply a result of the Adi Granth being a composite scripture, the work of several different people with differing linguistic emphases. But the point that we are trying to make here is that the variety of the Adi Granth language that we encounter in the works of the Gurus was primarily linked with its universal appeal and significance. This issue may be examined from the actual linguistic structure of certain hymns of the Gurus, particularly those of Guru Nanak and Guru Arjan.

Guru Arjan's *Var Jaitsari*, for instance, provides an excellent example of contrasting styles yet thematically parallel expressions of a single theme, in its linguistic structure. The first of each pair of shaloks preceding the pauris, is written in the *Sahaskriti* style[62] and the second in the south-western style. Christopher Shackle has reproduced a pair of shaloks from this var in medieval Latin and the language of Scots' lyric respectively to make the point that a certain significance lay behind the differing linguistic emphases. The relevant passage reads in the original as:

[60]Shackle, 'The South-Western Style,' p. 86.

[61]Christopher Shackle, 'Modern Standard Punjabi,' in Joseph T. O'Connell et al., *Sikh History and Religion in the Twentieth Century* (Toronto: University of Toronto, Center for South Asian Studies, 1988), p. 105.

[62]Christopher Shackle defines *Sahaskriti* as 'an amalgam of sahaskrta with samskrta, in other words a "grandified speech" which recalls Sanskrit without attempting to identify itself with most of its difficulties.' C. Shackle, 'The Sahaskriti Poetic Idiom in the Adi Granth,' *Bulletin of the School of Oriental and African Studies* (1978), 41(2): 310.

Salok//
raj kapatam rup kapatam dhan kapatam kul garabataha// sanchant bikhia chhalam chhidram nanak binu hari sang na chalate//1//
pekhandaro ki bhulu tuma disam sohana// addhu na lahandaro mulu nanak sath na chalai maya//2//
Pauri//
chaladian nali na chalai so kium sanjiai// tisu ka kahu kia jatanu jis te vanjiai// hari bisariai kium tripatavai na manu ranjiai// prabhu chhodi ana laggai naraki samanjiai// hohu kripal dayal nanak bhau bhanjiai//10//

Shalok
Falsum regnum, falsa forma, falsae opes et familia. Fructus mali consequentur, si cum eis non sit Deus. (1)
What fault is in the tumma-gourd, That it seems luvely to your e'e—Yet siller nane ye'll get for it, Nor maun your fortune gang wi' ye. (2)
Pauri
Why heap up that you may not take with you? Why speak of 'effort' which just parts from him? Forgetting God how can one's heart be glad? By leaving him one sends oneself to hell. If you show mercy all my fears are gone. (10)[63]

(M5, *Var Jaitsari*, 1–2 (10), AG, p. 708)

Here the meaning of the original is reproduced with great virtuosity. Through the use of different linguistic styles on the theme of the evanescence of worldly goods, Guru Arjan was surely appealing to a wider audience from different regions. In doing so, he was also making the claim that the variety of the Adi Granth language is primarily linked with its universal appeal and significance.

More recently, Michael Shapiro has skilfully demonstrated that much of gurbani 'exhibits an internal unity in which the formal aspects of texts, including their metrical, poetic, and linguistic structures are fully at one with their content.'[64] His arguments are based on an analysis of a series of words and verses in the locative case. In particular, he focuses on the surprising number of instances from Guru Nanak's *Japji* and *Var Asa* that are in the locative case. He cites, as example, the following words: *gurmukhi* (in/through the voice of the Guru), *gurprasadi* (in/through the grace of the Guru), *hukami* (in/through the divine order), *adi* (in the beginning), *sochai* (through introspection or through ritual purity), *chupai* (in/through silent

---

[63]Shackle, 'The South-Western Style,' p. 86.
[64]Michael C. Shapiro, 'The Theology of the Locative Case in Sacred Sikh Scripture (Gurabani),' in David N. Lorenzen, ed., *Bhakti Religion in North India: Community Identity and Political Action* (Albany: State University of New York Press, 1995), p. 157.

meditation), *suniai* (through having heard [the word]), *mannai* (through having accepted [the word]), *akhani* (in/through speaking/ saying), *karami* (through [one's] actions) and so on. Shapiro compellingly argues that many words of theological or doctrinal significance within the discourse of the Sikh Gurus are grammatically locative. Indeed, the works such as *Japji* and *Var Asa* are prolonged meditations that are deeply concerned with, *inter alia*, the nature of divine grace, the means of achieving awareness of higher realities through progressively hearing, accepting, and speaking the true word, and means for differentiating between things that are ultimately false and those that are true.[65] Thus the language of the Adi Granth plays a significant role in carrying out the religious, moral, doctrinal, and poetic ends of the teachings of the Sikh Gurus.

The inclusion of the bhagat bani in the Adi Granth is another point to justify the inclusive ideal of Sikh religion. To a certain extent, it represents the pan-Indian stance of the Sikh Gurus. One of the most significant reasons for the inclusion of the bhagats is that they experienced a vision of Akal Purakh by following the discipline of meditation on the divine name (nam simaran) in spite of their low caste. The most striking example in this context is Guru Arjan's *Basant Astapadi* in which he illuminates the spiritual attainment of all the sant poets.[66] Although the academic issues raised by the inclusion of the bhagat bani will be discussed in more detail in Chapter 6, our primary focus here will be a hymn of Guru Arjan inserted between two hymns of Dhanna. It is included in a section marked *Asa Bani Bhagat Dhanne Ji Ki* (Bhagat Dhanna's utterances in the *Asa* mode), and therefore, it must be regarded as a comment on Dhanna.

Mahala 5
In Gobind, Gobind, Gobind was Namdev's *man* absorbed. A calico-printer worth half a farthing became worth many hundred thousands! (1) rahau. Abandoning weaving and stretching thread, Kabir devoted his love to [Akal Purakh's] feet. Though a poor weaver of low family, he obtained untold virtues. (1)[67] Ravidas, who always carried carcasses, discarded attachment to worldliness (maya). He became prominent in the holy fellowship and beheld the divine sight. (2) Sain the barber, who was running errands, became known in each and every house. The moment the supreme lord took abode in his heart, he was numbered with the bhagats.(3) Listening to such happenings, the poor Jat [Dhanna] also engaged in devotion. Such

[65]For details, see ibid., pp. 145–59.
[66]See M5, *Basant Dutukian* 1, AG, p. 1192.
[67]The translation of these verses is adapted from Vaudeville's *Kabir*, pp. 29–30.

was Dhanna's good fortune that the lord himself became manifest to him in person. (4)

(M5, *Asa* 2, AG, pp. 487–8)

The use of Dhanna's 'signature' here has confused many scholars. For instance, Charlotte Vaudeville wrongly attributes this hymn to Dhanna, which in fact is Guru Arjan's comment on Dhanna.[68] Similarly, Winand Callewaert and Peter Friedlander argue that there has been some controversy whether this hymn 'should be attributed to Dhanna or Guru Arjan.'[69] They further argue that there is no reason to doubt the accuracy of the editing of the Adi Granth and that the inscription mahala 5 should be taken literally. Hence this hymn should be regarded as a song by Guru Arjan about Dhanna and other bhagats rather than a hymn by Dhanna.[70] In fact, this whole controversy has resulted from ignorance of the editorial interventions of Guru Arjan. By employing the signature of the bhagat, the fifth Guru is addressing the contemporary followers of the bhagat.[71]

Evidently, through this hymn Guru Arjan inspired his own audience with the example of the bhagats achieving their status through the transforming power of the divine name. He also refers to the imitative behaviour of Dhanna, who was inspired by other low-caste bhagats and who therefore became deeply involved in the practice of the remembrance of the divine name (nam simaran). Guru Arjan's comment in fact reveals his own contemporary situation when a large number of Jats were attracted towards the Sikh faith, following the example of the various followers of the sant poets. They were apparently becoming Sikhs because of the universal appeal of the Gurus' message and specifically their emphasis upon equality. In this context, the author of the *Dabistan-i-Mazahib* (1655) noted that, although the Gurus had been Khatris, 'they have placed the Khattris under the authority of the Jats, who belong to the low caste of the Vaishyas, as the big Masands of the Guru are mostly Jats.'[72] In a similar vein, Irfan Habib makes the following observation:

It is quite clear what Guru Nanak and his successors preached was a universal faith, and not a narrow or sectional doctrine.... In such circumstances,

[68]ibid.

[69]Winand M. Callewaert and Peter G. Friedlander, *The Life and Works of Raidas* (New Delhi: Manohar Publishers, 1992), p. 12.

[70]ibid.

[71]For details, see Chapter 6, pp. 185–6.

[72]See 'Nanak Panthis,' p. 57.

Sikhism, which rejected in theory the entire system of caste and whose Gurus in practice raised Jatts to the highest positions without hesitation, could not but fail to win over and command the loyalty of large sections from amongst the Jatts.[73]

Clearly, the egalitarian spirit of the Gurus' teachings must be regarded as the motivating force behind the extensive Jat allegiance to the Panth.[74] One hymn of Dhanna in the *Dhanasari* mode was incorporated in the Kartarpur manuscript after it was bound in 1604. This is quite evident from the way it is recorded in folio 519/2 with an extended margin on the left-hand side of the volume.[75] Its later addition clearly indicates that not all of Dhanna's hymns were available earlier. Perhaps some travelling-singers sung this hymn in the congregation, and it was duly included in the Kartarpur manuscript after the approval of Guru Arjan. Thematically, this new hymn (*gopal tera arata*, 'O Lord, I am your afflicted servant [who comes to you for begging]') perfectly fits in the context of the liturgical texts on arti (adoration) composed by other bhagats in the *Dhanasari* mode.

Sometimes, it is suggested that the inclusion of the bhagat bani in the Adi Granth was motivated primarily by the popular impulse of the times in which different sectarian traditions (*sampraday*) were equally involved in moulding the poetry of the sants into collections of scripture.[76] But the kind of selection and treatment of the bhagat bani that we encounter in the Adi Granth collection would scarcely be found anywhere else. We shall return to this point in the next chapter. Although Kabir is prominently represented in the Sikh scripture, followed by Namdev, Ravidas and Shaikh Farid, eleven other figures from different regions and castes are included to reinforce the pan-Indian stance of the Sikh movement. These sants, sufis and bhagats hailed from Banaras (Kabir and Ravidas), Satara (Namdev), Sholapur (Trilochan and Parmanand), Pakpatan (Shaikh

[73]Irfan Habib, 'Jatts of Punjab and Sind,' in Harbans Singh and N. Gerald Barrier, eds, *Essays in Honour of Dr Ganda Singh* (Patiala: Punjabi University, 1976), pp. 99–100.

[74]W.H. McLeod made the point on the significance of Jats and Jat culture on the developing Panth in *The Evolution of the Sikh Community*, Chaps. 1 and 3. The most notable response to his tentative enquiry was offered by Jagjit Singh, *Perspectives on Sikh Studies* (New Delhi: Guru Nanak Foundation, 1985), section 2.

[75]Kartarpur MS, f. 519/2. Also see Dhanna, *Dhanasari* 1, AG, p. 695.

[76]For instance, the Fatehpur manuscript on Surdas (1582) contains a total of 149 padas by other poets including Kabir (15), Ravidas (8), Namdev (11). See Gopal Narayan Bahura, 'Surdas ka pada: Manuscript of 1639 V.S. (1582)', in Monika Thiel-Horstmann, ed., *Bhakti in Current Research, 1979–1982* (Berlin: Dietrich Reimer, 1983), pp. 19–23.

Farid), Tonk (Beni and Dhanna), Birbhum (Jaidev), Lucknow (Bhikhan), Oudh (Surdas), Rewa (Sen), Gagraun near Quetta (Pipa), Sindh (Sadhana), and Paryag (Ramanand). In this context, Surjit Hans argues that by including them, the Sikh faith claims to transcend and subsume the different regional and caste divisions of the bhakti movement.[77]

THE CONCERN FOR INDEPENDENT IDENTITY

The compilation of the Adi Granth was intimately linked with the process of Sikh self-definition. The Sikh Panth had indeed developed a strong sense of independent identity by the end of the sixteenth century. This concern for distinctive identity may well be seen in Guru Arjan's editorial policy. This is evident from the *Bhairau* hymn, where Guru Arjan makes a direct assertion of independent identity: 'We are neither Hindu nor Musalaman.' The complete hymn reads:

Bhairau Mahala 5
I do not keep the Hindu fasts or [the Muslim fasts during] the month of Ramadan. I serve him, and him alone, who is my ultimate refuge. (1) I believe in one lord, who is also Allah. I have broken off with the Hindu and the Turk. (1) rahau. I do not go to Hajj or worship at Hindu pilgrimage places. I serve only him and no other. (2) I offer neither Hindu worship (*puja*) nor Muslim prayers (*namaz*). Holding the only formless one in my heart, I worship him there. (3) We are neither Hindu nor Musalman. My body and soul belong to the one who is called Allah and Ram. (4) Kabir has uttered the truth; meeting with Guru and pir I have met the lord. (5.3)
(M5, *Bhairau* 3, AG, p. 1136)

The use of Kabir's signature has once again raised the issue of its authorship. It is no wonder that the *Bhairau* hymn has been variously interpreted by different scholars. W.H. McLeod, for instance, attributes this hymn to Kabir, although he appreciates the problem of its authorship.[78] This hymn has a parallel in the *Kabir-granthavali* (pad 338), but the last two verses are not to be found there.[79] On the authority of Sahib Singh's exegesis of this hymn, Harjot Oberoi has raised the issue that Guru Arjan is only reinforcing Kabir's thought. 'In line with a dominant theme in medieval *sant* poetics,' he argues, 'both Kabir and Arjan speak of rejecting the received Hindu

[77]Hans, *A Reconstruction of Sikh History*, p. 154.

[78]See McLeod, 'Religious Tolerance', pp. 238–9.

[79]See Hazari Prasad Dwivedi, *Kabir* (New Delhi: Rajkamal Prakashan, 3rd edn, 1985; 1st edn, 1971), p. 158.

and Muslim orthodoxies, of not taking part in their formal modes of worship and pilgrimage, of finally asserting that the mystery of the Supreme Being is to be resolved in one's heart.' Oberoi further asserts that 'it is oversimplistic to suggest that they are discounting one set of categories to embrace a new set of labels.'[80]

Oberoi has missed an important point in his line of argument. In order to understand the actual context of the *Bhairau* hymn, we need to understand the technique of textual commentary adopted by the Gurus in the Adi Granth. Here Guru Arjan seems to have adapted certain lines of Kabir in the first three verses and for this reason he employed his signature in his hymn. In fact, he had in mind a particular composition of Kabir on the same theme and in the same musical mode, when he composed his own hymn.[81] The last two verses are definitely Guru Arjan's own composition. He was in fact addressing the issue of independent identity being debated between the Sikh community and Kabir's followers. Thus the *Bhairau* hymn originated in the situation of conflict in which Guru Arjan made Kabir's followers realize their master's stance on the issue of independent identity. It provides an interesting example of how past documents could be adapted to suit the present needs of the Sikh community.

Moreover, in the *Bhairau* hymn, Guru Arjan is clearly defining Sikhs as separate from Hindus and Muslims. He is quite explicitly distinguishing himself (and by extension his followers, the Sikhs) from both the Hindus and the Muslims on the basis of belief as well as practice. While Kabir refers in his hymn to religious elites (Pandits and Mullas)[82] only, Guru Arjan refers to Hindus and Muslims as a whole. Thus, he is extending Kabir's rejection of religious elites to include a general rejection of Hindu and Muslim practices. In doing so, he is in fact asserting a separate, non-Hindu, non-Muslim identity. One may argue that a text does not always determine practice. However, the fact remains that the idea of a separate Sikh identity based on textual evidence dates from the period of the Gurus.

CONCLUSION

This analysis has clearly demonstrated that the creation of an authoritative text in Sikh scripture owes much to the prodigious

---

[80]Harjot Oberoi, *The Construction of Religious Boundaries: Culture, Identity and Diversity in the Sikh Tradition* (Delhi: Oxford University Press, 1994), pp. 56–8

[81]See Kabir, *Bhairau* 7, AG, pp. 1158–9.

[82]ibid.

efforts of Guru Arjan. He applied meticulous standards to give the scripture its distinctive form, both with regard to its content and style. Indeed, the formal aspects of texts of the Adi Granth, including their metrical, poetic, and linguistic structures are fully at one with their theological content. All these aspects provide an internal unity to the Sikh scripture. Moreover, Guru Arjan was mainly responsible for the final text of the Adi Granth. Some of the fundamental aspects of his editorial policy are reflected in the *rédaction* process itself. Five major guiding principles that emerge from an analysis of his editorial decisions are as follows: (1) doctrinal consistency, (2) the ideal of balanced life, (3) the spirit of optimism, (4) the inclusive ideal, and (5) the concern for a distinctive Sikh identity.

It is significant that as a young boy Guru Arjan witnessed the compilation of the Goindval pothis under the direction of his maternal grandfather, Guru Amar Das. As a careful observer he must have seen the minute details of selection and arrangement of the works of the first three Gurus and some bhagats. He inherited the technique of textual commentary on the works of the bhagats from the third Guru and applied it successfully at the time of the compilation of the Adi Granth. It would be naive to underestimate his background training during the period of his father and grandfather. Moreover, there was Bhai Gurdas to act as an amanuensis for him in the making of the scripture. In fact, Guru Arjan took the canonical process to new standards which are reflected in the structure of the Adi Granth. His editorial comments clearly indicate how frequently he read (and re-read) the original volume and then revised the canon in the process. His decision to insert occasionally his own couplet or hymn in the works of Guru Nanak reflects an editorial policy that was based on the claim that he carried the spiritual authority of the founder of the Sikh tradition.

6

SCRIPTURAL ADAPTATION IN THE ADI GRANTH
Issues of the Bhagat Bani

The dominant Church did not drop the Jewish-scripture idea, but adapted it rather. It did so with a *tour de force*, some might say: one accomplished over the next couple of centuries. There are partial parallels later in principle, though not in practice, in the Qur'an; a thousand years still later the Sikh scripture emulated this again in a minor fashion.[1]

The purpose of this chapter is to examine the place of the hymns of non-Sikh bhagats in the Sikh scriptural tradition. In this context, Wilfred Cantwell Smith raises an important issue of how one religious movement explicitly incorporates the scripture of another within its own, 'adding things new but making the old part and parcel—even though in ways to this day never fully clarified: a somewhat subordinate part and parcel, heavily re-interpreted.'[2] Although the author claims that the Christian scripture provides the 'only instance in world history', he cites the example of Sikh scripture, the Adi Granth, emulating the idea in a minor fashion. The Adi Granth, Smith argues, includes primarily the hymns and sayings of the Sikh Gurus, but also a relatively small percentage of passages by the bhagats of a slightly earlier time or of those who were not formally members of what has subsequently coalesced into the Sikh community.[3]

Traditionally, it is assumed that the bhagat bani was included in the Sikh scripture on the basis of complete doctrinal identity

---

[1]Wilfred Cantwell Smith, *What Is Scripture?*, pp. 54–5.
[2]ibid.
[3]ibid., p. 270, n. 33.

with the teachings of the Sikh Gurus. Karine Schomer, for instance, maintains that some selection of Kabir's sayings must have been made by the compilers of the Adi Granth on the basis of conformity to the 'moods and motivations' of the Sikh community.[4] It is partially true that the hymns of the bhagats are included in the Adi Granth because of a basic agreement with the beliefs of the Gurus. It is also true that Guru Arjan edited the bhagat material before incorporating it in the scripture and chose only those aspects of the bhagat bani that were in basic agreement with Sikh teachings. But these assertions may not tell the whole story. They tend to underscore the traditional view of absolute identity between the teachings of the bhagats and the Sikh Gurus. This is too simplistic a view of what may have been a complex phenomenon.

There are, for instance, some verses of the bhagats which are juxtaposed with the comments made on them by the Gurus. Particularly, the verses of Kabir, Shaikh Farid, Surdas and Dhanna have received direct comments from the Gurus. These comments are not always made because of agreement between the Gurus and the bhagats, but are sometimes made to register clear disagreements with the views of the bhagats. In both instances, that is, the instances of agreement and disagreement, the comments of the Gurus serve to define their own understanding of the developing Sikh community at that particular stage of its history. In an earlier study, I have examined in more detail the concerns behind the Gurus' comments on the verses of the poet-saints. These comments serve to do three things. First, they highlight the Gurus' self-understanding of particular themes contained in the verses of the bhagats and thereby promote a process of self-definition for the Sikh community. For instance, the Gurus recommend the ideals of moderate living and disciplined worldliness for the Sikh community in their comments on the verses of Shaikh Farid which emphasize the ideals of self-torture and asceticism.

Second, the Gurus' comments provide more clarity and understanding to obscure texts of the bhagats so that they become intelligible. The aim here is to render the whole of the bhagat bani coherent and its message meaningful to the Gurus' contemporary audience. Third, these comments voice emphatically the Gurus' differences from the vision of the bhagats on certain important issues.[5]

[4]Karine Schomer, 'Kabir in the *Guru Granth Sahib*: An Exploratory Essay', in Juergensmeyer and Barrier, *Sikh Studies*, p. 77.

[5]For details, see my 'Sikh Self-Definition and the Bhagat Bani' (M.A. thesis, University of Calgary, 1987), pp. 13–15, 110–16.

For instance, the Gurus differ from both Kabir and Shaikh Farid on the issue of the primacy of divine grace over personal effort in spiritual progress. The Sikh view of divine grace requires that one must have the belief that the whole of one's spiritual progress is a matter of divine grace, not of one's efforts alone. Thus, in their comments on the verses of the poet-saints, the Gurus emphasize that God's gifts are not ultimately dependent upon the merit of an individual. Divine grace is ultimately fundamental but is a mystery. In the light of these observations it may be stated that the selections from bhagat bani were not made exclusively on the basis of identity with the teachings of the Gurus. There is difference as well as identity. It is important to note that the Gurus were deeply concerned about cultivating a particular Sikh view of true teaching, practice and community by way of editing and commenting on the received tradition of the bhagat bani.

Here, I intend to deal more specifically with the doctrinal issues arising from the inclusion of the bhagat bani in the Sikh scriptural tradition. There are some specific examples in the Kartarpur manuscript where certain hymns of the bhagats are either erased with the use of hartal or simply crossed out with a pen. These deletions clearly illustrate Guru Arjan's readiness to exercise editorial discretion. An examination of old manuscripts indicates that hartal was normally used by scribes during the process of writing (when they were so directed to delete a particular verse or hymn), whereas the 'crossings' with a pen reflect a later decision of the editor to exclude a particular composition from the scripture. The latter was sometimes accompanied by a marginal note. Before proceeding to examine the issue of deletions, however, we must determine who was responsible for collecting the hymns of the bhagats in the first place and making them part of the Sikh scriptural tradition.

COLLECTION OF THE BHAGAT BANI

It is commonly assumed that the founder of Sikh faith, Guru Nanak (1469–1539), must have collected the bhagat material during his extensive travels. Sahib Singh, for instance, discusses this issue at length and asserts that a comparative analysis of some of Guru Nanak's works and those of Kabir clearly indicates thematic as well as verbal similarities which can be explained by the assumption that Guru Nanak had access to at least some of Kabir's works.[6] However,

---

[6]Sahib Singh, *Bhagat-Bani Steek*, Part 4 (Amritsar: Singh Brothers, 1980), pp. 26–43.

W.H. McLeod challenges this assumption by arguing that many of the resemblances which Sahib Singh perceives are too vague to warrant consideration as they concern common themes rather than actual correspondence.[7] He then quotes five brief passages of less than two lines each which possess verbal correspondence and asserts that they may simply be proverbial expressions which may have come from the religious language of everyday life of north India. The following examples from the hymns of Beni, Kabir and Guru Nanak will illustrate the point.

Says Beni: the Guru-directed thus meditates; without the true Guru, one does not find the way.

(Beni, *Prabhati* 1, AG, p. 1351)

Without the true Guru, one does not find the way; explaining the mystery, so says Kabir.

(Kabir, *Basant* 3, AG, p. 1194)

Says Nanak: with trusting-faith one meditates; without the true Guru, one does not find the way.

(M1, *Sahasakriti* 1, AG, p. 1353)

The expression *binu satgur bat na pavai* (without the true Guru, one does not find the way) is common to the hymns of Beni and Guru Nanak. Although it differs slightly in the case of Kabir's hymn, the meaning is retained. McLeod maintains that such examples are a type of epigram which could easily have gained common currency within the circle of the sants. He concludes that 'in all likelihood Guru Nanak and Kabir neither met nor knew each other's works.'[8]

There are two significant points which need to be made in the context of the present discussion. In the first place, Guru Nanak does not mention Kabir or any other bhagat in his own works. Secondly, he does not comment on any verse of Kabir or any other sant poet, as he does in the case of Shaikh Farid.[9] He was certainly familiar with the hymns of the sufi poet, and nine of Guru Nanak's hymns (*Siri* 24, *Siri Ast.* 5, *Asa Ast.* 14, *Vadahans* 1–3, *Suhi Kafi* 1, and *Maru Ast.* 9–10) are composed in the language characteristic of Farid-bani.[10]

---

[7]W.H. McLeod, 'Guru Nanak and Kabir,' *Proceedings of the Punjab History Conference*, 1st Session, November 1965 (Patiala: Punjabi University, 1966), pp. 89–90.

[8]ibid., p. 92. Also see his *Guru Nanak and the Sikh Religion*, p. 86, n. 2.

[9]Guru Nanak's comments on Shaikh Farid are examined in my 'Sikh Self-Definition,' pp. 37–46.

[10]For details, see Christopher Shackle, 'Early Muslim vernacular poetry in the Indus Valley: Its Contexts and Character,' *Islam and Indian Regions*, pp. 274–5, n. 27.

Thematically, these hymns of Guru Nanak are entirely at one with the emphases of the Farid-bani, whose actual verbal expressions are frequently recalled on the *memento mori* themes.[11] Shaikh Farid's mystical songs in old Punjabi were intended to be recited or sung as part of religious music in the sufi worship. They influenced the entire population of the Punjab, particularly women, who used to sing these simple verses while doing their daily work.[12]

There is some fresh evidence from the Khuldabad manuscript that can provide a new light on the issue of the authenticity and dating of the Farid bani in the Adi Granth. The original manuscript, probably an eighteenth-century copy of the *Hidayat al-qulub wa 'inayat al-guyub* by Mir Hassan (*c.* 1370), is in the collection of Fariduddin Saleem of Khuldabad.[13] There is one shared verse of Shaikh Farid which appears in both the Adi Granth (*farida jo tain maranhi mukkian tinhan na mare ghummi// apanarai ghari jaiai pair tinhan de chummi//*) and the *Hidayat al-qulub* (*jo tujh mare mukkiyan tissu na mare ghummi// tun jaen ghari apane pagg tinhanre chummi//*). Thus in the *Malfuzat* of Zain ud-Din Shirazi (d. 1371), successor to Burhan ud-Din Garib at Khuldabad, there are at least seven Hindawi verses of Farid ud-Din Ganj-i-Shakkar, one of which is found in the Adi Granth. It clearly indicates that a corpus of poems acknowledged to be Baba Farid's was in circulation in Chisti circles within a century after his death. This evidence certainly favours the strength of oral tradition of Punjabi sufi poetry, and the continuity of the Farid bani with the older poems of the sufi tradition.[14] These sufi songs certainly attracted the special attention of Guru Nanak for comment on what constitutes true religious belief and practice. There is, however, no documentary evidence to support the contention that Guru Nanak was primarily responsible for collecting the hymns of the sufi poets and other bhagats and making them part and parcel of Sikh scriptural tradition.

Shaikh Farid frequently expresses his anguish over lack of fulfilment through the symbol of a suffering lover, which, according to Schimmel, is one of the salient features of Indo-Muslim poetry.[15]

---

[11] For details, see ibid., p. 275.

[12] Annemarie Schimmel, *Mystical Dimensions of Islam* (Chapel Hill: The University of North Carolina Press, 1975), p. 348.

[13] For more details, see Shackle, 'Early Muslim Vernacular Poetry', p. 269, n. 18 and Carl W. Ernst, *Eternal Garden: Mysticism, History, and Politics at a South Asian Sufi Center* (Albany: SUNY Press, 1992), pp. 166–8.

[14] ibid.

[15] Cited in my 'Sikh Self-Definition', p. 32.

In one of his shaloks, for instance, he calls the state of separation kingly (*birha tun sultan*). The sovereign quality of the devotee encourages the suffering lover to plumb deeper and deeper into the wonderful mysteries of the divine beloved and thus creates the conditions of ineffable joy. This theme of intense longing for the beloved pervades the compositions of the Sikh Gurus. For instance, the following shalok of Guru Angad sounds very much like Shaikh Farid's:

Shalok Mahala 2
The head that bows not to the lord merits casting off. The body which is not charged with the agony of separation (*birha*), O Nanak, is worth being burnt.
(M2, *Var Siri Raga* 1(15), AG, p. 89)

Here, Guru Angad has employed certain phrases from the Farid bani. This close verbal correspondence is not accidental. Guru Angad was certainly familiar with the mystical songs of Shaikh Farid. One needs only to look at Shaikh Farid's shaloks 36, 71 and 72 for comparative purposes.

It was, however, Guru Amar Das who mentioned the names of Kabir and Namdev for the first time in his hymns. He also inserted a number of Kabir's shaloks in his own vars (ballads) and responded to them in his commentary verses for the sake of defining true teaching, practice and community from the viewpoint of Sikh doctrine.[16] Moreover, Guru Amar Das provides the reasons underlying the inclusion of the bhagat bani in the Sikh scriptural tradition in a particularly interesting verse.

Namdev the chhimba and Kabir the julaha obtained their spiritual status from the perfect Guru. In divine knowledge, recognizing the word, they spurned all self-centredness and caste. Even gods and men sing their bani and none can wipe it away, my brother. (3)
(M3, *Siri Ragu* 22, AG, p. 67)

Here Guru Amar Das acknowledges that Namdev and Kabir had the experience of the divine truth which they proclaimed in verbal form (shabad) in their compositions. Thus their inclusion in the Sikh scriptural tradition follows naturally from the doctrine of the universal bani, which appears perpetually in all ages in the works of the bhagats. What cannot be effaced deserves to be preserved, and thus collected alongside the works of the Gurus.

[16]For details, see my 'Sikh Self-Definition,' pp. 84–91.

The presence of bhagat bani in the two available copies of the Goindval pothis provides documentary evidence that Guru Amar Das was responsible for introducing the compositions of medieval saints into the early Sikh scriptural tradition. It should be emphasized, however, that the hymns of the bhagats were circulating in the Punjab through travelling professional singers who used them in kirtan sessions.[17] That was why they were taken as a starting point during the selection process, to be confirmed after Guru Amar Das had carefully gone through them. This process began with a sifting through the writings of those bhagats who shared the Sikh theological vision, a vision that involved a belief in one God (Akal Purakh) beyond all form and sectarian garb, the basic equality of human beings, the doctrine of the word, the spiritual discipline of nam simaran, the doctrine of God as true Guru immanent in human soul, the company of the saintly people, and the emphasis upon true inner religiosity. Those hymns that did not conform to these ideals were rejected in preliminary scrutiny.

In the Goindval pothis the clusters of hymns by Kabir and Namdev are entitled 'the hymns in *Bhairon* mode by Kamiru and Nama, the devotees of Guru Baba [Nanak]' (*bhairon kamiru nama bhagat babe de*).[18] Two explanations may be offered for this striking title concerning the status of the sant poets in the Sikh tradition. First, Kabir and Namdev were generally scorned by the learned and high-born and their compositions were ignored as being of no significance. Commenting on the low-born sants including Kabir and Namdev, for instance, Vaudeville writes: 'They are generally ignorant, if not always illiterate, workshop prophets and village saints whom the learned and high-born despise and ignore.'[19] This kind of attitude towards the sants was a result of their vigorous attack on the *smarta* tradition, that is, the social and religious order taught in the Dharamshastras and the Puranas and based on the Vedas. Tulsidas, for instance, referred to the sant poetry in the *Dohavali* (doha 554) as follows: 'In this dark age with sakhis, shabads and dohas, with tales and stories, these devotees expound devotion, while scorning

[17]For details, see Winand M. Callewaert, 'Singers Repertoires in Western India,' in R.S. McGregor, ed., *Devotional Literature in South Asia: Current Research, 1985–1988* (Cambridge: Cambridge University Press, 1992), pp. 29–35.

[18]Punjabi University Library, Photocopy of Volume I [of Goindval pothis]: f. 263a. Also see the photographs of such folios in Giani Gurdit Singh, *Itihas Sri Guru Granth Sahib: Bhagat Bani Bhag* (Chandigarh: Sikh Sahit Sansthan, 1990), pp. 3, 4, 555.

[19]Charlotte Vaudville, *Kabir*, Vol. I (Oxford: Clarendon Press, 1974), p. 99.

the Veda and Puranas.'[20] He considered all the sants as a serious threat to conventional Hindu tradition and accused them as follows: 'They leave the path of devotion to Hari and dream many new paths.'[21] In the wake of such criticism it may have been necessary for Guru Amar Das to own Kabir and Namdev as devotees of Guru Nanak so that he might establish them in the early Sikh scriptural tradition.

Second, the title in the Goindval pothis may reflect an editorial device that simultaneously incorporates and supersedes the sant tradition. To use Wilfred Cantwell Smith's phrase, it may also imply that the bhagat bani was held as 'a somewhat sub-ordinate part and parcel' of the early Sikh scriptural tradition. By making Kabir and Namdev 'devotees of Guru Nanak', the third Guru was in fact extending an open invitation to their followers to join the Sikh Panth. He was certainly responsible for the institutional expansion that included the establishment of the city of Goindval, the biannual festivals of Diwali and Baisakhi, providing an opportunity for the growing community to get together and meet the Guru, and a missionary system (*manjis*) for attracting new converts. It should be emphasized here, however, that the title in the Goindval pothis reflects the contemporary Sikh understanding of the status of Kabir and Namdev as devotees of Guru Nanak. This understanding may also be seen in the panegyrics by bards in praise of Guru Nanak.[22] It was part of the ancient triumphant (*digvijaya*) tradition.

Guru Arjan extended the precedent of Guru Amar Das when he compiled the first canonical text of the Adi Granth. He made further selection and dropped several hymns of Kabir and Namdev available in the copies of the Goindval volumes. In the case of the bani of Namdev, he seems to have done recasting of certain hymns to fit them in the context of the teachings of the Gurus and simplified the language of others originally composed in the Marathi dialect.[23] There are 148 hymns of the bhagats in the two extant copies of the Goindval pothis in eleven raga sections. Out of these 129 hymns were introduced in the Kartarpur bir in their revised form while nineteen hymns were excluded.[24] It is interesting to note that out of

[20]R. Allchin, *Kitavali* (London: Allen and Unwin, 1964), p. 49.

[21]doha 555, see ibid.

[22]See Kal, *Savayye Mahale Pahale Ke 8*, AG, p. 1390.

[23]Nirbhai Singh, *Bhagata Namadeva in the Guru Grantha* (Patiala: Punjabi University, 1981), pp. 190–1.

[24]Gurinder Singh Mann, *The Goindval Pothis*, pp. 38–9. For the text of the nineteen hymns that were excluded from the Adi Granth, see pp. 117–35.

the nineteen 'excluded hymns' only three hymns are in the hand of the primary scribe while the other sixteen are in the hand of the second scribe and are invariably written at the closing of raga sections. It is quite possible that these sixteen hymns were not part of the original Goindval volumes and that they were introduced in the two available copies by Baba Mohan later. Some of these hymns are coloured by Vaishnava ideals and hence they would not likely to be acceptable to Guru Arjan. Moreover, thirty-four other hymns that were included in the Kartarpur manuscript came from independent sources. It means that there existed some other manuscripts of the bhagat bani which were available to Guru Arjan at the time of the compilation of the first canonical text.

Guru Arjan arranged the works of the bhagats under the common title of 'the bani of the bhagats [such as] Kabir, Namdev and Ravidas in *Asa* mode' (*ragu asa bani bhagatan ki: Kabir jiu Namdeu jiu Ravidas jiu*).[25] This new title indicates that the bhagats were duly acknowledged as part and parcel of the Sikh tradition when their compositions were included in the final text of the Adi Granth. It also suggests that they all shared a common status because they were all adjudged to have spoken the divine word and confirmed as such by the Sikh Gurus. The most striking example in this context is Guru Arjan's *Basant Astapadi* in which he illuminates the spiritual attainment of all sant poets.[26] It is quite possible that by this time the followers of the bhagats had become part of the Sikh Panth.

Moreover, in contrast with Guru Nanak's comments on Shaikh Farid and Guru Amar Das's reflections on both Kabir and Farid, Guru Arjan's verses of commentary bear the signatures of the bhagats who are being commented upon. This new convention shows a more intimate relationship with bhagat bani. In these instances, Guru Arjan actually addresses the followers of Kabir and Farid directly, while commenting on a particular composition of the sant or sufi poet.[27] Through these comments he in fact addresses the issues that were being debated between the Sikh community and the followers of the bhagats. The most striking example of it is the use of Kabir's signatures in the *Bhairau* hymn, where Guru Arjan makes a direct assertion of independent Sikh identity: 'We are neither Hindu nor

[25]Kabir, *Asa* 1, AG, p. 475.

[26]M5, *Basant Dutukian* 1, AG, p. 1192.

[27]M5, *Salok Bhagat Kabir Jiu Ke*, nos 209–11, 214, 221, AG, pp. 1375–6 and M5, *Salok Shaikh Farid Ke*, nos 75, 82–3, 105, 108–11, AG, pp. 1381–4.

Musalman.'[28] There is another striking instance in the *Gauri* mode where a hymn of Kabir is entitled *Gauri Kabir Ji Ki nali ralae likhia Mahala 5* ('Kabir's hymn in the measure *Gauri* to which Guru Arjan's composition is added').[29] This title clearly indicates that Guru Arjan's comment is added to the hymn.

In the context of the present discussion, Gurinder Singh Mann's assertion that 'the technique of direct response to the writings of the saints seems to have begun with Guru Amardas' becomes questionable.[30] First, Guru Nanak's *Siddh Gost* (discourse with the Siddhas) in the *Ramakali* mode provides clear evidence that this technique began with him. The immediate influence in the Punjab was that of naths and sufis and Guru Nanak responded to them by making comments on their writings. Second, even if we accept Guru Amar Das's authorship of the *Suhi* hymn (*jap tap ka bandh berula*) there are still three shaloks of Guru Nanak which are direct comments on the works of Shaikh Farid.[31] Finally, Guru Amar Das adopted the technique of textual commentary from the writings of Guru Nanak. In fact, his whole bani is carefully modelled on the pattern of the bani of the first Guru.

To understand the technique of textual commentary more fully, let us examine Kabir's theme of self-withdrawal from active life. His autobiographical hymns in the Adi Granth clearly state that 'Kabir does not care for his profession' and 'he has ruined the whole business.'[32] His wife complains that 'our daughter and sons have nothing to eat' and 'he no longer speaks of his beam and shuttle.'[33] There is a sense in which passivity is raised to the level of normative behaviour for the mystic:

Kabir, whatever I propose, God disposes; so why propose and scheme? For, what God proposes, he does; and does he what one cannot even dream?

(Kabir, *Salok* 219, AG, p. 1376)

Rather than accepting the divine will with a positive attitude, Kabir here seems to want to escape from life, giving up all proposing and scheming for the sake of living.

[28]M5, *Bhairau* 3, AG, p. 1136. For more details, see Chapter 5.

[29]Kabir and M5, *Gauri* 14, AG, p. 326. For more details, see my 'Sikh Self-Definition,' pp. 98–100.

[30]Gurinder Singh Mann, 'The Making of Sikh Scripture' (Ph.D. thesis, Columbia University, 1993), p. 167.

[31]For details, see my 'Sikh Self-Definition,' pp. 41–6.

[32]Kabir, *Bilavalu* 4, AG, p. 856.

[33]Kabir, *Gond* 6, AG, p. 871.

This escapist attitude is in opposition to the Sikh vision of action-oriented life in the world and a joyous acceptance of the divine will in every situation whether favourable or not. For the Gurus, creative activity in the world is the yardstick of one's progress in the life of spirituality. Guru Amar Das responds to Kabir's view as follows:

M3
He himself puts care (*chinta*) in us, he himself makes us carefree (*achintu*): Nanak, give praise to that one who takes care of all.

(M3, *Salok* 220, AG, p. 1376)

The word chinta in the present context means care and anxiety that one experiences in one's life while participating in worldly affairs. Guru Amar Das asserts that one should put one's faith exclusively in the Akal Purakh who dwells within oneself and looks after everyone in their mundane concerns. Thus by submitting to the divine will cheerfully one can become carefree (achintu) and gain confidence to cope with any situation of anguish and despair, because every happening is then seen to be coming from Akal Purakh. Here the Guru clearly provides a corrective to Kabir's view of self-withdrawal by stressing the need to confront life with a positive attitude.

However, in order to guard against excessive indulgence or over-confidence in the things of the world, Guru Arjan adds a further comment as follows:

M5
Kabir! man meditated not on Ram, he wandered, following his desires. Whilst given to sin, he died: in one moment, his life span was over.

(M5, *Salok* 221, AG, p. 1376)

Here, Guru Arjan employs the signatures of Kabir and describes the nature of unregenerate man who is so attached to his passions for worldly pleasures that he forgets God and wastes his entire life in sin. The remark is clearly intended to create a harmonized balance between the extremes of withdrawal and excessive indulgence in the things of the world. Thus the Gurus' comments serve to highlight the distinctive Sikh way of life for the benefit of the Sikh community.

Finally, it is important to note that a clear distinction is always maintained between gurbani and the bhagat bani in the very structure of the Sikh scripture. The writings of the bhagats are kept separate from those of the Gurus and are placed at the end of each raga section. In other words, the primacy of the writings of the Gurus is always maintained, even though the hymns of bhagats are held in great esteem. Nevertheless, the issue of the status of bhagat bani has been surfacing in Sikh literature from time to time, revealing an ambiguity in the historical experience of the Sikh community. It will receive an extensive treatment in a separate study. Here, I shall focus on the process that went into the selection of the writings of the bhagats permitted into the Sikh scripture.

SELECTION OF THE BHAGAT BANI

Now let us turn to the issue of deletions of certain hymns of bhagat bani from the Sikh scripture. These hymns must have had considerable *a priori* status to get so far as being included in the final Kartarpur manuscript. Their subsequent deletion, however, raises the following important questions: why were these hymns included in the Sikh scripture in the first place, and why were they excluded later on? Could the later deletions reflect a tension between the followers of the bhagats and the Sikhs at that particular time? In order to find answers to these questions, let us begin with an examination of the issues arising from the deletion of certain hymns of Kabir who is otherwise prominently represented in the Adi Granth. There are four instances in the Kartarpur manuscript where Kabir's verses are either crossed out with a pen or deleted with the use of hartal. We shall discuss this issue in detail in order to assess Guru Arjan's editorial concerns leading to the exclusion of these verses.

1. Deletion of Kabir Material from the Adi Granth

1.1. *Kabir's Gauri Shalok*

A shalok was incorporated in a different hand on the right hand corner just below the invocation of Kabir's work entitled *Var Sat* (seven days) in the *Gauri* mode, but later on it was deleted with the use of hartal.[34] This shalok can still be read under the deletion paste. It reads:

Shalok
There is a pivotal axis (*belari*, circular rod) between the lower region and the sky, where there is a crimson fragrant flower. You have not learned those [potent] syllables (*akhar*) and yet you expect that your fast (*roza*, the Muslim fast of Ramzan) will be approved [by the lord].

---

[34]Kartarpur MS, f. 275/1.

Here the belari refers to the spinal cord, the main axis of the human body, which is called in yogic terminology *meru-danda* from the analogy of Mount Meru or Sumeru, believed to be the pivot of the universe.[35] There is a series of chakras or discs along the spinal cord in the shape of lotuses (padmas). The lower region (*dhari*) refers to the *muladhara-chakra*, whereas the sky (*ambar*) refers to the 'thousand-petalled lotus' (*sahasrara-chakra*).[36]

Evidently the shalok reflects the mystical state achieved through the successful performance of the hatha-yoga technique. It seems to be addressed to a Muslim, who may have been observing his fast of Ramzan without any idea of yogic knowledge and practices. Its theme does not fit in the context of Kabir's composition entitled *Var Sat*. Further, Guru Arjan would never approve of this couplet because of its emphasis on the discipline of hatha-yoga. Although it was originally recorded in the Kartarpur volume, it was subsequently deemed unworthy of inclusion and was deleted with the use of hartal.

1.2. Kabir's Asa hymn

There is a hymn of Kabir in the *Asa* raga, which is crossed out with a pen. It is quite certain that C.H. Loehin was referring to the verses of this hymn when he took notes on the Kartarpur manuscript on 7 July 1946: 'Several verses by Kabir in Rag Asa have been obliterated by someone.'[37] This hymn reads:

Asa Kabir.
Look O people! the betrothal of the lord. Mother has wed her son and she goes with her husband. I am the father and Ram is my son. I am his sister's husband (*bahinoi*) and Ram is my brother-in-law (*sala*). Why should I say 'Ram' now! Ram is my father-in-law (*sasur*) and I am Ram's son-in-law (*javayyia*). Says Kabir: Listen O son! Those people who repeat Ram are the real appraisers (*kuta*). (3.2.35)[38]

Clearly, this is one of Kabir's paradoxical (*ultabamsi*) sayings. Linda Hess maintains that the meaning of *ulta* is more like reversed rather than upside-down. Typical ultabamsi expressions are based on reversals of roles, personalities, laws of nature: a rabbit eats a lion, a quail conquers a hawk, an arrow strikes the hunter, fire burns in

[35]Vaudeville, *Kabir*, p. 130.

[36]For more details, see my 'The Text and Meaning of the Adi Granth' (Ph.D. thesis, University of Toronto, 1991), p. 73, n. 23.

[37]C.H. Loehlin, 'A Westerner Looks at the Kartarpur Granth', *Proceedings of the Punjab History Conference* (Patiala: Punjabi University, 1966), p. 94.

[38]Kartarpur MS, f. 374/2.

water, and rain falls from the earth to the sky.[39] In the present case a mother weds her son, Kabir is the father and Ram is his son. Or Kabir is Ram's sister's husband (bahinoi) and Ram is his brother-in-law (sala). Kabir seems to have inherited this language of paradoxes and enigmas from the sahajiyas and naths and adapted to his own purpose.[40] These paradoxical statements of Kabir may have been designed to stir up his audience with surprises (acharaj) so that he could engender in his hearers/readers a sense of immediacy of experience.

The reason for the deletion of this hymn in the Kartarpur volume does not appear to be linked with its paradoxical nature. There are a number of such hymns to be found in the Adi Granth.[41] Rather, the issue in the present case appears to be the use of such strong words as sala (brother-in-law) and sasur (father-in-law) for Ram, which form part of abusive language in the Punjabi culture. This is hardly the language of self-abasement or the poetics of humility or even respect, which is characteristic of the Adi Granth. Kabir, who had to face the daily scorn of the pandits of Banaras because of his low caste, developed a caustic and blunt style.[42] He frequently becomes offensive to his audience, but this could be afforded by a solitary spiritual seeker. It is, however, certainly not the style of the Sikh Gurus, who had a deep sense of social mission and the idea of an organized religious community. Whatever the original context of this hymn might have been, Guru Arjan, it seems, decided to exclude it because it did not match the spiritual tone and meaning of the Adi Granth.[43]

Piar Singh vehemently argued that 'this hymn of Kabir is so

[39]Linda Hess and Shukdev Singh, *The Bijak of Kabir* (San Francisco: North Point Press, 1979), p. 145.

[40]ibid., p. 14. For more details on Kabir's language, see Charlotte Vaudville, *A Weaver Named Kabir* (Delhi: Oxford University Press, 1993), pp. 109–30.

[41]Kabir, *Basant* 3, AG, p. 1194 and *Gauri* 14, AG, p. 326. The second hymn includes Guru Arjan's commentary verse at the end which is intended to clarify the meaning of Kabir's hymn.

[42]Hess and Singh, *Bijak*, pp. 10–11. For more details on Kabir's style, see Linda Hess, 'Three Kabir Collections: A Comparative Study', and 'Kabir's Rough Rhetoric', in Karine Schomer and W.H. McLeod, eds, *The Sants: Studies in a Devotional Tradition of India* (Berkeley and Delhi: Berkeley Religious Studies Series and Motilal Banarsidass, 1987), pp. 112–65.

[43]This hymn may have originated in response to a Vaishnava's suggestion to repeat the name of 'Ram', an incarnation of Vishnu. Kabir may have replied: 'Why on earth shall I say 'Ram' now when he is my brother-in-law (sala) or father-in-law (sasur)?' In his compositions, Kabir explicitly repudiates this anthropomorphic Ram. For him, Ram is primarily a sound, a mantra consisting of the long and short syllable Ra-ma. See Hess and Singh, *Bijak*, p. 4.

patently out of tune with the Sikh thought and ideology that no Sikh Guru, much less Guru Arjan, would ever countenance its inclusion in the Sikhs' Holy Scripture.'[44] He thus questioned the authenticity of the Kartarpur bir on the basis of its inclusion in the first place: 'How could then Guru Arjan have allowed the inclusion of such a libellous hymn in his Holy Scripture as the above piece is?'[45] Piar Singh seems to be working on the assumption that the manuscript prepared by 'so talented an amanuensis as Bhai Gurdas' under the direct supervision of 'an infallible Guru' must be perfect in every way. Such a manuscript does not exist. The Kartarpur bir was transcribed by human hands, and during the process of writing certain errors of omission and commission obviously occurred. When they were detected by Guru Arjan, they were rectified, and the deletion of Kabir's *Asa* hymn illuminates that process.

1.3. Kabir's Sorathi hymn

There are only two lines of Kabir's hymn in *Sorathi* raga that were recorded in the Adi Granth and were then crossed out with a pen. These two lines appear in the Kartarpur volume as follows:

O Audhu! That yogi is my Guru, who clarifies the meaning of this word (pad) to me. (1). Refrain.

Clearly, this verse is addressed to an *audhu*, one who has shaken off [the ties of *samsara*].[46] Here Kabir offers to become the disciple of a yogi who might reveal the esoteric meaning of a particular hymn (pad) to him. To entertain such an idea of accepting a yogi as Guru would amount to exposing the community of householders to the nath tradition. This seems to be the main reason why this particular verse was crossed out with a pen in the text of the Kartarpur manuscript and why the remainder of the hymn was not recorded. Some of the manuscripts of the Adi Granth do not contain even these two lines.[47]

It is important to note that the above verse of Kabir is a part of a hymn, the complete version of which is to be found in some later manuscripts of the Banno recension of the Adi Granth. The reading of the complete hymn is as follows:

[44]Piar Singh, *Gatha*, pp. 100–1.
[45]ibid.
[46]Vaudeville, *Kabir*, p. 125.
[47]For instance, see PUM, MS # 6, f. 298b. In the Una Sahib MS # 2, the verse is written in the margin of folio 253a in a different hand as a later thought.

Sorathi

O Audhu! That yogi is my Guru, who clarifies the meaning of this word (pad) to me. (1). Refrain. There is a tree standing without roots, which bears fruit without flowering. There are no branches or leaves of that [tree], still [a flower of] eight lotuses bloom. (1). There are two birds sitting at a pool, one of them Guru and the other disciple. The disciple has picked and eaten [the fruit of] the whole world; the Guru has enjoyed the sport within. (2). In the cave of the sky there is an inverted well which is the abode of the nectar. The intelligent one drinks the nectar to the fill, while the one who lacks a Guru (*nigura*) remains thirsty. (3). After reflection Kabir says: 'The sport of the bird is just like the way of a fish. I have seen a unique form (*murati*) within the external appearance (*surat*), for which I sacrifice myself to the true Guru.' (4.9)[48]

Evidently, the whole hymn is full of tantric language and concepts. The eight lotuses (*ast-kanwal*) refer to the highest of the astral nerve centres (chakras) through which the *kundalini* power rises. The references to the cave in the sky (*gagan gupha*) and the inverted well (*uradh mukh kua*) of nectar point towards the state of supra-consciousness to which the yogis aspire.[49] Further, there are some paradoxical statements (ultabamsi) too: the tree standing without roots and bearing fruit without flowering, and a bird following the way of a fish. Obviously these statements are intended to convey an experience which defies logic. These esoteric teachings of tantric yoga would scarcely be acceptable to Guru Arjan.

1.4. Kabir's Shalok

Although an extra shalok was incorporated in the Kartarpur volume at the end of Kabir's shaloks in a different hand, it was crossed out with a pen. An editorial comment explains that 'this shalok is just an ordinary one' (*ih salok aime hai*). Obviously it was not approved by Guru Arjan. The shalok reads:

What can one take in return, Kabir, for revealing the mystery of the divine name? What [gift of mine] could please the Guru who provides contentment? I am surrendering [my self] within.[50]

The word *patantara* stands for the 'contents of an official document'

[48]John Rylands Library, Panj. MS # 5, f. 216b. The whole hymn is erased with the use of hartal, but it could still be read with some help from the following manuscripts: Guru Granth Sahib Trust, Coventry, UK, MS # 504, f. 319a and Tarlok Singh Choudary's Private Collection, Harrow, UK, MS # 3, f. 277a.

[49]Schomer, 'Kabir in the Guru Granth Sahib', pp. 82–3.

[50]Kartarpur MS, f. 943/2. The analogue of this couplet appears in the *Kabir-granthavali* (1.1). See Vaudeville, *Kabir*, p. 151.

which are confidential in nature.[51] In the present context Kabir employs it in connection with the mystery of the divine name (*ram nam ke patantarai*), which refers to the contemporary esoteric practice of giving nam (name) to the disciples who belonged to the inner sant circles. He further proclaims that the divine name is itself a priceless gift and that no present could repay it. He may also be referring to the Indian tradition of *Guru-daksina*, according to which it is customary for the disciple to make an offering to his teacher once he has received the name in the form of a sacred mantra.[52]

There are at least two possible reasons why Guru Arjan disapproved of this couplet. First, the theme of the shalok is linked with the esoteric practice of giving the nam secretly, which had no place in contemporary Sikh practice. The Gurus freely distributed (vartae) the gift of the nam in holy congregation.[53] Guru Nanak's observation is particularly significant in this context: 'A curse on the life of those who write the nam [as an incantation on a piece of paper] and sell it [for profit].'[54] Secondly, it did not fit well into the total context of Kabir's shaloks in the Adi Granth. Its later addition at the end and subsequent deletion may suggest that it did not appeal to Guru Arjan who considered it less perceptive and thereby took the decision to exclude it.

2. The Mira Bai Hymn

Mira Bai's hymn is another textual problem in the Adi Granth which has drawn a great deal of scholarly attention in the Kartarpur–Banno debate. Although it is written in the Kartarpur volume in a different hand, it has been deleted with a pen. Obviously the hymn was originally present, but was subsequently deemed unworthy of inclusion and hence was crossed out. It is not to be found in the earliest extant copy of the Kartarpur manuscript, which was apparently prepared during Guru Arjan's period.[55] This indicates

---

[51]C. Shackle, *A Guru Nanak Glossary* (London: School of Oriental and African Studies, 1981), p. 179.

[52]See Vaudeville's interpretation in *Kabir*, p. 151, n. 2.

[53]M1, *Maru* 8, AG, p. 991; M3, *Var Vadahans* 2 (18), AG, p. 593; and M5, *Gauri Guareri* 100, AG, p. 185–6; *Sarang* 80, AG, p. 1220; *Gujari* 3, AG, pp. 495–6. Also see Surjit Hans, *A Reconstruction of Sikh History from Sikh Literature* (Jalandhar: ABS Publication, 1988), p. 68.

[54]M1, *Var Sarang* 1 (20), AG, p. 1245.

[55]Punjabi University Museum, MS # 7, f. 448b. This undated manuscript does not contain the compositions of Guru Tegh Bahadur. There are certain features of this manuscript which make it a copy of the Kartarpur volume. For details, see my 'The Text and Meaning of the Adi Granth', pp. 35–8.

that the decision to exclude Mira Bai's hymn must have been made by Guru Arjan himself. Also, there is a very significant marginal note in Ram Rai's bir (written in 1659), which belongs to the Kartarpur tradition, mentioning specifically that 'Mira Bai's hymn is not found in the granth of the fifth Guru' (*mira bai ka sabad panjavain mahallai ke giranth nahin*).[56] The manuscripts of both the Lahore and Kartarpur traditions of the Adi Granth do not contain the hymn of Mira Bai at all. Gurinder Mann's claim that Mira Bai's hymn was 'deleted from the canon only when the *Adi Granth* was compiled [during the period of Guru Gobind Singh]' is not correct.[57] The compiler of Baba Ram Rai's bir which was written during the period of Guru Har Rai had already found this hymn crossed out in Guru Arjan's original volume. It is difficult to pinpoint exactly (the day, the month and the year) when it was deleted.

All copies of the Banno version of the Adi Granth include the Mira Bai hymn. It reads as follows:

Mira Bai

The lotus-eyed lord [with his attributes][58] has entwined my *man* (heart-mind-soul) O mother. (1) Refrain. The sharp arrow [of his love] has pierced my body through, O mother. I did not know when it struck me; now it cannot be endured, O mother. (1) Though I use charms, incantations and medicines, the pain will not depart. Is there anyone who will treat me? Intense is the agony, O mother. (2) You are near to me, you are not distant; come quickly to meet me. Mira's lord is the mountain-lifter who has quenched the fire of my body, O mother. The lotus-eyed has entwined [my *man* with the twine of his] attributes, O mother.[59] (3)[60]

Evidently, the central theme of this hymn is Krishna bhakti. The lotus-eyed lord (*kaval nainu*) was an epithet used for Krishna, the object of Mira Bai's special worship. She further employs an expanded version of her signatures—'Mira's lord the mountain-lifter' (*mira*

---

[56]G.B. Singh, *Prachin Biran*, p. 169.

[57]See his 'The Making of Sikh Scripture,' pp. 188–9.

[58]The phrase *apane gun* (with his attributes) is not to be found in the Kartarpur MS, although it appears in later manuscripts of the Banno text. See Kartarpur MS, f. 811/1.

[59]This translation is adapted from Max Arthur Macaulifffe, *The Sikh Religion*, Vol. VI (New Delhi: S. Chand & Co., reprint, 1963; originally published in 1909), p. 356.

[60]Kartarpur MS, f. 811/1. This is the oldest record of Mira's poem to be found in the early seventeenth-century manuscript. For more details, see John Stratton Hawley and Mark Juergensmeyer, *Songs of the Saints of India*, pp. 202–3, n. 9.

giradhar suami)—which clearly indicates that the image of Krishna as the mountain-lifter is the one she holds most dear.[61]

The focus of the hymn is the theme of the pangs of separation from the divine beloved, Krishna. The intensity of this anguish reaches its climax in the symbolism of sharp arrows afflicting wounds on the body. The phrase *tan ki tapati bujhai* ('quenched the fire of my body') points towards the erotic nature of Mira's love for Krishna.[62] It is important to note that the erotic symbolism in the compositions of the Gurus is toned down from the romantic love expressed by Mira Bai in her poetry.[63] This may be one of the reasons why Guru Arjan excluded her hymn from the Sikh scripture. The second reason seems to be Mira Bai's emphasis on Krishna bhakti, which is contrary to the Sikh devotional approach towards the non-incarnated Akal Purakh.[64] A third reason may be linked with Guru Arjan's editorial policy to keep the Sikh tradition removed from the Vaishnava influence.

3. The Surdas Hymn

The third major issue in the Kartarpur–Banno debate is linked with the incomplete nature of Surdas's hymn, the first line of which is recorded in the Kartarpur manuscript in the *Sarang* mode, followed by Guru Arjan's comment on Surdas. It created a great deal of confusion for later scribes who struggled with this textual problem and offered varying solutions to it. First, most of the scribes of the Lahore tradition did not record even this single line in their copies of the Adi Granth.[65] Second, some scribes did record the single line after Guru Arjan's comment on Surdas (though this was not the convention).[66] Third, some scribes omitted the single line of Surdas, but they attributed Guru Arjan's hymn to Surdas instead.[67] Fourth,

[61]Hawley and Juergensmeyer, ibid., p. 131.

[62] 'I am playing hide and seek with him, robed in this smock of five colors. Disguised as I was, he caught me, and beholding his beauty I made myself over to him, body and soul.' See A. J. Alston, *The Devotional Poems of Mirabai* (Delhi: Motilal Banarsidass, 1980), p. 42.

[63]For marital imagery in Sikh bhakti, see Gurudharam Singh Khalsa, *Guru Ram Das in Sikh Tradition* (New Delhi: Harman Publishing House, 1997), pp. 47–9.

[64]W.H. McLeod, *Guru Nanak and the Sikh Religion*, p. 214.

[65]Guru Nanak Dev University Library, MS # 1084 (1666), f. 351b (or 337a, second numbering); Punjabi University Museum, Jograj MS (1667), PUM # 2, f. 583b; British Library, MSS OR. 2159 (1745), f. 721a (or 718a).

[66]Una Sahib MS # 2 (seventeenth century), f. 493b; PUM MS # 6 (1692), f. 525b; BL MSS OR. 2748 (early nineteenth century), f. 690b (or 680b).

[67]GNDU MS # 1084, f. 398b (or 384a); BL MSS ADD. 25,680 (early nineteenth century), f. 688a (721a).

later scribes of the Banno text recorded Surdas's complete hymn in their copies of the Adi Granth.[68] All of these scribes failed to understand Guru Arjan's editorial policy.

This single line of Surdas's hymn is to be found in the Kartarpur manuscript, followed by a blank space. It is worth noting that early manuscripts of the Banno recension also contain only this single line.[69] It reads as follows:

Soul (*man*), turn your back on those who shun the lord.[70]

The opening line of Surdas's hymn stresses the urgent need to completely cut oneself off from the company of those people who have shunned the lord. This line inspired a response from Guru Arjan, and this is the main reason why he retained it in the Adi Granth while he excluded the remaining lines of the hymn. This unique instance illuminates two different aspects of Guru Arjan's editorial policy, namely the exclusive and inclusive attitudes towards the compositions of the bhagats.

In order to find the reasons for excluding the remainder of Surdas's hymn, we must examine the complete version of it. It reads as follows:

Soul (*man*), turn your back on those who shun the lord. Tell me, what good is there in giving cobras milk? Serpents can never surrender their venom. (1) Refrain. Why waste camphor by feeding it to crows or squander the water of the Ganges on dogs? Why array an ass in an aromatic scent? Why bejewel a monkey? (1) Do you really think an arrow can pierce a fallen stone, even if you empty your quiver of them all? Says Surdas: Once you've dyed a blanket black, there's no point hoping for a different hue. (2)[71]

Clearly, Surdas, like Kabir, describes the obstinacy and heedlessness of sinners in the formulaic expressions: 'you can't pierce a stone with an arrow,' and 'if you dye a blanket black, the colour will never

[68]Kanpur MS (1642), f. 414a (originally there was only the single line, but some other hand completed the hymn much later); IOL MSS Panj. C5 (1727, f. 617a), C1 (1738, f. 516b), F1 (1758, f. 618b), D3 (1764, f. 906a), D1 (1848, f. 608b); BL MSS OR. 1125, f. 576a (608a); Trinity College Library, Cambridge, MSS R. 153 (1743–1843), f. 750b.

[69]Tikana Bhai Ramkishen, Patiala, Gurdita Sekhon MS (1653), f. 665b; DBSSK MS # 3 (1679), f. 556a; PUM MS # 1, f. 615b; IOL MSS Panj. D2 (eighteenth century), f. 615b and John Rylands Library, Panj. MS # 5 (late seventeenth century), f. 385a.

[70]Kartarpur MS, f. 885/2.

[71]Sri Guru Granth Trust, Coventry, MS # 506. I have adapted this translation from John Stratton Hawley, *Sur Das: Poet, Singer, Saint* (Seattle: University of Washington, 1984), p. 135.

change.'[72] Here Surdas appears to be strongly opposed to any kind of association with sinners. For him, sinners are totally lost and for them the doors of liberation are closed.

Surdas's view is directly opposed to the optimistic Sikh view that it is never too late to turn towards Akal Purakh and that every sinner is a potential sant. This seems to be the reason why Guru Arjan accepted only the first line of Surdas's hymn and edited out the rest of the hymn. However, he offered his response to the issue raised in Surdas's hymn. His comment reads:

Sarang Mahala 5 Surdas
There is one supreme being, known by grace through the true Guru.

The devotees of the lord abide with him (alone). They dedicate their mind, body and everything else to him and remain joyously intoxicated by the divine music of the word (*dhuni,* melody). (1). Refrain. They are relieved of all evil at the [mere] sight of the lord; [from him] they receive all that they need. They have nothing to do with anything else except for the sight of [his] beautiful form. (1) Those who, discarding the beauteous lord (*siam*), seek anything else are like leeches sucking leper's blood. O Surdas! the lord has grasped my *man* in his hand, and has granted me [the everlasting joy of] the spiritual world (*paralok*). (2.1.8.)

(M5, *Sarang Surdas*, AG, p. 1253)

Here, by employing the phrase *siam sundar* (beauteous lord), an epithet used for Krishna, Guru Arjan addresses Surdas in his own terms. But Giani Gurdit Singh wrongly attributes this hymn to Sur Das Madan Mohan, a different poet from Surdas. There is no thematic or verbal correspondence (except the rhyme-scheme) between this hymn and Sur Das Madan Mohan's hymn that he quotes from the Har Sahai pothi.[73] This hymn is clearly Guru Arjan's comment on Surdas.

Guru Arjan stresses the point that saintly people (*har lok*) always abide in the company of Akal Purakh who is mystically present in holy fellowship. In contrast with Surdas, Guru Arjan's emphasis falls upon highlighting the goodness of the saintly people rather than on the wickedness of sinners. He does employ the highly figurative expression of leeches sucking leper's blood (*kusti tani jok*) to describe the pathetic condition of those who shun the beauteous lord (siam sundar). In the final analysis, however, he provides them with the hope to come out of their present predicament, and invites them to

[72]ibid., p. 135.
[73]See his *Itihas Sri Guru Granth Sahib*, pp. 584–5.

become part of the Sikh sangat and to enjoy the state of blissful *sahaj*[74] through devotional singing.

4. Namdev's Dhanasari Hymn

One extra-canonical hymn of Namdev is usually found in the *Dhanasari* mode in some later manuscripts of the Adi Granth. It is not recorded in the Kartarpur volume, which clearly indicates that it was turned down by Guru Arjan at the time of the compilation of the scripture in 1604. It reads as follows:

Dhanasari
His [tortoise-form's] river (*kirani*) constitutes seven oceans, and his daughter is [this huge] earth. I cannot wash the feet of that lord, whose back is so vast! (1) I sacrifice myself to you, O father cowherd! I am lying on the ground [to worship you]! I am just as meek as one can be! (1) Refrain. The two and a half paces of land was asked [from the demon Bali] by the dwarf-form, whose limit cannot be known. I cannot wash the feet of that lord, whose cosmic feet are so huge! (2) The giant boar-form rescues the earth [by raising it out of the ocean depths] on one of his tusks. I cannot wash the feet of that lord, whose teeth are so strong! (3) The half-lion and half-man form of the lord emerges [from a pillar to destroy the infidel King Hiranykashipu]. I cannot wash the feet of that lord, whose nails are so sharp! (4) Namdev's master is Krishna of the Yadu clan, the most beautiful lord, the enemy of Mura the demon. He is the divine beloved, the wearer of the garland of wild flowers, the destroyer of pain and fear. (5)[75]

This hymn is the most striking example of Krishna bhakti. Here Namdev presents the four important incarnations (avatars) of Vishnu in his native Marathi style. In the first instance he refers to the creative power of the giant tortoise in relation to the earth. The original myth is better known as the tortoise-form (*kacchaparupa* or *kurmavatara*), for supporting Mount Mandara when gods and demons churn the sea to obtain the elixir of immortality.

Secondly, Namdev refers to the story of the dwarf-form (*bavanrup* or *vamanrupa*). Three cosmic strides of Vishnu form the basis of this myth. The demon Bali, usurper of Indra's power, grants two and a half paces of land to Vishnu when he comes to him in the guise of a dwarf. Bali hospitably washes Vishnu's feet to welcome his guest,

[74]According to the teachings of the Gurus, the ultimate condition of blissful sahaj is achieved when the spirit ascends to sach khand (the realm of truth), a goal which may be reached before the physical death which is its final seal.

[75]GNDU MS 1084, f. 222b (or 208a); DBSSK MS 3, f. 312a (written in the margin in a different hand); John Rylands Library, Panj. MS 5, f. 227a; University of Cambridge, Trinity College Library, MSS R.15.153, f. 412b.

and then Vishnu assumes his cosmic shape, traversing the earth, atmosphere, and heaven, and destroying the demon.

Thirdly, Namdev describes the myth of the boar-form (*barahurup* or *varahavatara*). According to this Vaishnava story, the giant boar rescues the earth by raising it out of the ocean depths on one of his tusks.

Finally, the Maharashtrian sant refers to the story of the man-lion form of Vishnu (*narasimhavatara*). It is this form which destroyed the infidel king Hiranyakashipu, who threatened his own son Prahlad with death because of the son's devotion to Hari. The king had been given a boon of invulnerability in day or at night, by god, man, or beast, inside or outside his palace. To overcome it the lord appears at twilight as a man-lion inside a pillar and reaches out to dismember the demon king with his nails.[76] These stories of Vaishnava incarnations played an important role in the devotional tradition of the Maharashtrian sants.

An analysis of Namdev's extra-canonical hymn may provide a clue to Guru Arjan's editorial insights. The most plausible reason why he did not accept this hymn in the first place seems to be its link with Krishna bhakti through the worship of the incarnations (avatars) of Vishnu. This was deemed contrary to the Sikh devotional approach of worship of the non-incarnated divine.[77] It is quite possible that Guru Arjan's outright rejection of certain hymns of the sants may have created some resentment among the followers of these sants who may have tried to interpolate those hymns in the Adi Granth text later. This may be the primary reason for the diversity that we encounter in the early manuscripts of the Adi Granth, especially the Lahore and Banno traditions.

5. Trilochan's Gujari Hymn

There is one extra-canonical hymn of Trilochan in the *Gujari* mode, which was first recorded in the Lahori bir written in sambat 1667 (1610) during the period of Guru Hargobind. It is important to note that this hymn of Trilochan is not to be found in the

[76]These four stories are adapted from the description of Krishna's tenfold form, given in Barbara Stoler Miller, ed. and trans., *Love Song of the Dark Lord: Jayadeva's Gitagovinda* (New York: Columbia University Press, 1977), pp. 21–2.

[77]For the explicit rejection of avatars in the Gurus' thought, see M1, *Asa* 7, AG, pp. 350–51; M3, *Vadahans* 3, AG, p. 559; M5, *Bhairau* 1, AG, p. 1136. Also see Norvin Hein, 'Guru Nanak's Comment on the Vaishanava Lila,' in Harbans Singh, ed., *Perspectives on Guru Nanak* (Patiala: Punjabi University, 1975), pp. 493–501.

Kartarpur volume. Evidently Guru Arjan had not approved its inclusion when he finally produced the authoritative text in 1604. It appears in some later manuscripts of the Adi Granth. It reads as follows:

Gujari

O [man]! Why [do you run after] the nine treasures and the touchstone? Why worry about the legendary tree (*kalap*) of plenty [which provides] unexpectedly? Who should I ask for boons when my lord preserves my honour and blesses me with abundance? (1) [My lord is] Gobind, Gobind, and Gobind alone! I do not seek any thing from any one else except Gobind. I praise the name of Gobind [alone]. (1) Refrain. [The state of] liberation is itself the slave-girl of Gobind, although the renouncers of the world are absorbed in Shiva [for it]. All the great eight magical powers are their slaves, but I have nothing to do with these things. (2) One must abandon this wrong thinking that the knavish tricks create delights [in life]. Why don't you look inside the *man* and contemplate? The devotion (*bhagati*) to Gobind is the only good [thing, which creates] pure delights. (3) One must listen to the stories of Gobind. Tell me who has seen [Gobind] with his own eyes? The name of Gobind is always wondrous and Gobind is always on the lips of the sants. (4) [The devotion to] Gobind is the devotion to bhagavata. Like a mosquito my mind is always intoxicated [with the love of Gobind?]. Trilochan says: Listen O man! I seek the one who is free from the world. (5.2)[78]

Clearly, the key word in the hymn is Gobind, which is an epithet for Krishna. This word is probably a Prakrit form of gopendra, which means chief of cowherds. The linkage of ardent devotion to Gobind with the 'Bhagavata' worship (*gobind keri bhau bhagavat*) further supports the Vaishnava context of the whole hymn.

The real issue here appears to be linked with the question of allegiance. Was Trilochan a *nirguna* sant or a *saguna* bhagat? It is a well-known fact that Trilochan was a contemporary of Namdev and that both of them were Maharashtrian sants. In this context, Vaudeville makes the following observation:

In the Maharashtrian tradition, the sants are not only thought of and referred to as Vaishnava bhaktas or bhagavatas, but are specifically identified as varkaris, the devotees of Lord Vitthala of Pandharpur. ... It is indeed the popular cult of Vitthala that gives the Maharashtrian sant tradition as a whole its characteristic Vaishnava flavour. The popular cult of Vitthala as a

---

[78]Jograj MS, PUM 2, f. 234b (written in the margin in a different hand); PUM MS 1, ff. 269b–269a (later deleted with hartal); British Library, MSS ADD.25, 680, ff. 322b–323a.

young cowherd boy merges into the cult of Krishna as cowherd, and Vitthala himself is identified with Krishna-Gopal.[79]

Clearly, there was a kind of hybrid sant tradition in Maharashtra. In the light of this observation it may be stated that Trilochan was both a nirguna sant and a saguna bhagat. Like Namdev, he may have had different allegiances at different stages of his life. In this context, John Stratton Hawley compellingly argues that we must 'exercise caution when we speak of the great contrast between *nirgunis* and *sagunis* in the early or "classical" period of North Indian bhakti, the *bhakti kal* [or the devotional period].'[80]

It was, however, Trilochan's sant outlook which was most acceptable to Guru Arjan and that was the main reason for including four of his hymns in the Adi Granth. The present hymn stressing the Vaishnava ideal of bhakti was, of course, not included at the time of the compilation of the scripture. It may have been the case that the later followers of Trilochan failed to understand this important editorial stance and were primarily responsible for interpolating this hymn in the earliest copy of the Lahore tradition. Clearly, the activity to include such extra-canonical hymns in the Sikh scripture began only after the execution of Guru Arjan in Mughal custody.

CONCLUSION

This study has revealed that it was Guru Amar Das who was primarily responsible for the introduction of the bhagat bani in the Sikh scriptural tradition. He seems to have done this to enlarge the base of the early Sikh community by stressing social equality. Guru Arjan made further selection of the bhagat bani when he prepared the first canonical text of the Adi Granth. Indeed, some of the bhagat material was edited out through the process of selection and deletion at that time. Guru Arjan was certainly concerned with identifying the circles from which a particular composition emanated as well as with its message.

The hymns of the bhagats from the saguna (with attributes) school, who place emphasis upon worship through image and myth,

[79]Charlotte Vaudeville, 'The Shaiva-Vaishnava Synthesis in Maharashtrian Santism,' in *The Sants*, p. 216.

[80]John Stratton Hawley, 'The Nirgun/Sagun Distinction in Early Manuscript Anthologies of Hindi Devotion,' in David N. Lorenzen, ed., *Bhakti Religion in North India: Community Identity and Political Action* (Albany: State University of New York Press, 1995), p. 174.

were least acceptable to Guru Arjan. Thus the hymns of Mira Bai and Surdas (except the opening line) were excluded mainly because they were both worshippers of the amorous and anthropomorphic Krishna. Guru Arjan even rejected those hymns of the sants of nirguna (without attributes) school that were coloured with Vaishnava or tantric ideals. It is important to note that these sants are otherwise included in the Sikh scripture. This process of the selection of bhagat bani highlights both the exclusive and inclusive aspects of Guru Arjan's editorial policy. In other words, the selection logic favours those poems of the medieval bhagats that stress nirguna (formless divinity) religiosity and social equality, and are in general conformity with the Sikh Gurus' line of thinking.

The inclusion of the bhagat bani in the Adi Granth further illuminates the doctrinal concerns of the Sikh Gurus. Evidently, the process of its integration in the Sikh scripture was based upon the recognition of two major points. First was its harmony with the Gurus' thought in its broad outlines. Second, its differences with the Gurus' thought at essential points were highlighted to demonstrate the distinctive Sikh viewpoints. These reflections of the Gurus on bhagat bani were crucial for shaping the emerging Sikh identity. These points become obvious from the Gurus' comments on the verses of Kabir, Shaikh Farid, Surdas and Dhanna. It should be emphasized here that the net effect of the Gurus' comments on the bhagats is to cement firmly the bhagat bani in the Sikh scriptural tradition. Although a clear distinction is maintained between the writings of the bhagats and those of the Gurus, the bhagat bani has always been part of Sikh worship in the congregational setting.

7

THE ADI GRANTH TRADITIONS AND CANON FORMATION

Thus, some scholars distinguish sharply between Scripture and canon, where the one is authoritative and open (that is, open to supplementation and constant revision), and the other is closed and fixed. Or, in other words, from the technical standpoint of literary or textual criticism, with its special concern for the final form of documents, canonization frequently refers simply to an official closing and fixing of texts in a form that is declared to be authoritative (for whatever particular tradition) against all prior, competing, eccentric, and subsequent books and versions.[1]

The creation of an authoritative text by Guru Arjan involved sustained labour and rigorous intellectual discipline over a considerable period of time. Sikh scholars frequently make the claim about the original Kartarpur bir 'to be the work of the infallible Guru Arjan and a meticulous amanuensis of the calibre of Bhai Gurdas.[2] They further claim that all the later manuscripts are copies of the Kartarpur bir, and that it was fixed, static in time, without families and recensions. This preconceived assumption becomes most problematic in any academic inquiry. It is a confessional statement which raises the expectations of the scholar who wants to see perfection in early manuscripts, or even in the Kartarpur manuscript itself. But this hope is belied in the actual survey of old manuscripts. In spite of Guru Arjan's remarkable editorial achievement in establishing the first canonical text in 1604, there emerged three different recensions of the Adi Granth in course of time. Was this due to scribal

---

[1]Gerald L. Bruns, *Hermeneutics: Ancient and Modern* (New Haven and London: Yale University Press, 1992), p. 65.
[2]Piar Singh, *Gatha*, p. 2.

errors committed in the process of copying by later scribes, or intentional tampering with the text by some groups within the Panth?
The issue of the origins of the Adi Granth traditions, therefore, needs
to be examined thoroughly in the light of the situation of the Sikh
Panth in the seventeenth century.

The existence of textual families hints at some period of isolated
development of texts. They developed in different geographical areas
in isolation from one another in the process of repeated copying
and correction over generations of scribal activity. They are
distinguished especially by different sets of readings, but also by other
features including orthographic and grammatical peculiarities. When
textual families come together they cross or conflate, or bring a textual
crisis in which recensional activity occurs.[3] The examination of early
manuscripts of the Adi Granth has revealed that in certain instances
later scribes simply failed to understand Guru Arjan's editing
principles. That is why they diverged from the text of the Adi bir. In
this context, Piar Singh's work becomes quite significant in that it
lays emphasis on independent collections and sporadic compilations
which throw 'a flood of light on the proclivities—preferences,
insights, and modalities of their compilers.'[4] Indeed, the scribal
activity was rather encouraged within the early Sikh community.
Once three recensions of the Adi Granth became popular in different
areas, the later scribes faithfully copied their manuscripts from the
versions of the Adi Granth available to them.

It is crucial to understand, however, that all kinds of scribal errors
caused by poor handwriting, failure to grasp the meaning of certain
words, fatigue, or just plain carelessness, are to be found in all the
extant manuscripts. A major work prepared under the auspices of
the Shiromani Gurdwara Prabandhak Committee (SGPC), Amritsar,
identified thousands of *sudh path* (correct reading) and *asudh path*
(incorrect reading) by collating old manuscripts of the Adi Granth.[5]
The numerous *path-bhed* (variant readings) identified by Sant
Gurbachan Singh Khalsa of Bhindran Taksal in the Kartarpur bir are

[3]Frank Moore Cross, 'Problems of Method in the Textual Criticism of the Hebrew
Bible,' in Wendy Doniger O'Flaherty, ed., *The Critical Study of Sacred Texts* (Berkeley:
Berkeley Religious Studies Series and Graduate Theological Union, 1979), p. 47.

[4]Piar Singh, *Gatha*, p. 35.

[5]Randhir Singh, Kundan Singh and Gian Singh Nihang, eds, *Sri Guru Granth
Sahib Ji dian Santha-sainchian ate Puratan Hath Likhit Pavan Biran de Parasapar Path-
bhedan di Suchi*, Parts I–IV (Amritsar: Shiromani Gurdwara Prabandhak Committee,
1977).

of the same nature, and can be explained easily.[6] Piar Singh, however, labelled them as 'grave errors', on the basis of which he questioned the authenticity of the Kartarpur bir itself.[7] In my view, it is not fair to raise the question of authenticity on the basis of scribal errors alone. More recently, James A. Bellamy has provided the results of a major survey on the Qur'an with the purpose of isolating copyists' errors in the text and emending them wherever possible.[8] He argues that most of the mistakes that we find in the Qu'ran are of the same sort that occur in other manuscripts. They give us some insight into how the Qur'an was composed and copied. Certain mistakes, he argues, resulted from misunderstood corrections in the text; that is, the copyist (or dictator) caught his mistake and corrected it, but a subsequent copyist misunderstood the correction and so produced a new error. Bellamy concludes his last article as follows:

Non-Muslim Koranic scholars agree that Muhammad, in one way or another, composed the Koran, so they tend to lay all the problems of the text at his doorstep, usually without considering that mistakes in the tradition of the text as well as in the sources from which parts of Koran were drawn might be at fault. Perhaps one may hope that this and the preceding articles will go some way toward setting the record straight.[9]

Indeed, the noteworthy point is that we cannot expect perfection in the manuscripts inscribed by human hands. In proposing some emendations to the text of the Qur'an, Bellamy has done a scholarly job, but he is not concerned with the issue of actually revising the text. That decision lies with the Muslim community. He further suggests that in order to be sacred a text does not have to be correct.[10] There are numerous mistakes in the texts of world religions, yet they are held as sacred scriptures by various religious communities. Scriptures are sacred because of human involvement.

Here, I propose to treat the issue of canon formation according to the more radical power criteria rather than literary criteria. According to this power hypothesis, significant textual variations may reflect the diversity of the Sikh Panth, but they occur due to either

---

[6]Gurbachan Singh Khalsa, *Gurbani Path Darshan* (Amritsar: Bhai Mehar Singh & Sons, 6th edn, 1985; 1st edn, 1970), pp. 252–4.

[7]Piar Singh, *Gatha*, pp. 104–6.

[8]James A. Bellamy, 'Some Proposed Emendations to the Text of the Koran', *JAOS*, Vol. 113, no. 4 (1993): 562–73; and 'More Proposed Emendations to the Text of the Koran', *JAOS*, Vol. 116, no. 2 (1996): 196–204.

[9]ibid., p. 203.

[10]Personal discussion with Professor James A. Bellamy.

factional divisions or external interference in the affairs of the Panth. As a result, different groups may have provided isolated contexts in which several textual families developed. In particular, the issue of external interference in the affairs of the Panth by the Mughal authorities became apparent when the Muslim revivalists celebrated Guru Arjan's death in Mughal custody. For instance, Shaikh Ahmad Sirhindi, leader of the Naqshbandi movement in the Punjab, rejoiced at the execution. In a letter to Shaikh Farid Bukhari (Mir Murtaza Khan), the most influential Mughal official of Jahangir and the persecutor of Guru Arjan, he wrote:

These days the accursed infidel of Goindwal was very fortunately killed. It is a cause of great defeat for the reprobate Hindus. With whatever intention, and purpose they are killed—the humiliation of infidels is for Muslims life itself.[11]

Guru Arjan's martyrdom definitely changed the course of the Sikh movement. Although the Sikh sense of identity was heightened as an immediate result of the crisis, it soon created a situation which was conducive to sectarian tendencies within the Panth. J.S. Grewal has suggested that during the century following the death of Guru Arjan, the Sikh Panth underwent a considerable degree of transformation, which was largely due to external interference in the affairs of the Gurus and their followers by the Mughal officials. This interference, he argues, introduced a strong element of disunity in the Sikh Panth.[12] The issues of external interference by Mughal officials and factional divisions, therefore, must be addressed here to discover their possible impact on various groups within the Panth that were seeking to promote their versions of the Adi Granth.

LAHORE RECENSION

The traditional Sikh sources are quite silent about the origin of the Lahore recension of the Adi Granth. It was prepared in Lahore in 1610 when Guru Hargobind was imprisoned in the fort of Gwalior by the order of Emperor Jahangir. In this context, the author of *Dabistan-i-Mazahib* writes:

[11]Friedman Yohanan, 'Shaikh Ahmad Sirhindi: An Outline of His Image in the Eyes of Posterity' (Ph.D. dissertation, McGill University, 1966), p. 111.

[12]J.S. Grewal, 'Legacies of the Sikh Past for the Twentieth Century' in Joseph T. O'Connell et al., *Sikh History and Religion in the Twentieth Century* (Toronto: University of Toronto, Center for South Asian Studies, 1988), p. 23.

The late Emperor [Jahangir] sent Hargobind to the fort of Gwalior on account of the balance of the dues of fine that he had imposed on Arjan Mal. He remained for twelve years in that place, where they did not allow that he might eat salty food. During this time the Masands and the Sikhs used to go and bow down to the wall of the fort. At last the late Emperor, by way of kindness, gave freedom to the Guru.[13]

Guru Hargobind was evidently arrested because of the shift in the role of the Guru in the direction of increasing political and military involvement. He traditionally donned two swords symbolizing the spiritual (*piri*) as well as the temporal (*miri*) investiture. He also built the Akal Takhat (throne of the immortal lord) facing the Harimandir (the Golden Temple of Amritsar), which represented the newly assumed role of temporal authority. From the Sikh perspective, this new development was not at the cost of abandoning the original spiritual base. Rather, it was meant to achieve a balance between temporal and spiritual concerns. From the Mughal perspective, however, Guru Hargobind's life-style posed a danger to the state. Once again, the author of *Dabistan-i-Mazahib* writes: 'Many hardships confronted him. One of them is that he (Guru Hargobind) adopted the form of soldiers, girded sword against the practice of his father, kept servants and took to hunting.'[14]

In the context of the present discussion, Bhai Gurdas makes it quite explicit that Guru Hargobind's way of life was indeed different from that of his father, Guru Arjan. The following famous stanza deals directly with the issue:

The earlier Gurus sat peacefully in dharamsalas; this one roams the land. Emperors visited their homes with reverence; this one they cast into gaol. No rest for his followers, ever active; their restless Master has fear of none. The earlier Gurus sat graciously blessing; this one goes hunting with dogs. They composed the bani for listening and singing; this one neither composes [the bani] nor sings. They had servants who harboured no malice; this one encourages scoundrels. Yet none of these changes conceals the truth; the Sikhs are still drawn as bees to the lotus. The truth stands firm, eternal, changeless; and pride still lies subdued.[15]

Here, Bhai Gurdas provides us with firm evidence of the change which

---

[13]See Ganda Singh, 'Nanak Panthis', *The Panjab Past and Present*, Vol. 1, part 1 (April 1967), p. 62.

[14]ibid., p. 62.

[15]*Varan Bhai Gurdas*, 26: 24. The translation is taken from the one given in Hew McLeod, *Sikhism* (London: Penguin Books, 1997), p. 35. I have added the translation of the fifth line, missing in McLeod's translation.

took place under Guru Hargobind. In the first six lines of the stanza he poses the problem as he sees it in the contemporary discussion among the Sikhs, and then provides his own answer in the remaining two lines. As a loyal disciple of the Guru he defends the new martial response as 'hedging the orchard of the Sikh faith with hardy and thorny *kikar* tree.'[16]

One of the most significant features of the Lahore recension is the omission of specified heroic tunes (dhunis, that is, instructions with regard to the musical style in which the particular vars were to be sung) at the beginning of the vars (ballads) in different raga sections of the Adi Granth.[17] Traditionally the recording of these tunes is associated with Guru Hargobind, who is generally credited with introducing the practice of singing the ballads of the Adi Granth to popular heroic tunes in order to infuse martial spirit in his followers. For instance, the following passage from the *Gurbilas Chhevin Patashahi* clearly points to the inclusion of the dhunis in the Adi Granth by the sixth Guru:

When the true Guru (Arjan) saw in the court all the prominent Sikhs including [Bhai] Buddha, sitting there in one place, he addressed Hargobind with his words of advice: 'Listen to my commandment attentively.' Then the master repeated [Bhai] Buddha's words [which he had traditionally spoken as a prophecy at the birth of Hargobind]: 'You have to fight fierce battles. Pay attention with single mind to the singing of the twenty-two ballads (vars), which we have recorded in the granth. You should include heroic tunes at the beginning of those vars, which you like most.'[18]

Although this *Gurbilas* is attributed to an eighteenth-century poet Sohan, the various references to Maharaja Ranjit Singh demolishing Nurdin's *sarai* (inn) to construct the pool of Tarn Taran and mentioning Harimandir as being golden, clearly place the document in the early nineteenth century.[19] The Sikh community of that period seems to have created the tradition of the inclusion of the heroic tunes in the Adi Granth as the result of the decision taken by Guru Hargobind.

The tradition of the inclusion of the dhunis in the Adi Granth by

[16]*Varan Bhai Gurdas*, 26: 25.

[17]The MS copies of the Adi Granth that do not contain the heroic tunes are: *Bure Sandhu vali bir* (1654), *Kanagarh vali bir* (1661), *Saranake vali bir* (1671) and *Burhanpur vali bir* (Guru Gobind Singh's period). See G.B. Singh, *Prachin Biran*, pp. 115, 183–7, 205 and 327–30. Also see Chapter 2 of this study, p. 101.

[18]Giani Inder Singh Gill (*samp.*), *Sri Gurbilas Patashahi 6* (Amritsar: Vazir Hind Press, 1977), p. 90.

[19]Surjit Hans, *A Reconstruction of Sikh History from Sikh Literature*, p. 270.

the sixth Guru does not explain the fact that these heroic tunes had already been entered alongside the vars in the Kartarpur manuscript in the same hand. In two instances, that of *Var Asa* and *Var Majh*, the writing appears somewhat finer because the specified tunes were written with a different pen by the same scribe. It is to be noted, however, that the tradition of entering directions about specific important musical tunes was already well established when the Goindval pothis were written. The two extant copies of these volumes provide a clear evidence in this respect.[20] Further, seven vars of the GNDU MS 1245, an earlier recension of the Adi Granth, are assigned the specific heroic tunes to which they are supposed to be sung. In most cases these tunes are mentioned in the index only. In the two cases of Guru Nanak's *Var Malhar* and Guru Ram Das's *Var Vadahans*, however, the tunes are specifically stated at the beginning of their texts in addition to the index-entries.[21] There is another significant note in the *Bilaval* mode, specifying that Guru Arjan's hymn (*upama jat na kahi mere prabh ki*) should be sung to the musical style of *Dhamal* (*dhamalai ki chal*).[22] The musical style of *Dhamal/Dhamar* in which the drum beats followed a particular rhythm of *dhamar tal* was a popular folk style in those days in north India. This folk style is commonly sung at the time of weddings or on other happy occasions.[23]

On the whole the dhunis are to be found in the beginning of the following nine vars in the Adi Granth:

1. Guru Nanak's *Var Majh* is to be sung to the tune of a popular ballad of Malik Murid and Chandarhara of the Sohian clan, two brave chiefs of Emperor Akbar who died fighting against each other.

2. Guru Arjan's *Var Gauri* is to be sung to the tune of Rai Kamaldi and Maujadi, a well-known ballad of the time, which narrates the story of a fight between two Muslim Rajput chiefs, who were related to each other as uncle and nephew.

3. The var in the *Asa* raga by Guru Nanak is to be sung to the tune of a popular ballad of the stump-armed (*tunda*) Asraj, the son of a king named Sarang, who fought a battle against his step-brothers to win the throne of his father.

---

[20]For details, see Chapter 4 of this study, p. 133.
[21] GNDU MS 1245, ff. 551a and 1171a.
[22]GNDU MS 1245, f. 798a.
[23]A famous Punjabi singer, Narinder Biba, who died on 28 June 1997, used to sing her songs in *Dhamal* style. See *Daily Nawan Zamana* (6 July 1997), p. 8.

4   Guru Amar Das's var in the *Gujari* mode is to be sung to the tune of a popular ballad of Sikander and Birahim, which narrates the story of a fight between two local chieftains.

5   Guru Ram Das's var in the *Vadahans* raga is to be sung to the tune of a ballad of Lallan and Bahliman, two Rajput farmers of Kangara who fought on the issue of sharing water during times of famine.

6   Guru Amar Das's var in the *Ramakali* mode is to be sung to the tune of a popular ballad about Jodha and Vira of the Purban clan, two Rajput brothers who fought valiantly against the forces of Emperor Akbar.

7   Guru Ram Das's var in the *Sarang* raga is to be sung to the tune of a ballad about Mahima and Hasna, which narrates the story of a fight between two Muslim Rajput chiefs.

8   Guru Nanak's var in the *Malhar* raga is to be sung to the tune of a popular ballad about Rana Kailash and Maldeo, two brothers who ruled over Jammu and Kashmir respectively and fought against each other at the instigation of the Mughal Emperor.

9   Guru Ram Das's var in the *Kanara* raga is to be sung to the tune of a ballad about Musa, a brave man who fought against a King who had married his fiancee.[24]

These vars must have been quite popular in the Punjab during the period of Guru Arjan or even before. The minstrels (dhadhis) used to sing them among the rural people, particularly the Jats, to amuse them with heroic stories. It was a favourite pastime of the people of the Punjab to listen to the singing of these ballads.[25]

Guru Arjan probably selected heroic tunes for the singing of the vars of the Adi Granth in order to reach out to the rural audience. That was why these dhunis became a part of the text of the Kartarpur manuscript. Presumably the tradition of singing the vars to heroic tunes may have begun during Guru Arjan's period or even before with the specific purpose of attracting rural people, especially the Jats, into the Sikh fold. It should be emphasized, however, that the dhunis were selected only for their musical directions, and not for the purpose of propagating the heroic stories behind them. There are other such poetic genres which are modelled on folk tunes in the Adi Granth. These folk tunes were adapted because of their social significance.[26]

It is entirely possible that the singing of the vars to the musical style of heroic tunes by the dhadhis was further encouraged by the sixth Guru. Also, the spirit of militancy was heightened within the

---

[24]*Shabadarath*, pp. 137, 318, 462, 508, 585, 947, 1237, 1278 and 1312.
[25]Sohan Singh, *The Ballad of God and Man* (Amritsar: GNDU, 1982), p. 10, n. 1.
[26]For details, see Chapter 4, p. 144

Sikh community after Guru Arjan was executed in 1606 in Lahore. This resulted in the consolidation of the community against the Mughal authorities who were responsible for the death of the Guru. This growing militancy must have alarmed the Mughal officials, who wanted to tone down this spirit by creating dissensions within the ranks of the Panth. This they would have done through indirectly influencing certain groups to exclude these dhunis from the text of the Adi Granth. The origin of the first bir of the Lahore recension in the city of Lahore may further lend support to this theory. An alternate explanation may be proposed: namely, that some groups within the Panth thought it unwise to be provocative and hence decided to omit these tunes from their copies of the Adi Granth. Presumably these groups still held sant beliefs and did not approve the shift towards militancy in the affairs of the Panth. Whatever the reasons, it is certain that the dhunis were consciously omitted from the text of the Lahore recension.

If the present illuminates the past in any understanding of historical processes, then it will be useful to look at a recent phenomenon. When militancy within certain sections of the Panth was heightened as a result of the Indian army's assault on the Golden Temple complex in 1984, the Government of India banned dhadhi music specifically and the playing of all var music in general.[27] Despite this ban bus drivers in Punjab had dhadhi tapes playing continually in their buses while driving from town to town and the music shops defiantly displayed dhadhi cassettes.[28] Notwithstanding the defiant attitude among the Punjabis in general, there are always certain individuals and groups in the community who support the policies of the government of the day. These people may be doing so to protect their own interests, but at the same time they can play a divisive role in the community at large.

Other distinguishing features of the Lahore tradition are related to the concluding section of its text and the two extra hymns by Trilochan and Namdev. Should the scripture end with the message of Guru Arjan in the *Mundavani* and the concluding shalok, or with the praise of the Gurus in the panegyrics by the bards, or with the shaloks of the bhagats? These were the concerns of the scribes who diverged from the text created by Guru Arjan. First, it is important to note that the epilogue of the GNDU MS 1245 ends with panegyrics by the bards. This was an earlier

---

[27]See Louis E. Fenech, 'Playing the "Game of Love": The Sikh Tradition of Martyrdom' (Ph.D. thesis, University of Toronto, 1994), p. 14, n. 5.

[28]For more details on dhadhi music, see Joyce Pettigrew, 'Songs of the Sikh Resistance Movement,' in *Asian Music* (Fall/Winter 1991–2), pp. 108–11.

sequence which was revised by Guru Arjan in the Kartarpur bir. In certain cases, the compilers of the Lahore recensions were just following an earlier convention. They were following 'first Gurus, then bhagats and then others' principle in deciding the sequence of the epilogue of the Adi Granth. Second, in certain other cases the compilers were following 'first Gurus and then bhagats' principle to end the epilogue with Shaikh Farid's shaloks. Finally, the presence of two extra hymns by Namdev and Trilochan strongly suggests that their followers were responsible for the insertion of these hymns into the scripture. These hymns were originally turned down by Guru Arjan.

The examination of the manuscripts of the Lahore tradition has revealed that a significant number of them originated in the Kiratpur area during the period of Guru Har Rai (1644–61). This tradition continued to be popular in some sections of the Panth right up to the beginning of the nineteenth century. A copy of the Lahore tradition that was written in the early nineteenth century is kept at the British Library in London.[29] This is perhaps the only copy of the Adi Granth which contains a solitary couplet attributed to Guru Har Rai. It comes after the *Mundavani* as follows:

There is one supreme being, known by grace through the true Guru.
Shalok Mahala 7: *Sri Har Rai Ji Ka Bolana* ('the voice of Sri Guru Har Rai')
Those on whom the true Guru bestows his benevolence, they are kept in his refuge. I am devoted to the one, Nanak, who goes to have a glimpse of the Guru (*jini kau satguru daia kare tini rakhe charni lae// nanak tisu baliharanai jin gur ditha jai/*).[30]

The introductory formula used in the beginning of this couplet ('the voice of Sri Guru Har Rai') clearly places it in the context of hagiographic material produced by the Sikh community. It is, therefore, a later incorporation in the text of the Adi Granth. The couplet may have had its origin in the oral tradition popular in the Kiratpur area where the people had been converted to the Sikh faith by Guru Har Rai. The scribe must have intended to have Guru Har Rai represented in the Sikh scripture.

BANNO RECENSION

The origin of the Banno recension of the Adi Granth is explained by at least two traditions. According to one, Bhai Banno got permission

---

[29]British Library, MS Or. 2748.
[30]British Library, MS Or. 2748, f. 746a.

from Guru Arjan to borrow the original volume for one night and to take it to his village, Mangat in Gujarat district, to show it to the Sikh congregation there. The lengthy journey afforded him the opportunity to make another copy. Another tradition states that Bhai Banno was entrusted with the responsibility of taking the original volume to Lahore for binding and he made his copy with the help of a number of scribes while on this mission.[31]

A passage from the *Mahima Prakash* (1776) contains the following observation on the origin of the Banno text:

> It so happened that many hands wrote the volume. Some hymns were dislocated from their proper places. This volume is known as the 'Khara missal.' It is different from the 'Gurdas missal.'[32]

The name Khara missal derives from Khara, which is said to be an earlier name of Mangat village. The above passage reflects the late eighteenth-century understanding of the Sikh community concerning the origin of the Banno text. It also reveals the existence of an ongoing debate within the community on the issue of its differences from the text of the Adi Granth inscribed by Bhai Gurdas at the dictation of Guru Arjan. The tradition that many hands wrote the Banno text cannot be sustained in the light of the actual examination of the manuscript kept at Kanpur. Pritam Singh states that 'the internal physiognomy of the MS does not support the story that different copyists had combined to prepare a quick copy.'[33]

The traditional explanations must be set aside at the outset in order to examine critically the origin of the Banno text. The name of Bhai Banno does not appear in Bhai Gurdas's list of prominent Sikhs of Guru Arjan.[34] Here, the primary issue is: who was responsible for the Banno text? The apocryphal texts inserted at the end of it may provide some help in answering this question. Sahib Singh has discussed this issue in detail in his book *Adi Bir Bare*. He adopted the method of comparing the parallel phrases, passages, and other linguistic expressions occurring in the apocryphal texts at the end of the Banno text and the *Bala janam-sakhis*, especially sakhi 125 concerning the discourse with Vira Nau Malar and sakhi 36 concerning

---

[31]Giani Rajinder Singh Bal, *Bhai Banno Darpan ate Khare vali Bir* (Jalandhar: 82/3-D Central Town, 1989), pp. 60–7.

[32]Sarup Das Bhalla, *Mahima Prakash* (Patiala: Bhasha Vibhag, 1971), p. 373.

[33]Pritam Singh, 'Bhai Banno's Copy of the Sikh Scripture,' *Journal of Sikh Studies*, XI(2) (1984): 111.

[34]See *Varan Bhai Gurdas* 11: 18–28.

Baba Nanak's visit to Mecca. He argues that in the old manuscripts of the Banno text, the apocryphal shaloks attributed to Guru Nanak are sometimes entitled *gost malar nali hoi*[35] which is the same title as that of sakhi 125 of the Bala tradition. Again, there is an actual verbal correspondence between them: the typical expression *vir salamalekh barai khudai sachu chau* (brother, peace be with you and may you speak the truth with the blessings of God!) of the Banno text resembles with the *yar salamalekh bara khudai sachu chau* of the earliest Bala janam-sakhi (1658).[36]

Further, the following apocryphal shaloks of the Banno text are actually cited in the sakhi 125 of the Bala text:

At whose (Akal Purakh's) door there are a hundred thousand Muhammads and a hundred thousand Brahmas, Vishnus and Shivas. There are hundreds of thousands of Ramas, who claim to be the greatest of all, and there are hundreds of thousands of 'ways' [religions] and hundreds of thousands of sectarian garbs. There are hundreds of thousands of celibates, philanthropists and ascetics. There are hundreds of thousands of Gorakhs and hundreds of thousands of masters of the master-jogis ...

These shaloks presumably had their origin in the hagiographic literature (janam-sakhis) produced by the Sikh community. They were primarily intended to exalt the image of Baba Nanak over the religious leaders of both Muslim and Hindu traditions. They are not to be found either in the two available copies of the Goindval pothis or in an earlier recension, the GNDU MS 1245. Moreover, the style of these shaloks does not match the authentic sayings of Guru Nanak.

Furthermore, there are verbal as well as thematic similarities between the second set of apocryphal shaloks attributed to Guru Nanak in the Banno text and the sakhi 36 concerning Guru Nanak's visit to Mecca:

Shalok M.1 (Banno text)
The air, the fire, the water and the soil are four elements which are used in the making of the human body. The fifth element is added by the spirit of 'pure god' (*pak Khuda'i*) to create people...

Bala janam-sakhi 36
The first *ruh* or spirit is the air, which is known as an angel (*farishta*). The second one is the fire, which is called by the name of a *jinn* or demon. The third spirit is the water, which is likened with the godly form. The fourth

---

[35]See Gurdita Sekhon MS, Index entry.
[36]See Kirpal Singh, *Janam-sakhi Prampara* (Patiala: Punjabi University, 1969), p. 318.

spirit is the soil, which is the secret evil spirit. The fifth spirit is God himself, who keeps the four filled with love. The four [elements] are thus established (in making the human body) by the total grace of God ...

Clearly, these passages reflect discussions with a Muslim audience about creation. On the basis of his analysis of verbal and thematic similarities, Sahib Singh concluded that the responsibility for the composition of the Banno text rests on the shoulders of the Hindalis, the authors of the *Bala* janam-sakhis, who inserted the extra material in the text of the Adi Granth.[37] The Hindalis formed a schismatic group which evidently regarded itself as Sikh but which accepted the leadership of a rival claimant, Bidhi Chand, son of Baba Hindal of Jandiala, in opposition to Guru Hargobind. Bidhi Chand had married a Muslim woman and evidently responded to the reproaches of the Sikhs by turning apostate.[38] In this context, J.S. Grewal has suggested that the Hindalis occasionally aligned themselves with the Mughal administrators.[39] If this is correct, Sahib Singh's theory that extra material was inserted in the Banno text by the Hindalis is valid because the Hindalis served the purpose of the Mughal officials of creating dissension within the ranks of the Panth.

Sahib Singh's theory about the origin of the Banno version still seems to be too simplistic a view of what was probably a complex phenomenon. It should be emphasized that he reached his conclusion about the Banno text by comparing the apocryphal shaloks attributed to Guru Nanak with the text of the Bala janam-sakhi, which is the work of the heretical Hindalis. However, when the apocryphal *Ratan-mala*, a composition of twenty-five stanzas in *Ramakali* raga, is examined, the conclusion seems to point in another direction. Consider, for instance, the following passage from the *Ratan-mala*:

The five senses should be kept under complete control. The tongue should never utter untruth. Thus one knows the secret of millions and millions of wisdoms. The mind should be focused in the realm of the sky [or the tenth door]. One should water the lower regions (of the body) and fill the pool of the sky (with the vital energy through the practice of hatha yoga). Then one should bathe at the Triveni. The seven (mind, intellect and five senses of

---

[37]Sahib Singh, *Adi Bir Bare* (Amritsar: Singh Brothers, fourth edn, 1987; first edn., 1970), pp. 176–83.

[38]W.H. McLeod, *Early Sikh Tradition* (Oxford: Clarendon Press, 1980), p. 17.

[39]J.S. Grewal, 'A Perspective on Early Sikh History', in Juergensmeyer and Barrier, eds, *Sikh Studies:* p. 37.

knowledge),[40] the five (senses of action) and the nine (bodily orifices) should be kept under control. Nanak thus describes the attributes of yoga. (4) The (vital energy) rises in the east and then comes to the west. Both the sun (considered in yoga to control the right-hand channel of the body) and the moon (considered in yoga to control the left-hand channel of the body) should be mingled together within oneself (in the sahaja state). In the city of the heart one should realize the way. There one should understand the mystery of the difficult way (of hatha yoga). One should thus see all the sides of east, west, north and south of the nine climes of the earth (within oneself). Nanak says: [these are] the attributes of the yoga. (5)[41]

Here the word Triveni represents the confluence of the Ganga, Jamuna and Saraswati. It is the most auspicious Hindu bathing-place at Prayag, Allahabad. In yogic terminology it represents the meeting-place of three important channels of vital winds (*pranas*): the *sushumna-nadi* or the innermost channel situated within the spinal chord, the *ida-nadi* and the *pingala-nadi*, respectively located on the left and the right of the spinal cord. The vital energy in a yogi's body is conceived as a female serpent (*kundalini-shakti*), resting at the *muladhara* chakra, the base of the spine between the anus and the genitals. She is awakened by various techniques of hatha yoga and passes to the tenth door (*dasam duar*) via the various chakras (lotuses) in the spinal channel (sushumna-nadi), where she unites with the *Param-shiva* (the primal teacher of the yogis). This merging of Shiva and shakti within one's own body is the final goal of kundalini-yoga, when the yogi experiences supreme bliss (*maha sukha*) and enters the mysterious sahaja state.[42]

Evidently the *Ratan-mala* is an exposition of hatha-yoga technique, which obviously cannot be the work of Guru Nanak. It is definitely an Udasi account, which was edited out of the earlier recension when Guru Arjan produced the first canonical text of the Adi Granth.[43] It is quite possible that the revision of the received texts may have caused some resentment among the Udasi Sikhs, who followed ascetic ideals and practised hatha yoga techniques. They may have joined forces with the Hindalis and members of the Bhatra community to insert

[40]*Shabadarath*, Vol. IV, p. 1332, n. 33.

[41]The meanings of the terms of this passage are taken from C. Shackle, *A Guru Nanak Glossary* (London: SOAS, 1981), pp. 7, 30, 105, 164, 179 and 252.

[42]For an analysis of the kundalini-yoga, see Harold Coward, *Jung and Eastern Thought* (New York: State University of New York Press, 1985), pp. 109–24. Also see M. Eliade, *Yoga: Immortality and Freedom* (London: McClelland, 1958).

[43]The *Ratan-mala* text attributed to Guru Nanak is already to be found in the GNDU MS 1245, f. 1257a.

the extra material in the Banno text.[44] This they would have done originally in Khara Mangat in Gujarat district, which ultimately became a fertile area for the proliferation of the Banno version. The first Banno bir was prepared in 1642 when the centre of Sikh activities had already shifted under Guru Hargobind from Amritsar to Kiratpur in the Shivalik hills. This theory of the origin of the Banno tradition, therefore, represents the union of Hindali, Udasi, Bhatra and brahminical interests. It supplements the factor of external interference by the Mughal officials with the internal pressure created within the Sikh community as a result of disagreements over Guru Arjan's editing principles. It is not simply a conspiracy theory, but rather a radical hypothesis which illuminates the power struggle between different groups within the Panth.

The Banno version came to the fore during the second half of the seventeenth century, as a result of political disturbance which promoted Hindali influence. During the eighteenth century, the situation of the manuscripts of the Adi Granth changed dramatically with the Banno version assuming predominance. Two decades ago W.H. McLeod employed the argument of the predominance of the Banno version amongst early manuscripts to support the theory that the Banno recension might actually represent the original text.[45] This theory cannot, however, be sustained in the light of the oldest manuscripts. Edwards Hobbs offers two arguments against the textual theory based on the majority of manuscripts. First, they are always the ones that are of recent origin than the older ones. Second, they are the ones that have gone through more copyings.[46] The real reason for the predominance of the Banno version during the eighteenth century is that that was a period of turmoil for the Sikh community. This provided ample opportunity for the Banno group, particularly the Hindalis, to exert their influence with the help of the Mughal officials. In those circumstances, the Khalsa had no time to bother with the issue of an authentic text of the Adi Granth, for they were preoccupied with fighting for survival. It was, therefore, the Banno

[44]The text of *Hakikat Rah Mukam Raje Sivanabh ki* has references to the Bhatra community. For a detailed analysis of the text, see W.H. McLeod, 'Hakikat Rah Mukam Raje Sivanabh Ki,' *Punjab History Conference Proceedings*, Fourth Session (March 14–15, 1969), pp. 96–105.

[45]W.H. McLeod, 'The Sikh Scriptures: Some Issues', in Juergensmeyer and Barrier, eds, *Sikh Studies*, p. 101.

[46]See Edwards Hobbs, 'An Introduction to Methods of Textual Criticism', in Wendy Doniger O'Flaherty, ed., *The Critical Study of the Sacred Texts* (Berkeley: Religious Studies Series and Theological Union, 1979), pp. 8–9.

version which was widely used in the Panth during the eighteenth
century, although other versions were also to be found occasionally.
We need to look at the actual survey of the manuscripts of the Adi
Granth from the eighteenth and early nineteenth centuries.

A rare manuscript of the Banno version written by Bhai Harijas is
preserved by 1st Battalion of the Brigade of The Guards Mechanical
(2 Punjab) of the Indian Army. I was able to examine this manuscript
through the courtesy of the Commandant of the Battalion, Colonel
Jatinder Singh, during my visit to India in the summer of 1994. The
following inscription is written on the Army display-board:

1st Bn Bde of The Guards Mech (2 Punjab)
The Holy Granth Sahib:
1   The Holy Granth was written during the times of Guru Gobind Singh Ji,
    The tenth Sikh Guru, By Shri Harijas Dass possibly before AD 1708. The
    Holy Granth has the following details:
    (a) Procedure for making ink used in writing the Holy book.
    (b) Names and dates of death anniversaries of all the Gurus except the
        tenth.
2   The Granth Sahib was possibly handed over to the Bn during partition
    for safe custody by refugees who were under grave threat.
Chandani [Canopy] *and Chibbas* [Arcs]:
1   The original Chandani was presented to Maharaja Ranjit Singh by Nizam
    of Hyderabad who in turn presented it to Golden Temple. This had seven
    golden chibbas.
2   The replica Chandani has one pure gold and seven silver Chibbas.

The Army Gurdwara has carefully preserved all these items, and they
have recently taken steps to preserve the manuscript of the Adi Granth
with special chemical treatment. The most beautiful chandani is
indeed the replica of the original which was unfortunately destroyed
during Operation Bluestar of 1984. Photographs of these rare
artefacts are in my possession. An actual examination of the
manuscript reveals the following details:

First, the actual date of the writing of the manuscript is given at
the end of the index in folio 1b as follows:

The autograph of the Guru was taken in sambat 1702 (1645) on the fifteenth
day of katik (November). The granth was written at Khuram through the
grace of the Guru by Harijas, a servant of the Guru. It was written at the
command of the Guru. Please forgive my mistakes. Read the letters carefully
by paying attention to the vowel-signs. Repeat: Guru! Guru! Guru! Guru!
Guru!, true! true! true! true! true! true! and thou! thou! thou!

This early date suggests that the manuscript was copied from a volume originally written in sambat 1702 (1645). Again, the second entry in the index folio claims that 'the index was prepared in sambat 1704 (1647) in the month of katik (October–November) when the Guru's autograph was taken.' However, there is no autograph of the Guru to be found in the volume. Harijas was simply copying the actual words from the earlier volume mentioning the autograph (*nisan*) of the Guru. He himself did not get any autograph when he prepared his copy at Khuram, a city on the bank of river Khuram in Afghanistan.[47] It certainly points towards the area where the Banno version was popular.

Second, the presence of the compositions of the ninth Guru at their appropriate places in all the raga sections clearly indicates that the manuscript was prepared during the period of Guru Gobind Singh. The only significant exception is that Guru Tegh Bahadur's raga *Jaijavanti* comes after *Jaitasari* raga in folios 283b–284a. Also, a single couplet attributed to Guru Gobind Singh is recorded in folio 538a among the shaloks of the ninth Guru.

Third, the text of *So Purakh* is not to be found in the introductory section of the volume on folio 5b. Guru Arjan's complete hymn in the *Ramakali* mode is recorded in folios 371b–372a. Similarly, Mira Bai's hymn and Surdas's complete hymn are to be found in folios 429b and 476a respectively. Another significant feature of this manuscript is that it has thirty-three shaloks of Guru Nanak recorded in the section of *Salok Varan te Vadhik* instead of the usual thirty-seven. The remaining four are included in the shaloks of Guru Amar Das. It clearly reflects the tradition when the final form of *Salok Varan te Vadhik* was already fixed.

Finally, all the usual apocryphal texts of the Banno version are included at the end of the volume. There is an important date with respect to the first *prakash* (splendour) of Sri Guru Granth Sahib given at the end of the volume as sambat 1784 (1727), followed by the symbol of *IK Oankar*. This symbol was usually regarded as the *bhog* mark which was written at the time of the complete unbroken reading (akhand path) of the scripture. This hand-written note may reveal that the liturgical tradition of akhand path may have started in the early decades of the eighteenth century.[48]

---

[47]Kahn Singh Nabha, *Gurshabad Ratanakar Mahan Kosh* (Patiala: Bhasha Vibhag, 4th edn. 1981), p. 383.

[48]Harijas MS, 1st Battalion of the Brigade of the Guards Mechanical (2 Punjab), Army Gurdwara.

There is a large number of manuscripts of the Banno version which are still extant at different places. The following table gives the date of writing and the location of these manuscripts:

Table 7.1 Manuscripts of the Banno Recension

No	MS #	Date	Location
1.	Panj. MS 5	1650 (?)	John Rylands Library, University of Manchester
2.	MS 504	1711	Guru Granth Sahib Trust (GGST), Coventry
3.	MS 506	18th century	GGST, Coventry
4.	Panj. MSS C5	1727	India Office Library (IOL), London
5.	Panj. MSS C1	1738	IOL, London
6.	MS 1	1740	Collection of Tarlok Singh, Harrow
7.	MS 2	1744	Collection of Tarlok Singh, Harrow
8.	MS Or. 2159	1745	British Library (BL), London
9.	MS 115594	1755	Punjabi University Library (PUL), Patiala
10.	Panj. MSS F1	1758	IOL, London
11.	Panj. MSS D3	1764	IOL, London
12.	MS 115464	1768	PUL, Patiala
13.	Panj. MSS D2	18th century	IOL, London
14.	MS R.15.153	1743–1843	Trinity College, Cambridge
15.	MS Or. 1125	19th Century	BL, London

An actual examination of these manuscripts has, however, revealed that there was no single text of the Banno version during the eighteenth century, since all of them varied from one another to some degree.

There were other versions that appeared during the eighteenth century as a result of interaction between the scribes of the Banno text and those of the Lahore text. For instance, a manuscript written in 1730 (sambat 1787 manghar vadi 5) and kept at Dr Balbir Singh Sahitya Kendra in Dehradun, follows the usual concluding sequence of the Lahore tradition, but it also includes the extra material of the Banno version.[49] G.B. Singh has given a detailed analysis of a manuscript, written in sambat 1826 (1769) and used by the Dhaka Sangat, founded by the missionary activities of a Sikh named Bhai Natha, which represents another variation of the union of the Banno

[49]Also see MS Add. 25,680, kept at the British Library. It was written in the nineteenth century and provides another example of the combination of the Banno and Lahore traditions.

and Lahore traditions.[50] In Dina and Kangar, another such version was used by the Sikh community of the Malwa area of the Punjab and its manuscript is preserved at the Punjabi University Museum. This manuscript was presented to Punjabi University by Sardar Jagmit Singh Brar, son of the late Sardar Gurmit Singh Brar, a former Minister in the Punjab Legislative Assembly. It is a beautiful manuscript representing the union of the Lahore and Banno traditions, with the whole of *Japji* in coloured artwork. It is claimed in the manuscript note to be a late eighteenth-century document. Its artistic style, however, reveals that it was written in the early nineteenth century.[51]

Tradition records that Bhai Mani Singh prepared a new granth in the early eighteenth century by adding the bani of the Dasam Granth to the Adi Granth. He changed the sequence of the contents by arranging all the hymns according to their authors instead of the ragas. For instance, all the works of Guru Nanak are placed collectively at the beginning of the volume and are followed by the works of other Gurus in the order of their succession. As a result of this new scheme, bhagat bani was separated from the works of the Gurus, which appeared at the end of the volume after the works of the tenth Guru. It was followed by the var by Satta and Balwand, the *Saddu* or dirge by Sunder, the panegyrics in praise of the Gurus by the Bhatts, and the apocryphal texts of the Banno version. A manuscript bearing the date sambat 1770 (1713) is still extant and it is preserved by the family of Raja Gulab Singh Sethi of New Delhi. It is believed to be the copy written by Bhai Mani Singh, although its date is given unconventionally at the end in a different hand. Rattan Singh Jaggi, who examined this manuscript in the 1980s, considers this volume to be 250 years old, dated to Bhai Mani Singh's period.[52]

According to tradition, the Sikh community of that period did not approve Bhai Mani Singh's innovation and they placed on him a curse that he be cut limb by limb in the same manner as he had broken the sequence of the Adi Granth.[53] This story may well be an attempt to subvert the understanding of the contemporary Sikh community concerning the death of Bhai Mani Singh, according to which the actual blame for his death was placed on his own conduct

[50]G.B. Singh, *Prachin Biran*, pp. 292–7.

[51]See PUM, MS # 4.

[52]A detailed description of this manuscript is given in Rattan Singh Jaggi, *Bhai Mani Singh: Jivani te Rachana* (Patiala: Punjabi University, 1983), pp. 39–43.

[53]See Rattan Singh Jaggi (*samp.*), 'Kesar Singh Chhibbar da Bansavali-nama Dasan Patshahian Ka,' *Parakh*, Vol. II (Chandigarh: Panjab University, 1972), pp. 135–6.

rather than on the Mughal officials, who were primarily responsible for his death. The tradition of Bhai Mani Singh's involvement in the creation of the new version of the Sikh scripture thus appears to be well founded. Moreover, the existence of a manuscript which combined the Adi Granth and the Dasam Granth into one volume, clearly points out that during his period a new version appeared in the Sikh community. Obviously there were several different versions of the Adi Granth, all of them differing to some degree, which were being used by various Sikh sangats in the eighteenth and early nineteenth centuries.

DAMDAMA RECENSION

The origin of the Damdama version of the Adi Granth is explained traditionally in the *Gur bilas* (pleasure of the Guru) literature. According to this explanation, Guru Gobind Singh prepared the final recension of the Adi Granth at Damdama Sahib, Talvandi Sabo in Bhatinda district, in sambat 1762 (1705), when he added the works of the ninth Guru for the first time. For instance, the following passage from the *Gurbilas Chhevin Patashahi*, written in the early nineteenth century, says:

Having gone to the Malwa land [the Guru] then established there the Kanshi [the centre of learning]. He named it Damdama, the provider of liberation and sustenance. There he dictated the Adi Granth, and included the bani of the ninth Guru in it. There are fifty-nine sabads and fifty-seven shaloks [of the ninth Guru]. Anyone who reads them with a spirit of detachment from the world rises above the desire to kill. Like Kanshi, Damdama removes sufferings. The people there become scribes, perfect in every way. The Damdama bir was manifest for the whole world. Anyone who learns to read and write there will not be born again.[54]

It is claimed here that Guru Gobind Singh prepared the final recension of the Adi Granth at Damdama by adding a collection of works by the ninth Guru to the original compilation. This is not correct, since the bani of Guru Tegh Bahadur had already been incorporated in a number of manuscripts immediately after his death. The point to be noted is that a single couplet, attributed to Guru Gobind Singh in earlier manuscripts, became part of the fifty-seven shaloks of the ninth Guru.[55]

[54]Giani Inder Singh Gill (*samp.*), *Sri Gurbilas Patashahi 6*, p. 170.

[55]The following shalok (no. 54) is attributed to Guru Gobind Singh in PUM MS 6, written in 1692: 'Strength has come, the bondage is broken and all the resources are there. Lord! everything is in your power, You are my only refuge.'

Giani Gian Singh records a similar tradition in his *Sri Guru Panth Prakash* (1870) that Guru Gobind Singh dictated the whole of the Adi Granth from memory to Bhai Mani Singh:

Mani Singh was appointed amanuensis. Every day two watches of time were fixed for the purpose [of creating the scripture]. As the true Guru kept dictating, so the Sikh kept recording the bani. The project was completed in several months. Thus was prepared the Adi Granth. A new volume of the original Guru Granth was prepared in this way. This is how that volume came to be known as the Damdama bir or recension.[56]

The author further claims that he had learned this story from oral tradition. This final version or the Damdama bir, he says, was lost to the Sikhs during their war with the Afghans in 1762.[57] This traditional story of the loss of the Damdama bir, however, is already to be found in Rattan Singh Bhangu's *Sri Gur Panth Prakash* written in 1841.[58]

There is certain evidence that Guru Gobind Singh made an attempt to standardize the text of the Adi Granth and thus correct the problem of the circulation of three different versions of the Adi Granth during his period. Although he approached Dhir Mal's descendants at Kartarpur to obtain the Adi Bir, he did not succeed in persuading them to part with the volume.[59] A number of copies of the Kartarpur text, however, were available at that time, along with two other versions of the Adi Granth. It was these that he used to prepare the Damdama version of the Adi Granth at a resting-place (damdama) in Anandpur Sahib in the last quarter of the seventeenth century. Further, the bani of Guru Tegh Bahadur had also become part of all the different recensions of the Adi Granth immediately after his death.

Harbhajan Singh briefly mentions two manuscripts of the Adi Granth, written in sambat 1739 (1682) and sambat 1748 (1691), which contained the works of the ninth Guru at appropriate places with raga *Jaijavanti* following the *Prabhati* mode in the standard way. He calls them Damdama versions because they were written at a

[56]Giani Kirpal Singh (*samp.*), *Sri Gur Panth Prakash*, Vol. 3 (Amritsar: Manmohan Singh Brar, 1973), pp. 1678–80.

[57]ibid., verses 61–2.

[58]Rattan Singh Bhangu, *Sri Gur Panth Prakash*, ed. Jeet Singh Sital (Amritsar: Sikh Itihas Research Board, SGPC, 1984), p. 459.

[59]W.H. McLeod, *The Chaupa Singh Rahit-nama* (Dunedin, New Zealand: University of Otago Press, 1987), p. 210.

place called by that name in Anandpur Sahib.[60] These two volumes did not contain the extra material of the Banno text. These copies (nos 97 and 14) were housed in the Sikh Reference Library, Amritsar, and were destroyed in 1984 during Operation Bluestar.

However, we have other testimony concerning the manuscript written in sambat 1748 (1691) that comes from Udasi Harnam Das, who examined the manuscript held at the Sikh Reference Library in 1969. He writes the following brief notes:

1 The *Japu* [of Guru Nanak] is copied from the manuscript written in Guru Ram Das's hand (*japu Guru ramdas jiu kian dasakhatan ka nakalu*).
2 The works of the ninth Guru are available in the volume (*mahala 9 di bani maujud hai*).
3 The volume follows the sequence of the Damdama version (*bir damadami yathakram di hai*).[61]

Clearly, the first point refers to the convention that is generally followed in the copies of the Kartarpur tradition. When the works of the ninth Guru were added to this volume it became the Damdama bir of the Adi Granth. It is evident from these brief reports that the copies of the Damdama version, the manuscripts of which existed before Operation Bluestar in 1984, were current during the period of Guru Gobind Singh along with other versions of the Adi Granth. Khushwant Singh has also mentioned the presence of two manuscripts of this version compiled before Guru Gobind Singh's arrival at Talvandi Sabo, Damdama Sahib, in 1704.[62] I have recently examined an eighteenth–century manuscript of the Damdama version of the Adi Granth, written in 1796 (sambat 1854 poh vadi 10), which is preserved at the Reference library of Punjabi Sahit Akademi at Ludhiana.[63] This manuscript was donated to the Library by Dr. Gurmukh Singh Bedi.

THE STANDARD VERSION OF THE ADI GRANTH

A careful survey of the early manuscripts reveals that there was no one version of the Adi Granth that was accepted by all the Sikhs in

---

[60]Harbhajan Singh, *Gurbani Sampadan Nirnai* (Chandigarh: Satnam Prakashan, 1982), pp. 121–2.

[61]Swami Harnam Das Udasi, *Adi Sri Guru Granth Sahib Ji dian Puratan Biran te Vichar*, Part II (Kapurthala: Kantesh Ayurvedic Pharmesi, 1970), p. 76.

[62]Khushwant Singh, *A History of the Sikhs*, Vol. I (Delhi: Oxford University Press, fifth impression, 1984), p. 93, n. 35.

[63]MS Acc # 1686, Punjabi Sahit Akademi Reference Library, Punjabi Bhavan, Ludhiana.

the eighteenth century. By the beginning of the nineteenth century the Sikhs were using more than four different versions of the Adi Granth. Maharaja Ranjit Singh's rule (1799–1839) brought settled conditions for the Sikh community. Further expansion of his territories brought people from different backgrounds into the fold of the Sikh faith. It also created a situation where different groups within the Panth began to argue over the text of the Adi Granth. This development provided an opportunity for the standardization of the written text. Moreover, in order to consolidate his power Maharaja Ranjit Singh abolished the institution of gurmata (intention of the Guru as expressed in the collective decision of the Sikh community) and tried to downplay the doctrine of Guru-Panth, a doctrine that affirms the mystical presence of the Guru within the corporate body of the Sikhs.[64] He also made efforts to bring forward the doctrine of Guru-Granth, a doctrine that affirms the religious authority of a scriptural Guru, and therefore he needed a standard version for this purpose.

Maharaja Ranjit Singh patronized the Sodhis and Bedis, the direct descendants of the Gurus, who received veneration because of their distinguished origins. He was able to procure the original volume of the Adi Granth from Sodhi Sadhu Singh of Kartarpur by using his political influence, for the purpose of having a sole authorized canon prepared. This is evident from the testimony of a contemporary source, *Suraj Prakash*, written in 1843 by Kavi Santokh Singh.

From that day onwards the most beautiful Granth Sahib has remained with Dhirmal's establishment. His descendants have been receiving offerings [from the devotees]. Now the Khalsa (Maharaja Ranjit Singh) has brought this original granth, the pool of nectar [of the divine word], to Lahore by force to keep it with him. Whatever offerings of money and other gifts are made by him, all of these are received by the descendants of Dhirmal. He has shown compassion in that he did not grab it [from them]. He is prudent and knows the teachings of the true Guru. I do not know what will happen [to the Adi Granth] in the future, whether the Panth takes possession of it or it still remains with them.[65]

Here Santokh Singh's claim that Maharaja Ranjit Singh received the Adi Granth from the descendants of Dhirmal by using force may indicate initial resistance to part with the original volume. He has further expressed uncertainty about the issue of ownership and

[64]Teja Singh maintains that the last gurumata was held in 1809. See *Sikhism: Its Ideals and Institutions* (Amritsar: Khalsa Brothers, reprinted 1978), p. 44.

[65]Translation of the original cited in G.B. Singh, *Prachin Biran*, pp. 250–1.

custody of the Kartarpur manuscript, which was being debated in the Sikh community at that time.

The Kartarpur volume, which Maharaja Ranjit Singh acquired in 1818, was ceremonially installed daily in the Moti Mandir of his palace in Lahore.[66] It was used there for the purpose of standardization of the Adi Granth text, which apparently took place during the 1820s. Other testimony on this matter, which comes from the Gazetteer of Jalandhar District, published under the authority of the Punjab Government during the British rule, states as follows:

Sadhu Singh, an ancestor of the present Guru, took the volume to Lahore at Ranjit Singh's request in 1830, and received the highest honour as its guardian. A daily offering was made of Rs 86; and special doles of Rs 600 were received at each festival of the amawas (end of a moon) and sankrant (beginning of a calendar month); while once a year a valuable shawl and horse were presented in the Maharaja's name. The Granth Sahib was always taken into camp whenever a military expedition of importance was to be undertaken.[67]

The date given here appears to be based on some other event that took place in 1830 concerning Sodhi Sadhu Singh. As the guardian of the original Adi Granth, Sadhu Singh evidently made his fortune and increased his influence to a great extent in the Maharaja's court. Even his family tree (*bansavali-nama*) appears on a golden page in the Persian chronicle *Iqbal-nama*, which gives eyewitness reports of Maharaja Ranjit Singh's court along with the Sikh history starting from the period of the Gurus. It is still in manuscript form. The first part of this Persian manuscript, written by Raja Ram Tota, covers events up to 1849. The second part, written by his son Kaul of Kashmir, covers the British rule up to 1868.[68]

Maharaja Ranjit Singh had also acquired the Banno bir from Bhai Ram Singh and Bhai Nidhan Singh of Khara Mangat, the descendants of Bhai Banno, in 1820.[69] This was obviously done for the purpose of consulting it during the process of preparing a standard version of the Adi Granth. This was also intended to resolve the Kartarpur–Banno debate that must have been going on in the Sikh community

---

[66]Shamsher Singh Ashok, 'Maharaja Ranjit Singh da Pustakalia,' in C.S. Chan Sandhu, ed., *The Sikh Heritage* (Southall: Sri Guru Singh Sabha, 1984), p. 63.

[67]Lepel H. Griffin et al., *Chiefs and Families of Note in the Punjab*, Vol. 1 (Lahore, 1940), p. 167.

[68]The manuscript of *Iqbal-nama* is kept at Sri Guru Granth Sahib Trust, Coventry (UK).

[69]See *Bhai Banno Darpan ate Khare vali Bir*, p. 27.

during that period. It is quite possible that the date of writing of the manuscript of the Banno text was tampered with at that time for the purpose of making a claim to an earlier origin. Although the descendants of Bhai Banno lost such a claim, they won a *jagir* (grant) of Rs 7500 per annum from the generous Maharaja.[70]

It is quite possible that Maharaja Ranjit Singh appointed a council of prominent Sikh scholars to prepare an authorized version of the Adi Granth. Although we do not have any historical evidence to know the actual details of this operation, we do have the manuscripts coming from that period. As it is always the case, those responsible for the actual editing of the text did their best to obscure their own identity. The following characteristic features of this canonical text may be noted. First, a standard convention was employed to introduce the text of the Adi Granth with the words *japu nisanu*, signifying that the *Japu* of Guru Nanak has become the autograph of the Guru. It clearly signals a new emphasis on the doctrine of word as Guru.

Second, the new version was based solely on the original Kartarpur bir with the addition of the works of Guru Tegh Bahadur. The Kartarpur bir thus became the touchstone for correcting the copies of the Adi Granth.[71] Sodhi Sadhu Singh even presented a direct copy of the original bir to Queen Victoria in 1859. The manuscript note on this volume, by the Deputy Commissioner of Lahore reads: 'Transcribed from the original copy, said to bear the signatures of one or more of the five Gurus themselves, in the possession of Guru Sadhu Singh of Kartarpur and by him presented.' Another note by G.B. Singh reads: 'A copy made by Sodhi Sadhu Singh Ji (Guru of the Gaddi at Kartarpur) and presented to Queen Victoria in 1859. It is a copy of the volume at Kartarpur (Jallundhar).' This manuscript (MSS Panj. E 2), kept at the India Office Library (London), has coloured margins throughout, and folios 1b–2a of the text are written in alternate lines of gold and black, with finely illuminated margins.[72] An examination of this manuscript reveals that it is, in fact, a copy of the Damdama version, since it includes the works of the ninth Guru in the usual places. The following two points, however, make it a copy of the original bir. First, some folios

[70]ibid.

[71]'The original granth is in the possession of Guru Jawahir Singh, of Kartarpur, in Jullundur district, and this is often referred to for correcting of copies or erasure of interpolations; this book is most carefully guarded.' See *Gazetteer of the Lahore District 1883–4* (Calcutta: Calcutta Central Press, 1884), p. 58.

[72]IOL, MSS Panj. E 2.

(545a–b and 567a–b) in the *Maru* raga were replaced with new ones to bring the texts (*kudarati karanaihar apara* and *agam agochar veparavahe*) into line with the original bir, although the marginal comments of the Kartarpur volume, explaining the position of these texts, were not written down. Second, in folio 730b, a shalok of Guru Amar Das (*bhai vichi sabhu akaru hai*), which is crossed out with a pen in the Kartarpur volume, is written here in the margin. The most significant point is that the total number of letters in this volume is given at the end in another hand: 'There are nine lakhs ninety-one thousand and thirty-two letters in this volume, all of which are the limbs (*ang*) of the Guru Granth Sahib Ji.'[73] This note clearly suggests the self-understanding of the contemporary Sikh community, and how it perceived the Guru Granth Sahib as the 'living embodiment of the Guru.'

Third, the new version was, in fact, a revival of the earlier Damdama version, compiled during the period of Guru Gobind Singh in the late seventeenth century, which went out of circulation due to the turmoil during the eighteenth century. However, in this version the place of *Jaijavanti* raga and the sequence of the shaloks of the ninth Guru were fixed. In certain instances, the language of the shaloks was modified. The solitary couplet that was attributed to the tenth Guru in early manuscripts lost its authorship and became part of Guru Tegh Bahadur's shaloks. This may have been done intentionally to keep Guru Gobind Singh's authorship limited to the bani in the Dasam Granth. It would also indicate that the canon was closed by the tenth Guru himself.

Fourth, neither was the table of the dates of the Gurus' death included in the volume, nor was its date of writing mentioned anywhere. Perhaps this was done intentionally to create the impression that this particular version represented the everlasting presence of the Gurus. Further, this would also help to promote the Damdama version among the Sikhs as coming directly from the time of Guru Gobind Singh. The later Damdama tradition was actually intended for that purpose.

Finally, Maharaja Ranjit Singh patronized the scribes who made beautiful copies of this new version, which were sent as gifts to all the Sikh Takhats (thrones) and other major gurdwaras. He presented a beautiful copy of the Adi Granth, with two coloured illustrations and finely decorated margins with art work, to Baba Sahib Singh Bedi, which is now in the possession of Baba Sarabjot Singh Bedi of

---

[73]IOL, MSS Panj. E 2, f. 735b.

Una Sahib.[74] This is indeed the most beautiful of the manuscripts of the Adi Granth that I have ever seen. A number of photographs of this manuscript are in my possession.

There is no doubt that Maharaja Ranjit Singh promoted the copying and distribution of the Damdama version of the Adi Granth in the Sikh community. In response to his initiative, some people changed their copies of the Banno version by deleting the extra material in order to bring them into line with the new Damdama version. For instance, a manuscript of the Banno version written in sambat 1847 (1790) was later converted into the Damdama version through the use of hartal (deletion) and by replacing the folios containing extra-canonical material.[75] Evidently the Damdama version was coming to the fore in the Sikh community in the early nineteenth century. At least two contemporary Sikh sources, *Gurbilas Chhevin Patashahi* and *Suraj Prakash*, which were written after the standardization of the text of the Adi Granth, provide detailed accounts of the compilation of the Adi Granth by Guru Arjan.[76] They specifically record the number of bhagats included in the Adi Granth as fifteen without mentioning Mira Bai of the Banno version.[77] This fact alone indicates that they were written after the final canonical text was prepared. It is quite possible that their authors were members of the Sikh council responsible for the project undertaken with the specific approval of Maharaja Ranjit Singh. In fact, Santokh Singh had been associated with the Lahore Darbar for sometime and was entrusted with the service of Harimandir Sahib after the death of his elder brother, Bhai Gurmukh Singh. There he came in contact with Bhai Sant Singh, a scholar of great repute, and received instruction from him. He lived in his *bunga* (educational centre) and remained there till the end of the first decade of the nineteenth century.[78]

[74]One such manuscript (MS # 503) with coloured margins is preserved at Sri Guru Granth Sahib Trust, Coventry, and another is in the possession of Sardar Tarlok Singh Choudhary of Harrow (U.K.). Other manuscripts of the Damdama version are: Punjabi University Library, MS # 115460; MS PUM # 7; MS # 115466; MS # 115593; MS # 115463 and a manuscript kept at Gurdwara Sahib Kuthala, Malerkotala.

[75] Punjabi University Library (Patiala), Special Collections: MS # 11565.

[76]Giani Inder Singh Gill (*samp.*), *Sri Gurbilas Patashahi 6*, pp. 52–91; and Bhai Vir Singh (*samp.*), *Sri Gur Pratap Suraj Granth*, Vol. 6 (Amritsar: Khalsa Samachar, 4th edn, 1963), pp. 2038–145.

[77]See *Sri Gurbilas Patashahi 6*, p. 76 and *Sri Gur Pratap Suraj Granth*, p. 2087. Compare it with the account given in the *Mahima Prakash* (1776), where Mira Bai is included in the list of the bhagats. See *Mahima Prakash*, p. 371.

[78]Sabinderjit Singh Sagar, *Historical Analysis of Nanak Prakash* (Amritsar: Guru Nanak Dev University, 1993), p. 37.

Some sections of the Sikh community, especially in the area of Gujrat district, continued to use the Banno version despite the standardization of the text of the Adi Granth. This is evident from the fact that a number of such manuscripts coming from that period still survive.[79] Indeed, a copy of the Banno text, claimed to be an immediate copy from the original and written by Ram Mrigi in sambat 1905 (1848), was sent to the Imperial Exhibition at Paris in 1855 as part of works of art and industry by the Punjab committee at Lahore.[80] In this context, Christopher Shackle makes the following observation: 'It is interesting that the Banno text should be, even at this relatively late date, still considered a standard version, suitable for exhibition overseas.'[81] This may have been an effort on the part of the protagonists of the Banno text to regain their lost prestige at a time when the Sikh kingdom of Lahore had come under British rule.

Printed Version of the Adi Granth

The coming of the printing press in the Punjab provided another impetus for the Damdama version to be universally accepted by the Sikh community. The Christian Mission at Ludhiana had already made history by setting up a printing press in 1835, and its press was the proud owner of the only Gurmukhi typefaces in India for many years.[82] The annexation of the Punjab in 1849 by the British introduced the printing press into the region, which brought the Sikhs together as never before. In this context, Harjot Oberoi skilfully argues that the new print culture brought three major developments in the Punjabi society. First, it enabled communication across different local and social groups. Second, the printing process encouraged homogenization by standardizing scripts, lexicons and grammatical rules, by promoting uniformity in tastes and by encouraging linear modes of thinking. Third, the print culture removed the authors of printed texts from the realm of direct public contact and endowed them with an anonymous power to circulate their message in a way that might be the envy of a scribe or oral performer.[83]

[79]I have in my possession a manuscript of the Banno version (the second half of a two-volume copy) which was written in sambat 1889 (1832).

[80]IOL, MSS Panj. D 1.

[81]C. Shackle, *Catalogue of the Punjabi and Sindhi Manuscripts in the India Office Library* (London: India Office Library and Records, 1977), p. 6.

[82]Harjot Oberoi, *The Construction of Religious Boundaries: Culture, Identity and Diversity in the Sikh Tradition* (Delhi: Oxford University Press, 1994), p. 220.

[83]ibid., pp. 263–4.

It was in 1860 that Lala Harsukh Rai, the proprietor of the Kohinoor Printing Press, Lahore, approached the Sikh authorities at Amritsar for the purpose of printing an authentic version of the Adi Granth. He was advised to print the Damdama version, the first printed edition of which eventually appeared in 1864.[84] It was printed through lithographic press. Other publishers followed the lead of Kohinoor Press. Thus another printed edition of Sri Guru Granth Sahib (28 by 32 cms in size, with a total of 1574 pages of text and 64 extra pages of index) was published by Matbai Aftab Press in sambat 1925 (1868) at Lahore.[85] It is clearly a standard Damdama version with a beautiful illustration of Guru Nanak, with Guru Angad sitting by his side, which appears in the text of *Japji*. Still another printed edition of 'Sri Guru Granth Sahib Ji Adi' of the Damdama version (with 1775 pages of text and an extra 47 pages of index) was published by Yantralya Press in sambat 1942 (1885) at Lahore.[86] A second edition appeared in sambat 1949 (1892).[87]

Bhai Sankar Singh Ragi of Gujranwala, however, made an effort to revive the Banno text by getting a copy of the 'Sri Adi Granth Sahib Ji' printed at Gian Press by Brij Lal in sambat 1938 (1881) at Gujranwala. The writing that appears on its title page as well as at the end is significant.

1. Om Narayan (*om narayan*)
   By the grace of Parmbraham, who is the supreme lord, the volume of Sri Adi Granth Sahib Ji is written (*prambraham paramisar ki kirapa se sri adi giranth sahib ji likhayate*).
2. [The volume] is authorized under the signatures of Bhai Sankar Singh Ragi, a resident of Gujranwala (*dasakhat bhai sankar singh ragi rahane vala gujranvale ka*).[88]

The Sikhs of Gujranwala were still under brahminical influence, as indicated by the expression om narayan in the above text. They continued to use the Banno version of the Adi Granth. Incidentally, this volume contains only the first two lines of Guru Arjan's hymn in the *Ramakali* raga on page 754. It does, however, contain Mira

---

[84]Piar Singh, *Gatha Sri Adi Granth*, pp. 33–4, n. 3. A copy of this first edition is preserved at Guru Nanak Dev University, Amritsar, with Accession No. R 2846. Also see Harnam Singh Shan, *Guru Granth Sahib di Koshkari* (Patiala: Bhasha Vibhag, 1994), p. 52.
[85]IOL, Panj. H 26.
[86]IOL, Panj. H 25.
[87]IOL, Panj. H 12.
[88]IOL, Panj. H 21.

Bai's hymn and Surdas's complete hymn, along with other apocryphal texts. The Banno bir, however, had already been branded as *khari* (brackish), which means in this context spurious or apocryphal. This usage appears to have come into vogue after the standardization of the written text of the Adi Granth. The Singh Sabha reformers picked up the term and excluded the use of the Banno version for good. They were mainly responsible for sanctifying the standard Damdama version, setting aside all other versions that were used earlier.

The printing of the Adi Granth also created tension among different groups within the Panth. This may be gauged from the most interesting advertisement by Bhai Hira Singh of Damdama Sahib, which is inserted in the printed version of the 'Panj Granth Adi,' published by Yantar Mustafai, Lahore. The advertisement reads:

Advertisement:
Let it be known that this pothi (volume) of Sri Panj Granth has been published with great effort and care. And, 'Sri Guru Granth Sahib Ji Adi, written in the hand of Bhai Hira Singh of Damdama Sahib, will be published [very soon]. It will be ready within a year. Those granths which have already been published are very incorrect. For, the title of *So Dar Rahiras* has been written in the wrong order in them.
Bhai Hira Singh of Damdama Sahib.[89]

Clearly, Bhai Hira Singh was fully aware of other printed versions of the Adi Granth. He was making the claim for writing the correct version of the Adi Granth, and thereby asserting his authority on behalf of 'Sri Darbar Damdama Sahib Kanshi.' The publishers were also running these advertisements beforehand so that people should buy their printed versions of the Adi Granth. This seems to have been the situation in the late nineteenth century. Thus the new print culture and the control of printing and public discourse by specific people were largely responsible for the popularity of the standard Damdama version of the Adi Granth.

The most significant development in the printed version of the Adi Granth, however, took place in the beginning of the twentieth century when the standard pagination of 1430 was established permanently. Primarily, it was the result of printing uniformity based on what William Graham calls 'the use of accurate citations because of the invariance of paginations and page-by-page content in all

[89]*Pothi Panj Granth Adi* (Lahore: Yantar Mustafai, n.d.), p. 62. This pothi is preserved at the Army Gurdwara of 1st Battalion of the Brigade of The Guards Mechanical (2 Punjab).

copies of a given edition set in type.'[90] Charan Singh Shahid seems to have played a major role in this new development. He was concerned to prepare the most authentic and correct copy of the Adi Granth by consulting both the Kartarpur and the Damdama versions. He spent five years comparing the readings of the Damdama version of the Adi Granth with the Kartarpur bir. The printed copy of this most correct recension (sudh bir) of 'Adi Sri Guru Granth Sahib Ji' was published in the second decade of this century by Rai Sahib Munshi Gulab Singh and Sons.[91] This version was then published by other Sikh organizations such as the Shuddh Gurbani Trust of Amritsar. The title page of this version carried the following statement:

Correct Recension of Adi Sri Guru Granth Sahib, pages 1430
The world-wide famous Kartarpur bir of the fifth king, Satguru Arjan Dev Ji and the Damdama bir were consulted by the servant of the Panth, the late S.S. Charan Singh Shahid, with dedicated service, and this bir was prepared after five-years' hard work. This bir is correct to the minute details of vowel-signs.
Publishers:
Shuddh Gurbani Trust, Sri Amritsar Ji[92]

This version of standard pagination was followed by the compilers of the *Shabadarath Sri Guru Granth Sahib Ji*, which was first published in four volumes between 1936 and 1941. This standard version is now published by the Shiromani Gurdwara Prabandhak Committee, Amritsar, and it is used by the Sikh community all over the world.

In the 1950s, the SGPC prepared standard photo-blocks of each page of the Guru Granth Sahib, and placed all the *mangalacharan* (invocations) at the beginning of the titles of various raga sections and sub-sections. This created a storm of controversy within the Panth, and the matter was eventually resolved in a meeting held at Gurdwara Sri Karamsar, Rara Sahib on 4 April 1964, under the chairmanship of Sant Chanan Singh (President, SGPC). Other signatories to the unanimous decision were: Singh Sahib Giani Chet Singh (Head Granthi, Darbar Sahib, Amritsar), Singh Sahib Giani Sharam Singh (Jathedar, Takhat Sri Kesgarh, Anandpur), Principal Satbir Singh, Sant Niranjan Singh, Arjan Singh Muni (Takhat Sri

[90]Graham, *Beyond the Written Word,* p. 22.
[91]Piar Singh, *Gatha Sri Adi Granth,* p. 185. There is one copy of this version preserved at Rare Collections Section, Guru Nanak Dev University Library, with Accession No. 2889. It was published between 1913 and 1918.
[92]*Adi Sri Guru Granth Sahib* (Amritsar: Shuddh Gurbani Trust, n.d.). This beautiful volume with coloured margins is preserved at the Army Gurdwara of 1st Battalion of the Brigade of The Guards Mechanical (2 Punjab).

Hazur Sahib, Nander), Gian Singh Nihang, Sant Balbir Singh, Sant Ishar Singh of Rarevale, and Sant Gurbachan Singh Khalsa of Bhindran Kalan. The decision of the committee reiterated the earlier position to follow the guidelines available from the Kartarpur manuscript.[93] It was indeed a victory of the Sikh sants over the Singh Sabha scholars.[94]

CONCLUSION

This analysis has revealed that the process of canon formation in the Sikh tradition conceals a politically unstable situation in which there was not one but several competing versions of the Adi Granth used by different sections of the Panth in the earlier centuries. The different recensions of the Adi Granth originated as a result of factional divisions in the Panth and external interference in its affairs. Guru Arjan's martyrdom led to a heightening of the spirit of militancy and resulted in the consolidation of the Sikh community against the Mughal authorities. The growing militancy alarmed the Mughal officials, who wanted to tone down this spirit by creating dissensions within the ranks of the Panth. This they appear to have done through indirectly influencing certain groups to tamper with the text of the Adi Granth. There were other groups who still held sant beliefs and who did not approve the shift towards militancy in the affairs of the Panth. They created an internal pressure within the Panth. Further, Guru Arjan's open but cautious approach to the selection of the bhagat bani appears to have created a tension within some sections of the Panth. No one would have even thought of challenging the decision of the Guru while he was alive, but later on, when the situation became unstable after Guru Arjan's martyrdom, the followers of the sants seem to have succeeded in inserting those hymns (which were earlier turned down by the fifth Guru) in their copies of the Adi Granth. This may explain the origin of the three versions of the Adi Granth in the seventeenth century.

This analysis offers the following theories of the origins of different versions of the Adi Granth. The Lahore recension was prepared in 1610, when Guru Hargobind was imprisoned in the Gwalior fort by the orders of Emperor Jahangir. The followers of the sants must have

[93]See Harbhajan Singh, *Gurbani Sampadan Niranai* (Chandigarh: Satinam Prakashan, 1982), pp. 152–62.

[94]For details, see Chapter 3, pp. 89–90

played a role in the creation of this recension. The Banno recension originated in the area of Khara Mangat in Gujrat district in 1642, when the centre of Sikh activities shifted from Amritsar to Kiratpur in the Shivalik hills under Guru Hargobind. This provided ample opportunity to the Banno Group—which included Hindalis, Udasis, Bhatras and Brahmins[95]—to insert extraneous material in the text of the Adi Granth. Apart from reflecting internal pressure within the Sikh community, the Banno group was also reacting to external pressures by the Mughals on the Sikhs.

Although the Damdama version of the Adi Granth was prepared by Guru Gobind Singh at Anandpur in the last quarter of the seventeenth century, different versions of the Adi Granth were used by the Sikh community in the eighteenth century. The Banno recension was predominant. The standardization of the text of the Adi Granth, based on the Damdama version, took place during the reign of Maharaja Ranjit Singh, who was able to procure the Kartarpur volume for this purpose. The first printed edition of the standard Damdama version appeared in 1864, which gave a fillip to its universal acceptance. The Singh Sabha reformers sanctified this standard version and set aside all other versions used in earlier centuries.

It should be emphasized here that apart from a small number of disputed passages (which I have discussed in this study) there has always been complete agreement on the contents of the bani in all three versions of the Adi Granth, even in the seventeenth-century manuscripts. This was due to Guru Arjan's editorial insights, whereby he devised certain checks and balances, which made it extremely difficult for anyone to interpolate any extraneous matter in the text. Each entry in the Adi Granth is numbered and its position is further determined by its raga, authorship, metrical form and so on.[96] Guru Arjan gave to Sikhs an authoritative scripture, which provided a framework for the shaping of the community. How the Sikh community received it will be discussed in the following chapters.

[95]See Chapter 3, pp. 120–1.

[96]Pritam Singh, 'Bhai Banno's Copy of the Sikh Scripture,' *Journal of Sikh Studies,* Vol. XI, no. II (August 1984), p. 115. On the numbering system of the Adi Granth, see Mohinder Kaur Gill, *Sampadan-Kala,* pp. 67–85.

Opening folio of the Guru Nanak Dev University Manuscript (GNDU MS) # 1245 (*c* 1599 CE). Photograph courtesy the author.

SECTION TWO

MEANING

8

THE MEANING OF GURBANI:
A Focus on Hermeneutic Techniques

> The true meaning of scripture is the solid historical reality of
> the continuum of actual meanings over centuries to actual
> people. It is as mundane, or as transcending, or both, as have
> been those actual meanings in the lives and hearts of
> persons.[1]

As a scriptural text the Adi Granth achieved high status within
the Sikh community when its first canonical form was
established by Guru Arjan in 1604. It achieved further dignity,
however, when Guru Gobind Singh closed the canon in the form of
the Damdama recension (bir) in the last decades of the seventeenth
century. It soon became the focus of oral as well as written exegesis,
each generation of Sikh interpreters drawing out its meaning from
their particular angles. In discussing the category of canon in the
history of religions, Jonathan Z. Smith has argued that 'canon is
best seen as one form of a basic cultural process of limitation and
the overcoming that limitation through ingenuity.'[2] He further argues
that the task of overcoming the limitation posed by a closed canon
is accomplished through the exegetical enterprise, in which the task
of the interpreter is 'continually to extend the domain of the closed
canon over everything that is known or everything that exists without
altering the canon in the process.'[3]

[1]Wilfred Cantwell Smith, *What Is Scripture?* p. 89.
[2]Jonathan Z. Smith, 'Sacred Persistence: Toward a Redescription of Canon,' in his
Imagining Religion: From Babylon to Jones-town (Chicago: University of Chicago Press,
1982), p. 52.
[3]ibid., p. 48.

Here it should be emphasized that all interpretative activity is subject to particular cultural predispositions, the historical situation of the interpreter, inevitable change in the modes of attention and the nature of interaction between the past and the present. We shall try to address the following questions while looking at these issues: Does the author's intention alone define the meaning of a text? Is there an objective meaning if each new reader/hearer brings different experiences and awareness to bear on the interpretation? How do different theological presuppositions affect the understanding of a text? Are there levels of meaning in a text? How is scriptural exegesis to be done? How and why do interpretations of religious texts vary from one historical period to another and even from person to person in the same period? How does the scriptural interpretation become the focus of dissent that leads to sectarian tendencies in a religious community? What are the recent trends in the field of scriptural interpretation within the Sikh community?

Let us begin with certain preliminary remarks and definitions. In its basic sense, hermeneutics is a systematic, procedural approach to the texts of our cultural past, and it is a mode of interpretation or exegesis to understand the meaning of those texts. In Sikh usage, the interpretation of the hymns of the Gurus is called *gurbani vichar* or 'reflection upon the utterances of the Gurus.' It is also referred to as *shabad vichar* or reflection upon the word. There are four standard techniques of Indian scriptural tradition that are employed in Sikh exegetical methods. The first is *shabadarath* (meanings of the words), which provides synonyms as well as the meanings of difficult words in a particular hymn. The second is *tika* (commentary), which provides the meaning of a particular hymn with comments in simple language. The third is *viakhia* (exegesis), which provides a detailed exegesis and extended commentary on a particular hymn from a particular angle. The last is *paramarath* (sublime meaning), which provides the spiritual meaning of a particular hymn.[4] Thus, interpretation begins at the discursive level, at which one deals with the literal sense of gurbani, but goes deeper and deeper as one contemplates the divine mysteries by gradually penetrating into subtler levels of meaning. Each encounter with the text of the Adi Granth thus provides a fresh experience of unfolding a divine mystery.

Guru Nanak himself placed great emphasis on the understanding

---

[4]Taran Singh, *Gurbani dian Viakhia Pranalian* (Patiala: Punjabi University, 1980), p. 1.

of the meaning of bani as the fundamental characteristic of the life of a person who has turned towards the Guru (*gurmukh*). For instance, he proclaims: 'Rare is the one who contemplates the meaning of the *bani* and thus turns towards the Guru. This *bani* belongs to the Exalted One and makes one realize one's true self.'[5] Guru Nanak emphasizes the point that a vast majority of people usually do not care to understand the full richness and depth of meaning contained in the bani. He adds that those rare ones who care to do so will certainly have their reward in achieving their true spiritual status.

The Sikh Gurus have repeatedly emphasized that the potentiality of the meaning contained in gurbani is inexhaustible. No matter how much one studies and interprets it, an infinity of meaning remains yet to be fathomed. In this context, Guru Ram Das says: 'The great ocean is full of the wealth of jewels and pearls. This is attainable by such [people] as are devoted to gurbani'.[6] Guru Ram Das thus compares the meaning of gurbani with an unbounded ocean of jewels. Those individuals who dive deep into that ocean through reflection and meditation find within themselves a treasure trove of jewels and realize their true spiritual status. Others who remain on the surface level of that ocean may be dealing only with the literal sense of gurbani, without having any deeper understanding of its meaning. Bhai Gurdas echoes a similar understanding of the depth and richness of the meaning of gurbani: 'In the same way [as the ocean], all treasures are contained in gurbani. Whatever one seeks from it, the same will one attain.'[7]

Our primary concern here is to introduce briefly the different approaches adopted by various schools of interpretation within the Sikh tradition. A thorough examination of all or any of these, however, would require a major scholarly project of its own. The first attempt in this field was made by the late Professor Taran Singh in his *Gurbani dian Viakhia Pranalian* (schools of interpretation of gurbani).[8] Here, the traditional Sikh school of interpretation is referred to as *pranali* or technique of learning. As all interpretative activity is historically conditioned, we shall try to reconstruct the linguistic and historical context of an interpretation. This process will involve an understanding of the interplay between the spirit of the interpreter and the spirit of the age. In this way we shall try to find

---

[5]M1, *Ramakali Dakhani Oankaru* 40, AG, p. 935.
[6]M4, *Asa Chhant* 1, AG, p. 442.
[7]*Kabitt Bhai Gurdas*, 546.
[8]For details, see Taran Singh, *Gurbani dian Viakhia Pranalian*.

out how an interpretation of a text relates to the issues of its epoch. Further, we shall try to keep in mind Mircea Eliade's distinction between the internal meanings of textual and symbolic systems and the ways their use and interpretation are influenced by the 'vicissitudes of social life.'[9] In other words, to determine the religious and social significance of texts, hermeneutics must be coupled with an inquiry concerning the ways readers interpret and use texts.

MAJOR SCHOOLS OF SCRIPTURAL INTERPRETATION

Although there have been occasional attempts to understand the meaning of certain works from the Adi Granth, a strong scholarly tradition of scriptural interpretation did not develop early. In fact, the first complete vernacular commentary on the Adi Granth appeared only at the beginning of this century. It was the celebrated *Adi Sri Guru Granth Sahib Satik*, commonly known as the Faridkot Tika because it was commissioned by the Raja of Faridkot and published in four volumes under his patronage in 1905. The best commentary, however, was to appear under the Singh Sabha influence in the name of *Shabadarath Sri Guru Granth Sahib Ji* in four volumes. This was largely the work of Teja Singh, although it was published anonymously between 1936 and 1941. This work gives the complete Adi Granth text, with commentary on all difficult words on the facing pages. Another excellent work with much fuller exposition of the Adi Granth text is Sahib Singh's *Sri Guru Granth Sahib Darpan*, published in ten volumes between 1962 and 1964. Nevertheless, interpretative activity has been going on within the Sikh tradition since the days of the Gurus. Here we shall introduce seven major schools of interpretation of gurbani.

1. Sahaj Pranali

This special mode of spontaneous interpretation (sahaj pranali) is attributed to the Gurus themselves, who sought to clarify and expound the meaning of certain words, concepts and themes contained in the bani of their predecessors. This exegetical process may be seen to be at work as one proceeds from the bani of Guru Nanak to that of the succeeding Gurus. It should be emphasized that Guru Nanak's bani was the main inspiration behind the bani of the later Gurus, who were also responding to the needs of the growing

---

[9]Mircea Eliade, *Images and Symbols: Studies in Religious Symbolism* (New York: Sheed and Ward, 1969), pp. 24–5.

Sikh community in their own historical situation. In this context, Taran Singh cites certain passages from Guru Nanak's works that were interpreted by Guru Angad, Guru Amar Das, Guru Ram Das and Guru Arjan respectively in their own works.[10] For instance, the exposition of two stanzas of Guru Nanak's *Japji* (nos 17 and 18) may be seen in the first two stanzas of the tenth octave of Guru Arjan's *Sukhmani*.[11]

The sahaj pranali is based upon the celebrated principle of interpretation of scripture by means of scripture. Accordingly, the scripture is regarded as a self-interpreting text, based on the ordinary philological principle that what is plain in one place can be used to clarify what is obscure in another. In other words, it would mean to apply to the text the words of the text itself, using one verse as commentary upon another. This method is frequently employed in almost all religious traditions. In the hermeneutics of midrash, for instance, the rabbis treated the Torah as a self-interpreting text: 'Words of Torah need each other. What one passage locks up, the other discloses.'[12] Similarly, Luther's formulation of the great reform principle of *sola scriptura* was based on the following assertion: 'Scripture is in itself the most certain, most easily understood, most plain, is its own interpreter.'[13] In the same vein, one can cite the qur'anic principle of interpretation that 'the meaning of the Qur'an is understood through the Qur'an itself.'[14] There are thus striking parallels between western and Indian discussions about the interpretation of scripture by means of scripture.

The inclusion of sahaj pranali among the schools of interpretation, it may be stated, was challenged by Piar Singh on the assumption that the bani of the later Gurus was equally inspired and that it must not be placed under the category of any mode of interpretation.[15] He criticized Taran Singh's categorization as arbitrary. He excluded sahaj pranali from his own suggested tripartite scheme: (1) sampardai pranali, traditional school, (2) shastri pranali, brahminical school, and (3) adhunic pranali, modern school. Piar

[10]Taran Singh, *Gurbani dian Viakhia Pranalian*, pp. 26–34.

[11]See M1, *Japu* 17–18, AG, pp. 3–4 and M5, *Gauri Sukhmani* 1–2 (10), AG, p. 275.

[12]Gerald L. Bruns, *Hermeneutics of Ancient and Modern* (New Haven: Yale University Press, 1992), p. 109.

[13]ibid., p. 146.

[14]Taran Singh, *Gurbani dian Viakhia Pranalian*, p. 24.

[15]Piar Singh, 'Gurbani Tika Pranalian,' *Nanak Prakash Patrika*, Vol. 20, no. 2 (Patiala: Punjabi University, December 1985), pp. 108–9.

Singh's scheme may be equally objectionable, since it reduces the diversity of interpretations into three fixed categories. In fact, Taran Singh's categorization reflects the historical development of various schools of interpretations. More than the issue of categorization what should be emphasized is that Guru Nanak's bani was the main inspiration behind the bani of the later Gurus, who were also responding to the needs of the growing Sikh community in their own historical situation.

Let us consider, for instance, the issue of the coining of the divine word (*ghariai* sabad) in the true mint (*sachi taksal*) as described in the last stanza of Guru Nanak's *Japji*:

Continence the forge and tranquillity the goldsmith, intelligence the anvil and knowledge the tools. Let fear be the bellows, austerities the fire, and love the crucible in which nectar is poured. In such a mint the divine word is cast, the daily task for all who receive divine grace. They who receive this grace, Nanak, are blessed with a joy transcending all.[16]

Here, Guru Nanak is describing his self-understanding of how the divine word (shabad) becomes manifested in the life of a person based upon the eight-fold ethical virtues of continence, tranquility, intelligence, knowledge, fear, austerities, love and the nectar (amrit) of divine name. In this whole process of spiritual development, personal effort and divine grace go hand in hand, although the latter is of primary importance and the final arbiter. Guru Nanak employs the celebrated metaphors of furnace, crucible and mint to describe the purgatorial process, from which the redeemed emerge purified like metal in a smelting operation. Images of refinement and purification in a furnace recur in almost all the religious traditions.[17]

Guru Ram Das had in mind Guru Nanak's last stanza of *Japji* when he composed his *Bhairau* hymn. Especially notable is his spontaneous interpretation of the ghariai shabad in the sachi taksal:

They who faithfully performed the self-less service (*seva*) through the grace of the Guru have run their course, their labours done. The divine word is cast in such a true mint.[18]

Here, Guru Ram Das employs the key word seva as the true basis of the life of spirituality. Accordingly, all the ethical virtues flow from

---

[16]M1, *Japji* 38, AG, p. 8. Translation is taken from W.H. McLeod, *Sikhism*, p. 281.
[17]Northrop Frye, *Words with Power: Being a Second Study of 'The Bible and Literature'* (San Diego, New York and London: Harcourt Brace Jovanovich, 1990), pp. 296–7.
[18]M4, *Bhairau* 3, AG, p. 1134.

the faithful performance of self-less service of the Guru and thus one becomes the channel of the divine word. By his time seva and simaran (remembrance of the divine name) had become the two pillars of the teachings of the Gurus. In fact, Guru Amar Das designated Ram Das to the throne (gaddi) of Guru Nanak because of his self-less service. Thus Guru Ram Das interprets the last stanza of Guru Nanak's *Japji* in the light of his personal experience.

The adoption of the word taksal (mint) to refer to a school of traditional Sikh learning within the Panth is highly significant. It was taken from the last stanza of Guru Nanak's *Japji*. The intention here is that the method of scriptural interpretation at any taksal is based upon the true teachings of Guru Nanak and the succeeding Gurus. However, in course of time there emerged a number of such taksals or schools within the Panth with different orientations and backgrounds. Each taksal seeks to impart a particular version of gurmat (teachings of the Guru). The most famous school of learning is known as the Damdami Taksal, believed to have been started by Guru Gobind Singh at Damdama Sahib in Talvandi Sabo.

2. Bhai Pranali

This school of interpretation is linked with the name of Bhai Gurdas, whom Guru Arjan chose to act as his amanuensis during the final recording of the Adi Granth text. He received the honorific title bhai (brother) for his contribution to the Sikh faith, and for this reason his typical approach of interpretation is known as bhai pranali. He was a poet and a theologian whose works are generally regarded as the key to the Guru Granth Sahib. The most influential among his works are the thirty-nine lengthy poems called vars, which provide an extensive commentary on the teachings of the Gurus.[19] He is also the author of a series of 675 poems, which he wrote in Braj in the kabitt style.[20]

Bhai Gurdas provides an example of theological interpretation. He faithfully expounds the key terms and theological concepts of early Sikh doctrine. For instance, one may see his exposition of the Mul Mantar in *Var* 3:15. Again, the meaning of the epilogue of the *Japji* is clearly brought out in the light of the Sikh doctrine of word as Guru (Guru sabadu) as follows:

[19]Hazara Singh and Vir Singh, eds, *Varan Bhai Gurdas* (Amritsar: Khalsa Samachar, 9th edn, 1977).

[20]Vir Singh, ed., *Kabitt Bhai Gurdas*, Parts 1 and 2 (Amritsar: Khalsa Samachar, 3rd edn, 1966). The first part contains 556 poems and the second the remaining 119.

Shalok
Air is the Guru, water the father, and earth the mighty mother of all ...
(M1, *Japji*, AG, p. 8)

Bhai Gurdas (*Var* 2:19)
Air is the Guru in the sense of word as Guru, and [this knowledge comes from] the contemplation of the music of the word. Water is the father and earth the mother, which give birth to the whole creation ...

The real issue here is to understand the identification of Guru with air. It is instructive to note that in all languages the metaphorical kernel of spirit is air (*pavan*) or breath. Breathing is the most primary of all concerns of life, the act marking the transition from embryo to baby, and our most continuous activity thereafter. In this context Northrop Frye makes an important observation: 'The transition from the embryonic to the ordinary world suggests by analogy a second transition from a natural world to a spiritual world, which we reach by taking a second breath or inspiration in a higher kind of air. This process is a rebirth or a higher birth.'[21]

Guru Nanak's identification of Guru with air (pavan Guru) makes perfect sense when we apply the notion of transition from a natural world to a spiritual world. In his *Siddh Gost* he makes the same assertion that as life begins with air so does the life of spirituality begin with the word (shabad) of the Guru.[22] Bhai Gurdas's interpretation of Guru Nanak's shalok elaborates on this from a doctrinal standpoint, since by his time the doctrine of word as Guru was well established within the Sikh tradition.

Throughout his works, Bhai Gurdas deals with the essential doctrines taught by the Gurus (gurmat): unity of guruship, Sikh way of life (*sikhi*), Sikh morality (*sadachar*), holy fellowship (sadh sangat), the ideal Sikh who has turned towards the Guru (gurmukh), and so on.[23] From his earliest days Bhai Gurdas was closely associated with four Sikh Gurus, serving successively Guru Amar Das, Guru Ram Das, Guru Arjan and Guru Hargobind. In his works, therefore, one may also find the source material for the early history of the Panth. Bhai Gurdas's approach to gurbani may be termed what Paul Ricoeur defines as the 'hermeneutics of affirmation.'[24] That is, he begins the process of scriptural exegesis with the power of affirmation of Sikh

[21] Frye, *Words with Power*, p. 126.
[22] M1, *Siddh Gost* 44, AG, p. 943.
[23] Taran Singh, *Gurbani dian Viakhia Pranalian*, p. 45–8.
[24] Charles E. Reagon and David Stewart, eds, *The Philosophy of Paul Ricoeur: An Anthology of His Work* (Boston: Beacon Press, 1978), p. 215.

doctrines from the orthodox standpoint. It is no wonder that Bhai Gurdas is commonly referred to as the first interpreter of the Sikh way of life.[25]

3. Paramarath Pranali

This school of interpretation is associated with the Miharban tradition. It was mainly responsible for the didactic variety of discourse (gost). W.H. McLeod draws two significant conclusions from an analysis of the Miharban janam-sakhi: first, the work is not sectarian polemic, and secondly, it is not strictly a janam-sakhi, but rather an exegetical tradition.[26] The name of this tradition is derived from the conventional formula *tis ka paramarath* (its sublime meaning) used by the commentator after each quotation of Guru Nanak before giving its actual exegesis.[27] Unlike Bhai Gurdas who employed the medium of poetry for his exposition of Sikh doctrines, Miharban took prose as his medium. This should not, however, conceal the fact that he concludes his didactic discourse with a shalok of his own in which he tries to recapture the spirit of the original verse of Guru Nanak.

In his analysis of Sikh hagiography, W.H. McLeod suggests that the Miharban janam-sakhi begins with the narrative setting and the introduction of interlocutors, which provide a context suitable to the basic pedagogical purpose. This purpose, he argues, is to provide an explanation or interpretation of Guru Nanak's own works.[28] For instance, the detailed description of Guru Nanak's marriage-party in the wedding-discourse provides the setting for the interpretation of *Suhi Chhant* 1:

Suhi Chhant Mahala 1
Loved friends have arrived at my home. The true one has brought about the union ...

(M1, *Suhi Chhant* 1, AG, p. 764)

Its sublime meaning [is as follows]:
Then Guru Baba Nanak Ji said, 'Loved friends have arrived at my home.' Who are these loved friends who have come? Well, all these that are good actions are the loved friends of this soul. And, all those that are bad actions are its enemies. When the true lord showed benevolence towards this [soul],

then these good actions have become its loved friends, through which this soul has achieved excellence ....[29]

Here Miharban's method of exegesis is clearly reflected in his allegorical interpretation of loved friends (*sajan*) as good actions (*sukrit*) and home (*ghar*) as soul (*jia*). In this way he goes beyond the literal sense of Guru Nanak's verse and tries to provide its spiritual meaning through the medium of homilies which he delivered to his followers in simple language during the early decades of the seventeenth century.

From a hermeneutical standpoint Miharban emerges as one of the great allegorists in the history of interpretation, someone who deals with alien discourses by recontextualizing them within his own conceptual framework. In this context, interpretation does not mean recovering or preserving an original message, rather it means integrating a text (and its meanings) into a radically new cultural environment. It is interesting to note how Philo of Alexandria interpreted the literal historical narratives of the Hebrew Bible as spiritual paradigms. For instance, the story of the exodus from Egypt, the wanderings in the desert for forty days, and the entry into the promised land, was really an allegory of the individual soul's emancipation, tribulations, and final deliverance. Interpretation in this case presupposes a discrepancy between the plain meaning of the text and the demands of readers from a new Hellenistic environment. It seeks to resolve that discrepancy. The situation is that a dead text has become unacceptable; yet it cannot be discarded because of its scriptural status. Interpretation is thus a radical strategy for conserving the old text, which is thought too precious to be repudiated, by revamping it. The interpreter, without actually erasing or rewriting the text, alters it. But he cannot admit doing this. He claims to be only making it intelligible, by disclosing its true meaning.[30]

The Miharban school of interpretation points towards the existence of a strong tradition of scriptural exegesis in the form of religious discourse. After Miharban's death in 1640 his exegetical method was followed by his sons Hariji and Chatarbhuj.[31] Their particular emphasis on the 'spiritual meaning', based on allegorical interpretation of a scriptural passage, makes sense only in the context

---

[29] Taran Singh, *Gurbani dianViakhia Pranalian*, p. 57.

[30] Susan Sontag, *Against Interpretation and Other Essays* (New York: Farrar, Strauss & Giroux, 1966), p. 6.

[31] For more details, Taran Singh, *Gurbani dian Viakhia Pranalian*, pp. 69–89.

of their historical situation. It is important to note that Guru Arjan's death in 1606 in Mughal custody became a turning point in the history of the Sikh Panth. This resulted in the rise of the spirit of militancy and the consolidation of the Sikh community against the Mughal authorities who were responsible for the death of the Guru. The sixth Guru, Hargobind traditionally donned two swords symbolizing the spiritual (piri) as well as temporal (miri) aspects of the guruship. In fact, the main centre of Sikh activities finally shifted from Amritsar to Kiratpur in 1634 under Guru Hargobind, who had to withdraw to the Shivalik hills due to the pressure of Mughal authorities. It was then that the Miharban group, popularly branded as the Mina sect, took control of Amritsar and preached their spiritual discourses with the blessings of the Mughal authorities. W.H. McLeod has remarked that Mina literature suggests that 'this particular group may have been seeking to restrict the Panth's concern to more limited religious aspects of Nanak's teachings, that they were opposed to the wider social concern which increasingly occupied the Panth's interest and which increasingly was being used to define its nature.'[32] Here McLeod does not take into account the issue of Mughal interference in the affairs of the Panth, an issue which is highly significant for an understanding of the complexity of that historical period. It is no wonder that when the Khalsa took control of Amritsar in the early years of the eighteenth century, the Mina sect became extinct since there was no Mughal support to sustain it.

4. Udasi Pranali

This school of interpretation is linked with the Udasi Sikhs, the followers of Baba Sri Chand, Guru Nanak's elder son. Their ascetic ideals are reflected in their writings. They were basically itinerant sadhus who delivered their own interpretation of Guru Nanak's message orally among people throughout India. The first written record of the Udasi school of thought may be seen in Sadhu Anandghan's commentary on the *Japji* and other works of Guru Nanak, which he completed in 1825 during Maharaja Ranjit Singh's reign. Sadhu Anandghan received his education in brahminical thought at Kashi, the influence of which may be seen in his interpretation. He maintained that Guru Nanak's whole bani was written according to the Hindu shastra tradition.[33] That was why he

---

[32]W.H. McLeod, *The Evolution of the Sikh Community*, p. 43.
[33]Taran Singh, *Gurbani dian Viakhia Pranalian*, p. 96.

stressed upon its interpretation in the context of Vedic thought.

In his commentary on the *Japji*, Sadhu Anandghan manipulated the text with the subtle tools of linguistics and forced it to yield the meaning that fitted with his theological presuppositions. Note, for instance, his interpretation of a line from the fifth stanza of *Japji*:

Shiva, Vishnu, Brahma and Parvati, all are but manifestations of the one divine Guru.

(M1, *Japji* 5, AG, p. 2)

Anandghan's interpretation runs as follows:

In this line Guru Nanak himself acknowledges that he is the disciple of six Gurus. Those six Gurus are as follows: Shiva, Vishnu, Brahma, Parvati, *ma* (Lakshmi) and *i* (Sarasvati). [34]

One can see how Guru Nanak is actually reducing the status of all gods by saying that they are but manifestations of the one divine Guru. In this context, W.H. McLeod makes a highly significant observation: 'Guru Nanak does refer to Brahma, Vishnu, and Shiva in ways which suggest that he accepted their existence as real, but they appear as the creatures of God, deprived of all functions and subject to *maya* and to death.'[35] Sadhu Anandghan, on the other hand, makes Guru Nanak a disciple of those six gods, by interpreting the line from the *Japji* from the perspective of Vedantic thought. One can see here that the process of the Hinduization of the Sikh tradition was at work through the efforts of the Udasis.

Further, the most striking instance in Sadhu Anandghan's commentary may be seen in his method of hermeneutics of reduction when he declares that the actual text of *Japji* ends at the twenty-fifth stanza and that the remainder of it is just its extra (*khil*) portion:

The king of kings [in the twenty-fifth stanza] must be the supreme lord himself ...
According to this interpretation *Japji* is perfect and according to our traditional lineage its name is *Japji* ...
The following [stanza that begins with the words] priceless virtues (*amul gun*) is just an extra (khil) portion of the *Japji* ... [36]

In method and style Sadhu Anandghan reflects in his interpretation of gurbani a Vedantic Hindu perspective influential in Varanasi at

[34]See ibid., p. 105, n. 3.
[35]W.H. McLeod, *Guru Nanak and the Sikh Religion*, p. 166.
[36]Taran Singh, *Gurbani dian Viakhia Pranalian*, p. 96.

that time. It seems that the Udasi tradition was completely assimilated to Hindu philosophical thought by the time it reached the nineteenth century.

Although the Udasis did not reject the line of succession from Guru Nanak to Guru Gobind Singh, they attached greater importance to the chain of succession from Guru Nanak, through his eldest son Sri Chand and the Adi Udasis, to the reigning Mahant of Udasi establishment. They showed greater respect to the Adi Granth, but interpreted its essential message in Vedantic terms, shifting the focus from a personal God, Akal Purakh, to an impersonal reality. They did not subscribe to the twin doctrine of Guru-Panth and Guru-Granth. In the process they produced an interpretation of Sikhism that made them unorthodox from the viewpoint of the Singhs of the Khalsa.

It is important to understand the historical context in which Udasis acted as readers of the Adi Granth and attendants of Sikh *dharamsalas* in the eighteenth and nineteenth centuries. Under Ranjit Singh's rule the Udasi centres flourished more in terms of influence and resources than under Sikh rulers of the eighteenth century. In particular, the Udasis wielded considerable influence among ruling and landowning classes. Commenting on Maharaja Ranjit Singh's patronage to the Udasis, Sulakhan Singh writes:

No doubt the Maharaja was liberal and catholic in matters of revenue-free grants, but we cannot ignore his interest in consolidating his power among different social elements. The Udasis could be patronized therefore, partly for their influence among various sections of the society, and partly to make themselves influential with people. They could serve as a counterpoise to orthodox religious groups among the Sikhs.[37]

The Udasi interpretation of gurbani was in a certain sense, part of the complex process of state formation. After all, how could 1.5 million Sikhs, that is, 12 per cent of the Punjabi population, rule over the vast majority of Hindus and Muslims? The Vedantic perspective of Udasis helped in strengthening the ties between the Hindus and the Sikhs. Moreover, the boundaries between different religious communities were not clearly marked in the nineteenth century. That process was to begin later in the colonial period.

[37]Sulakhan Singh, 'State Patronage to the Udasis under Maharaja Ranjit Singh,' in J.S. Grewal and Indu Banga, eds, *Maharaja Ranjit Singh and His Times* (Amritsar: Guru Nanak Dev University, 1980), p. 115.

5. Nirmala Pranali

The origin of the Nirmala sect within the Panth is obscure, although there is some evidence that it existed during the Misal period in the late eighteenth century.[38] There is no evidence to support the traditional claim that Guru Gobind Singh himself deputed five Sikhs to Kashi for Sanskritic learning. The first recognized Nirmala scholar was Kavi Santokh Singh, who wrote the celebrated works *Nanak Prakash* and *Suraj Prakash* in the first half of the nineteenth century. He also wrote a commentary on *Japji*, popularly known as *Garbganjani Tika*, 'A Commentary to Humble the Pride [of Udasi Anandghan].' Santokh Singh took strong exception to Anandghan's interpretation that Guru Nanak acknowledged six Gurus in a line from *Japji*. He was also strongly critical of the esoteric interpretation of gurbani presented in the Udasi work. It appears that the scriptural interpretation was one focus of conflict among various sects within the Panth in the nineteenth century.

Like Udasis, however, the Nirmala scholars were equally inclined towards Vedantic interpretations of gurbani. They maintained that gurbani was essentially an expression of the Vedic teachings in the current vernacular language (*bhakha*).[39] In his commentary on *Japji*, for instance, Santokh Singh frequently employed the Puranic myths and examples from the Vedas to make a point. Basically, he interpreted certain key Sikh doctrines from a brahminical perspective. For instance, note the following interpretation of the expression Karta Purakh from the Mul Mantar:

The Brahman who is truth, consciousness and bliss becomes creator-person through maya—for the sake of maya itself. By means of his conscious creative power, maya, he creates the world again and again. He who is truth is called by the name of creator through the power of maya.[40]

Here, the celebrated expression *sat chit anand* (truth, consciousness and bliss) from the Vedantic thought is superimposed on the Mul Mantar. Further, maya (illusion) is presented as the cosmic power which makes the Brahman appear as Karta Purakh (creator-person) for the sake of creating the world again and again. In other words, the Brahman is the only ultimate reality, and the world is just cosmic illusion which is unreal (*asat*). The whole interpretation

---

[38]Rai Jasbir Singh, 'Nirmal Bhekh da Arambh', in Pritam Singh (*samp.*), *Nirmal Sampradai* (Amritsar: Guru Nanak Dev University, 1981), pp. 30–7.

[39]Taran Singh, *Gurbani dian Viakhia Pranalian*, p. 130, n. 1.

[40]ibid., p. 133, n. 5.

becomes meaningful only when it is seen through the lens of Vedanta. In order to understand the true nature of scriptural interpretation, therefore, it is of utmost importance to understand the theological presuppositions of the interpreter. Santokh Singh was strongly influenced by the Vedantic doctrines of the Udasis and the Nirmalas. It was indeed the result of his basic training at Amritsar where 'Vedant was also in the curriculum of Gurmukhi schools.'[41] There were other such scholars, like Pandit Tara Singh Narotam, Bhai Dal Singh Gyani, Giani Gian Singh, Sant Deva Singh Nirmala, Pandit Gulab Singh, Sadhu Gurdit Singh and Sant Sampuran Singh, who were all interpreting gurbani from the Nirmala perspective in the late nineteenth and early twentieth centuries.[42]

6. Giani Pranali

Traditionally, this school of interpretation is associated with Mani Singh Giani who is credited with having learned the exposition of scriptures from Guru Gobind Singh at Damdama Sahib in Talvandi Sabo. However, there is no authentic work that may be consulted for understanding his approach towards scriptural interpretation. The first major work from this school, in fact, appeared in the form of a complete commentary on the Adi Granth, the *Faridkot Tika*, in 1905. Its author was Giani Badan Singh of Sekhwan, who was responding to the situation created by the offensive remarks made by Ernest Trumpp in his incomplete translation of the Adi Granth in 1877.[43] In fact, M.A. Macauliffe also undertook his monumental work *The Sikh Religion* (1909) to 'make some reparation to the Sikhs for the insults which Trumpp offered to their Gurus and their religion.'[44] It is important to note that the giani school of thought put great emphasis on strict adherence to the sacred text and on the received tradition of the Khalsa.

The chief characteristic of the Faridkot tika is its emphasis on intuitive (*anubhab*) interpretation.[45] Giani Badan Singh maintains that an interpreter's intuitive faculties are developed only in the

---

[41]Sabinderjit Singh Sagar, *Historical Analysis of Nanak Prakash by Bhai Santokh Singh* (Amritsar: Guru Nanak Dev University, 1993), p. 13.

[42]See Taran Singh, *Gurbani dian Viakhia Pranalian*, pp. 138–88.

[43]Ernest Trumpp, *The Adi Granth* (New Delhi, reprint, 1970; 1st edn, London, 1877), p. CXX.

[44]Harnam Singh Shan, 'Macauliffe and his Contributions to Sikh Studies and Contacts between Cultures' (a paper presented at the 33rd ICANAS, University of Toronto, 19–25 August 1990).

[45]Taran Singh, *Gurbani dian Viakhia Pranalian*, pp. 206–7.

company of ideal Sikhs, who can pass on the Guru's correct intention of a particular passage through oral transmission. He further stresses that a single meaning of a line of gurbani should be preferred to multiple meanings achieved through various interpretative techniques. In his approach, however, he goes beyond the literal sense. For instance, note the following interpretation of a line from *Japji*:

Past actions determine the nature of our birth but grace alone reveals the door to liberation.

(M1, Japu 4, AG, p. 2)

Through the lord's gracious glance one achieves the robe of honour in the form of loving devotion (bhakti), by means of which one reaches the door to liberation in the form of knowledge.[46]

Here there is no mention of the role of past actions (*karami*) in the interpretation of this line from *Japji*. Rather, emphasis is placed on the dual function of divine grace which paves the way for loving devotion in the first place and then for the knowledge of the door to liberation.

A prominent institution of the giani school was established at Amritsar by Sant Ameer Singh (1870–1954), who frequently offered many new meanings of a single line of gurbani on the basis of etymological possibilities of different words. Indeed, he employed the ancient Indian technique of 'etymology' (*nirukat*) as a science of interpretation. He generally observed the rules for deriving etymologies formulated by the ancient Indian scholar Yaska. On occasion, however, Ameer Singh was creative in his interpretations. His creativity was prefigured by Yaska's admission that etymology may be derived in accordance with the desired effect. It is no wonder that Ameer Singh's interpretations frequently became strained and out of context, and his audience became confused with his message.[47]

Another giani school, which later became popular as Bhindran Taksal, was established by Sant Sunder Singh of Boparai Kalan in 1906. Commenting on his exegetical skills, Harjot Oberoi argues that Sundar Singh's strategy was to negate differentiation among Sikhs by abolishing all polysemous interpretations of Sikh scriptures and cultivating a univocal reading of texts in order to shape a more homogeneous community.[48] Oberoi seems to be stretching the argument too far in order to make a case for the rise of Sikh

---

[46]ibid., p. 208.

[47]For details, see ibid., pp. 223–34.

[48]Harjot Oberoi, 'Sikh Fundamentalism: Translating History into Theory', in

fundamentalism in the early decades of the present century. In my opinion, Sundar Singh's emphasis on a single meaning was more a reaction against the multiple meanings offered by the Nirmala scholars of the day, rather than a conscious strategy to create a monolithic Sikh community. Moreover, his successor, Giani Gurbachan Singh Khalsa (1902–69) of Bhindran Kalan, was known for offering many possible meanings of the same scriptural passage.[49] He was the one who trained a large number of gianis through his mobile seminary, popularly known as Bhindran Taksal.

Gurbachan Singh Khalsa devoted his entire life to teaching correct enunciation and intonation in reciting the Sikh scriptures. He maintained that the sacred sounds of gurbani have transformative power only if they are replicated exactly as they were first enunciated by the Sikh Gurus. Verne Dusenbery calls this approach the non-dualistic understanding of the Guru's inspired words. The non-dualistic ideology of language 'recognizes the material as well as cognitive properties of language (especially articulated speech) and refuses to privilege semantico-referential meaning at the expense of other properties that language is thought to possess.'[50]

The influence of the Bhindran Taksal is attested by the fact that its alumni include the head granthi (reader) at the Golden Temple, jathedars (commanders) of all the takhats, and granthis of major gurdwaras of historical significance. In the recent past, an incumbent of a branch of this school, Sant Jarnail Singh Bhindranwale, achieved world-wide attention when he died along with many other Sikhs during the Indian Army's assault on the Golden Temple complex in June 1984. Since then the interpretation of the Bhindran Taksal seems to have moved towards a fundamentalist position with emphasis on scriptural literalism.

7. Singh Sabha Pranali

This school of interpretation is linked with the Singh Sabha, which began in 1873 as a reform movement dedicated to the revival of traditional Sikh values following a period of apparent decay. It was greatly influenced by the British presence in the Punjab, a presence

Martin E. Marty and R. Scott Appleby, eds, *Fundamentalisms and the State* (Chicago: The University of Chicago Press, 1993), p. 267.

[49]See Gurbachan Singh Khalsa, *Gurbani Path Darashan* (Amritsar: Bhai Mehar Singh and Sons, 6th edn, 1985).

[50]Verne A. Dusenbery, 'The Word as Guru: Sikh Scripture and the Translation Controversy', *History of Religion*, 31(4) (May 1992): 388–9.

which, among other things, provided the technology for dissemi-
nating literature. The Singh Sabha scholars adopted an approach to
scriptural interpretation which was primarily guided by the scientific and rationalistic influence of western education. Through this
process of reinterpretation of the received tradition they were able
to produce detailed commentaries on the Adi Granth from a purely
Sikh perspective. For instance, Teja Singh (1894–1958), the author
of *Shabadarath*, brought out rationally the meaning of scriptural
words, phrases and passages in exclusively Sikh terms.[51]

Bhai Vir Singh (1872–1957), the most prolific writer of the Singh
Sabha school of interpretation, emphasized the need to practise nam
simaran in order to understand the deeper levels of meaning of
gurbani. In his *santhia* (lesson) he provided an excellent combination
of all the four techniques of interpretation, comprising shabadarath,
paramarath, tika and viakhia, from a strictly orthodox Sikh
standpoint. His typical approach was to explore the meaning of every
line in the context of the whole hymn or composition. He frequently
used quotations from the Adi Granth, the Dasam Granth and Bhai
Gurdas's vars to elaborate the meaning of particular passages of
gurbani, thus following the principle of interpreting the scripture by
means of scripture.[52]

Unlike Bhai Vir Singh, Sahib Singh (1893–1977) was quite
adamant on the principle of 'a single meaning' of a scriptural passage.
His approach is based upon a grammatical explanation of gurbani,
which he developed fully in his *Gurbani Viakaran* in 1939. The idea
that gurbani has its own grammar was suggested for the first time by
the much-maligned linguist Ernest Trumpp in his introduction to
The Adi Granth. In his letter of 5 October 1870, to India Office,
London, Trumpp noted in his examination of two lithographed
copies of the Adi Granth that 'the final vowels are frequently dropped,
because they are now no longer pronounced by the Sikhs, though
they are very important for the right understanding of the text and
grammatical structure of the language which Bhais do not seem to
be aware.'[53] This knowledge and study of the orthographic
grammatical vowel-signs was carried forward to a great extent by

---

[51]Taran Singh, *Gurbani dian Viakhia Pranalian*, pp. 323–48.

[52]For more details, see ibid., pp. 295–300.

[53]Cited in Trilochan Singh, *Ernest Trumpp and W.H. McLeod as Scholars of Sikh
History, Religion and Culture* (Chandigarh: International Centre of Sikh Studies, 1994),
p. 47. Also see Harnam Singh Shan, *Guru Granth Sahib di Koshkari* (Patiala: Bhasha
Vibhag, 1994), pp. 29–31.

Teja Singh in his *Shabadarth*, but was fully developed by Sahib Singh.[54] He also maintained that there is complete identity between gurbani and bhagat bani. In his commentary, Sahib Singh argues that the refrain-verse of a hymn provides its central meaning. That is why he begins his explanation with it and weaves the whole meaning of a hymn or composition around it. He tries to free the explanation of gurbani from history. He also maintains that there is always a theme running as a continuous thread throughout a composition. In order to justify this he sometimes offers strained interpretations.[55]

RECENT TRENDS IN SCRIPTURAL INTERPRETATION

In this section, we shall briefly examine the recent trends in scriptural interpretation within the Sikh tradition. Western-trained interpreters are now applying historical-critical method to reconstruct the linguistic and historical context of an utterance. This is only the first step to an understanding that requires us to work back through the utterance to the person who originally produced it. The historical-critical method is further sharpened by a 'hermeneutics of suspicion' what Paul Ricoeur defines as 'set[ting] out from an original negation, advanc[ing] through a work of deciphering and ... struggl[ing] against masks, and finally ... put[ting] in the quest of new affirmation.'[56] It is important to note that personal and official biases may be removed to a large extent once the text is subjected to the hermeneutics of suspicion. But the recent welcome that such a method has received within the Sikh scholarship is not a favourable one.

An examination of recent literature, originating from such circles as the Institute of Sikh Studies, Chandigarh, and the Centre of Sikh Studies, California, clearly indicates that certain groups within the Panth are busy in projecting 'a correct image' of Sikhism and the Sikh community in India and abroad. They perceive critical scholarship as an attack on their faith and are always ready with their defensive approach to rebut perceived distortions or misrepresentations of Sikh religion and history. Their emphasis on a single correct meaning of gurbani is the result of a distinctive doctrinal approach of certain Singh Sabha scholars, particularly the grammatical approach of Sahib Singh.

[54]See Taran Singh, *Gurbani dian Viakhia Pranalian*, p. 350.
[55]ibid., pp. 351–62.
[56]Reagon and Stewart, eds, *The Philosophy of Paul Ricoeur*, p. 217.

In the context of the present discussion, it will be useful to note the following remarks of W.H. McLeod on the potentiality of meaning of the text of the Adi Granth:

Many Sikhs are quite adamant about the meaning of the Guru Granth Sahib. The sacred scripture is indeed the Guru, but it conveys its message in different ways to different people, communicating with some on one level of perception and with others on a different level. It is foolish to imagine that the scripture will speak at the same level and degree of understanding to the ordinary villager as opposed to the person who has devoted many years to meditation. Clearly it will speak in different ways, the one to a person requiring a simple meaning and the other to someone of deep perception. All people will derive a message from the Guru Granth Sahib, but not all receive the same one. The range is indeed infinite as people differ in their perception and their diversity. Non-Sikhs are certainly encouraged to consult the scripture, but the Guru's message for a person of western background will be distinctively different from that of a Punjabi Sikh.[57]

Here McLeod is challenging the assumption of certain sections within the Panth, who maintain that the text of the Adi Granth contains a single correct meaning. He is in fact referring to those fundamentalists in the Sikh community who believe in the doctrinal mode of interpretation. Such a doctrinal mode of interpretation, it may be stated, has lost its credibility in present-day scholarship because of its limited utility in an ecumenical era. McLeod is suggesting an approach that maintains that the process of unfolding the meaning of the Adi Granth text depends upon the level of understanding of human beings. His appeal is to the scholarly emphasis on text reception as reader-response (a focus that accepts and assumes the printed text as the form of the message).

Further, recent scholarship has brought a new awareness of the function of the oral dimension of a scripture in world religions. This shift stimulates reflection on text reception as 'hearer-response' (a focus that accepts and assumes the 'oral/aural text' as the form of the message). In this context, Harold Coward makes the following observation:

Rather than there being one correct meaning for a text, the hearing and reading of a Vedic poem or New Testament parable may convey many different meanings or insights depending on the listener, the time, and the place. Instead of a hermeneutics of reduction, based on the assumption

---

[57]W.H. McLeod, 'Sikh Fundamentalism,' *Journal of the American Oriental Society,* Vol. 118(1) (January–March 1998): 23.

that the text has only one correct meaning, the oral experience of scripture paves the way for a hermeneutics of unfolding (*Entfaltung*), an opening up of the richness of the word in terms of its symbolic potentialities.[58]

Coward's suggestion of adopting a 'hermeneutics of unfolding' through the oral experience of scripture may be conveniently applied to the Sikh experience of the Adi Granth. There is ample justification for this approach in Sikh tradition. We shall return to this rich tradition of oral/aural experience of gurbani in the next chapter.

To conclude the discussion, let us now put our inquiry into a theoretical framework in order to make sense of various hermeneutic techniques. For convenience, we shall make use of a schematic diagram shown in Figure 8.1. From the theoretical schema given in Figure 8.1, we notice that in the case of doctrinal interpretation there is a screen of beliefs and other theological presuppositions in front of the eye of the observer. The interpreter is approaching the text with preconceived intentions. In other words, there is a world before the text through which the interpreter is trying to make sense of the text. This mode of interpretation may be seen in almost all the major schools of interpretation within the Sikh tradition, although the theological presuppositions will be different in each individual case.

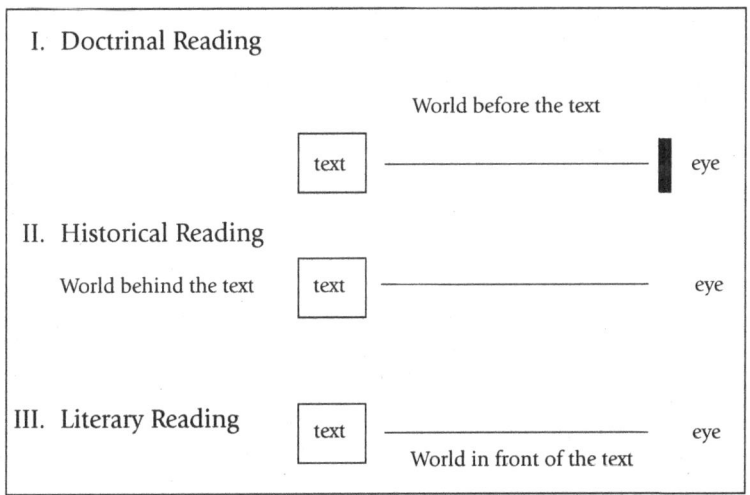

Figure 8.1 Theoretical Schema for Various Hermeneutic Techniques

[58]Coward, *Sacred Word and Sacred Text*, p. 182.

In certain instances, this approach turns into a fundamentalist variety that leaves no room for any other interpretation.

In the case of historical reading, the critical historian is trying to make sense of the world behind the text. That is, one is interested in understanding the cultural, historical, and literary influences that gave rise to individual texts. One is further interested in knowing the author's original intention. The interpreter in this case approaches the text through the new lens of historical reason and research rather than through the perspective of theology and traditional formulations. It should be emphasized here, however, that it is not entirely possible for any historian to be absolutely free from any preconceived intention. At times, one might not be aware of one's own unconscious subjectivity. But the goal of the historian should always be to utilize the rigours of investigation based on the principles of truth and detachment, and to offer no more than tentative claims based on historical probability. Indeed, true scholarship aspires to do no more. The nature of historical knowledge is always limited by the character and extent of evidence, and can be altered by the discovery of new evidence or by the development of new methods in analysing data. In this context, Robert W. Funk et al. make a very significant observation: 'Even the more exact knowledge of the physical sciences must settle for something less than absolute certainty. Human knowledge is finite: there is always something more to be learned from the vast and complex workings of the universe. And this view makes room for faith, which seems to be in short supply for those who think they have the absolute truth.'[59]

Finally, in the case of literary interpretation one approaches the text without preconceived intention in order to explore the many possibilities of its meaning, and confronts the world in front of the text. Each act of hermeneutic encounter with the Adi Granth text is unique since it is the encounter with the eternal Guru as disclosed in it. Thus it is the text that illumines the interpreter like radiance, not the interpreter who illumines the text. In order to appreciate this phenomenon we need to look at Paul Ricoeur's magical looking-glass theory of textual meaning. He asserts that the meaning of a text does not lie behind it, in the region of intention and ostensive reference, but in front of it in the space of interpretation. He says:

[59]Robert W. Funk, Roy W. Hoover, and the Jesus Seminar, trans. and comment., *The Five Gospels: The Search for the Authentic Words of Jesus* (New York: Macmillan Publishing Company, 1993), p. 6.

The moment of understanding corresponds dialectically to being in a situation: it is 'the projection of our ownmost possibilities,' applying it to the theory of the text. For what must be interpreted in a text is a *proposed world* which I could inhabit and wherein I could project one of my own most possibilities. This is what I call the world of the text, the world proper to this unique text.[60]

Thus the understanding of a text begins to show itself only in action and conduct.

CONCLUSION

In this chapter we have argued that the Adi Granth text has an inexhaustible hermeneutic potential. Each generation of scholars has tried to unfold its meaning from its particular angle. If one looks at the sheer number of books and commentaries on Guru Nanak's *Japji* alone one can easily sense the diverse possibilities of various levels of its meaning. Both Sikh and non-Sikh scholars have employed their skills to understand its meaning. In fact, plurality of interpretations has remained part and parcel of Sikh tradition throughout its history. The Adi Granth will have future meanings too, the meanings which have not yet been determined. It is only recently that emphasis is being placed upon a single correct meaning, which is the result of Singh Sabha interpretation, particularly the grammatical approach of Sahib Singh.

The trend in recent scholarship is focused on the literary approach to understand the meaning of a scripture. This is an approach that treats the scripture 'like any other piece of literature', and through it the reader encounters the text without preconceived notions in order to explore the possibilities of its meaning. This approach can show the plausibility of a wider range of meanings and can also demonstrate the implausibility of certain fixed interpretations. But the question still remains: What is the real meaning of gurbani? The answer may be found in the opening citation of this chapter in which Wilfred Cantwell Smith has aptly suggested that the 'true meaning of scripture is the solid historical reality of the continuum of actual meanings over centuries to actual people.' Thus the real meaning of gurbani is not any one meaning but a dynamic process of meanings, in variegated and unending flow.

---

[60]Cited in Bruns, *Hermeneutics Ancient and Modern*, p. 238.

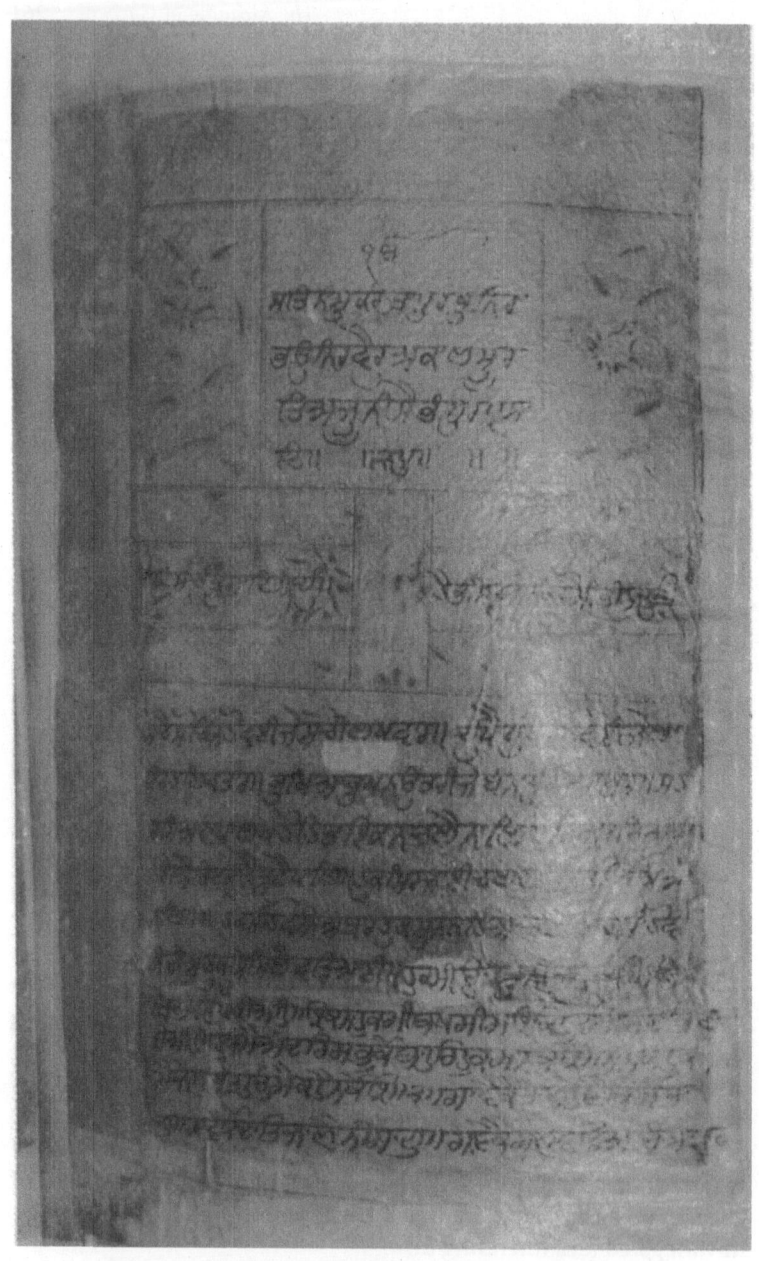

Opening folio of the Kartarpur Manuscript (1604 CE).
Photograph courtesy the author.

SECTION THREE

AUTHORITY

9

THE GURU GRANTH SAHIB:
The Place of Scripture in the Sikh Tradition

The Word enshrined in the Holy Book was always revered by
the Gurus as well as by their disciples as of Divine origin.
The Guru was the revealer of the Word. One day the Word
was to take the place of the Guru. The line of personal Gurus
could not have continued forever. The inevitable came to pass
when Guru Gobind Singh declared the Guru Granth Sahib
to be his successor. It was only through the Word that
Guruship could be made everlasting.[1]

It is now commonly held that the study of a text as scripture
focuses upon its contextual meaning, interpretation, and use.
What matters is the ongoing role the text has played in a tradition,
not only in formal exegesis but in every sector of life.[2] Perceived
from this angle, the reception of the Adi Granth as Guru by the Sikh
community is highly significant. In his *Sacred Word and Sacred Text*,
Harold Coward aptly remarks:

While most religions have scriptures, the place and function of [the] Sikh
scripture seems unique. In no other religion can one find a human Guru
founder, followed by a series of human Gurus living parallel with a collection
of scripture, ending in a breaking of the human succession and the scripture
attaining full authority as Guru.[3]

The Sikh scripture is believed to be the actual embodiment of

---

[1]Harbans Singh, 'Guru Granth Sahib: Guru Eternal for the Sikhs', *Sikh Courier*,
26(61) (Summer 1986): 8.

[2]William A. Graham, *Beyond the Written Word*, p. 6.

[3]Harold Coward, *Sacred Word and Sacred Text*, p. 130.

the eternal Guru and that is why it is known as the 'Guru Granth Sahib'. As the living word of the eternal Guru it participates in divine reality, whereby its meaning assumes central importance in the life of the Sikh Panth. One must try to keep this basic understanding in mind while one explores the place of scripture in the Sikh tradition.

The Guru Granth Sahib has indeed functioned as a supratextual source of authority within the Sikh Panth throughout its history. For instance, the daily Sikh prayer, *Ardas* ('Petition') concludes with an exhortation to acknowledge the Adi Granth as Guru. The concluding passage, the earlier version of which originated in the eighteenth century, expresses with greater clarity the doctrine of the spiritual Guru embodied in the scripture:

From the timeless one there came the bidding, in accordance with which was established the Panth. To all Sikhs there comes this command: acknowledge as Guru the Granth. Acknowledge the Granth as Guru, for it is the manifest body of the Masters. Ye who seeks the union with the Lord, seek him in the word! The Khalsa shall rule, no enemy shall remain. All who endure suffering and privation shall be brought to the safety of the Guru's protection.[4]

Here, it will be interesting to note that the first two couplets appear in an earlier form as separate parts of the Prahilad Singh/Rai *rahit-nama* as follows: Firstly, 'Accept the Khalsa as Guru, for it is the manifest body of the Guru. The Sikh who wishes to find me should seek me in its midst' (*Guru khalsa maniahi paragat Guru ki deh// jo sikh mo milabo chahai khoj inahu mahi leh//*); and secondly, 'The Panth was founded at the command of Akal Purakh. Every Sikh is bidden to accept the Granth as Guru' (*akal purakh ke bachan siun pragat chalayo panth// sabh sikhan ko bachan hai Guru maniahu granth//*).[5] The third couplet (*raj karega khalsa*) occurred in the *Tanakhah-nama* of Bhai Nand Lal. A comparison of these couplets with their modern versions clearly indicates how the doctrine of Guru Granth came to the fore in the first decades of the nineteenth century after replacing the original emphasis on the doctrine of Guru Panth in the eighteenth century. This may have happened when Maharaja Ranjit Singh abolished the institution of gurmata after 1809.[6] We shall return to this issue in the final section.

---

[4]The translation is slightly adapted from W.H. McLeod, *The Evolution of the Sikh Community*, p. 66.

[5]W.H. McLeod, *The Sikhs: History, Religion, and Society*, p. 75.

[6]For details of the gurmata of 1805, see John Malcom, *Sketch of the Sikhs* (London, 1812), pp. 120–3.

Our primary concern here is to understand the ongoing role that the Guru Granth Sahib has played in the cumulative tradition of the Sikh community. In fact, the Sikhs had already become a 'textual community,' to use Brian Stock's terminology, when Guru Arjan compiled the first canonical text in 1604.[7] Since then they have sought to shape and articulate the central norms of their tradition through codifying symbol systems and practices in the form of scriptural canon. In other words, as a textual community the Sikhs have always organized their religious and social practices in accordance with the teachings of the Adi Granth. They have experienced the eternal Guru in their life through the words of the scripture: 'The word of the Guru is an intimate companion of my soul.'[8] It is immaterial to argue whether Guru Gobind Singh made the decision unilaterally to declare the Adi Granth as Guru before his death (as the Sikh tradition asserts) or the community made this decision in response to the needs of the historical situation after the death of the tenth Guru (as critical historians assert).[9] The most significant point is that during the period of the ten Gurus the Sikhs felt that the authority lay with their leader, but once the new decision to accept the authority of the scriptural Guru was made, the community faithfully accepted it. Here, we shall examine in more detail the cohesive role of the Guru Granth Sahib in the ever-evolving Sikh tradition.

ORAL EXPERIENCE OF THE SIKH SCRIPTURE

The oral experience of scripture has received much attention in recent scholarship. Both scholars and common people are now involved in a process in which they make an attempt to recapture the spirit of 'personalism' that has been lost in the transition away from oral/aural language. Here the word personalism is employed in the sense in which Wilfred Cantwell Smith has used it: 'To memorize, to recite, even to hear, have always been more deeply personal ways of relating to the meaning of words than to look at them on the page.'[10] In order to understand this oral dimension more thoroughly we need to look at the actual practice within the Sikh tradition.

[7]For a theoretical discussion of the notion of 'textual community,' see Brian Stock, *The Implications of Literacy* (Princeton: Princeton University Press, 1983), pp. 88–240.

[8]M5, *Dhanasari* 32, AG, p. 679.

[9]For two recent perspectives on this issue, see Harbans Singh, *Berkeley Lectures on Sikhism* (New Delhi: Guru Nanak Foundation, 1983), pp. 24–32 and W.H. McLeod, *Who is a Sikh?*, pp. 52–5.

[10]Wilfred Cantwell Smith, *What Is Scripture?*, p. 166.

Oral Recitation of the Bani

Oral recitation of the bani has always played a significant role in Sikh life since the days of Guru Nanak. It began during the Kartarpur period in individual and corporate settings as a part of daily discipline. Since then the memorization of the bani has remained a devotional activity among the Sikhs. In this context, William Graham aptly observes: 'Memorization is a particularly intimate appropriation of a text, and the capacity to quote or recite a text from memory is a spiritual resource that is tapped automatically in every act of reflection, worship, prayer, or moral deliberation, as well as in times of personal and communal decision or crisis.'[11] In fact, the memorization of gurbani by heart (*kanth*) has always been compared in the Sikh lore with the possession of money that is readily available for use (*gurbani kanth paisa ganth*).

Guru Ram Das, for instance, prescribes the daily routine of early morning devotion for a 'Sikh of the true Guru', who must meditate on the divine name after rising and bathing, and recite Guru Nanak's *Japji* from memory.[12] It is interestingg to note that the name of the fourth Guru is particularly associated with the daily routine of oral recitation of liturgical prayers as part of Khalsa rahit or code of conduct. For instance, an eighteenth-century text, the *Chaupa Singh Rahit-nama* explicitly states: 'According to Guru Ram Das, he who recites *Japji* five times will acquire the radiance of [true] enlightenment. Thereafter let him recite whatever bani he may know by heart.'[13] Even in modern times Sikh parents make an effort that their children learn Guru Nanak's *Japji* and other prayers by heart in childhood.

A key principle here is the Sikh belief that the recitation of daily prayers by heart has the power to transform and unify one's consciousness. As Coward puts it: 'For the Sikh, as for the Hindu, participation in the divine word has the power to transform and unify one's consciousness. The purifying power of the sacred scripture is understood as a combing of negative thoughts from one's heart and mind that occurs as a regular part of one's daily discipline.'[14] Through this personalized experience one is able to understand the subtler levels of meaning of various passages of gurbani. It is quite

---

[11]Graham, *Beyond the Written Word*, p. 160.

[12]M4, *Var Gauri* 2 (11), AG, pp. 305–6. Also see *Varan Bhai Gurdas* 1: 38.

[13]W.H. McLeod, *The Chaupa Singh Rahit-nama*, p. 149. Also see p. 187 for the rahit injunction against an offender: 'Any Sikh who does not know *Japji* by heart'.

[14]Coward, *Sacred Word and Sacred Text*, p. 133.

possible that one may have a different understanding of a particular passage at different times in one's life, since its spiritual sense is not so constant as it is often perceived. This normally happens in the life of those individuals who are always exploring infinite possibilities of meaning contained in the divine word.

Devotional Singing (Kirtan)

In the Adi Granth itself the names of the raga and rhythm to be used in singing are stated at the beginning of each section of hymns. The hymns are also classified according to the gharu, or 'musical clef', in which each hymn is to be sung. According to the Indian method of singing, the accent falls, and the voice rises and falls, in different positions, according to the gharu in which hymns are sung.[15] There are seventeen different positions of gharu employed in the Adi Granth. These musical instructions in the written text fulfil the same function as that of a musical score in relation to performed music. Like written music, the written text of the Adi Granth has spiritual power only as it is sung.[16] Guru Arjan, for instance, stresses the spiritual power of kirtan as follows: 'The false thinking of both performers and hearers is destroyed when they participate in devotional singing.'[17]

Thus the singing of hymns in congregational worship is the heart of Sikh devotional experience. Through such kirtan the devout Sikhs attune themselves to the divine word and thereby immerse themselves in the deeper levels of its meaning. It is based upon the assumption that the melody in the singing of gurbani evokes the divine word of which it is an earthly resonance. According to this assumption: 'A direct correspondence is seen as existing between the physical vibration of the phenomenal chant and the noumenal vibration of the transcendent. The more the physical vibrations of the uttered chant are repeated, the more transcendent power is evoked in experience until one's consciousness is purified and put into a harmonious relationship or even identity with the Divine.'[18] For instance, Guru Nanak's *So Dar* presents his personal experience of heavenly joys in the company of all liberated ones, who sing eternally at the door of Akal Purakh's ineffable court, the praises of his glory.[19]

[15]See Frederic Pincott, 'The Arrangement of the Hymnss of the Adi Granth', *JARS* (1885), p. 443.

[16]Coward, *Sacred Word and Sacred Text*, p. 134.

[17]M5, *Kanara* 1, AG, p. 1300.

[18]Coward, *Sacred Word and Sacred Text*, p. 175.

[19]M1, *So Dar*, AG, pp. 6, 8–9 and 347–8.

In a gurdwara, Sikh worship consists mainly of the singing of scriptural hymns set to music with the accompaniment of instruments. It is normally led by a group of four singers (ragis), who are often joined by the sangat in the singing.[20] The appropriation of the meaning of the divine word, however, depends to a large extent upon the capacity, preparation and interest of the audience.

Oral Exegesis of the Adi Granth

The exegesis of the bani had its beginning in the oral context during the period of the Sikh Gurus. For instance, Guru Arjan proclaims: 'The true aim of my life lies in absorption in religious discourse, kirtan and vibration of the divine word through singing and music'.[21] Here the use of the word *katha* (homily) by Guru Arjan is very significant. The devotional singing of gurbani was normally followed by the Guru's spontaneous oral interpretation of the meaning of a particular scriptural passage. It could also take the form of a formal response to the questions raised by the sangat concerning that passage. Thus a living dialogue was established between the Guru and the Sikh in the oral context, in which the Guru would provide the necessary instruction suitable to the existential situation of the disciple.

At the beginning of the *Dhanasari* raga, for instance, Guru Nanak proclaims: 'My Lord is new every morning'.[22] Similarly, as a living force in the lives of the Sikhs, the Guru Granth Sahib has functioned as an ever-fresh fountain of timeless truth. Writing about the timeless message of the Adi Granth, W. Owen Cole observes: 'It [the Adi Granth] emphasizes a universal message. It is a scripture which enables the Sikh to live in the sixteenth or twentieth century, in India or in Britain, with equal ease or difficulty'.[23] Nevertheless, the process of interpretation certainly provides an opportunity for it to remain dynamic, relevant and immediate to the changing times without being a dead letter.

It should be emphasized that oral interpretation of scripture has always been a part of Sikh worship. In the congregational setting, it begins in the performance of katha, which consists of an exposition of the Sikh scriptures. Its actual format may be explained as follows:

[20]On the paramount importance of Sikh kirtan, see G.S. Mansukhani, *Indian Classical Music and Kirtan* (New Delhi: Oxford and IBH, 1979), esp. Chapter 10.

[21]M5, Bilaval 6, AG, p. 818.

[22]M1, Dhanasari 1, AG, p. 660.

[23]W. Owen Cole, *Sikhism and its Indian Context 1469–1708* (London: Darrton, Longman & Todd, 1984), p. 280.

Katha is generally delivered in the presence of the Guru Granth Sahib. The *kathakar*, the performer, will in fact recite reverentially the hymn he proposes to expound from the Holy Book itself. The choice may have been premeditated or utterly impromptu. To describe the format, which certainly allows for variation, after a well-punctuated, clean, melodious and rhythmic recitation of the hymn, its central theme is brought into focus and explained. Then, the difficult words are explicated and verse-wise paraphrase of the entire *sabad* is given. Care is taken to sustain the context and point out the relevance of each verse to maintain the argument. This is followed by a thematic analysis of the hymn, bringing out its spiritual and doctrinal significance. Notice may also be taken of its literary graces. To support his interpretation, the *kathakar* quotes, all from memory, passages from the religious texts, and anecdotes from the lives of the Gurus. Before concluding the discourse, the argument is summed up and the original text recited again.[24]

There is always the possibility of several interpretations in this process of religious discourse, since each individual giani (traditional Sikh scholar) may be offering his/her own interpretation specific to the situation of a particular audience. This may be testified by listening, for instance, to the katha-performances of Giani Sant Singh Maskeen and Ragi Darshan Singh.

To conclude the discussion on the oral experience of the Sikh scripture we must take note of recent developments in science and technology. Modern-day innovations have led to an influx of electronic media that is intended to replace old-world traditions. Multimedia is, in fact, in the forefront of technology and within the reach of an average household. It has already gone so far as CD-ROM versions of the Guru Granth Sahib. Internet sources also contain transcriptions of the scriptural passages with translations and meanings. In the modern print culture and computer-assisted programs, therefore, there is a need to recapture the sense of the central importance of the oral dimension of Sikh scripture.

THE WORD AS GURU

The most significant point in the Sikh experience of accepting the Adi Granth as living Guru may be seen in the practice of *vak laina* (taking the Guru's word) or *hukam laina* (taking a commandment). The procedure functions in a liturgical fashion of opening the scripture at random. During the process the first hymn at the top of

---

[24]Harbans Singh, ed., *The Encyclopaedia of Sikhism*, Vol. II, pp. 459–60.

the left-hand page (or when a hymn begins on the preceding page, as is usually the case, one turns back to its actual beginning) is read aloud as the proclamation of Guru's vak for that particular moment or situation in life. It is then appropriated by the audience through 'hearing'. In the case of individual early morning prayers, the whole family gathers in the presence of the Guru Granth Sahib to receive the divine command which serves as an order of the day. This vak becomes the inspiration for personal meditation throughout the day. Again during evening prayers, one takes the vak to conclude the day with its particular joys and sorrows.[25] Similarly in the congregational setting, the whole sangat receives the vak as a divine command (hukam) at the conclusion of different ceremonies.

The origin of this liturgical tradition may be traced in Guru Nanak's own bani: 'The Guru's word (vak) is pure and it shines eternally as the light [of divine wisdom]. Its contemplation is truly the daily bath at the everlasting holy place.'[26] Presumably the first Sikhs would normally have looked to Guru Nanak for advice, which they would have received in the form of a vak or commandment. Rather than depend upon the efficacy of external observances they were encouraged to meditate on the divinely inspired vak. During the period of Guru Ram Das, his vicars (masands)[27] were probably keen to have a written vak from him for the sake of establishing their credentials in the new sangats: 'Only a trader in the divine treasure deals with the wealth of divine treasure. A raw dealer cannot take the vak of divine wealth.'[28] There is another instance of clear evidence from the life of Guru Har Rai, who proclaimed his first vak in the written form when he assumed the office of guruship at Kiratpur.[29]

During the eighteenth-century struggles, the Sikh Panth continued to seek guidance from the Guru Granth Sahib through the process of 'taking the Guru's word' (vak). The *Chaupa Singh Rahit-nama*, for instance, specifically mentions that 'authority lies with the [Guru] Granth Sahib' (*agaia giranth sahib ji di*).[30] Teja Singh and Ganda Singh record a historical event as follows:

---

[25]For an analysis of the vak in Sikh life, see W. Owen Cole and Piara Singh Sambhi, *The Sikhs: Their Religious Beliefs and Practices* (London: Routledge and Kegan Paul, 1978), pp. 54–5.

[26]M1, *Dhanasari Chhant* 1, AG, p. 687.

[27]See W.H. McLeod, *Who is a Sikh?*, p. 12.

[28]M4, *Suhi* 3, AG, p. 734.

[29]See Chapter 2, p. 71.

[30]See McLeod, *The Chaupa Singh Rahit-nama*, pp. 77–8, 165.

While the Sarbat Khalsa were gathered at the Akal Takhat on the occasion of Baisakhi on April 10, 1763, some Brahmins of Kasur came and complained against the Afghan inhabitants of their city, especially against Usman Khan who had carried away the wife of one of them and converted her to Islam.'[31]

It will be interesting to note how the Sarbat Khalsa (entire khalsa) arrived at the decision to attack Kasur. Rattan Singh Bhangu narrates the incident as follows:

Then the 'Entire Khalsa' went to the court [of the Guru Granth Sahib], and they prayed single-mindedly with folded hands: 'Give us the *vak* ('command') what to do. You are the True Guru and we are your Sikhs. Give us the command to attack Kasur, a task to be performed by the Sikhs.' The whole sangat stood with folded-hands. After bowing, some of them sat on the ground. 'You are the Guru Granth, a living embodiment [of the True Guru]. Give the true *vak* to the Sikh sangat.' Then they looked at the Granth after lifting (or opening) the folios [at random]. The appropriate hymn came from *Var Basant*.

Pauri ('Stanza'):
'The five great enemies were bound by seeking the True divine prop. By inspiring devotion to His feet the Lord stood by [his devotees] in [resolving the matter]. All maladies and sufferings are gone, and one becomes ever-fresh and strong. One who meditates on the divine Name day and night never dies again.' Dohara ('Couplet'):
[The Singhs] became happy after listening to the words of the Granth, and they conquered Kasur at once. They beat the battle-drums and raised the shouts of Guru's victory. [32]

The words in the expression *panje baddhe mahabali* (the five great enemies were bound) from *Var Basant* provided sufficient divine hint for the Singhs to attack Kasur and rescue the wife of the Brahmin from the captivity of Usman Khan. Rattan Singh Bhangu was closer to the eighteenth-century events, and he has provided us with minute details of the process of taking a vak from the Guru Granth Sahib before any major undertaking.

Further, there is evidence that even during the Anglo–Sikh wars, the Sikh soldiers would take the scripture along and would set up a separate tent for their devotional experience of taking the Guru's command before going to fight. For instance, the following note by Henry Erskine is noteworthy:

[31]Teja Singh and Ganda Singh, *A Short History of the Sikhs*, p. 163.
[32]Rattan Singh Bhangu, *Sri Gur Panth Prakash*, ed. Jeet Singh Sital (Amritsar: Shiromani Gurdwara Prabandhak Committee, 1984), p. 479.

After the Infantry charging the enemy at Goojerat the Cavalry and Light Artillery pursued the fugitive Sikhs and Afghans. The Infantry then advanced steadily in line until clear of the blazing Camp, when they filed arms. It was there I found this Book in a tent of one of the hostile Chiefs—probably Shere Singh's. This is called the *Grunth* or Code of Sikh Religion. It is highly prized by the Sikhs, and I have many solicitations for it from the Sikh gentlemen.[33]

More evidence of this nature may be seen from another manuscript of the Sikh scripture, preserved at John Rylands University of Manchester Library. The introductory note in this manuscript reads: 'The fine manuscript of its kind was wrested out of the hands of a Sikh Priest at the battle of Guzerat by an officer of the 52nd Bengal Native Infantry, who was offered a very large sum in India for it, but he preferred bringing it home as a trophy.'[34] Evidently, each unit of Khalsa army would carry a copy of the Guru Granth Sahib for receiving the vak at the time of undertaking a military expedition.

The most striking instance in Sikh history concerning the effectiveness of the vak in the affairs of the Panth, however, is related to an event that took place in 1920. Large groups of Punjabi outcasts were becoming members of the Khalsa in the hope of improving their social status. These outcast converts proceeded to the Golden Temple in the expectation that they would be permitted to offer and receive *karah prasad* there. The administrators of the Golden Temple had already made it quite explicit that they would be refused. The Singh Sabha reformers pressed the issue on the basis of the teachings of the Gurus that any Sikh could share in offering prasad to the congregation. Eventually it was agreed that advice should be taken from the Guru Granth Sahib through the process of vak. The revealed passage of Guru Amar Das put the issue beyond all doubt:

Upon the worthless he bestows his grace, brother, if they will serve the true Guru. Exalted is the service of the true Guru, brother, to hold in remembrance the divine name. (1) The lord himself offers grace and mystic union. Worthless sinners are we, brother, yet the true Guru has drawn us to that blissful union. (1) rahau ... [35]

(M3, *Sorathi Dutuki* 2, AG, pp. 638–9)

---

[33]See Henry Erskine's manuscript note of April 1849 at British Library, MSS.OR.1125.

[34]John Rylands University of Manchester Library, Panj. MS # 5.

[35]The translation is adapted from McLeod, *The Evolution of the Sikh Community*, p. 68.

With the hearing of these words it was clear to all that the Guru had accepted the new converts and their prasad was distributed by the triumphant reformers among all the Sikhs present on the occasion. This event typifies the Sikh experience of the Adi Granth as a living Guru who always speaks with power and truth on the situation at hand. From the purely human perspective the appropriateness of the passage is a mere coincidence, or at best an example of a public oracle. From the Sikh perspective, however, the random choosing of the passage functions to remove the sinful haumai (self-centredness) so as to allow the true Guru to choose.[36]

THE ROLE OF THE SCRIPTURE IN SIKH CEREMONIES

The central feature of every Sikh ritual and ceremony is always the Guru Granth Sahib, installed ceremoniously every morning in the gurdwara. When a child is to be named, the family takes the baby to the gurdwara, and offers karah prasad. After offering thanks and prayers through Ardas (petition), the Guru Granth Sahib is opened at random, and a name is chosen beginning with the same letter as the first composition on the left-hand page. Thus, the process of vak laina functions to provide the first letter of the chosen name. The underlying principle is that the child derives his/her identity from the Guru's word and starts his/her life as a Sikh. To a boy's name, the common surname 'Singh' (lion) is added and to a girl's name 'Kaur' (princess) at the end of the chosen name. However, in certain cases, particularly in North America, Singh and Kaur become middle names when people employ their caste names (such as Dhaliwal, Grewal, Sethi, Sawhney, Kalsi and so on) at the end of their names.

A Sikh wedding, according to the Anand (bliss) rite, also takes place in the presence of the Guru Granth Sahib and the performance of the actual marriage requires the couple to circumambulate the sacred scripture four times. Commenting on the significance of the Anand ceremony, for instance, W.H. McLeod remarks:

The bridegroom is addressed first by the officiant and enjoined to be 'the protector of [the bride's] person and her honour.' Then comes the address to the bride, wherein she is counselled to accept her future husband as 'a master of all love and respect.' The hem of one of groom's garments is then placed in the bride's hand and *she* follows *him* round the sacred scripture four times. The ceremony is a beautiful one and it indicates symbolically

[36]Coward, *Sacred Word and Sacred Text*, p. 133.

what the nature of the union is intended to be. It very definitely is what modern Panth regards as ideal.[37]

Here, McLeod is actually addressing gender issues in the Sikh Panth and arguing that Sikh society, like any other religious community, is still dominated by the centuries-old patriarchal system. In order to make the point he puts emphasis on the symbolic significance of the Anand marriage ceremony and that '*she* follows *him* round the sacred scripture four times.' Anyone who follows the linear mode of thinking will understand the Sikh wedding-ceremony essentially in this way.

However, we need to understand the ritual of circumambulation of the couple in the actual Anand marriage ceremony in its proper perspective. Figure 9.1 presents symbolically the clockwise movement of the bridegroom (G) and the bride (B) round the Guru Granth Sahib (GGS). Figure 9.1 indicates that in the original position (shown at the bottom in the figure) the couple sit before the Guru Granth Sahib, both being at equal distance from the centre. Before they make each round they listen to a verse of Guru Ram Das's *Suhi Chhant 2*

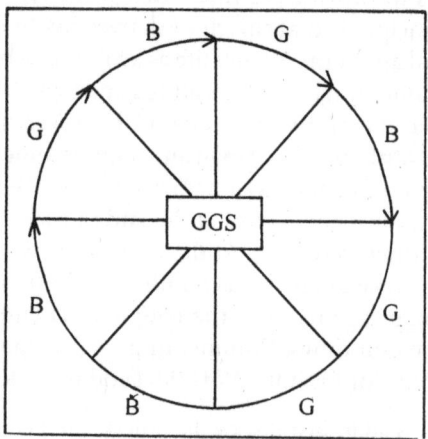

Figure 9.1 Movement of the Bridegroom (G) and the Bride (B) Around the Guru Granth Sahib (GGS)

[37]W.H. McLeod, 'Gender and the Sikh Panth,' in Pashaura Singh and N. Gerald Barrier, eds, *The Transmission of Sikh Heritage in the Diaspora* (New Delhi: Manohar Publishers, 1996), pp. 39–40.

being read by a scriptural reader.[38] Then they bow before the Guru
Granth Sahib and get up to make the round while the same verse is
sung by the ragis and the congregation. During the process of their
clockwise movement round the Guru Granth Sahib four times, they
are always at equal distance from the centre, that is, they stay within
the same orbit. In the actual movement of lavan (circumambulations),
if the bride (B) follows the groom (G), then the groom follows the
bride, although there is a long way between them. The symbolic
significance of the Sikh wedding ceremony, therefore, makes sense
only if we apply the model of the cyclical movement of various plan-
ets in our interpretation. Moreover, the pattern of circumambulation in the Anand marriage ceremony is in fact the reactualization
of the primordial movement of life in which there is no beginning
and no end.

The initiation ceremony (amrit sanskar) must take place in the
presence of the Guru Granth Sahib. In order to understand the full
significance of the amrit ceremony let us examine it from a theoretical
perspective which explains the place of the initiation rite in human
cultures. In this context, Mircea Eliade explains that the central moment
of every initiation is represented by the ceremony symbolizing the
death of the novice and his/her return to the fellowship of the living
through a new birth. He says:

This birth requires rites instituted by Supernatural Beings: hence it is a divine
work, created by the power and will of those Beings; it belongs, not to nature
but to sacred history. ... To attain the initiate's mode of being demands
knowing realities that are not a part of nature but of the biography of the
Supernatural Beings, hence of the sacred history preserved in the myths.[39]

In the majority of initiation rites, Eliade argues, the rhythm is similar:
an initial movement into death through which the previous existence
is discarded and a culmination of the ritual in a reformation as well
as a new creation in the image of the divine being. He further maintains
that whenever the rite of initiation is performed it is the reactualization
of the primordial event.[40] In fact, whenever the amrit ceremony takes
place it is always conducted by five Khalsa Sikhs representing the
original 'Five Beloved Ones' (*panj piare*) in the presence of the Guru
Granth Sahib. Also, the pattern of death and rebirth during the amrit

[38]M4, *Suhi Chhant* 2, AG, pp. 773–4.
[39]Mircea Eliade, *Birth and Rebirth: The Religious Meaning of Initiation in Human
Culture* (New York: Harper, 1958), p. xiv.
[40]ibid., pp. xii–xiii.

ceremony is singularly evident in the popular understanding of the Sikh community.

Hymns from the Guru Granth Sahib are also sung at funerals. This is followed by a reading of the entire scripture. The celebration of the anniversaries associated with the births and deaths of the Sikh Gurus (*gurpurb*) is marked by an 'unbroken reading' (*akhand path*) of the scripture by a relay of readers in approximately forty-eight hours on week-ends. Further, the Guru Granth Sahib always presides over the audience in the congregational worship. It is installed on the throne (*manji* or lectern) under a canopy, and an attendant always waves a *chauri* (a fan made from yak hair or peacock feathers) over it to accord royal honour and dignity to the sacred volume. The devotees bow before the Guru Granth Sahib and make offerings. If one really wants to understand the reverence bestowed upon the scripture in the Sikh tradition, one should visit the Golden Temple at Amritsar early in the morning around 3 a.m. This is the time when thousands of devotees participate in the procession in which the sacred volume is carried in a golden palanquin. The procession starts from the Akal Takhat and ends at the Golden Temple where the daily installation (*parkash karna*) of the Guru Granth Sahib takes place every morning. The volume is ceremonially closed in the late evening, wrapped in *rumalas* ('clothes,' normally ornate) and then transported back in procession to the resting-place (*sukh asan*) at the Akal Takhat.[41] A similar kind of activity takes place at every gurdwara around the world. The sacred volume is always carried respectfully on the head by a Sikh into the gurdwara from the resting-place and installed ceremonially early each morning. All present at that time sing devotional hymns. Thus one can witness the reverent liturgical zeal with which the physical copy of the Adi Granth is treated as Guru.

THE ULTIMATE AUTHORITY

We now turn to the final question of the ultimate authority within the Sikh Panth. The statement by Professor Harbans Singh quoted at the beginning of this chapter continues as follows: 'It was only through the Word that the Guruship could be made everlasting.' This

[41]For details, see McLeod, *Evolution of the Sikh Community*, pp. 63–4 and Patwant Singh, *The Golden Temple* (New Delhi: Times Books International, 1988), pp. 145–64.

statement is straightforward but can have significant implications regardless of whether or not the author intended so. Here, the doctrine of Guru Panth has not been regarded as a factor that makes the guruship everlasting. It comes as no surprise since it reflects the Singh Sabha mode of interpretation. In this context, W. Owen Cole has aptly shown that 'with the success of Maharaja Ranjit Singh, representative of the Sarbat Khalsa, paradoxically the concept of corporate guruship passed into obscurity.'[42] He further argues that 'when, in the nineteenth century, a revival of the Khalsa ideal took place, the notion of corporate guruship was not revived.'[43] In order to understand the dynamic process by which the doctrine of Guru Granth was broadly accepted within the Panth, we need to briefly examine two significant developments.

First, during the eighteenth century the twin doctrines of Guru Granth and Guru Panth successfully provided cohesiveness within the Sikh tradition. The gurmata (Guru's intention) system provided an effective means of passing resolutions in the presence of the Guru Granth Sahib. However, in order to consolidate his power Maharaja Ranjit Singh abolished political gurmatas in 1809 and downplayed the doctrine of Guru Panth in order to reconcile the growing social inequalities in the Panth. J.S Grewal has aptly remarked that 'every Sikh was equal in the presence of the Granth Sahib, in the *sangat* and the *langar*, but in the life outside social differences were legitimized.'[44] Thus the process was set in motion by which the doctrine of Guru Granth came to the fore in place of the doctrine of Guru Panth. It gained further momentum during the Singh Sabha period.

Second, the Dasam Granth enjoyed an equal status with the Adi Granth in the eighteenth and the nineteenth centuries. In fact, both the Granths were installed side by side on the same platform. Kesar Singh Chhibber, the author of the *Bansavalinama* (1769), maintained that the two Granths were like 'real brothers' and that the Adi Granth, being the older, was entitled to greater respect and veneration.[45] However, with the rise of the Tat Khalsa, the dominant wing of the Singh Sabha movement, the Dasam Granth was relegated to a lower

[42]W. Owen Cole, *The Guru in Sikhism* (London: Darton, Longman & Todd, 1982), p. 84.

[43]ibid.

[44]J.S. Grewal, *The New Cambridge History of India*, p. 118.

[45]Cited in J.S. Grewal, 'Legacies of the Sikh Past for the Twentieth Century,' in Joseph T. O'Connell et al., eds, *Sikh History and Religion*, p. 20.

status. In this context, Harjot Oberoi makes an important observation that 'the Dasam Granth, which enshrined the "great code" of Sanatan tradition, was gradually eased out of Sikh rituals, and by the early twentieth century it no longer enjoyed the textual hegemony it once enjoyed.'[46] Here, we must apply the definition of canon as a collection of texts, the authority of which is related to the authority of other texts from the same religion as absolute to relative. Thus the Guru Granth Sahib came to be universally accepted as the sole and absolute source of authority within the Sikh Panth as a result of the Tat Khalsa reforms in the late nineteenth and early twentieth centuries.

In order to address the issue of the ultimate authority in Sikhism, McLeod poses the question: Where do Sikhs find the ultimate authority for the religious belief they uphold? He then offers the following answer:

Sikhs normally find it by turning to the Guru Granth Sahib and accepting it alone as supreme and absolute authority. Through the scripture the Guru speaks. Those who are not Sikhs may question its sufficiency, but they are bound to acknowledge that Sikhs have a better record of harmony and accord than other religious systems can claim. Sectarian divisions and continuing controversies must be acknowledged, yet what other religion is without these? By maintaining their trust in the Guru which is the Granth, the Sikh people uphold a belief that stands them in abundantly good stead.[47]

McLeod provides an objective assessment of the role of the Guru Granth Sahib as the source of ultimate authority within the Sikh Panth. He is fully aware of factional divisions and continuing controversies on certain fundamental issues that arise within the Panth from time to time. Nevertheless, the Sikh people, he argues, have resolved those issues by turning to the Guru Granth Sahib and accepting it alone as the supreme and absolute authority.

CONCLUSION

This analysis has revealed how the Guru Granth Sahib has functioned as a supratextual source of authority in the Sikh tradition. Indeed, as a sacred symbol it has played the central role in the life of the Sikh community. The more significant the symbol, as Northrop Frye argues, the more quickly it is transformed into the next stage of symbolism, the stage of epiphany or manifestation of a divine

---

[46]Harjot Oberoi, *The Construction of Religious Boundaries*, p. 319.
[47]McLeod, *Sikhism*, p. 266.

presence, a real presence appearing as a symbol itself.[48] The truth of this statement may be seen in the veneration of the text of the Adi Granth as Guru. As the manifest body of the Guru, the Adi Granth is indeed heir to the line of ten personal Gurus, possessing the same status and authority as they did and commanding the same reverence accorded to each successive Guru.

There is a rich tradition of oral/aural experience of Sikh scripture. Each individual Sikh tries to understand the meaning of life in the light of his/her daily experience of immersing himself/herself in gurbani. This happens through oral recitation and devotional singing. Further, the process of vak laina confirms the function of the scripture as Guru. For instance, each day early in the morning thousands of devotees gather at the Golden Temple in Amritsar to listen to the Guru's vak and each one of them derives from the same hymn a message suitable to his level and degree of understanding. In fact, the daily vak proclaimed at the Golden Temple may now be viewed from anywhere in the world with the use of Internet and the World Wide Web through electronic media.

In sum, the place and function of the Adi Granth as Guru has inspired Sikhs throughout their history in personal piety, liturgy, ceremonies and communal solidarity. It has given them a sacred focus upon which to reflect and in the process discover the meaning of life as Sikhs. It has provided a framework for the shaping of the Panth and has been a decisive factor in shaping a distinctive Sikh identity. Thus the ultimate authority within the Sikh tradition, for a wide range of personal and public conduct, lies in the Guru Granth Sahib.

[48]Northrop Frye, *Words with Power: Being a Second Study of 'The Bible and Literature'* (San Diego, New York, London: Harcourt Brace Jovanovich, Publishers, 1990), pp. 109–10.

10

CONCLUSION

T he process of the formation of the Sikh canon began with the use of Guru Nanak's hymns in Sikh liturgy at Kartarpur during the last decades of his life. These hymns were committed to memory by his first disciples, who passed them on to the next generation through oral transmission of a singing tradition. It is entirely possible that Guru Nanak himself wrote these down. Although the manuscript of Guru Nanak's pothi is not available, it must have been originally an *aide-mémoire*, a mnemonic device, to facilitate the memorization of his inspired utterances by singers and the newly emerging Sikh community. In fact, the initial impetus for the preparation of this original pothi must have been to preserve the bani as a legacy for future generations. In its basic sense, the bani has always remained functional as an oral text. Nevertheless, the writing of gurbani was also regarded as a devotional activity in the early Sikh community. Thus oral and written transmission of the bani has simultaneously taken place within the Sikh tradition since perhaps, the last years of Guru Nanak's life at Kartarpur. Guru Angad, it seems, popularized the Gurmukhi script which had already been developed from the lande and takari characters by Guru Nanak himself. He also composed sixty-two shaloks, some of which are found independently recorded in the Guru Har Sahai pothi.

A four-volume written collection appeared in the form of the Goindval pothis during the period of the third Guru. These volumes may have been cast on the model of the four Vedas of the Hindu tradition. The two extant copies of the Goindval pothis at Jalandhar and Pinjore provide us with the earliest writings of the first three Gurus and the bhagats. Their structure reveals that the key organizing principle was based on ragas, keeping in mind the needs of the singers. The Gurmukhi script of these two volumes represents the earlier stage of orthography when vowel-signs were not yet fully developed. The Goindval pothis indeed provided a substantial nucleus for the compilation of the Adi Granth by Guru Arjan. Bula and Pandha, the renowed scribe and singer of Guru Amar Das's period prepared anthologies of devotional literature called *gutakas* (breviaries) and pothis for various Sikh congregations (sangats).

Guru Ram Das provided a new musical dimension to the Sikh scriptural tradition by adding eleven new ragas to the existing system of nineteen ragas employed by Guru Nanak for his compositions. There is clear internal evidence that he had the works of the earlier Gurus in his possession. For instance, Guru Nanak's *Pahare* in the *Siri* raga provided the model for Guru Ram Das's composition in the same genre and the same metre.[1] Further, Guru Ram Das composed a lengthy composition in *rayasa* (romantic tale) genre in the *Tilang* mode on the model of Guru Nanak's rayasa in the same mode.[2] Furthermore, Guru Nanak's *Japji* was copied from the manuscript written in Guru Ram Das's own hand at the time of the compilation of the first canonical text of the Adi Granth. Although no manuscript of his works has survived, Guru Ram Das frequently encouraged the professional class of scribes to write gurbani for the purpose of distribution among the various Sikh sangats. Certain pre-canonical texts (such as the Bahoval pothi) throw a flood of light on independent scribal activity. These independent collections reflect the fluid state from which the various structures of organizations and the final form of various hymns emerged in the 'first' canonical text of the Adi Granth.

The compilation of the Adi Granth evidently owes much to the enormous energies of Guru Arjan. He prepared an authoritative scripture in 1604, primarily in response to the process of consolidation of the Sikh tradition that was taking place during his period. Secondly, he updated the existing collection by substantially increasing it. Thirdly, the cultural environment of Mughal India, which stressed upon the presence of a revealed scripture as part of the definition of a religious community, provided the historical context for the compilation of the Adi Granth. It is no wonder that the creation of a unified scripture for the Sikh community was suggested by the surrounding Islamic tradition. Fourthly, Guru Arjan created an authoritative text for the Sikh community whereby it could understand and assert its unique identity. By doing so he affixed a seal on the sacred word to preserve it for posterity, and also frustrate any attempts by

---

[1]See M1, *Siri Ragu Pahare* 1–2, AG, pp. 74–6 and M4, *Siri Ragu 3*, AG, pp. 76–7.
[2]See M1, *Tilang 1*, AG, pp. 724–5 and M4, *Tilang 2*, AG, pp. 725–6.

schismatic groups to circulate spurious hymns for sectarian ends. Finally, Guru Arjan appointed his faithful disciple and poet Bhai Gurdas as the main scribe, although there were other scribes like Jagana Brahman who provided additional help in the making of the Sikh scripture. The whole project was completed at a peaceful location beside a pool named Ramsar in Amritsar.

The Gurmukhi script was standardized with the introduction of proper vowel-signs during Guru Arjan's period. As the writing system developed so did the use of proper grammatical constructions. It is in this context that the GNDU MS 1245 provides us with a rare insight into the textual process through which the evolution of the Sikh scripture took place. Guru Arjan organized the works of the Gurus, the bhagats and other poet-bards into a coherent pattern reflecting both theological and musicological perspectives. In particular, he employed classical and folk traditions side by side in various ragas so that both styles of singing were balanced in the musical performance. He applied meticulous standards to give the scripture its unique form, with regard to its content and style. In the process he frequently revised the received texts to achieve linguistic modifications, especially through the substitution of synonyms for certain words. He took extraordinary care to maintain the original meaning and rhythm of those hymns which he revised for the final text. No theological change was introduced in the editorial process. Guru Arjan used the best possible words to crystallize the divine message. As fifth 'Nanak', he had the authority to do so. Thus any decision taken by him with respect to the *rédaction* process was regarded as final.

Guru Arjan carefully directed the whole operation of recording of the Adi Granth. This is evident from his personal approval of the content, form and organization of the bani in particular raga sections, as indicated by the use of the word sudh (correct) in the margins of the text. He devised certain checks and balances which made it extremely difficult for anyone to interpolate extraneous matter in the text without being identified. Each entry in the Adi Granth is numbered and its position is further determined by its raga, authorship and metrical form. Guru Arjan's achievement can be seen from the remarkably consistent structure of the Adi Granth. There are, however, certain instances where he consciously diverged from consistency. It was meant to provide a deeper theological coherence to the text, a coherence which is not visible on the surface level. For this purpose, he sometimes added his own couplet or stanza to the celebrated works of his predecessors.

Some of the fundamental aspects of Guru Arjan's editorial policy are reflected in the actual processes by which he created the first canonical text of the Adi Granth. Five major guiding principles that emerge from an analysis of his editorial decisions are as follows: (1) doctrinal consistency, (2) the ideal of balanced life, (3) the spirit of optimism, (4) the inclusive ideal, and (5) concern for a distinctive Sikh identity. The formal aspects of texts of the Adi Granth, including their metrical, poetic, and linguistic structures are fully at one with their theological content. All these aspects provide an internal unity to the Sikh scripture. On the remarkable consistency of the message of the entire scripture, McLeod makes a perceptive observation that this is 'a result of the volume having been almost all assembled by one person at one particular time.'[3] That one person was none else than Guru Arjan. There may be other aspects of his editorial policy which may be identified through competent textual analysis of certain portions of the Adi Granth in future research. This study stands by the claims of the Kartarpur manuscript as the final text of the Adi Granth as compiled by Guru Arjan in 1604.

The inclusion of the bhagat bani in the Adi Granth illuminates the process of scriptural adaptation in the Sikh tradition. The selection logic favours those poems of the medieval bhagats that stress nirguna (formless divinity) religiosity and social equality, and are in general conformity with the Sikh Gurus' line of thinking. It should be pointed out, however, that this selection was not made exclusively on the basis of identity with the teachings of the Gurus, for there is difference as well as identity. Indeed, the process of the integration of the bhagat bani in the Sikh scriptures was based upon the recognition of two major points. First, there was its harmonization with the Gurus' thoughts in broad outlines. Second, its differences with the Gurus' thoughts at essential points were highlighted to demonstrate the distinctive Sikh viewpoints. These additional reflections of the Gurus were crucial for shaping the emerging Sikh identity. They played an important role in defining what it meant to be a Sikh in relation to the commonly held sant, sufi or bhagat ideals. These points become clear from the Gurus' comments on the bhagat bani, the net effect of which is to firmly cement its inclusion in the Sikh scriptural tradition. Some of the bhagat material was edited out at the time of the compilation of the Adi Granth. Guru Arjan was concerned not only with identifying the circles from which a

---

[3] McLeod, *Sikhism*, p. 174.

particular composition emanated, but also with the details of its message. The hymns of the Vaishnava bhagats were least acceptable to him. He even rejected those hymns of the sants (who are otherwise included in the scripture) which were coloured with Vaishnava ideals or hatha yoga techniques. The selection of the bhagat bani thus highlights both the exclusive and inclusive aspects of Guru Arjan's editorial policy.

Guru Arjan's open but cautious approach in selecting the bhagat material appears to have created a tension within certain sections of the Sikh Panth who still held Vaishnava ideals. There must have been an ongoing debate on his editorial policy among those groups. There were other groups who held sant beliefs and who did not approve the shift towards militancy in the affairs of the Panth. They created an internal pressure within the Panth. They took advantage of the unstable situation created by Guru Arjan's death and reinserted those hymns (which earlier were turned down by the Guru) in their copies of the Adi Granth. They also omitted the heroic tunes (dhunis) from their volumes. The first such bir was prepared in Lahore in 1610 when Guru Hargobind was imprisoned in the Gwalior fort by Jahangir. This manuscript tradition became popular as the Lahore recension of the Adi Granth in the seventeenth century.

This study offers the following theory of the origin of the Banno recension. The main centre of Sikh activities shifted from Amritsar to Kiratpur under Guru Hargobind, who had to withdraw to the Shivalik hills due to the pressure of Mughal authorities. This provided ample opportunity for the Banno group, which represented the union of Hindali, Udasi, Bhatra and brahminical interests, to exert its influence within the Panth in the area of Khara Mangat in Gujrat district. This was the time (1642) when the Banno recension of the Adi Granth appeared. Apart from reflecting internal pressure within the Sikh community, the Banno group was also reacting to the external pressure of the Mughals upon the Sikhs. Out of the three competing versions of the Adi Granth text, the Banno recension gradually came into prominence at the end of the seventeenth century. It reigned supreme throughout the eighteenth century because of the Banno group's increasing influence within the Panth during this period of turmoil.

Guru Tegh Bahadur himself took the decision to add his own bani to the earlier text of the Adi Granth before he left for Delhi to face the Mughal challenge in 1675. His son and successor, the tenth and the last Guru, Gobind Singh, further made an attempt to close the canon due to the problem of the circulation of three different versions of the Adi Granth during his period. He approached Dhir Mal's descendants to obtain the Kartarpur volume, but did not succeed in persuading them to part with it. However, a number of copies of the Kartarpur text were available at that time, and it was these that he used to make the Damdama version of the Adi Granth at Anandpur in the last quarter of the seventeenth century. Guru Gobind Singh thus closed the canon, marking a significant completion of a matrix of revelation for the Sikh community. It was believed that core truths of the tradition had been established irrevocably, and the documents included in the canon were a witness to these truths in an authoritative way. The closing of the canon, however, did not prevent the circulation of other versions in the eighteenth and nineteenth centuries.

The standard version of the Adi Granth now available was prepared during the reign of Maharaja Ranjit Singh, who promoted its copying and distribution among the Sikh community. It is based on the Kartarpur manuscript with the addition of Guru Tegh Bahadur's bani. In other words, it is the standard Damdama version of the Adi Granth. Although the Banno version was still popular in some sections of the Sikh community, particularly in the south-western area of Gujarat district, it soon came to be branded as a spurious recension (khari bir). The first printed copy of the standard Damdama version of the Adi Granth appeared in 1864. This gave a fillip to its universal acceptance. A complete consensus in the Sikh community on the text of the Adi Granth was achieved, however, only as a result of the Singh Sabha reforms in the late nineteenth century, which sanctified the standard Damdama version and set aside all other versions used earlier. At the beginning of the twentieth century, the Adi Granth text even attained a standard pagination as a result of printing uniformity. All modern printed editions have a total of 1,430 pages, and all correspond exactly in terms of the material printed on the individual pages.

The Adi Granth as a scriptural text has inexhaustible hermeneutic potential. In oral as well as written exegesis, each generation of Sikh interpreters has drawn its meaning from differing perspectives. In fact, plurality of interpretations has remained part and parcel of the Sikh approach to the Adi Granth throughout its history. Each encounter with the text of the Adi Granth provides a fresh experience of unfolding a divine mystery. Recent emphasis on a single 'correct' meaning is a result of the distinctive doctrinal approach of certain

Singh Sabha scholars. An even more recent phenomenon of scriptural literalism, in the form of a fundamentalist interpretation, seems to be emerging in certain sections of the Panth as a result of post–1984 events in the Punjab, but its articulation is not yet clear. It is still in the process of development and is related to the larger process of religious fundamentalism that is taking place in India, particularly Hindu fundamentalism.

The Adi Granth has played a unique role as Guru in the personal piety, liturgy and corporate life of the Sikh community. It has provided a framework for the shaping of the Panth and a distinctive Sikh identity. It occupies a central position in all Sikh ceremonies and its oral/aural experience has provided the Sikh tradition with a living presence of the divine Guru. The daily process of vak laina inspires Sikhs throughout the world and confirms the function of the scripture as Guru. Indeed, the Guru Granth Sahib has given the Sikhs a sacred source to reflect upon and discover the meaning of life as Sikhs. It has functioned as a supratextual source of authority within the Sikh tradition. Thus the ultimate authority within the Sikh Panth for a wide range of personal and public conduct lies in the Guru Granth Sahib.

It is hoped that this study will stimulate research in other areas related to the Adi Granth, an important focus for scholarship which until now has been rather neglected by historians, philologists, theologians and scholars of religious studies. At the same time the study of the pattern of assimilation, *rédaction*, and canonization in Sikh tradition can be useful in the study of the scriptural histories of Christian, Jewish, Muslim, Buddhist, and other religious communities. The emergence of Sikh scripture tells us much about the process of canonization in general, as well as the particular dynamics of the Sikh tradition. The study of the Adi Granth can offer its own contribution to the study of world religions in an ecumenical era. In any situation of a religious dialogue, for instance, it can offer an approach which is based on an open attitude, an attitude which allows not only true understanding of other traditions but also disagreement on crucial theological issues. In such a dialogue, all participants will be able to maintain their differences in dignity and mutual respect.

BIBLIOGRAPHY

A. Early Pothis and Manuscripts of the Adi Granth

Goindval Pothi, Volume I (late sixteenth century). Lajpat Nagar, Jalandhar, Punjab, India.

Goindval Pothi, Volume II (late sixteenth century). Sundar Kutia, Pinjore, Haryana, India.

Guru Har Sahai Pothi (c. sixteenth century–1635). This precious pothi was lost in 1970.

GNDU MS # 1245 (c. 1599). Bhai Gurdas Library, Rare Books, Guru Nanak Dev University, Amritsar, Punjab. A photocopy of this manuscript is preserved at Anant Education and Rural Development Foundation, Inc., 914 Waxen Way, Grandledge, Michigan – 48837, USA.

Bahoval Pothi (early seventeenth century). Bhai Vir Singh Sahitya Sadan, New Delhi, India.

Kartarpur MS (1604). Gurdwara Shishmahal, Kartarpur Estate, Kartarpur, Jalandhar, Punjab, India.

PUM MS # 8 (early seventeenth century). Punjabi University Museum, Patiala, Punjab.

Lahori Bir (1610). Sikh Reference Library, Amritsar, India. Destroyed in Operation Bluestar of 1984.

Kanpur MS (1642). Gurdwara Bhai Banno Sahib, Jawahar Nagar, Kanpur, UP, India.

Gurdita Sekhon MS (1653). Tikana Sri Bhai Ramkishan, Sheranwala Gate, Patiala, Punjab, India.

Una Sahib MS # 2 (seventeenth century). Baba Sarabjot Singh Bedi, Kila Bedi Sahib, Una Sahib, Himachal Pradesh, India.

Baba Ram Rai's Bir (1659). In the possession of Mahant Inderesh Chandar Das of Baba Ram Rai's dera, Dehradun, UP, India.

GNDU MS # 1084 (1666). Bhai Gurdas Library, Rare Books, Guru Nanak Dev University, Amritsar, Punjab, India.

Jograj MS PUM # 2 (1667). Punjabi University Museum, Patiala, Punjab, India.

DBSSK MS # 3 (1679). Dr Balbir Singh Sahitya Kendra, 20–Pritam Road, Dehradun, UP, India.

PUM MS # 1 (1687). Punjabi University Museum, Patiala, Punjab, India.

PUM MS # 6 (1692). Punjabi University Museum, Patiala, Punjab, India.

Harijas MS (late seventeenth century). 1st Battalion of the Brigade of The Guards Mechanical (2 Punjab), Army Gurdwara. This MS is the copy of a manuscript prepared in 1645.

MS Copy of Baba Ram Rai's Bir (late seventeenth century). Gurdwara Dasmesh Bhavan, Sri Guru Singh Sabha, Dehradun, UP, India.

Panj. MS # 5 (late seventeenth century). John Rylands University of Manchester Library, Manchester, UK.

MS # 504 (1711). Dr Chanan Singh Chan, Sri Guru Granth Sahib Trust, 91 Mantilla Drive, Coventry CV3 6LJ, UK.

MS # 506 (early eighteenth century). Sri Guru Granth Sahib Trust, Coventry, UK.

Panj. MSS C5 (1727). India Office Library (IOL), London, UK.

MS # 2 (1730). Dr Balbir Singh Sahitya Kendra, Dehradun, UP, India.

Panj. MSS C1 (1738). India Office Library, London, UK.

MS # 1 (1740). Private Collection of Sardar Tarlok Singh Choudhary, 49 Brook Drive, Harrow, Middlesex HA1 4RT, UK.

MS # 2 (1744). Private collection of Sardar Tarlok Singh Choudhary, Harrow, UK.

MS Or. 2159 (1745). British Library, London, UK.

MS # 115594 (1755). Punjabi University Library, Special Collections, Patiala, Punjab, India.

Panj. MSS F1 (1758). India Office Library, London, UK.

Panj. MSS D3 (1764). India Office Library, London, UK.

MS # 115464 (1768). Punjabi University Library, Special Collections, Patiala, Punjab, India.

MS Acc. # 16686 (1794). Punjab Sahit Akademi Reference Library, Punjabi Bhavan, Ludhiana, Punjab, India.

Panj. MSS D2 (eighteenth century). India Office Library, London, UK.

MS R.15.153 (1743–1843). Trinity College, Cambridge, UK.

MS # 115461 (late eighteenth century). Punjabi University Library, Special Collections, Patiala, Punjab, India.

MS Or. 2748 (early nineteenth century). British Library, London, UK.

MS Add. 25680 (early nineteenth century). British Library, London, UK.

PUM MS # 4 (early nineteenth century). Punjabi University Museum, Patiala, Punjab, India.

Una Sahib MS # 1 (1820–30). Kila Bedi Sahib, Una Sahib, HP, India.

MS # 503 (nineteenth century). Sri Guru Granth Sahib Trust, Coventry, UK.

MS # 115462 (nineteenth century). Punjabi University Library, Special Collections, Patiala, Punjab, India.

MS # 3 (nineteenth century). Private collection of Sardar Tarlok Singh Choudhary, Harrow, UK.

MS # 1 (1832). Private collection of Pashaura Singh, 3212 Foxway Court, Ann Arbor, Michigan – 48105, USA.

PUM MS # 7 (nineteenth century). Punjabi University Museum, Patiala, Punjab, India.

MS # 1041 (nineteenth century). Bhai Gurdas Library, Rare Books, Guru Nanak Dev University, Amritsar, Punjab, India.

MS # 11560 (nineteenth century). Punjabi University Library, Special Collections, Patiala, Punjab, India.

MS # 115466 (nineteenth century). Punjabi University Library, Special Collections, Patiala, Punjab, India.

MS # 115593 (nineteenth century). Punjabi University Library, Special Collections, Patiala, Punjab, India.

MS # 115463 (nineteenth century). Punjabi University Library, Special Collections, Patiala, Punjab, India.

MS # 1 (nineteenth century). Gurdwara Sahib, Kuthala, Malerkotla, Punjab.

Panj. MSS D1 (1848). India Office Library, London, UK.

Panj. MSS E2 (1859). India Office Library, London, UK.

B. Printed Editions of the Adi Granth

Sri Guru Granth Sahib (1864). Accession No. R 2846. Guru Nanak Dev University Library, Amritsar.

Panj. H 26 (1868). India Office Library, London, UK. This is the standard Damdama version of the Adi Granth, published by Matbai Aftab Press, Lahore.

Panj. H 25 (1885). India Office Library, London, UK. This was also the standard Damdama version of the Adi Granth, published by Yantralya Press, Lahore.

Panj. H 12 (1892). India Office Library, London, UK. The second edition of Panj. H 25.

Panj. H 21 (1881). India Office Library, London, UK. This was the first Banno version of the Adi Granth, printed by Brij Lal at Gian Press, Gujranwala.

Adi Sri Guru Granth Sahib (pages 1430). Amritsar: Shuddh Gurbani Trust, n.d. This beautiful volume with coloured margins is preserved at the Army Gurdwara of 1st Battalion of the Brigade of The Guards Mechanical (2 Punjab).

Adi Sri Guru Granth Sahib (pages 1430). Dayal Singh Trust Library, 25 Nisbet Road, Lahore, Pakistan. This standard version of the Adi Granth was printed in Sukhar (Sind) by Swami Ishvranand Udasin. It was corrected with the Kartarpur granth.

Pothi Panj Granth Adi. Lahore: Yantar Mustafai, n.d. This pothi is preserved at the Army Gurdwara of 1st Battalion of the Brigade of The Guards Mechanical (2 Punjab).

C. Punjabi Works

Akali Kaur Singh. *Guru Shabad Ratan Prakash.* Patiala: Punjab Language Department, reprint, 1963.

Avtar Singh and Gurcharan Singh. *Gurbani Sangat Prachin Rit Ratanavali.* 2 vols. Patiala: Punjabi University, 1979.

Bawa Kirpal Das. *Mahima Prakash.* Patiala: Bhasha Vibhag, 1971.

Badan Singh Giani, ed. *Adi Sri Guru Granth Sahib Ji Satik (Faridkot Vala Tika).* Patiala: Punjab Language Department, reprint, 1970.

Balbir Singh. *Raga-mala da Saval te Jodh Kavi ate Alam.* Amritsar: Khalsa Samachar, 3rd edn,1969.

——— *Nirukat Sri Guru Granth Sahib.* 2 vols. Patiala: Punjabi University, 1972–4.

Charan Singh. *Sri Guru Granth Bani Biora.* 1902. Amritsar: Khalsa Tract Society, reprint, 1945.

Darshan Singh. *Bhai Gurdas: Sikhi de Pahile Viakhiakar.* Patiala: Punjabi University, 1986.

Davinder Singh Vidiarthi. 'Gurbani ate Raga.' *Khoj Patrika.* No. 26. Patiala: Punjabi University, 1985.

——— *Kirtan: Sandarabh te Sarup.* Patiala: Punjabi University, 1992.

Ganda Singh, ed. *Hukam-name.* Patiala: Punjabi University, 1967.

Gian Singh. *Sri Guru Panth Prakash.* Delhi: 1870; rev. edn, Amritsar: Khalsa Samachar, 1923.

——— *Tvarikh Guru Khalsa.* 2nd edn. Patiala: Punjab Language Department, reprint, 1970.

Gurbachan Singh Khalsa. *Gurbani Path Darashan.* Amritsar: Bhai Mehar Singh and Sons, 5th edn, 1985.

Gurbakhsh Singh (G.B. Singh). *Sri Guru Granth Sahib dian Prachin Biran.* Lahore: Modern Publishers, 1944.

Gurcharan Singh. *Adi Granth Shabad-anukramanika,* 2 vols. Patiala: Punjabi University, 1971.

Gurdas Bhalla (Bhai Gurdas). *Varan Bhai Gurdas, samp.* (editor). Hazara Singh and Vir Singh. Amritsar: Khalsa Samachar, 1962.

Gurdit Singh Giani. *Itihas Sri Guru Granth Sahib: Bhagat Bani Bhag.* Chandigarh: Sikh Sahit Sansthan, 1990.

——— ed. *Singh Sabha Patrika: Path-Bodh Ank,* Parts 1–3 (August–September–October 1979).

Gurmohan Singh Ahluwalia. *Sodhi Har Ji: Jiwan te Rachana.* Patiala: Punjabi University, 1985.

Gursharan Kaur Jaggi, ed. *Babe Mohan valian Pothian.* Delhi: Arsi Publishers, 1987.

——— *Varan Bhai Gurdas.* Patiala: Punjabi University, 1987.

Harbhajan Singh. *Gurbani Sampadan Nirnai.* Chandigarh: Satnam Prakashan, 1981.

Harnam Das Udasi. *Adi Sri Guru Granth Sahib dian Puratan Biran te Vichar,* 2 vols. Kapurthala: Kantesh Ayurvedic Pharmesi, 1969–70.

Harnam Singh Shan. *Guru Granth Sahib Di Koshkari.* Patiala: Bhasha Vibhag, 1994.

Janam-sakhi Sri Guru Nanak Dev Ji, Vol. 2. Amritsar: Khalsa College, 1969.

Jodh Singh. *Prachin Biran Bare: Bhullan di Sodhan*. Lahore: Lahore Book Shop, 1947.

Sri Kartarpuri Bir de Darshan. Patiala: Punjabi University, 1968.

Joginder Singh. *Sri Guru Granth Darpan*. New Delhi: Punjabi Prakashan, 1966.

Kahn Singh Nabha. *Gurushabad Ratnakar Mahan Kosh*. Patiala: Bhasha Vibhag, 2nd edn, 1960.

Kesar Singh Chhibbar. *Bansavali-nama Dasan Patashahian ka, samp*. (editor). Chandigarh: Rattan Singh Jaggi, 1972.

Kirpal Singh, ed. *Janam-sakhi Sri Guru Nanak Dev Ji*. Amritsar: Khalsa College, 1962.

Janam-sakhi Prampara. Patiala: Punjabi University, 1969.

Manohar Das Miharban: Jivan te Rachanavan. Patiala: Punjabi University, 1974.

Kirpal Singh, Giani, ed. *Sri Guru Panth Prakash*, 5 vols. Amritsar: Manmohan Singh Brar, 1973.

Kuir Singh. *Gur-bilas Patshahi 10*. Ed. Shamsher Singh Ashok and Fauja Singh. Patiala: Punjabi University, 2nd edn, 1986; 1st edn, 1968.

Mahan Singh, Giani. *Param Pavittar Bir da Sankalan Kal*. Amritsar: Khalsa Samachar, 1952.

Mani Singh, Bhai (?). *Sikhan di Bhagatmal*. MS 2827. Patiala: Public Library, 1826.

Mohinder Kaur Gill. *Guru Arjan: Jivan te Bani*. Delhi: National Book Shop, 1975.

Guru Granth Sahib di Sampadan Kala. Amritsar: New Age Book Centre, 2nd edn, 1982.

Piar Singh, ed. *Adi Sakhian*. Ludhiana: Lahore Book Shop, 3rd edn, 1983.

Bhai Jodh Singh: Jivan te Rachana. Patiala: Punjabi University, 1983.

'Gurbani Tika Pranalian.' *Nanak Prakash Patrika*, 20(2). Patiala: Punjabi University, 1985.

ed. *Bhai Jodh Singh Gadd Saurabh*. Patiala: Punjabi University, 1986.

Gatha Sri Adi Granth. Amritsar: Guru Nanak Dev University, 1992.

Piara Singh Padam. *Punjabi Sahit di Ruprekha*. Patiala: Kalam Mandir, 1971.

Guru Granth Sanket Kosh. Patiala: Punjabi University, 1977.

Sri Guru Granth Prakash. Patiala: Kalam Mandir, 2nd edn, 1990.

Pritam Singh, ed. *Ahiyapur Vali Pothi*, Vol. 1, Amritsar: Guru Nanak Dev University, 1998.

Pritam Singh, ed. *Nirmal Sampradai*. Amritsar: GNDU, 1981.

Raijasbir Singh, ed. *Guru Amar Das: Sarot Pustak*. Amritsar: Guru Nanak Dev University Press, 1986.

Randhir Singh. 'Adi Granth da Kal.' *Punjabi Duniya*. Patiala: Punjab Language Department, May 1952.

ed. *Guru-Pranalian*. Amritsar: SGPC, 1977.

Rajinder Singh Bal. *Bhai Banno Darapan ate Khare vali Bir*. Jalandhar: 82/3 D Central Town, 1989.

Rattan Singh Jaggi, ed. *Parkh*, Vol. II. Chandigarh: Punjab University, 1972.
  Bhai Gurdas Jivan te Rachna. Patiala, 1974.
  Bhai Mani Singh: Jivani te Rachna. Patiala: Punjabi University, 1983.
Sahib Singh. *Adi Bir Bare*. Amritsar: Singh Brothers, 4th edn, 1987; 1st edn, 1949.
  Sri Guru Granth Sahib Darapan, 10 vols. Jalandhar: Raj Publishers, 1962–4.
Santokh Singh. *Suraj Prakash, samp*. (editor). Vir Singh. *Sri Gur Pratap Suraj Granth*. Vols. V–XIII. Amritsar, 1927–35.
Sarup Das Bhalla. *Mahima Prakash*. Patiala: Bhasha Vibhag, 1971.
Satbir Singh. *Sri Guru Granth Sahib da Sar-visthar*, 3 vols. Jalandhar: New Book Company, 1985–90.
  and Gurnam Singh, eds. *Simriti Granth: Aduti Gurmat Sangit Samelan— 1991*. Ludhiana: Sant Sucha Singh, Gurdwara Gur Gian Prakash, 1991.
  and Bibi Jasbir Kaur, eds. *Simriti Granth: Aduti Gurmat Sangit Samelan— 1992*. Ludhiana: Sant Sucha Singh, Gurdwara Gur Gian Prakash, 1992.
Seva Das Udasi. *Parchi Patshahi Dasavin Ki*. Ed. Piara Singh Padam. Patiala: Kalam Mandir, 1988.
Seva Singh. *Shahid Bilas*. Ed. Giani Garja Singh. Ludhiana: Sahitya Academy, 1961.
Shabadarath Sri Guru Granth Sahib. 4 vols. Amritsar, SGPC, 5th edn, 1979.
Shamsher Singh Ashok. *Madav Nal Kam Kandala te Raga-mala Nirne*. Amritsar: Singh Brothers, 1981.
  Punjabi Hath-Likhatan Di Suchi, 2 vols. Patiala: Punjab Language Department, 1961–3.
Sohan Kavi (?). *Sri Gurbilas Patashahi 6*. Ed. Inder Singh Gill. Amritsar: Vazir Hind Press, 1977.
Taran Singh. *Sri Guru Granth Sahib da Sahitak Itihas*. Amritsar: Faqir Singh and Sons, 1963.
  Guru Angad Dev Ji. Patiala: Punjabi University, 1975.
  Guru Granth Ratnavali. Patiala: Punjabi University, 1975.
  Gurbani dian Viakhia Pranalian. Patiala: Punjabi University, 1980.
  Guru Tegh Bahadur: Jivan, Sandesh te Shahadat. Patiala: Punjabi University, 1976.
Vir Singh. *Santhya Sri Guru Granth Sahib*, 7 vols. Amritsar: Khalsa Samachar, 1958–62.
  Sri Guru Granth Kosh, 3 vols. Amritsar: Khalsa Samachar, 4th edn, 1950.
  Sri Asht Gur Chamatakar, 2 vols. Amritsar: Khalsa Samachar, 1952.

D. Hindi Works

Bahura, Gopal Narayan, ed. *The Padas of Surdas*. Jaipur: Maharaja Savai Man Singh II Museum, 1982.
Callewaert, Winand M. and Mukund Lath, eds. *The Hindi Padavali of Namdev*. Delhi: Motilal Banarsidass, 1989.

Chaturvedi, Parashuram. *Kabir Sahitya ki Parakh*. Allahabad: Leader Press, 1974.

Dvivedi, Hazari Prasad. *Kabir*. New Delhi: Raj Kamal Prakashan, 3rd edn, 1985.

Gupta, Mataprasad, ed. *Kabir Granthavali*. Allahabad: Lokbharti Prakashan, 1969.

Harji. *Goshti Guru Miharvanu*. Ed. Gobindnath Rajguru. Chandigarh: Panjab University, 1974.

Maini, Dharam Pal. *Santon ke Dharmik Vishvas*. Malerkotla: Navjot Publications, 1966.

Mishr, Jayaram. *Sri Guru Granth Darshan*. Allahabad: Sahitya Bhavan, 1960.

Narula, D.S. *Guru Nanak Sangitaggya*. Jalandhar: New Book Company, 1978.

Paintal, Gita. *Punjab ki Sangit Prampara*. New Delhi: Radha Publications, 1988.

Sharma, Harbans Lal. *Bharatiya Darshan-prampara aur Adi Granth*. Delhi: National Publishing House, 1972.

E. ENGLISH WORKS

Ahluwalia, Jasbir Singh. *The Sovereignty of the Sikh Doctrine*. New Delhi: Bahri Publications, 1983.

Allchin, F.R. *Kitavali*. London: George Allen & Unwin, 1964.

Alston, A.J. *The Devotional Poems of Mirabai*. Delhi: Motilal Banarsidass, 1980.

Archer, John Clark. *The Sikhs in Relation to Hindus, Moslems, Christians, and Ahmadiyyas*. Princeton: Princeton University Press, 1946.

'The Bible of the Sikhs'. *The Review of Religion* (January 1949).

Arora, R.K. *The Sacred Scripture: Symbol of Spiritual Synthesis*. New Delhi: Harman Publishing House, 1988.

Attar Singh, ed. *Socio-Cultural Impact of Islam on India*. Chandigarh: Panjab University Press, 1976.

Avtar Singh. *Ethics of the Sikhs*. Patiala: Punjabi University, 1970.

Bellamy, James A. 'Some Proposed Emendations to the Text of the Koran'. *Journal of the American Oriental Society*. 113(4) (1993): 562–73.

'More Proposed Emendations to the Text of the Koran'. *Journal of the American Oriental Society*. 116(2) (1996): 196–204.

Bhatkhande, V.N. *A Comparative Study of Some of the Leading Music Systems of the 15th, 16th, 17th and 18th Centuries*. Delhi: Low Price Publications, reprint, 1990; originally published in 1934.

Blumhardt, J.F. *Catalogue of the Hindi, Panjabi and Hindustani Manuscripts in the Library of the British Museum*. London: British Museum, 1899.

Bruns, Gerald L. *Hermeneutics: Ancient and Modern*. New Haven and London: Yale University Press, 1992.

Callewaert, Winand M., ed. *Early Hindi Devotional Literature in Current Research*. Leuven: Katholieke Universiteit, 1980.

and Mukund Lath. *The Hindi Padavali of Namdev: A Critical Edition of Namdev's Hindi Songs with Translations and Annotations*. Delhi: Motilal Banarsidass, 1989.

and Peter G. Friedlander. *The Life and Works of Raidas*. New Delhi: Manohar Publishers, 1992.

Childs, Brevard S. *Introduction to the Old Testament as Scripture.* Philadelphia: Westminster Press, 1979.

Cole, W. Owen. *The Guru in Sikhism.* London: Darton, Longman & Todd, 1982.

  Sikhism and Its Indian Context 1469–1708. London: Darton, Longman & Todd, 1984.

  and Piara Singh Sambhi. *The Sikhs: Their Religious Beliefs and Practices.* London: Routledge & Kegan Paul, 1978.

Coward, Harold G. *Sacred Word and Sacred Text: Scripture in World Religions.* Maryknoll: Orbis Books, 1988.

  Jung and Eastern Thought. Albany: State University of New York Press, 1985.

  and David Goa. *Mantra: Hearing the Divine in India.* Chambersburg, PA: Anima Press, 1991.

Cunningham, Joseph Davey. *A History of the Sikhs.* 1849. Reprint. New Delhi: S. Chand and Company, 1985.

Daljeet Singh. *Essays on the Authenticity of Kartarpuri Bir and the Integrated Logic and Unity of Sikhism.* Patiala: Punjabi University, 1987.

Danielou, Alain. *The Ragas of Northern Indian Music.* London: Barrie and Rockliff, 1968.

Dass, Nirmal. *Songs of Kabir from the Adi Granth.* Albany: State University of New York Press, 1992.

Dhillon, Balwant Singh. 'Myth of an Early Draft of the Adi Granth'. *Abstracts of Sikh Studies.* Chandigarh: Institute of Sikh Studies, July 1993. *Early Sikh Scriptural Tradition: Myth and Reality.* Amritsar: Singh Brothers, 1999.

Dhillon, Dalbir Singh. *Sikhism: Origin and Development.* New Delhi: Oriental Publishers, 1988.

Diwana, Mohan Singh. *A History of Punjabi Literature.* Jalandhar: Bharat Prakashan, 1971.

  'Discoveries in Sikh Culture I–IV.' *Journal of Sikh Studies.* Vols. I–II, nos. 1–2 (1974–5).

Dusenbery, Verne A. 'The Word as Guru: Sikh Scripture and the Translation Controversy.' *History of Religions.* 31(4) (May 1992): 385–402.

Eliade, Mircea. *Birth and Rebirth: The Religious Meaning of Initiation in Human Culture.* New York: Harper, 1958.

  Images and Symbols: Studies in Religious Symbolism. New York: Sheed and Ward, 1969.

Ernst, Carl W. *Eternal Garden: Mysticism, History, and Politics at a South Asian Sufi Center.* Albany: State University of New York Press, 1992.

Fauja Singh. *Guru Amar Das: Life and Teachings.* New Delhi: Sterling Publishers, 1979.

Fenech, Louis E. *Martyrdom in the Sikh Tradition: Playing the 'Game of Love'.* New Delhi: Oxford University Press, 2000.

Fernhout, Rein. *Canonical Texts: Bearers of Absolute Authority: Bible, Koran, Veda, Tipitaka.* Amsterdam, Atlanta, GA: Editions Rodopi, 1994.

Friedman, Yohanan. *Shaykh Ahmad Sirhandi: An Outline of His Image in the Eyes of Posterity.* Montreal: Institute of Islamic Studies, McGill University, 1966. Forthcoming from Oxford University Press, Delhi.

Frye, Northrop. *The Great Code: The Bible and Literature.* New York: A Harvest/ HBJ Book, 1982.

Words with Power: Being a Second Study of 'The Bible and Literature.' New York: Harcourt Brace Jovanovich, 1990.

Funk, Robert W., Roy W. Hoover, and the Jesus Seminar, trans. and comment. *The Five Gospels: The Search for the Authentic Words of Jesus.* New York: Macmillan Publishing Company, 1993.

Ganda Singh, trans. 'Nanak Panthis' (selection from *Dabistan-i-Mazahib* by Zulfiqar Ardastani). *The Panjab Past and Present.* Patiala: Punjabi University, 1967.

Guru Arjan's Martyrdom (Re-interpreted). Patiala: Guru Nanak Mission, 1969.

Gangoly, O.C. *Ragas and Raginis.* Bombay: Nalanda Publications, 1958; 1st edn, 1935.

Giani, Bachittar Singh, ed. *Planned Attack on Aad Sri Guru Granth Sahib: Academics or Blasphemy.* Chandigarh: International Centre of Sikh Studies, 1994.

Grewal, Jagtar Singh (J.S. Grewal). *Guru Nanak in History.* Chandigarh: Panjab University, 1969.

The New Cambridge History of India II.3: The Sikhs of the Punjab. Cambridge: Cambridge University Press, 1991.

Gopal Singh, trans. *Sri Guru Granth Sahib.* English translation of the Adi Granth, 4 vols. Delhi: Gur Das Kapoor, 1962.

A History of the Sikh People, 1469–1978. New Delhi: World Sikh University Press, 1979.

Gottlieb, Roberts S. *Solo Tabla Drumming of North India: Its Repertoire, Styles, and Performance Practices,* Vol. I: Text and Commentary. Delhi: Motilal Banarsidass, 1993.

Graham, William A. *Beyond the Written Word: Oral Aspects of Scripture in the History of Religion.* New York: Cambridge University Press, 1987.

Griffin, Lepel H. and Charles Francis Massy. *Chiefs and Families of Note in the Punjab.* Lahore: Government Press, 1909.

Harbans Singh. *Guru Nanak and Origins of the Sikh Faith.* Bombay: Asia Publishing House, 1969.

ed. *Perspectives on Guru Nanak.* Patiala: Punjabi University, 1975.

Berkeley Lectures on Sikhism. New Delhi: Guru Nanak Foundation, 1983.

The Heritage of the Sikhs. 2nd rev. edn. Columbia, Mo. and New Delhi: South Asia Books and Manohar Publisher, 1983.

Sri Guru Granth Sahib: Guru Eternal for the Sikhs. Patiala: Academy of Sikh Religion and Culture, 1988.

Hawley, John Stratton. *Sur Das: Poet, Singer, Saint.* Seattle: University of Washington Press, 1984.

'Author and Authority in Bhakti Poetry.' *The Journal of Asian Studies* 47(2) (1988): 269–90.

and Mark Juergensmeyer. *Songs of the Saints of India.* New York: Oxford University Press, 1988.

Hess, Linda and Shukdev Singh. *The Bijak of Kabir.* San Francisco: North Point Press, 1979.

Holdrege, Barbara A. *Veda and Torah: Transcending the Textuality of Scripture.* Albany: State University of New York Press, 1996.

Holm, Jean and John Bowker, eds. *Sacred Writings.* London: Pinter Publishers, 1994.

Irwin, Joyce, ed. *Sacred Sound: Music in Religious Thought and Practice.* Chico: Scholars Press, 1983.

Jairazbhoy, N.A. *The Rags of North India: Their Structure and Evolution.* London: Faber and Faber, 1971.

Juergensmeyer, Mark and N.G. Barrier, eds. *Sikh Studies: Comparative Perspectives on a Changing Tradition.* Berkeley: Berkeley Religious Studies and Graduate Theological Union, 1979.

Kaufmann, Walter. *The Ragas of North India.* Bloomington: Indiana University Press, 1968.

Khalsa, Gurudharam Singh. *Guru Ram Das in Sikh Tradition.* New Delhi: Harman Publishing House, 1997.

Khushwant Singh. *A History of the Sikhs.* 2 vols. Princeton: Princeton University Press, 1963–6.

Kohli, Surinder Singh. *A Crtical Study of the Adi Granth.* New Delhi: Punjab Writers' Cooperative Industrial Society, 1961.

Lambert, Neal E. *Literature of Belief.* Salt Lake City: Brigham Young University Religious Studies Center, 1981.

Levering, Miriam, ed. *Rethinking Scripture: Essays from a Comparative Perspective.* Albany: State University of New York Press, 1989.

Loehlin, Clinton H. *The Sikhs and Their Scriptures.* Lucknow: Lucknow Publishing House, 1958.

'A Westerner Looks at the Kartarpur Granth.' *Proceedings of the Punjab History Conference.* Patiala: Punjabi University, 1966.

Lopez, Donald S., Jr., ed. *Religions of India in Practice.* Princeton, New Jersey: Princeton University Press, 1995.

Lorenzen, David N., ed. *Bhakti Religion in North India: Community Identity and Political Action.* Albany: State University of New York Press, 1995.

Macauliffe, Max Arthur. *The Sikh Religion: Its Gurus, Sacred Writings, and Authors.* 6 vols. Oxford: Clarendon Press, 1909.

Madanjit Kaur. *The Golden Temple: Past and Present.* Amritsar: Guru Nanak Dev University, 1983.

Malm, William P. *Music Cultures of the Pacific, the Near East, and Asia.* Upper Saddle River, New Jersey: Prentice-Hall, 3rd edn, 1996; 1st edn, 1967.

Mansukhani, Gobind Singh. *Indian Classical Music and Sikh Kirtan.* New Delhi: Oxford and IBH, 1982.

Mann, Gurinder Singh. 'The Making of Sikh Scripture.' Ph.D. Thesis, Columbia University, 1993.

——— *The Goindval Pothis: The Earliest Extant Sources of the Sikh Canon.* Cambridge, MA: Department of Sanskrit and Indian Studies, Harvard University, 1996.

Manmohan Singh, trans. *Sri Guru Granth Sahib.* English and Punjabi translation of the Adi Granth. 2nd edn, 8 vols. Amritsar: SGPC, 1981–3.

McGregor, R.S., ed. *Devotional Literature in South Asia: Current Research, 1985–1988.* Cambridge: Cambridge University Press, 1992.

McLeod, W.H. 'Guru Nanak and Kabir.' *Proceedings of Punjab History Conference,* 1st session, November 1965. Patiala: Punjabi University, 1966.

——— *Guru Nanak and the Sikh Religion.* Oxford: Clarendon Press, 1968.

——— 'Hakikat Rah Mukam Raje Sivanabh Ki'. *Proceedings of the Punjab History Conference.* 4th session (March 1969). Patiala: Punjabi University, 1970

——— *Evolution of the Sikh Community.* Oxford: Clarendon Press, 1975.

——— *Early Sikh Tradition: A Study of the Janam-sakhis.* Oxford: Clarendon Press, 1980.

——— trans. *The B40 Janam-sakhi.* Amritsar: Guru Nanak Dev University Press, 1980.

——— trans. and ed. *Textual Sources for the Study of Sikhism.* Manchester: Manchester University Press, 1984.

——— trans. *The Chaupa Singh Rahit-nama.* Dunedin: University of Otago Press, 1987.

——— *Who is a Sikh?: The Problem of Sikh Identity.* Oxford, Clarendon Press, 1989.

——— *The Sikhs: History, Religion and Society.* New York: Columbia University Press, 1989.

——— *Popular Sikh Art.* Delhi: Oxford University Press, 1991.

——— *Historical Dictionary of Sikhism.* Lanham, MD, & London: The Scarecrow Press, 1995.

——— *Sikhism.* London: Penguin Books, 1997.

——— 'Sikh Fundamentalism.' *Journal of the American Oriental Society.* 118(1) (January–March 1998): 15–27.

Miller, Barbara Stoler, ed. and trans. *Love Song of the Dark Lord: Jayadeva's Gitagovinda.* New York: Columbia University Press, 1977.

Moutal, Patrick. *A Comparative Study of Selected Hindustani Raga-s: Based on Contemporary Practice.* New Delhi: Munshiram Manoharlal, 1991.

Nahar Singh. 'Some Documents Regarding Sacred Sikh Relics in England.' *The Panjab Past and Present* 8:2 (1974): 304–13.

Nikky-Guninder Kaur Singh. *The Feminine Principle in the Sikh Vision of the Transcendent.* Cambridge: Cambridge University Press, 1993.

——— trans. *The Name of My Beloved: Verses of the Sikh Gurus.* San Francisco: HarperCollins, 1995.

Nirbhai Singh. *Bhagat Namdeva in the Guru Grantha*. Patiala: Punjabi University, 1981.

'The Collection of the Hymns of the *Guru Granth.*' *Journal of Sikh Studies*. 8 (1981): 9–22.

Nripinder Singh. *The Sikh Moral Tradition*. New Delhi: Manohar Publishers, 1990.

Oberoi, Harjot. 'Sikh Fundamentalism: Translating History into Theory.' *Fundamentalisms and the State*. Eds. Martin E. Marty and R. Scott Appleby. Chicago: The University of Chicago Press, 1993.

Construction of Religious Boundaries. Delhi: Oxford University Press, 1994.

O'Connell, Joseph T., Milton Israel et al. *Sikh History and Religion in the Twentieth Century*. Toronto: University of Toronto, Centre for South Asian Studies, 1988.

O'Flaherty, Wendy Doniger, ed. *The Critical Study of Sacred Texts*. Berkeley: Berkeley Religious Studies Series, 1979.

Pashaura Singh. 'Sikh Self-Definition and the Bhagat Bani.' M.A. thesis. University of Calgary, 1987.

and N. Gerald Barrier, eds. *The Transmission of Sikh Heritage in the Diaspora*. New Delhi: Manohar Publishers, 1996.

Patwant Singh. *The Golden Temple*. New Delhi: Time Books International, 1988.

Pettigrew, Joyce J.M. *The Sikhs of the Punjab: Unheard Voices of State and Guerrilla Violence*. London: Zed Books, 1995.

'Songs of the Sikh Resistance Movement.' *Asian Music* (Fall/Winter, 1991–2).

Piar Singh. *Gatha Sri Adi Granth and the Controversy*. Grandledge, Michigan: Anant Education and Rural Development Foundation, 1996.

Pincott, Frederic. 'The Arrangement of the Hymns of the Adi Granth.' *Journal of the Royal Asiatic Society*. Vol. XVIII. Calcutta, 1878.

Prajnananda, Swami. *A History of Indian Music*. Delhi: Munshiram Manoharlal, 2nd edn, 1981.

Pritam Singh. 'Keertana and the Sikhs.' *Journal of Sikh Studies* 3:2 (1976): 5–8, 182–5.

'Bhai Banno's Copy of the Sikh Scripture.' *Journal of Sikh Studies*. XI(II) (August 1984).

Sikh Concept of the Divine. Amritsar: Guru Nanak Dev University Press, 1985.

Ray, Niharranjan. *The Sikh Gurus and the Sikh Society*. New Delhi: Munshiram Manoharlal, 1975.

Rebecca, Stewart. 'The Tabla in Perspective.' Ph.D. Dissertation. Los Angeles: University of California, 1974.

Rowell, Lewis. *Music and Musical Thought in Early India*. Chicago: The University of Chicago Press, 1992.

Sagar, Sabinderjit Singh. *Historical Ananlysis of Nanak Prakash by Bhai Santokh Singh*. Amritsar: Guru Nanak Dev University, 1993.

Schimmel, Annemarie. *Mystical Dimensions of Islam*. Chapel Hill, NC: The University of North Carolina Press, 1975.
    Deciphering the Signs of God: A Phenomenological Approach to Islam. Albany: The State University of New York Press, 1994.

Schomer, Karine and W.H. McLeod, eds. *The Sants: Studies in a Devotional Tradition of India*. Berkeley and Delhi: Berkeley Religious Studies Series and Motilal Banarsidass, 1987.

Shackle, Christopher. 'Approaches to Persian Loans in the Adi Granth.' *Bulletin of the School of Oriental and African Studies* 41(1) (1978): 73–96.
    'The Sahaskriti Poetic Idiom in the Adi Granth.' *Bulletin of the School of Oriental and African Studies* 41(2) (1978): 313.
    'The South-Western Style in the Guru Granth Sahib.' *Journal of Sikh Studies*. Vol. 1. Amritsar: Guru Nanak Dev University, 1978.
    A Guru Nanak Glossary. London: School of Oriental and African Studies, 1981.
    An Introduction to the Sacred Language of the Sikhs. London: School of Oriental and African Studies, 1983.
    'The First Restatement of the Bani.' *The Sikh Courier*. London: Sikh Cultural Society of Great Britain, Autumn–Winter 1985.
    'Early Muslim Vernacular Poetry in the Indus Valley: Its Contexts and its Character.' In Anna Libera Dallapiccola and Stephanie Zingel-Ave Lallemant, eds. *Islam and Indian Regions*. Vol. I. Stuttgart: Franz Steiner Verlag, 1993.

Shapiro, Michael C. 'Observations on the Core Language of the Adigranth.' *BIS*, 3 (1987).

Smith, Jonathan Z. *Imagining Religion: From Babylon to Jones-town*. Chicago: University of Chicago Press, 1982.

Smith, Wilfred Cantwell. *On Understanding Islam*. New York: Mouton Publishers, 1981.
    What Is Scripture?: A Comparative Approach. Minneapolis: Fortress Press, 1993.

Sohan Singh. *The Ballad of God and Man*. Amritsar: Guru Nanak Dev University, 1982.

Sontag, Susan. *Against Interpretation, and other Essays*. New York: Farrar, Strauss & Giroux. 1966.

Surjit Hans. *A Reconstruction of Sikh History from Sikh Literature*. Jalandhar: ABS Publication, 1988.

Talib, Gurbachan Singh, ed. *Guru Tegh Bahadur: Background and Supreme Sacrifice*. Patiala: Punjabi University, 1976.
    trans. *Sri Guru Granth Sahib*. Vols. 1–4. Patiala: Punjabi University, 1984–90.

Taran Singh. *Guru Nanak: His Mind and Art*. New Delhi: Bahri Publications, 1992.

Teja Singh. *Sikhism: Its Ideals and Institutions*. Rev. edn. Bombay: Orient Longman, 1951.

Teja Singh and Ganda Singh. *A Short History of the Sikhs.* Rev. edn. Patiala: Punjabi University, 1989.

Thiel-Horstmann, Monika, ed. *Bhakti in Current Research, 1979–1982.* Berlin: Dietrich Reimer Verlag, 1983.

Timm, Jeffrey R. *Texts in Contexts: Traditional Hermeneutics in South Asia.* Albany: The State University of New York Press, 1992.

Trilochan Singh. *Ernest Trumpp and W.H. McLeod: As Scholars of Sikh History, Religion and Culture.* Chandigarh: International Institute of Sikh Studies, 1994.

Trumpp, E., trans. *The Adi Granth.* London, George Allen & Unwin, 1877. New Delhi: Munshiram Manoharlal, reprint, 1970.

Uberoi, J.P.S. *Religion, Civil Society and the State: A Study in Sikhism.* Delhi: Oxford University Press, 1996.

Vaudeville, Charlotte. *Kabir.* Vol. I. Oxford: Clarendon Press, 1974. ·
A Weaver Named Kabir. Delhi: Oxford University Press, 1993.

Ward, Keith. *Religion and Revelation.* Oxford: Clarendon Press, 1994.

Widdess, Richard. *The Ragas of Early Indian Music: Modes, Melodies and Notations from the Gupta Period to c. 1250.* Oxford: Clarendon Press, 1995.

INDEX

Abul Fazal, 135
Adi bir, 23, 58, 67, 74-6, 114, 204,
  223
Adi Granth, 3-4, 6-7, 11-16, 18-26,
  28-31, 34-5, 37, 40-1, 44,
  46-8, 51, 53, 55, 57, 59-
  61, 64-7, 69-71, 73, 75-
  85, 89-90, 92-3, 95-100,
  102-6, 111-12, 114-15,
  118-20, 122-4, 126, 129,
  136-8, 140-1, 143-52,
  154-5, 157, 159, 161, 165,
  169-78, 181, 184-6, 188,
  190-1, 193-6, 198-204,
  206, 208-12, 215, 217-18,
  223, 225, 227-35, 239-40,
  242, 251, 253, 256, 258-
  61, 265-7, 269-71, 275,
  278-9, 281, 283-8
addhan-shahi ink, 76
adhunik-pranali, modern school, 243
Adi Sri Guru Granth Sahib, 233
Adi Sri Guru Granth Sahib Satik/
  Faridkot Tika, 242, 253
Adi Udasis, 251
Aduti Gurmat Sangit Samelan, 149
Afghans, 58, 223, 273-4
Afghanistan, 138, 219
Agra, 61, 124
Ain-i-Akbari, 135
Ajit Singh Paintal, 129, 136
Akalis, Akali Movement, 66
Akal, timeless one, 85
Akal Purakh, 6-8, 10, 12, 14, 16, 84,
  86, 88-9, 119, 129, 153,
  155, 160, 163, 171, 183,
  187, 195, 197, 214, 251,
  266, 269
Akal Takhat, 207, 273, 278
Akbar, Mughal Emperor, 22, 45, 103,
  135-6, 148, 209-10
akhand path, unbroken reading, 219,
  278
akhar, letters, 8, 188
alahanian, 144, 157, 162
Alexandria, 248
Allah, God, 109-10
Ameer Khusrau, 135, 145
amrit, nectar, 11, 116
amrit bani, 9
amrit sanskar, Khalsa initiation, 277
amrit vela, ambrosial time, 90, 97
Amritsar, 33, 58, 61, 81, 97, 112, 120,
  156, 204, 217, 231, 233, 235,
  249, 253-4, 281, 284, 286
Amritsari Granth, 58
amsa, tone, 127
Anand, hymn of joy, 47, 98-102,
  118, 144, 152, 162
Anandghan, Udasi, 249-50, 252
Anand Karaj, Sikh marriage, 275-6
Anandpur Sahib, 81, 223-4, 235,
  287
Anglo-Sikh wars, 273
anubhav, intuition, 253
anup balak, unique son, 117
Archer, J.C., 21
Ardas, Sikh Prayer, 166, 275
Arjan Singh Muni (Hazur Sahib),
  233

arti, adoration, 91, 144, 173
Arya Samaj, 29
Arya Samajis, 28
Asa mode, 14, 16, 43, 47, 56, 96–7,
        117, 132, 135–6, 138, 146,
        157, 171, 180, 185, 189,
        191
Asa Ki Var, see *Var Asa*
asavari mode, 135
Asiatic Society of Bengal, Calcutta,
        147
astapadi, 47, 134, 144, 152, 157, 180
astakari chakkar, octagonal circle, 41
ast-kanwal, eight lotuses, 192
asudh-path, incorrect reading, 203
Audhu, 191–2
avatar, 13, 120, 198–9
Avtar Singh, 64
Azrael, 109–10

Baba, 33, 36, 37, 103–5, 183, 214
Baba
    Farid, 181
    Gurdita, 73
    Hindal, 215
    Prem Singh Hoti Mardan, 35–6
    Ram Rai, 58, 66
    Sahib Singh Bedi, 228
    Sarbjot Singh Bedi, 30, 69, 228
    Sri Chand, 249, 251
Baba Ram Rai's *bir*, 23, 64–7, 194
Babur, Mughal Emperor, 7
badd parvaru, big family, 164
bahinoi, brother-in-law, 189–90
Bahoval pothi, 53, 82, 283
bairagis, ascetics, 143
Bairari mode, 47
Baisakhi festival, 184
Bala janam-sakhis, 213–15
Bali, demon, 198
Balvand, Rai, 47, 49
Balwant Singh Dhillon, 43, 50
bani, divine Word, 6–11, 13–19, 23,
        28, 38, 73, 78, 92, 95, 107,
        119, 123, 125–6, 130–1,
        134, 136, 157, 161, 165,
        171, 182, 184, 186, 207,
        223, 235, 242–4, 268, 270,
        272, 282, 284, 286–7
Bani Biora, 26
Banno *bir* (version), 28, 30, 61, 72,
        74–6, 78–80, 82, 114–21,
        191, 194, 196, 199, 212–14,
        217, 219–21, 224, 226–7,
        229–32, 235, 241, 286–7
Bansavalinama, Chhibar text, 20, 279
Bansavali-nama, Sodhi Sadhu Singh,
        226
bar, blessing, 36–7
baraha-rup, boar form, 199
barah mahan, twelve months, 144
Basant mode, 35, 47, 50, 131–2,
        134, 143, 146–7, 171, 185
Basant Singh Rekhi, 59n
Bavan Akhari, fifty-two letters, 8
bavan-rup, dwarf form, 198
Bawa Arjan Singh, 68
Bazar Mai Sevan (Amritsar), 41
Bedi family, 70
belari/meru danda, 187–8
Bellami, James A., 205
benati chaupai, 98–9
Beni, bhagat, 174, 180
bhaddanu unet, tonsure ceremony,
        116, 118
bhagats, 6–7, 19, 31, 40–1, 49–50,
        55, 57, 66, 79, 134, 171–3,
        176–9, 182–5, 187–8, 200–
        2, 211–12, 229, 282, 284–6
bhagat bani, 24, 30–1, 49–50, 70,
        152, 171, 173, 176–9, 182–
        5, 187–8, 200–2, 211–12,
        234, 257, 285
Bhagavata worship, 200
Bhai, honorific title, 245
Bhai
    Addhan Sahib, 76
    Banno, 28, 74, 212–13, 226–7
    Buddha, 23, 42–3, 208
    Durga Singh, 64

Ghanahyya, 76
Gurdas Bhalla, 17–18, 23, 28, 53–
4, 60–1, 74, 76, 91, 98, 124,
129, 133, 139, 164, 176,
191, 203, 207, 213, 240,
245–7, 256, 284
Gurmukh Singh, 229
Harijas, scribe, 218–19
Hira Singh, 232
Jodh Singh, 45, 47, 53, 54, 57,
59, 117, 157
Lorinda Sahib, 77
Mani Singh, 223, 253
Milkhi, 68
Nand Lal, 266
Natha, 220
Nidhan Singh, 226
Ram Singh, 226
Sant Singh, 229
Sankar Singh Ragi, 231
Seva Ram, 77
Vir Singh, 256
Wazir Singh, 66
Bhai-pranali, 245
bhakha, 252
bhakti, loving devotion, 24, 105, 129,
135, 254, 285
Bhalla family, 35, 38, 40, 43,
Bhatra/s, 120, 216–17, 235, 286
Bhairon/Bhairau mode, 35, 47, 50,
52, 55, 132–3, 143, 174–
5, 244
bhat, bard, 51, 120
Bhikhan, bhagat, 174
Bhindran Kalan, 234, 255
Bhindran Taksal, 254–5
Bhog mark, IK Onkar symbol, 219
Bhuvanesvara, 136
Bible, 14
bibhas-prabhati, 138
Bidhi Chand, Hindali, 215
Bihagara mode, 47
Bilaval mode, 47, 135–6, 146
bilaval-gaund, 138
biraha, pangs of separation, 182

birahare, 144
Birbhum, 174
Bopa Rai Kalan, 254
Brahman, ultimate reality, 252
Brahma, god, 214, 250,
Brahmins, priests, 235, 273
brahminical influence, 118, 119–20,
122, 217, 231, 249, 252,
286
Braj, 124, 245
Brhad-desi, 138
Brij Lal, 231
Bruns, Gerald, 25
Bula, singer, 18, 40, 283
Bunga, educational centre, 229
Bura Sandhu, scribe, 68, 69
Burhan ud-Din Garib, 181

Callewaert, Winand, 135, 147, 149,
172
chakaras, discs, 189, 192, 216
Chandani, canopy, 218
Charan Singh, 26
Charan Singh Shahid, 233
Chaturbhuj, 248
chaubara, balcony, 133
Chaubole, 51, 66, 68–70, 144
chaudan ratan, fourteen jewels, 84
chaunkis, sittings, 141–2
Chaunki
    Anand di, 141–2
    Asa di Var di, 141–2
    Bilaval di, 142
    Charankanval di, 141–2
    Kalyan di, 142
    Kanare di, 141–2
    Kirtan Sohile di, 142
    Rahiras di, 142
    Ramakali di, 142
    Sarang di, 142
    So Dar di, 97, 141–2
Chaupa Singh Rahit-nama, 20, 268,
272
chaupada/e, 144, 153–4
chauri, whisk, 278

chavala, rice, 164
chhant/chhand, 47, 114, 117, 129, 133–4, 144, 152, 276
chhibbas, arcs, 218
Chhimba, calico-printer, 182
Childs, Brevard, 24
Chisti, sufi order, 181
Christian chant, 127
Christian Mission, Ludhiana, 230
Christian Scripture, 177
Church, 177
Cole, W. Owen, 95, 279
Coward, Harold, 13, 258–9, 265, 268

Dabistan-i-Mazahib, 71, 164, 172, 206–7
dakkhana, shalok, 112, 144
dakkhani, south-western style, 85, 87, 112–13, 134, 169
Dakkhani
  Bilaval-dakkhani, 143
  Gauri-dakkhani, 143
  Maru-dakkhani, 143
  Ramakali-dakkhani, 143
  Prabhati-dakkhani, 143
  Vadahans-dakkhani, 143
Daljeet Singh, 59, 61
Damdama *bir* (version), 78, 89, 223–4, 227, 228–33, 235, 239, 287
Damdama Sahib (Anandpur), 81, 223
Damdama Sahib (Talvandi Sabo), 81, 224, 232, 245, 253
Damdami Granth, 58
Damdami Taksal, 245
Danielou, Alain, 128
Darbar Sahib, Golden Temple, 141
dasam duar, tenth door, 216
Dasam Granth, 98, 228, 256, 279, 280
Dastur al-'Aml Sri Darbar Sahib, 141
Dayanand, Swami, 29
Deccan, 143
Dehra Dun, 23, 66, 220

Delhi, 78, 286
Dervishes, 106
Devanagari script, 17, 47
dhadds, 144
dhadhi, minstrel, 16, 144, 210–11
Dhaka sangat, 220
dhamar, 129
Dhanasari mode, 47, 55, 70, 132–4, 136, 158–9, 173, 198, 270
Dhanna, bhagat, 171–4, 178
Dharam-raj/rai, 56, 163
dharamsalas, 207, 257
Dharmshastras, 183
Dhir Mal, 23, 58, 65, 223, 225, 287
Dhir-malias, 59
dhrupad style, 128–9
dhunis, heroic tunes, 48, 69, 73, 197, 208, 210–11, 286
Dhuni
  Ballad of Asraj Tunda, 209
  Ballad of Jodha and Vira, 210
  Ballad of Lallan and Bahiliman, 210
  Ballad of Mahima and Hasna, 210
  Ballad of Malik Murid and Chandarhara, 209
  Ballad of Musa, 210
  Ballad of Rai Kamaldi and Maujdi, 209
  Ballad of Rana Kailash and Maldeo, 210
  Ballad of Sikander and Birahim, 210
dhur ki bani, 6, 11–12
didar, 109
digvijaya tradition, 184
din raini, day-night, 144
Dipak mode, 145–6
diva, lamp, 118
Divali festival, 184
Doctrinal reading, 259
Dohavali, 183
Dohra/Doha, 98, 183, 273
Dr. Balbir Singh Sahitya Kendra, Dehra Dun, 30, 78, 220

dukkar, 136
dukkh, suffering, 165
Dusenbery, Verne, 255

Egypt, 248
Eliade, Mircea, 242, 277
Erskine, Henry, 273

Farid-bani, 180–2
Farid ud-Din Ganj-i-Shakar/Shaikh
    Farid, 181
Fariduddin Saleem, 181
Friedlander, Peter, 172
Fatehpur MS, 131
farishta, angel, 214
Frye, Northrop, 75, 246, 280
Funk, Robert W., 260

gaddi, throne, 160, 245
gagan gupha, 192
Gagraun (Quetta), 174
Ganda Singh, 272
Ganga river, 216
Garbganjani Tika, 252
Gatha, 51, 66
Gauri mode, 47, 56, 67, 140, 143,
    186, 188
Gauri
    Gauri-bairagan, 138, 143
    Gauri-dipaki, 138, 145
    Gauri-guareri, 138, 143
    Gauri-majh, 138
    Gauri-mala, 138
    Gauri-malva, 138
    Gauri-purbi-dipaki, 138
    Gauri-sorathi, 138
G.B. Singh, 26, 28, 29, 64, 68, 75,
    78, 117, 123, 220, 227
Ghannaya Singh, 64
ghar, musical clef, 144–5, 154, 248,
    269
gharanas (family traditions), 148
ghazal, 109
ghorian, 144, 162
gian, knowledge, 7, 8

Gian Singh Nihang, 234
gianis, traditional Sikh scholars, 255,
    271
Giani
    Badan Singh Sekhvan, 253
    Dal Singh, 253
    Gian Singh, 37–8, 132, 223, 253
    Gurdit Singh, 27, 32–5, 38, 91
    Sant Singh Maskeen, 271
Gita Govinda, 131
GNDU MS # 1245, 30, 41, 43, 45–
    50, 52, 57, 81, 91–3, 99–
    100, 102–3, 106–7, 110–11,
    115, 137, 144, 155, 162,
    209, 211, 214, 284
Goindval, 37, 91, 184, 206
Goindval Pothis, 17, 19, 27, 30–1,
    33–5, 37–42, 44, 46–8, 50,
    52, 57, 81, 84–6, 91–2,
    100–3, 122–3, 126, 131–3,
    137, 144, 159, 162, 176,
    183–5, 209, 214, 284
Golden Temple, 97, 99, 138, 141–
    3, 211, 218, 255, 274, 278,
    281
Gond mode, 47
Gond-bilaval, 47
Gopendra/Gobind, 200
gopis, 146
Gorakh, nath yogi, 214
Gorakh-bani, 131
gost, discourse, 247
Gosti Guru Amar Das Ki, Mina text,
    99
gost malar nali, discourse with Malar,
    77, 213
Grahm, William A., 4, 232, 268
Granth, 3
Granth Sahib, 21, 68, 226
granthis, readers, 255
Grewal, J.S., 16, 105, 206, 215, 279
Gujar tribe, 146
Gujari mode, 47–8, 67–8, 72, 146,
    199–200
Gujranwala, 231

Gujrat district, 78, 120, 213, 217, 230, 274, 286–7
Gulam Sadasevak, 38–9
Gunavanti, virtuous woman, 112, 118
gurbani, Guru's Word, 6, 11, 30–1, 33, 40, 42, 126, 155, 170, 187, 239–41, 246, 250, 252–7, 259, 268–70, 281–3
Gurbani dian Viakhia Pranalian, 241
Gurbani Viakaran, 256
gurbani vichar, 240
Gurbilas Chhevin Patashahi, 59, 141, 208, 229
Gurdas missal (version), 58, 213
Gurdita Sekhon, scribe, 30, 76, 77
gurdwara, 4, 228, 275, 278
Gurdwara Bhai Banno Sahib, Kanpur, 74
Gurdwara Dasmesh Bhavan, Dehra Dun, 66
Gurdwara Gur Gian Prakash, Jawaddi Kalan, Ludhiana, 149
Gurdwara Sri Karamsar, Rara Sahib, 233
Gurinder Singh Mann, 27, 34, 36, 38–9, 45, 49, 58, 101, 119, 131–2, 186, 194
gurmat, Gurus' teachings, 245–6
gurmata, corporate decision, 225, 266, 279
gurmukh, ideal Sikh, 9, 241, 246
Gurmukh Singh Bedi, 224
Gurmukhi script, 16, 17, 37, 44, 57, 63, 70, 123–4, 282, 284
Gurmukhi Schools, 253
Gurmukhi typefaces, 230
Gurnam Singh, 144
gurpurb, 278
Gupta age, 128
Gursharan Kaur Jaggi, 35
Guru, divine, 86, 88, 250, 260, 267, 270, 288
Guru/s, personal, 4–7, 9–11, 14–16,

19, 34, 36–45, 47, 49–51, 55, 58–61, 64–5, 67, 71, 73, 76–7, 79–80, 92, 95, 103–5, 110–16, 118, 122, 129, 139, 144–5, 149, 153, 161, 163, 169, 171–3, 175–9, 182, 184–1, 187, 190–2, 195, 212, 219, 226, 227, 233, 239, 241–6, 265–6, 270–2, 275, 281–2, 284, 288
Guru Amar Das, 10–11, 18, 20, 33, 35–7, 39–40, 42–3, 47–8, 50, 55, 65, 75, 81, 85, 99, 101–2, 119, 131, 133–4, 137, 139, 151–2, 157, 159, 162, 164, 182–4, 186–7, 201, 210, 219, 228, 243, 245–6, 274, 283
Guru Angad, 8, 9, 17, 32–3, 36, 93–6, 101, 151, 153, 182, 231, 243, 282
Guru Arjan, 11–12, 16, 18–21, 23, 28–31, 34–7, 40, 44–57, 59–64, 66–9, 71, 76, 79–80, 82–4, 88, 90, 92–4, 96–102, 104–22, 124, 136, 138–41, 148–9, 151–7, 159–65, 169–70, 172, 174–6, 184–6, 188–98, 200–4, 206–13, 217, 233–5, 239, 243, 245–6, 249, 267, 269–70, 283–6
Guru Arjan's Ramakali hymn, 57, 62, 66, 69, 70, 72–4, 77–8, 80, 115, 119, 122, 219, 231
Guru Arjan's Svayye, 66, 73,
Guru Gobind Singh, 3–4, 22, 23, 60, 64, 69, 72–3, 78–81, 126, 218–19, 223–4, 228, 235, 239, 245, 251–3, 265, 267, 286
Guru-Granth, doctrine of scriptural Guru, 11, 25, 225, 251, 266, 273, 279

Guru Granth Sahib, 3, 11, 26, 219, 228, 233, 245, 258, 25-7, 271-81, 288
Guru Granth Sahib Trust, Coventry, 220
Guru Hargobind, 42, 45, 54, 58, 61, 67, 69-70, 73, 117-18, 120-22, 199, 207, 208, 216-17, 234-5, 246, 249, 286
Guru Harkrishan, 58, 66
Guru Har Rai, 58, 65, 67, 71-2, 76-7, 194, 212, 272
Guru Har Sahai village, 18, 32
Guru Har Sahai Pothi, 27, 33, 34, 81, 87, 91, 197, 282
Guru Nanak, 4, 6, 8, 10, 14, 15-18, 20, 32-4, 36-7, 39, 46, 48-51, 55, 65-6, 68, 71, 75, 81, 84-6, 88, 90-9, 101-6, 111-12, 119, 125, 129-31, 134, 138, 145-6, 149, 151-60, 162, 169-70, 176, 179-81, 184-6, 209-10, 214, 219, 231, 240-52, 268-70, 272, 282-3
Guru Nanak's Pothi, 30, 32, 34, 126, 282
Guru Panth, doctrine of corporate guruship, 225, 251, 266, 279
Guru Ram Das, 11, 19, 33, 36-8, 40, 46, 49-50, 61, 65, 76, 86-8, 92, 97-9, 101, 133-6, 151, 160, 209-10, 224, 241, 243-6, 268, 272, 276, 283
Guru Tegh Bahadur, 42, 61, 66, 69-73, 75, 77, 78-81, 140, 219, 223, 228, 286-7
gutakas, breviaries, 283

Habib, Irfan, 172
hajj, Muslim pilgrimage, 174

Hazur Sahib, Nander, 234
Hakikat Rah Mukam, apocryphal text, 77
Harbans Singh, 151, 278
Harbhajan Singh, 223
Harbhajan Singh Chavla, 41
Harcharan Singh Chavla, 41
Hari Bhagati Premakar Granth, 142
Harimandir, Golden Temple, 12, 101, 141, 155-7, 207-8, 229
Harji, 100, 248
Harji's *Japu Parmarath*, 43
Harjot Oberoi, 174-5, 230, 254, 280
hartal, deletion, 56, 179, 229
Hatha Yoga, 51, 189, 215-16, 286
haumai, self-centredness, 275
Hawley, J.S., 105, 201
Hebrew Bible, 248
Hellenistic culture, 248
Hess, Linda, 189
Hindalis, 120, 215-17, 235, 286
Hindawi/Hindui, 168, 181
Hindol mode, 146-7
Hindur (Nalagarh), 72
Hindustani musical theory, 127, 144-5
Hiranyakashipu, 199
Historical-critical method, 257
Historical reading, 259
Hobbs, Edwards, 29, 217
Hola Mahalla festival, 143
hukam, divine Order, 6, 9
hukam laina, random reading, 271-2
hundi, official document, 37

ida-nadi, 216
Imperial Exhibition, Paris, 229
Iqbalnama, 226

Jagana Brahmin, 60-1, 124, 284
jagir, grant, 227
Jahangir, Mughal Emperor, 206-7, 234, 286
Jaidev, bhagat, 174

Jaijavanti mode, 72–3, 78, 80, 140, 219, 223, 228
jajamani system, 119
Jaitsiri mode, 47, 72–3, 78, 80, 140, 219
Jalandhar/Jullundhar, 35, 226, 282
Jalandhar Pothi, 39, 131–3
Jamuna river, 216
janam-sakhis, birth narratives, 32, 87, 105, 129, 214
Jandiala, 215
janeu, sacred thread, 118
Japji/Japu, Morning Prayer, 8, 14, 19, 33, 43, 46, 65, 90–5, 97–9, 101, 170–1, 224, 227, 231, 243, 245, 249–50, 252, 254, 261, 268, 283
Japu nisan, 227
Jarnail Singh Bhinderanwale, 255
Jat, rural caste, 172–3
Jathedars, commanders, 255
Jatinder Singh (Colonel), 218
javayyia, son-in-law, 189
Jawahar Nagar, Kanpur, 74
Jayadeva, bhagat, 131
Jeth Chand, 35, 38
jevanvar, ritual feast, 116, 118
Jewish Scripture, 177
jia, soul, 248
jinn, demon, 214
Jog mode, 146
Jograj, scribe, 71, 72
Jograj MS, 71
Julaha, weaver, 182

Kabir, bhagat, 8, 24, 34, 50, 56, 61, 67, 119, 162–4, 171, 173–5, 178–80, 182–93, 196
Kabir-granthavali, 174
Kabir's shaloks, 50, 61, 66, 68, 69, 70, 73
Kabitt, 124, 245
Kabul, 7
kachi bani, spurious hymns, 18, 38
kafi, genre, 112, 129, 144, 149

Kafi
   Asa-kafi, 138, 144
   Maru-kafi, 138, 144
   Suhi-kafi, 138, 144, 180
   Tilang-kafi, 138, 144
Kahn Singh Nabha, 59
Kal bard, 50
Kali Nath music system, 139
Kalyan mode, 47, 143
kambalari, sufi dress, 164
Kanara mode, 47, 143
Kangarh, 73
Kanpur, 74, 76, 213
Kanpur MS, 76
karah prashad, 275
karahale, 144
karma, 8, 9, 254
Karta Purakh, 88, 252
Karnatak, 134
Kartar, Creator, 86–7
Kartarpur (Jalandhar district), 23, 58, 74, 223, 225, 227
Kartarpur (Ravi), 15, 23, 31–2, 86–7, 89, 91, 94–5, 98, 125, 268, 282
Kartarpur-Banno debate, 28–9, 114, 121–2, 193, 195, 226
Kartarpur *bir* (version), 23, 27–31, 39, 42, 44–5, 47–54, 56–63, 65–8, 75, 82, 92, 96–7, 101–2, 110, 114–15, 117–18, 121–4, 137, 141, 145, 147, 156, 159, 161, 173, 179, 184–5, 187, 189–96, 198, 200, 203–5, 209–10, 212, 223–4, 226–8, 233–5, 285, 287
Kashi, 252
Kashmir, 226
Kasur, 273
katha, homily, 270–1
kathakar, 271
Kaul of Kashmir, 226
Kaur (Khalsa female name), 275
Kavi Santokh Singh, 225, 229, 252

Kedara mode, 47, 137
Kesar Singh Chhibber, 279
Khalsa, order, 99, 121, 217, 251, 253,
   260, 268, 274, 277, 279
Khara Mangat, 120, 213, 217, 226,
   235, 286
Khara missal, Banno version, 213
khari, brackish, 232,
khari bir, 232, 287
Khatri/s, urban caste, 17, 172
Khayal style, 128
Khuda'i, 109–10, 214
Khuldabad, 181
Khuram, 218–19
Khushwant Singh, 146, 224
Kiratpur, 58, 72, 73, 120, 212, 217,
   235, 249, 272, 286
kirtan, 97, 107, 135, 138, 141–2, 183,
   269–70
Kirtan Sohila, see Sohila
kitab, book, 17
Krishna, 146, 194–5, 197, 200–2
Krishna bhakti, 194–5, 198–9
Kshema Karna/ Pathaka, 147
Kuchajji, uncultured woman, 112
Kundalini shakti, 192, 216
kuramavatara, tortoise form, 198
kushta/bhasam, 63

Lahina, 95
Lahore, 59, 206, 211, 213, 225–7,
   230–2, 286
Lahore *bir* (version), 30, 61, 67, 72,
   79, 114, 194–5, 199, 201,
   206, 208, 211–12, 220, 234,
   286
Lahore Darbar, 229
Lakshmi, 250
Lala Harsukh Rai, 231
Lalo, 7
lande, business shorthand, 17, 126,
   282
langar, communal meal, 122, 279
Lath, Mukund, 135, 147, 149
Latin Scots' lyric, 169

lavan, wedding hymn, 104, 277
Literary reading, 259
Locative case
   adi, in the beginning, 170
   akhani, by speaking, 171
   chupai, through silence, 170
   gurmukhi, through the Guru, 170
   gurprasadi, by Guru's grace, 170
   karami, by actions, 171
   mannai, through reflection, 171
   suniai, by listening, 171
Lochan Pandit, 138
Loehlin, C.H., 189
Lucknow, 174
Luther, 243

Macauliffe, Max Arthur, 253
Madan Mohan Sur Das, 34, 197
Maghi festival, 143
Magical looking-glass theory, 260
mahal/mahalu/mahala, Gurus' sign,
   33, 55, 91–2, 103–4, 164,
   172, 186
mahajani, business shorthand, 17
maha-sukha, ultimate bliss, 216
Mahant/s, 250
Mahant Gopal Singh, seva-panthi,
   30, 76
Maharaja Ranjit Singh, 59, 208, 218,
   225–9, 235, 249, 251, 266,
   279, 287
Maharashtrian Sants, 199–201
Mahima Prakash, 213
Majh mode, 47, 132, 137, 143, 146,
   157–8
Majha, region, 143, 158
Malar/Malhar mode, 35, 47, 73, 132,
   134, 136, 143, 146
Malfuzat, 181
Mali-gaura mode, 47
man, heart/mind/soul, 19, 106–7,
   145, 153, 171, 194, 197
mangal, song of joy, 144
mangalacharan, invocations, 233
mangeva, betrothal, 116, 118

manji/s, 184, 278
manji-bardar, Sikh preacher, 43
mantra, sacred formula, 89, 193
Marathi dialect, 184
Marathi style, 198
Mardana, 49, 129
Maru mode, 35, 39, 57, 62, 64–5, 67, 69, 72–3, 75, 77–8, 80, 94, 137–8, 149, 153–5, 180, 228
Maru-kedara, 137
Masands, 70, 172, 207, 272
Matanga, sage, 138
maya, 130, 171
McLeod, W.H., 6, 15, 39, 40, 67, 97, 103, 114, 121–2, 142, 151, 155, 180, 217, 247, 249–50, 258, 275–6, 280, 285
Mecca, 214
Megh mode, 146
Mesha Karana (Kshema Karana), 130
midrash, Jewish interpretation, 243
Miharban, 43, 247–8
Miharban janam-sakhi, 20, 247
Mina/s, schismatic sect, 20, 43, 249
Mina literature, 100–1, 249
Mira Bai, female bhagat, 57, 62, 64, 67, 69, 70, 72–3, 75, 77–8, 80, 193–5, 202, 219, 229
Mir Hasan, 181
miri-piri, doctrine, 207, 249
misl, warrior band, 252
Mohan, Baba, 34–5, 37–8, 86, 133–4, 185
Mohan Pothis (Goindval Pothis), 28, 34, 99, 149
Mohan Singh Diwana, 91, 154
Mohari, Baba, 37, 133
Mohinder Kaur Gill, 26
Moti Palace, Lahore, 59, 226
Mount Mandara, 198
Mount Sumeru, 189
Muktesvara, 136

Mughals, Mughal authorities, 22, 72, 103, 122, 201, 206, 211, 215, 217, 234–5, 249, 283, 286
Mughal army, 58, 72
Muhammad, Prophet, 13, 205, 214
Mullas, Muslim priests, 175
muladhara-chakra/dhari, 189, 216
Mul Mantar, 32–4, 42, 71, 73, 75, 77, 84–6, 88–90, 92, 153, 245, 252
Multan, 112–13, 134
Mundavani, 51, 62, 66, 68–9, 71, 73, 75, 77, 79–80, 98, 211–12

nada, mystic sound, 127
Nahan, 71
Najabat Khan, 71
nam, divine Name, 6, 85, 193
Namdev, bhagat, 24, 70, 78–9, 171, 173, 182–5, 198–200, 211–12
namakaran, name-giving ceremony, 116, 118
nam-simaran, 110, 171–2, 183, 256
Nanak Prakash, 252
Nanakana Sahib, 66
Naqshbandi movement, 206
naqqara, 136
narasimhavatara, man-lion form, 199
Narda, 130
Nat-narain mode, 47, 135–6
Naths, 186, 190
Nath tradition, 191
Nawab of Lahore, 107
New Testament parable, 258
Nihang, 99
Nikky-Guninder Kaur Singh, 6
nirguna sants/nirgunis, 200–2, 285
nirankar, formless Lord, 10, 85–6, 88
Nirmala sect, 252–3, 255
nirmala pranali, 250
nirukat, etemology, 254
nirvair, without enmity, 87–8
nisan, autograph, 219

Nizam of Hyderabad, 218
North Indian bhakti, 201
Nurdin's sarai (inn), 208

Onkar, 85, 87
Operation Blue Star (1984), 68, 81,
    99, 218, 224, 255
Oudh, 174

pad genre, 105, 129, 145, 174, 191–
    2
pada-prabandha, 128
padmas, lotuses, 189
pahare, 144, 283
Pahinda Sahib's *bir* (version), 53
Panchama-sara-samhita, 130
Panj Granth Adi, 232
Panj Piare, Cherished Five, 277
pakhavaj, 135–6
Pakpattan, 173
Pandha, scribe, 18, 40, 283
Pandharpur, 200
pandit, 118, 190
Pandit Gulab Singh, 253
Pandit Tara Singh Narotam, 253
Panth, Sikh community, 8, 10, 15,
    18, 20–1, 25, 29, 58, 65,
    70, 72, 76, 80, 82, 90, 120,
    174, 184–5, 204–6, 211–
    12, 217–18, 225, 232–4,
    245–6, 249, 252, 258, 266,
    276, 279–81, 286, 288
para ras rakhsu, medicinal prescrip-
    tion, 63
Paramanand, bhagat, 173
paramarath, sublime meaning, 240,
    247, 256
paramarath pranali, 247
paratal, change of drum-rhythms,
    135–6
parkash karna, installation, 278
Parvati, 250
Paryag, 174
patal, 118
patantara, 192–3

path-bhed, variant readings, 204
Path-bodh-samagam, 33
Patiala, 35, 37, 132
Patna, 23, 60
Patti Likhi, 8, 16, 144
pauris, stanzas, 48, 99, 160–1, 163
Persian, 17
Peshawer, 68
Philo, 248
Phunahe, 51, 66
Piar Singh, 14, 27, 34, 38, 41, 44,
    46, 49, 53–4, 56, 58–60,
    64, 67, 88, 90, 100–1, 119,
    190–1, 204–5, 243, 244
Piara Singh Padam, 26, 68
pind, 118
pingla-nadi, 216
Pinjore, 35, 38, 282
Pinjore Pothi, 132
Pipa, bhagat, 174
Pothi, 34, 53, 68, 132, 282
Prabandha style, 128
prabhat, dawn, 140
Prabhati mode, 35, 47, 78, 132, 134,
    136, 139, 140–1, 143, 223
Prabhati-bibhas, 138
Prahilad, bhagat, 199
Prahilad Singh/Rai, 266
prakash, splendour, 219
Prakriti, 89
pranali, school, 241
pranas, breaths, 216
Prayag, Allahabad, 216
Preservation Operation of Kartarpur
    MS, 59n
Pritam Singh, 40, 74, 213
Prithi Chand, 18, 20, 43, 54, 101, 120,
    160
Puhkar (Pushkar) Granth, 60–1
puja, Hindu worship, 174
Pundarika Vitthala, musician, 132,
    148
Punjab, 129, 144, 181, 186, 211, 230,
    288
Punjabi/s, 181, 211, 251, 274

Punjabi culture, 190
Punjabi society, 230, 258
Punjabi Sahit Akademy, Ludhiana, 224
Purakh, personal God, 88
Puranas, ancient texts, 183–4, 252
puran-mashi, full moon, 38
Puratan janam-sakhis, 94
Purusha, 89
Purvang/Purba, 128, 132
Puskara, 136
putra, son, 130

qafias, 154
Queen Victoria, 227
Qur'an, 12–13, 21–2, 42, 63, 174, 205, 243
Qur'anic *fatiha*, 42

rabab, rebeck, 129
Rababi, 129, 141–2
ragas, musical modes, 6, 11, 39, 46, 89–90, 125–8, 131–2, 134–5, 141, 143–6, 152, 184, 187, 208, 231, 282, 284
raga-ragini-putra system, 130, 147, 148
Raga-mala, 63–4, 66, 70–3, 75, 79–80, 130, 139, 145–8
Raga Trangini, 138
ragis, Sikh musicians, 136, 141–2
Ragi Darshan Singh, 271
rahau, refrain, 106–8, 154
rahit, code of conduct, 268
Rahit-nama, 266
Rai Sahib Munshi Gulab Singh, 233
Raja Karam Prakash, 72
Raja Ram Tota, 226
Raja Sivanabh, 63–4, 75
Rama, 214
Ram Rai, son of a goldsmith, 23, 60
Ram Mrigi, scribe, 230
Ramadan/Ramzan, 174, 187–8
Ramakali mode, 35, 37, 40, 47, 49, 70, 73, 77–8, 80, 85, 87,
98–9, 114, 116, 118, 121, 132, 134, 136, 146, 149, 162, 186, 215
Ramanand, bhagat, 174
Ramsar, 284
Ratan-mala, 51, 75, 77, 215–16
Rattan Singh Bhangu, 58, 223, 273
Ravidas, bhagat, 24, 65, 171, 173, 185
Ray, Niharranjan, 161
rayasa, romantic genre, 283
Rewa, 147, 174
Ricoeur, Paul, 246, 257, 260
ruh, spirit, 214
rumalas, 278
Ruti, seasons, 114, 144

sabad (shabad), Word, 6, 11–12, 16, 20, 85, 136, 154–5, 157, 182–3, 244, 246, 271
Sach Ji, 69
sach/u, 85, 92
Sacha Patisha, 103
sachu-namu, 85
Sacred Language of the Sikhs, SLS, 169
sadachar, morality, 246
sadara, call, 153
Saddu, 40, 47, 49, 144, 162
sadh, saint, 162–3
Sadhana, bhagat, 174
Sadhu Gurdit Singh, 253
sagunis/saguna bhagats, 200–1
sahaj, 198
sahaj pranali, 242–3
sahaja state, 216
Sahajiyas, 190
Sahans Ram, 35–6
sahasrara-chakra/amber, 189
Sahib Singh, 26, 179–80, 213, 215, 242, 256–7, 261
Sain, bhagat, 171
Sair-i-Punjab, 142
Sajada Mal Ji, 69
sajan, friend, 248
sakat, sinner, 156, 162–3

Sakhis, 183
sala, brother-in-law, 189–90
Salok Sahaskriti/Sahanskriti, 51, 65, 153
Salok Varan te Vadhik/Bahari, 50, 62, 66, 68, 69–70, 219
sama, sufi dance, 129
sambadi, 127
sampardai pranali, 243
sampraday, sect, 173
samsara, 191
Sanatan Sikh tradition, 280
sangat, Sikh congregation, 18, 76, 118, 162, 164, 246, 270, 272–3, 279, 283
sangrand/sankrant festival, 226
sankar raga, 145
Sanskrit, 17, 124
Sanskritic learning, 53, 61, 124, 252
sant/s, medieval saint/s, 15, 24, 171–4, 183–5, 197, 200–2, 211, 285–6
Sant beliefs, 234, 286
Sant Bhasha, 168
Sants, Sikh saints, 89, 90, 99, 234
Sant
  Ameer Singh, 254
  Balbir Singh, 234
  Chanan Singh, 233
  Darshan Singh, Baba, 43
  Deva Singh Nirmala, 253
  Gurbachan Singh Khalsa, 204, 234, 255
  Ishar Singh Rarewala, 234
  Niranjan Singh, 233
  Sampuran Singh, 253
  Sham Singh, 142
  Sundar Singh, 254–5
Santokh Singh, Kavi, 229
Sarang mode, 17, 35, 47, 57, 67, 72, 132, 136, 143, 146
Sarangi, a string instrument, 144
Saraswati, 216, 250
Sarbat Khalsa, entire Khalsa, 273, 279

Sardars, Sikh chiefs, 141
Sarup Das Bhalla, 34
sat chit anand, Vedantic doctrine, 252
sasur, father-in-law, 189–90
Satara, 174
Satbir Singh, Principal, 233
Satta, 47, 49
Savayye, 49, 51, 98
Schimmel, Annemarie, 181
Schomer, Karine, 178
Sen, bhagat, 174
seva, service, 244–5
Seva-panthi sect, 30, 76, 77
shabad vichar, 240
shabarath, meanings, 240, 256
Shabadarath Sri Guru Granth Sahib Ji, 233, 256–7
Shabad Hazare, 102
shabad-kirtan, 129
Shackle, Christopher, 11, 93, 111, 158, 169, 229
Shah Jahan, Mughal Emperor, 58, 72
Shah Rukh Mirza, 71
Shahpur, Sargodha, 77–8
Shaikh Ahmad Sirhindi, 206
Shaikh Farid, 61, 72, 164–5, 173–4, 178–82, 185–6, 212
Shaikh Farid Bukhari/Mir Murtaza Khan, 206
sha'ir, Muslim poet, 111
Shaiva devotees/school, 129, 139
shakti, 216
Shalok/s, 8, 9, 17, 33, 48, 50–1, 61, 65, 68, 71, 73, 79, 92–6, 99, 114, 118, 145, 153–5, 165, 169, 182, 186, 188–9, 192–3, 213, 228, 282
Shapiro, Michael, 169, 171
Sharda script, 44
Sharifpura, 68
Shastra tradition, 243, 249
Sher(e) Singh, 274
Shiromani Gurdwara Prabandhak Committee (SGPC), 26, 204, 233

Shiva/Param Shiva, 214, 216, 250
Shivalik hills, 217
Sholapur, 173
Shudh Gurbani Trust (Amritsar), 233
Siddh (Siddha), 186
Siddh Gost, 47, 91, 134, 144, 152, 162, 186, 246
Sikh Reference Library, Amritsar, 30, 67, 81, 224
sikhi, 246
Sindh, 134, 174
Singh/s, 251, 273, 275
Singh Sabha *pranali*, 255
Singh Sabha scholars, 26, 59, 89–90, 99, 232, 234–5, 242, 256–7, 261, 274, 279, 287–8
Singh Sahib
    Giani Chet Singh, 233
    Giani Sharam Singh, 233
Singhladip, 63–4
Siranda, 142
Siri Gur Panth Prakash (Prachin), 223
Siri Guru Panth Prakash, 223
Sirhind, 72
Siri mode, 34, 38, 46–7, 139–41, 149, 180
Sirmur/Sirmor, 71
smarta tradition, 183
Smith, Jonathan Z., 239
Smith, Wilfred Cantwell, 5, 12, 21–2, 177, 184, 261, 267
So Dar, 14, 46, 62, 91, 96–8, 269
So Dar Rahiras, 14, 96–7, 232
Sodhi family, 18, 32, 225
Sodhi Amarjit Singh, 59n
Sodhi Sadhu Singh, 225–7
Sohila (Kirtan Sohila), 46, 144
Solaha/Solahe (pl.), 55, 75, 94, 155–7
So Purakh, 219
Sorathi mode, 35, 47, 56, 132, 140, 145, 191–2
Sri Adi Granth Sahib Ji, 231

Sri Darbar Damdama Sahib, Kanshi, 232
Sri Guru Granth Sahib, 27
Sri Guru Granth Sahib Ji Adi, 231
Sri Guru Granth Sahib Darpan, 242
Sri Vahiguru Ji, 68
Staal, Frits, 21
sthai, 107
Stocks, Brian, 267
Suchajji, cultured woman, 112
sudh, correct, 49, 55, 61–2, 123–4, 284
Sudhang, pure notes, 135
sudh bir, correct recension, 233
sudh kichai, make corrections, 49, 62
sudh kita, corrected, 62
sudh path, correct reading, 204
sufis, Muslim mystics, 24, 106, 110–11, 129, 144, 149, 164, 180–1, 185–6, 285
Suhi mode, 35, 47, 102, 104, 111–12, 130–2, 134, 146, 186, 247, 276
Suhi-lalit, 138
sukirt, good actions, 248
Sukhamani Sahansarnama, 120
Sukhmani, 93, 120, 144, 162, 243
sukh asan, 278
Sulakhan Singh, 257
Sulhi Khan, 43
Sundar, 40, 47, 49, 162
Suraj Prakash, 59, 225, 229, 252
Surdas, bhagat, 34, 57, 62, 67, 69–70, 72–3, 75, 77–80, 131, 174, 178, 195–7, 200, 219, 232
Surinder Singh Kohli, 26
Sur Sagar, 47
sushumna-nadi, 216

tabla, a pair of drums, 135–6
takari, 17, 44, 126, 282
Takhats, thrones, 228, 255
taksal, mint, 245
tala/s, drum rhythms, 136

Tala
   ada/ara, 136
   chanchal, 136
   chautal, 136
   dadra, 136
   dip chandi, 136
   dhamar, 136
   jhaptal, 136
   kahirava, 136
   sulphakte, 136
   tintal, 136
Talvandi Sabo,
tan, melodic figuration, 146
Tanakhah-nama, 266
Tansen, musician, 148, 150
Tantric Yoga, 192, 202
Tara Chand, 72
Taran Singh, 26, 146–7, 241, 243, 244
Tarlok Singh, 200
tasakar, thieves, 163
Tat Khalsa, 279–80
Teja Singh, 26, 242, 256–7, 272
Thapal/Thapul, dera, 71–2
tika, commentary, 240, 256
Tikana Sri Bhai Ram Kishan, 30, 76, 78
Tilang mode, 7, 35, 47, 106–9, 111, 131–2, 146, 283
Todi mode, 47
Tonk, 174
Torah, 12, 243
Trilochan, bhagat, 67–8, 72, 78–80, 199–201, 211–12
Triveni, 215–16
Trumpp, Ernst, 253, 256
Tulsidas, 183
tukh, husk, 174
Tukhari mode, 33, 47, 132, 137–8

Udasi/s, 70, 120, 235, 249–53, 286
Udasi Harnam Das, 224
Udasi *pranali*, 249
Udhovala, 76
ultabamsi, upside-down, 189, 191

Una Sahib, 30, 69
upakaram-upasanhar, 140
urdh mukh kua, inverted well, 192
Usman Khan, 273
Uttam Chand, goldsmith, 60
uttrang/uttra, 128, 132

Vadahans mode, 47, 132, 138, 157, 162, 180
Vadda Ghalughara, great holocaust, 59
vadda granth, 60, 82
vadi, 127–8
Vahiguru, 68
Vaishnava/s, 120, 129, 149, 185, 195, 200, 202, 286
Vaishnava bhakti, 201, 286
Vaishyas, caste, 172
vak, 71, 95, 161, 271–4, 281
vak laina, 271, 275, 281, 288
vanajara, 144
var/s, ballads, 47–9, 69, 73, 122, 124, 129, 144, 152, 182, 208, 211, 256
Var
   Asa, 33, 138, 153, 170–1, 209
   Basant, 48, 66, 69, 122, 273
   Gauri, 62, 160, 209
   Gujari, 50, 99, 210
   Kanara, 210
   Jaitsiri, 169
   Majh, 49, 94, 153, 209
   Malhar, 17, 48, 49, 209–10
   Ramakali, 47, 49–50, 99, 162, 210
   Sarang, 210
   Vadahans, 49, 209–10
   Vihagara/Bihagara, 42, 50
Varanasi/Banaras, 124, 173, 190, 250
Várkaris, 200
Var sat, seven days, 56, 67, 188–9
vand, distribution, 118
Vaudville, Charlotte, 172, 183, 200
Vedas, 9–10, 12, 15, 21, 183–4, 252, 282
Vedic teaching, 251–2, 258

Vedantic perspective, 250–1, 253
viakhia, exegesis, 240, 256
vibhasas, 138
Vidya Sagar Suri, 59n
Vishnu, 198–9, 214, 250
Vitthala, lord, 200–1

Wulff, Donna, 129

Yaska, 254
Yoga, 216
Yogis, 146, 149

Zain ud-Din Shirazi, 181
Zohar, 12